JOSEPHINE BAKER'S SECRET WAR

JOSEPHINE BAKER'S BAKER'S SECRET WAR

The African American Star Who Fought for France and Freedom

HANNA DIAMOND

YALE UNIVERSITY PRESS
NEW HAVEN AND LONDON

For information about this and other Yale University Press publications, please contact:
U.S. Office: sales.press@yale.edu   yalebooks.com
Europe Office: sales@yaleup.co.uk   yalebooks.co.uk

Set in Freight Text Pro by IDSUK (DataConnection) Ltd
Printed and bound in Great Britain by Bell & Bain Ltd, Glasgow

Library of Congress Control Number: 2025931214
A catalogue record for this book is available from the British Library.
Authorized Representative in the EU: Easy Access System Europe, Mustamäe tee 50, 10621 Tallinn, Estonia, gpsr.requests@easproject.com

ISBN 978-0-300-27998-6

10 9 8 7 6 5 4 3 2 1

For Kelsie, Hugo and Isabelle

CONTENTS

ILLUSTRATIONS

Plates

Maps

ABBREVIATIONS

AVF	Association des amis des volontaires français (Association of Friends of the French Volunteers)
BCRA	Bureau central de renseignements et d'action (Gaullist Free French Intelligence Service)
CFLN	Comité français de libération nationale (French Committee of National Liberation)
CFT	Corps féminin des transmissions (Women's Signal Corps)
CIA	Central Intelligence Agency
CIC	Counter Intelligence Corps
DSM	Direction de la sécurité militaire (Directorate of Military Security)
DSR-SM	Direction des services de renseignement et de sécurité militaire (Directorate of Military Intelligence and Security)
DSS	Direction des services spéciaux (Directorate of Special Services)
ENSA	Entertainments National Service Association
FAFL	Forces aériennes françaises libres (Free French Air Forces)
FFA	Forces féminines de l'Air (Women's Air Force)
FFL	Forces françaises libres (Free French Forces)
IPSA	Infirmières pilotes secouristes de l'air (Pilot Nurses for Medical Services)
LICRA	Ligue internationale contre le racisme et l'antisémitisme (International League against Racism and Antisemitism)

NAACP	National Association for the Advancement of Colored People
OSS	Office of Strategic Services
RG	Renseignements généraux (French security intelligence service)
SR	Service Renseignements (French intelligence service)
TR	Travaux ruraux – 'rural works engineers' (clandestine counterespionage)
USO	United Service Organizations

ACKNOWLEDGEMENTS

First and foremost, I wish to thank the Leverhulme Trust for funding the twenty-month Research Fellowship that made it possible for me to do this research and to produce this book. It has been a privilege and a joy to be able to take this project forward. I am deeply grateful to Greg Nichols and the team at Truly*Adventurous for commissioning me to do some initial research and writing about Josephine Baker's life during this period. It was this work that seeded my interest in her story. I feel very lucky that Jo Godfrey of Yale University Press took the initiative to contact me after seeing a newspaper report about my research. She has followed me through the research and has guided me through the publishing process with careful attention and expertise. Her remarkable colleagues Rachael Lonsdale, Katie Urquhart and Chloe Foster, as well as my peer reviewers, have all played a crucial part in bringing the book to fruition.

I am deeply indebted to the archivists and librarians I have encountered. In France, at the Service historique de la Défense in Vincennes, Géraud Létang smoothed my way to seeing the key documents, and his colleague Jean-Charles Foucrier provided me with helpful material. Nicolas Cournil at the Archives départementales de la Dordogne, Patricia Gillet at the Archives nationales, and the team at the Centre des Archives diplomatiques de Nantes all helped enormously. In the US, my thanks go to Tim Noakes for sending material from the Special Collection at Stanford University, Malea Walker at the Library of Congress, Mary Ellen Budney and other archivists at the Beinecke Library, Yale University. Thanks go to Eric Van Slander and Tab Lewis, who acted as a lifeline in helping me navigate the National Archives at College Park in Maryland. Finally, closer to home, our own Luisa Tramontini and the inter-library loans team at the Arts and Social Studies Library at Cardiff University were incredibly efficient in tracking down materials.

My thanks also go to Madame de Labarre, owner of the Château des Milandes, and to Ian Reed, Director of the Allied Forces Heritage Group, who kindly provided me with a photograph from their archive of Josephine Baker's visit to RAF Elvington in May 1945, and gave me permission to publish it.

Many wonderful friends and colleagues have supported me along this journey. Special mention goes to Sylvie Zaidman, who never tired of discussing Josephine and helping me to unravel the challenges of the sources. Others who have had invaluable input include Simon Kitson, Sébastien Albertelli, Claire Andrieu, Ben Shepherd, Benjamin Haase, Robert Pike, Robin Leclercq, Claudia Hillebrand, Charles Forsdick, Debra Kelly, Jenny Nelson, Charlotte Hammond, Loredana Polezzi, Rachael Langford, Claire Gorrara and David Clarke. Olive Colman came with me to visit Marrakech, where we walked in Baker's footsteps and my eyes were opened to the wonders of Morocco. Warm thanks go to Mike Wood, owner of the Riad Star, the boutique hotel at the site where Baker lived in Marrakech, who went out of his way to be helpful, and to Ahmed Alcadi at the Hotel La Mamounia, for his time and hospitality.

Finally, in dedicating this book to Kelsie, Hugo and Isabelle, I am paying tribute to all the members of my family who have been my rock and my refuge through the research and writing process. They have kept me grounded, have been tolerant about my need to disappear to write for frequent periods, and have always been available to play when I came up for air. I could not have done it without you all.

AUTHOR'S NOTE

My interest in Josephine Baker's wartime life arose from my work as a historian of France and the Second World War. Some years ago, I was commissioned to carry out research on Baker's war record, and was astonished to discover the remarkable lack of material relating to her activities during this fascinating period of her life. While it was apparent that Baker had been actively involved in French intelligence as an operative serving the Allied cause, there was little work in English or in French that dealt with her wartime service extensively, or that explored it with an eye to the existing field of research on France and the Second World War. This book sets out to tell her wartime story via a critical engagement with the sources, and to offer insights that examine her activities in the light of the wider social and political context of the time. All translations from French sources are my own.

Baker's Black heritage is central to her wartime experiences. She invariably operated in a landscape where she was the sole woman of colour in a predominantly white male world. When I refer to Baker's racial identity in my writing, I use the term African American or Black (with a capital 'B') to show a recognition of the Black community's shared sense of ethnic identity and history.[1] Any exploration of Baker's life reveals that she experienced many forms of racism, and one way in which this was evident was in the language used to describe her. Terms were used that today we would find inappropriate, or even offensive. The book cites language that was current at the time and that Baker also sometimes used to describe herself. While her skin colour is never referenced in any of the official archival documents relating to her actions, it was discussed frequently, openly and explicitly by others, particularly in the press.

When referring to the inhabitants of North Africa and the Middle East, contemporary commentators reference 'Arab', 'native' and 'Moslem' populations to distinguish them from the French, Spanish and other Europeans who lived there. In my writing, I identify them as Moroccans, North Africans or local populations. In this region, Black Africans were very much a part of the diverse ethnic landscape, and Baker's heritage and transnational identity made it possible for her to fit in and gain acceptance across a range of social groups in ways which facilitated her intelligence-gathering activities.

Throughout this project I have been conscious of my own position as a white woman and a professor in a British university, and that my own breadth of experience bears no relation to Baker's. As historians, we have a responsibility to portray as accurately as possible the experiences of our subjects, based on close reading, analysis and research. I have made every effort to represent appropriately the challenges that Baker experienced as a Black woman, while showing the profound impact that she had in supporting the Allied war effort.

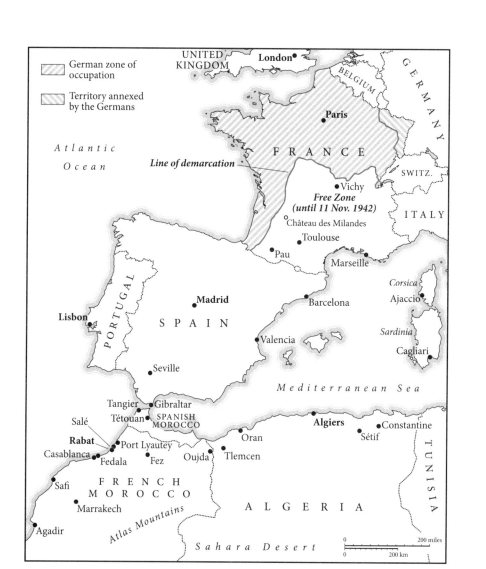

Map 1. Southwest Europe and Morocco (late 1940).

INTRODUCTION

When celebrated music-hall star Josephine Baker arrived in Madrid in March 1941 to take up her four-day residency at the Teatro de la Zarzuela, she knew she would have to keep her wits about her. She had grown used to the double life she had been leading since the outbreak of the war, but she still found it unnerving dealing with missions on her own, without the support of her trusted handler, Jacques Abtey. A counter-intelligence agent with the French military, and Baker's lover, Abtey had taught her all she knew about espionage and prepared her well to operate in a landscape where suspicion and duplicity were the norm. She had been a good pupil and knew she would need to draw on all the knowledge she had acquired during this sensitive and dangerous mission to the Spanish peninsula. She had become skilled at identifying and playing those individuals she suspected were operatives, but she still marvelled at how resourceful they were, particularly the agents of the Abwehr, the German military intelligence service.

She missed Abtey when they were apart, but he had been unable to acquire the necessary papers to be able to accompany her. Determined nonetheless to carry on their important work to advance the cause of the Allies, they had pressed ahead with making plans for her tour. Getting travel papers was never a problem for Baker – then one of the most famous celebrities in the world. Officials would go out of their way to help. She had never been refused a visa and her unique freedom to move around facilitated her missions at a time when vigorous border controls were in place across Europe. The tour had been organised in record time. Everyone they had approached to secure the bookings for her performances had shown an astonishing willingness to overcome the difficulties brought about by the ongoing conflict. Following her shows in Madrid, she had agreed to engagements in Seville, Valencia and Barcelona.

Baker loved performing; but on this occasion, travelling across Spain to these venues was a pretext to spend time in the country and carry out her mission. The three-week concert tour was a ruse to collect intelligence and report on any signs that preparations were being laid for an incursion into Morocco by the German or Spanish military. She knew that her life depended on staying out of the hands of the Abwehr and that if anything went wrong and her espionage work was discovered, she would be on her own.

On checking in to her hotel room in Madrid, Baker had collected a mountain of invitations to events and receptions. She would prioritise those from embassies and consulates. Diplomats tended to be in the know, and she knew where she was with them. They loved to talk and were often indiscreet after a few drinks. It would be easy for her to turn conversations to the topics that interested her. She would gently probe them about the German presence in the country and whether they thought the Spanish were planning joint military action. Then, when she returned to her hotel, she would note down the names of all those she had seen and everything that she had heard. At the end of the tour, as she prepared to travel back to Morocco where she was based, she would hide these precious notes on her person, carefully attached with safety pins to the inside of her clothes so they were not visible. She knew that getting through the frontier would not be a problem. The border guards would be much more interested in asking for her autograph than inspecting her identity papers. It certainly would not cross their minds to carry out a body search. Once she was back in the safety of her opulent Marrakech residence, she would deliver the information to Abtey, who would ensure that it reached those who needed it.

And so it was that Josephine Baker was able to conduct missions like this one, collecting and transmitting intelligence using her celebrity as a cover to support the Allied cause. While her fame made her the centre of attention wherever she went – a rather unusual attribute for a spy, who would normally aim to pass unnoticed – she worked undercover effectively for the French intelligence services throughout the war, later mobilising a heavy programme of troop concerts across North Africa and the Middle East to disguise her clandestine activities. Baker knowingly took dangerous risks to support the Allied war effort and held a passionate devotion to the Gaullist Free French resistance movement (known from July 1942 as the Fighting French to mark its fusion with movements and networks of the Resistance); yet her wartime actions have received remarkably little serious attention. Although she was decorated by post-war French governments, the citations for these honours only offer limited detail of her activities. In the ensuing years, despite the tardy award of a Légion d'honneur in 1957, the exact nature of her wartime contribution continued to be overlooked. Since her death in 1975, the focus of Baker's memorialisation has been on her accomplishments, first as an exotic dancer, then the career she made for herself as a music-hall star and ultimately her involvement in the civil rights movement in the US. This account deals with the overlooked period of the Second World War, drawing on original archival research to tell the story of Josephine Baker's wartime life and to assess its importance.

~

Baker had found herself in the public eye in France almost from the first moment of her arrival in the country. Freda Josephine McDonald alias Josephine Baker disembarked in Cherbourg on 25 September 1925 with just ten days to rehearse before her first performance. On 2 October, she was due to appear in the 'Revue nègre' at the Théâtre des Champs-Élysées, one of the capital's most glamorous nightspots. On opening night, her dancing immediately drew a huge amount of attention. These venues had been promoting exclusively Black performers, musicians and dances (including jazz and the Charleston) for some years, but their popularity was starting to wane. Josephine

Baker's first appearance changed all that. As soon as she came off the stage, she literally became the talk of the town. It was her 'danse sauvage' which electrified her audience. She portrayed Fatou, a seductive and bewitching African girl, mistress to a French explorer from Pierre Loti's popular nineteenth-century novel, which would have been known to her audience. It was not her partial nudity, which was common in French nightclubs, but the way she danced with frenetic abandon in a wildly suggestive display that captivated the onlookers. At the end of the show, the audience members sat stunned, and then rose to their feet, some hissing and booing, but most applauding and cheering. A new life was about to open up for Baker.

An African American born into poverty in East St Louis, Missouri, in 1906, she had succeeded in getting herself onto the stage in Broadway, largely due to her clowning at the end of the chorus line and her creation of a 'unique funny-glamorous persona'.[1] She was noticed in 1925 in a revue at New York's Plantation Club by Caroline Dudley Reagan, a socialite and wife of the commercial attaché to the US ambassador to France, who was recruiting talent to take to Paris. She wanted to create a new show to feed the popular 'negrophilia', a passion for Black art and culture that had led to an explosion of Black talent in the capital. Parisians had a fascination, not just for Black art and sculpture, but also for Black entertainers, jazz artists and dances. The Charleston, for example, which had originated in the rural South of the US among African Americans, had become extremely popular. The 'Revue nègre' was designed to cater to this demand.

From that very first opening night, Baker's appearances became a sensation and propelled her into the limelight in ways she could never have imagined. She performed tirelessly, first in evening shows; then she opened her own nightclub, which she would visit late at night to sing in a more intimate setting after her music-hall shows had closed. Her appearance in a banana skirt in a revue the following year only cemented her reputation. The girdle of bananas swung and vibrated to the frenzy of her dancing and the costume became one of the most celebrated of all theatrical outfits.[2] Baker gained the kind of fame that African American artists at home in the

US could only dream of, their own careers stymied by the limitations of segregation. Her dancing attracted the attention of the literati of the day, who waxed lyrical about her talents. As the money rolled in, she enjoyed every facet of the luxurious lifestyle it offered her.

When she arrived in Paris in 1925, Baker could hardly read or write.[3] But she was intelligent and she used her new celebrity to surround herself with people who could aid her in improving herself and boosting her career. Key to her success was her association with Count Pepito Abatino, a curious character whom she met in autumn 1926. He was not actually a count, but he did have a remarkable talent for understanding how to promote Baker to her best advantage and manage her image. It was he who masterminded her advertising campaigns for the hair product Bakerfix, and helped to shape her public identity. She was very fond of him, and in June 1927 they announced a 'pretend' marriage as a publicity stunt to cover for their close involvement. By 1928, there was clamour for Baker to visit venues abroad. Under Abatino's direction, for the following two and a half years, she performed mostly outside France. First, there was a European tour which took in Austria, Germany, Hungary, Yugoslavia, Denmark, Romania and Czechoslovakia.[4] Then, after a short break, they departed for South America, where she appeared in Argentina, Brazil, Chile and Uruguay. Even if Baker was not universally lauded at every stop, she still caused a sensation wherever she went.

When they finally returned home to Paris at the end of 1929, the theatre scene was struggling and, along with music hall, was adjusting to competition from the new talkie cinema. Baker (and Abatino) had long harboured the ambition that she should move on from just dancing to become a more rounded performer. During their travels, he had arranged intensive coaching for her to learn to sing and – importantly – to improve her French. These new-found accomplishments were revealed to excited spectators in her new revue at the Casino de Paris in 1930, 'Paris qui remue' ('Paris When It Sizzles'), where Baker revealed the ballad that would become her anthem: 'J'ai deux amours' ('Two Loves Have I') written by Géo Koger, Henri Varna and Vincent Scotto.

Baker made a recording of the song with the jazz band of the Casino de Paris to coincide with the opening of 'Paris qui remue'. The Columbia Records release marked the beginning of her new musical and performative image. Originally about an African girl torn between her love for a Frenchman and her attachment to her people and her homeland, Baker shifted the meaning to symbolise her identity between France and the US.[5] 'J'ai deux amours' established Baker's Parisian roots and sophisticated image.[6] The recorded version of the song was performed in duet with another singer whose voice Baker encircles and dominates with her refrain. The tune became an immediate bestseller, selling over 300,000 copies.[7] Although the song was ostensibly about Baker's two loves – her native country and Paris – as early as the mid-1930s she began to play with the words and change the concluding refrain of the song. 'J'ai deux amours, mon pays et Paris' translates as 'I have two loves, my country and Paris'; but now the last clause became 'mon pays c'est Paris', 'my country is Paris', thereby conferring on France a loyalty that she felt the US no longer deserved. The song would become a central part of Baker's public presence.

Baker also increased her acting credits. Her first silent film, *La Sirène des Tropiques*, had been made in 1927 and she now went on to make two speaking films, *Zouzou* in 1934 and *Princesse Tam Tam* in 1935. These showcased her new-found singing and French-speaking abilities. In these films, she adopted her music-hall persona as a French colonial subject, which made sense to French audiences because of her skin colour. In accordance with the existing social mores around race, despite romantic storylines, Baker's characters never got their (white) man.[8] The films met with considerable success; but it was the comic opera *La Créole*, in which she starred between these shoots, that attracted the most admiration. Critics hailed this performance not just because it showcased her new talents, but also because it was seen as emblematic of her transformation from her 'African primitivist' phase and perceived embrace of French culture.[9] For some critics, this change was conflated with an apparent transformation in her skin colour.[10]

In her last appearances, we suspected that something was happening, Josephine, the negress, was no longer so black. Josephine was growing paler . . . And she was starting to change her delightful tropical songs. Now [in *La Créole*], her skin is [even] lighter . . . And Josephine sings delightfully. She sings with profound art.[11]

Her move towards French operetta exemplified her transition to 'whiteness' for many commentators. It was seen as a reassertion of French cultural values and 'it evinced the continued effectiveness of France's idea of its civilising mission in the colonies'.[12] Beyond her performances, Baker had become a potent symbol of France, its commitment to freedom and the accomplishment of its colonial project.

On the crest of this wave, now a recognised film star as well as a celebrated music-hall performer, Baker planned a visit to the US, counting on the fact that all the attention she was getting in Europe would enhance her reputation there. She longed for recognition at home. But her star turn in a 1936 revival of the 'Ziegfeld Follies' on Broadway was a flop commercially. Reviews were harsh. She was poorly received by American audiences, who saw her act as both stale and too erotic.[13] Largely blaming Abatino, who had organised her visit, for her failure, she sent him home in disgrace. By the time Baker returned to Paris some weeks later, convinced that she had no future in her home country, he had died rapidly of a cancer that he had chosen not to reveal to her. Despite their falling-out, she was devastated. He had been her mainstay, providing her with professional and emotional support for years.

In the years leading up to the outbreak of the war, Baker turned away from the US and focused on performing in France and across Europe, where she was widely solicited and adored by her audiences. By 1939, Baker had remarried and taken French nationality. She returned from an extended South American tour just as war once again threatened to hit the European continent. When it broke out, she chose not to leave, but to participate in the war effort, mobilising her own distinctive armoury to advance the interests of the Allies and particularly those of her adopted country. These wartime experiences would represent a pivotal chapter in Josephine Baker's life and would set her on a completely new course after the war, as this book will reveal.

~

Baker herself remained remarkably silent about her wartime exploits. This is not unusual when considering the actions of women in the Resistance, who often downplayed their own contribution. They would often summarise their participation in terms of having done what was normal or expected in the circumstances, when in fact this was far from the truth.[14] Baker expressed her own engagement in similar terms after the war. In 1949, she said of being awarded the Resistance medal, 'I cannot see that I did anything extraordinary to merit this honour. Everything was just as it had to be.'[15] In later life, Baker continued to be reticent on the subject when we might have expected her to be more open. Typically, when asked about her medals by a *Guardian* reporter in August 1974, she brushed off the question, saying, 'I told them, why give it to me. I didn't do much. Others deserve it more.'[16] She would often assert that she just did what was necessary. In recent years, progress has been made in crediting women for their extensive and multi-faceted contribution to resistance. One of the reasons that their work remained overlooked and undervalued for so long was because of its very invisibility at the time. This was even more the case for those who acted as intelligence agents; of necessity, their wartime stories contain many areas where the full picture may never be uncovered.[17] In addition, in Baker's case, the intelligence landscape within which she operated after the fall of France in 1940 was a highly complex one. In French intelligence alone there were overlapping agencies that disagreed about where national loyalties should lie; and all this was further complicated in a clandestine landscape where operatives from other Allied and Axis countries were also working. It also seems highly likely that Baker did not always know the full content or importance of the intelligence she was transmitting. What is certain, however, is that she acted with a full understanding of the dangers, and she appears to have run the risk willingly and enthusiastically.

While her own accounts of her life, her (auto)biographies, provide important insights, they are fraught with difficulty for the historian. Baker was just twenty-one when her earliest autobiographical account appeared in 1928. It focuses on her arrival in France and her ensuing success, and was the result of a collaboration with the literary critic Marcel Sauvage. From it, Baker learnt the power of her story to enhance her celebrity status, and she continued to practise this approach throughout her life. This is not to say that she was a consummate fabricator, but she knew how to create stories that would draw in her public. She understood that her 'private' life could be of interest and fed into her stage persona. These documents therefore tend to be a bizarre mixture of fact and fiction, telling stories which Baker updated over the years, depending on the mood of the time. They have the advantage that they present us with her 'version' of the narrative, and we can hear her voice commenting on events. The last of the three Sauvage *Mémoires*, published in 1949, includes her life during the war period. While this account tends to be somewhat anecdotal, it is not devoid of interest.

In 1948, just before the appearance of the last of the books in the Sauvage collection, Baker's handler, Jacques Abtey, who had spent most of the war period with her, published his version of events.[18] This is often taken to be the 'true' story of their wartime activities, and to date has been the most highly quoted source for Baker's war record.[19] While it offers detail and insight, and we can certainly learn a good deal from it, there are embellishments, and Abtey had his eye on managing his own post-war reputation.[20] Soon after her death in 1975, Baker's estranged husband, Jo Bouillon, published a semi-autobiographical account of her life.[21] His book pieces together memoirs, some extended passages of writing by Baker herself, supplemented with contributions from members of her close entourage. Designed to make money and to foster a heroic version of her memory, historical accuracy was not the priority. While this, too, includes insightful material, when it comes to the events of the war it follows a very similar narrative to Abtey's 1948 account. Apart from these sources, it is rare to have access to Baker's authentic voice or to have insight into her activities from reliable first-hand witnesses. The key ambition of this study, therefore, has been to take these personalised accounts of Baker's wartime life as a starting point, and cross-check them with other relevant sources, following an archive trail across France, the UK, Morocco and the US.

The collections in France were the starting point. I worked closely with staff at the French military archives in the Château de Vincennes in Paris to unearth documents relating to Baker's work for French intelligence and the work of her senior officers. The material included recordings of revealing interviews with the key protagonists, including Major Paul Paillole and Major Alla Dumesnil, Baker's senior commanding officers. Dumesnil's files offer valuable insight into Baker's role in the Armée de l'Air in 1944–45 in North Africa. Documents about Baker held in the National Archives in Paris were also consulted, including Baker's correspondence with General de Gaulle when he was president of the French Republic. Beyond Paris, I consulted holdings in the local archives in Dordogne, where Baker spent time in 1940 at her Château des Milandes, and in the French diplomatic archives in Nantes, where the Morocco protectorate archives are held.

In the US, archives relating to the Office of Strategic Services, the American intelligence services present in North Africa at the time Baker was there, held in the National Archives in Washington were consulted. However, the documents that have survived are patchy and do not cover the full period. By contrast, the Josephine Baker Collection held at the Beinecke Library at Yale University is a rich holding. Of particular interest to this study was the Henry Hurford Janes Collection, which documents in detail the time Janes spent with Baker in North Africa in 1943, when she was touring the Allied troops. While he was obviously unaware of the intelligence work she was undertaking at the time, his correspondence proved particularly useful. The Eugene Lerner Josephine Baker Collection at Stanford University provided valuable supplementary details. Finally, in the UK, holdings in the National Archives, Kew, on the Entertainments National Service Association (ENSA) and its president Basil Dean, helped provide background into Baker's entertainment work for the association, as did the work of other entertainers – including, for example, Noël Coward and Alice Delysia, who toured North Africa and the Middle East at the same time as Baker.

Press archives proved very fruitful. These include local and national French and North African daily press, Allied military forces press and the British and American press (including African American press), as well as the entertainment press throughout the period which regularly reported on Baker's performances.[22] The *Afro-American* newspaper was particularly valuable: it had closely followed Baker's rise to success in France, updating a US readership with a keen interest in her story, which engendered hope and feelings of pride in her achievements. Baker was one of their own who had made good, despite segregation and the hostile environment it represented. Throughout the war, these editions continued to carry regular updates documenting the challenges and experiences of the star. Baker loved being interviewed: in wartime, as in peacetime, she made a point of meeting reporters, and their articles became a valuable platform for her to promote and amplify her ideas. Baker's exploits entertaining the troops provided them with valuable copy. The African American press was particularly conscientious and kept its readers updated about her movements, although the extent of her wartime activities was only revealed at the end of the war and in very generic terms. This is not to say that some of the reports were not speculation reported as fact to create copy and entertain readers; but for the most part, the material they carried tallies with other sources and represented serious journalism.

It is also worth highlighting the value of the African American press in offering insights into how Baker was seen within the Black community. This is particularly beneficial as, other than these press articles, almost all the sources present Baker through white male eyes. There is just one notable exception: Baker's superior officer in the army, Major Alla Dumesnil, whose archives, a previously unexploited source, provided useful insights for this research. There are aspects of Baker's wartime life that we can never know. But all the sources described here, along with the memoirs of other characters who appear in her story – such as, for example, the British entertainer Noël Coward – have made it possible for this study to draw a compelling picture of the life of the star during this traumatic period.

~

There is a longstanding link between espionage and entertainment, and Baker was not the first to mobilise her celebrity to support her work as a spy.[23] She had several predecessors during the First World War, the most notorious being Mata Hari. Baker was, however, the first woman of colour in the French context to do so. This book is informed by gender,[24] race,[25] celebrity[26] and intelligence[27] scholarship. It explores how Baker claimed, performed and enacted her French identity throughout the period. While the book follows a chronological approach to relating her wartime life, three interlinked themes are developed across the chapters. The first is the theme of celebrity. The book tracks how Baker gradually learnt to exploit her celebrity as a cover to enable her to play her part in the battle to free Europe from Nazi oppression. Her ability to move between countries without arousing the suspicion of the enemy allowed her to become a remarkably effective undercover intelligence agent for the Allies and for France. Secondly, while Baker had distanced herself from other African Americans present in Paris between the wars, the book traces the way in which her contacts with American troops in North Africa led her to 'rediscover' her own identification with the African American cause and to realise that she had a platform to transmit her views that could allow her to act to counter the inequality and injustice represented by segregation. This culminated in a public commitment to join the anti-racist and civil rights movements after the war, first in France and later in the US. Thirdly, the book shows how Baker's social fluidity, her ability to gain acceptance across different social groups and nationalities, allowed her to play an invaluable international role as a cultural facilitator and diplomatic intermediary working tirelessly in the interests of France and the Gaullists until the end of the war.

Baker's unique story continues to resonate today, as is shown by French President Macron's decision in August 2021 to honour her by transferring her ashes to the Panthéon. The *Panthéonisation* ceremony in November of that year celebrated all the achievements of Baker's life as a performer and activist, and brought her war record to the attention of a global public for the first time. But it added little to existing knowledge about her life during this period. This book sets out to go further. In drawing on all the available sources, it offers an extensive exploration of the wartime life of this committed entertainer and espionage agent, who did great service for the Allies and her country.

1

BECOMING AGENT BAKER
(1939–1940)

On 7 August 1939, Josephine Baker returned to Paris from an extended four-month concert tour of South America. She was particularly eagerly awaited by Henri Varna, director of the Casino de Paris, the music hall where she was due to start rehearsing her next show, 'Le soleil de Paris', a Brazilian-style extravaganza scheduled to open at the end of the following month. Determined not to miss any opportunities to promote his star, and keen to celebrate her return, he decided to transform her arrival platform at the Gare de Lyon into a makeshift stage. Decorating it with huge orchid flower arrangements, he arranged for several of his chorus girls bearing colourful bouquets to be there, as well as a handful of his musicians. He even organised for her to be presented with a fox, captured that very morning from his garden – Baker was renowned for her love of animals and maintained a large menagerie. The unfortunate animal refused to cooperate, however, forcing his handler to drag him down the platform on a lead. As planned, Josephine Baker alighted from the train onto the crowded platform to huge applause. Dressed in a white-and-blue striped suit, she wore a charming little straw hat adorned with two swallows, one white and the other black. She was serenaded by members of Varna's orchestra as she greeted all those who were assembled to meet her individually. The welcoming committee included her husband, Jean Lion, Varna, his team and several of the dancers who were due to perform with her. She took her place in the middle of the carefully arranged group behind an array of cages containing the creatures of all kinds that had been gifted to her during her trip. She beamed obligingly at the sea of photographers as she struggled to control the confused fox, who was determined to escape from her arms.

The South American tour had been a huge success. Baker explained to the waiting reporters that she had expected to spend three weeks in Rio after their first stop in Buenos Aires, but had ended up staying for three months, delighting audiences every night with her French repertoire. 'I was worried!' she exclaimed. 'I hadn't been there for ten years. At that time, I was a savage,' she said, referencing her earlier reputation for dancing with abandon in virtually non-existent clothing. 'This time they were waiting to see my dresses so they could copy them,' she announced proudly, going on: 'I've brought so much back home with me.'[1] According to the evening paper, *Ce soir*,[2] she was not exaggerating. Baker's luggage allegedly included: a lion, a kangaroo, six monkeys, around a hundred birds, two hens, ten pigeons and a little frog who unfortunately never made it to French soil – even though Baker had 'travelled with the little creature in my hands to keep her warm'. The party then left the station for the Casino de Paris to indulge in a champagne cocktail reception, which members of the press were also warmly invited to attend.

Images of Baker's extravagant return to the capital adorned the front pages of most of the French papers the following day.[3] Even the communist paper *l'Humanité* carried a large photograph of the scene,[4] bearing testimony to Baker's appeal to a range of different publics at that time. Only the Paris evening paper and the American entertainment paper *Variety* later reported on how her joyful homecoming had been overshadowed by the death of all the tropical birds she had transported. They were discovered dead in their cages by her cook, unable to survive the 'unsuitable Paris climate'.[5]

The staging at the Gare de Lyon was typical of the kind of celebrity moment that Josephine Baker was known for. She and those around her had long understood exactly how to orchestrate situations designed to engage public attention in ways that had allowed her to build unparalleled fame. Varna was particularly expert at this. It was he who had given her a cheetah to publicise its appearance with her in a show at his music hall.[6] She would parade the animal down the Champs-Élysées, clinging on to the lead attached to its diamond collar. It was touches like these that had enabled her to fashion her unique celebrity persona. Baker's success was linked to her ability to feed her audience's fascination with Americanness and Africanness and draw on a range of fantasy-driven colonial stereotypes. The fact that she was from St Louis and had never even been to Africa did not prevent her from playing scenes as a young native girl from somewhere in the French empire, be it Black Africa, the Caribbean (French Antilles), North Africa or even Indochina, in love with a dashing Frenchman.[7] Her skill in embodying this 'colonial pastiche'[8] and 'using nudity and provocative costuming to add to her impact',[9] allowed her to claim a unique position in French interwar music hall. Initially, she was greatly influenced by managers and promoters, but later had more control of her own performances and her image construction.[10] She took the stereotypical views held by the French towards Black Africans and developed an artistic lexicon which subverted and repurposed those very attitudes, playing on them to her own advantage. Her success at this tactic was demonstrated by her nomination as 'Queen of the Colonies' at the Colonial Exhibition in Paris in 1931, a nomination which was later withdrawn after protests that she was from the United States, which was not a French colony.[11]

Baker had not been alone in leaving the US to try her luck in Paris. By the late 1930s, there was a small but well-established thriving community of African American jazz artists, musicians and dancers in the capital, including Baker's friend Ada Louise Smith, known as 'Bricktop', a nickname she acquired owing to her red hair. She had arrived in France in the early 1920s and had built herself a reputation as Queen of the Paris nightclubs, becoming the cornerstone of the African American jazz community in the city. But over the years, Baker had seemed to distance herself from this community and set herself apart from being closely identified with it. When Mussolini invaded Abyssinia during a colonial expedition in

1935, she rather ill-advisedly publicly expressed her support for him. She had taken him at his word when he proclaimed that he would end slavery in the country, and this move led to hostility on the part of the Parisian Black press.[12] Then, in 1937, she moved her nightclub away from Montmartre, known to be a centre for African American community life, and opened a new one in the Rue François 1er, near the Champs-Élysées. To other Black musicians and singers, she appeared to surround herself with white French performers in her shows at the Folies Bergère and the Casino de Paris.[13] They also viewed her performances with some hostility, due to her 'performative eroticism and her willingness to uncritically reproduce colonial stereotypes for the French public'.[14] Mixing in predominantly white circles, Baker appeared to be keen to display her attachment to France and to take every opportunity to publicly demonstrate that she identified as French, rather than American.

In the year after the catastrophic 1936 US tour, as she recovered from Abatino's sudden death, Baker put the trip behind her and began planning another show. She decided to stay in France, where audiences adored her and applauded her talents. It was at this time, when Baker was perhaps a little vulnerable, that she met and married a Paris-based broker, Jean Lion. She appears to have fallen for him very rapidly.[15] Accounts of their meeting differ. Some claim that the two had met while riding in the Bois de Boulogne, others when Lion became a regular visitor to her nightclub (as was reported by the *Daily Mail*).[16] Lion was Jewish, and Baker took to the family and became particularly fond of his mother. She embraced their way of life, gaining first-hand insight into the Jewish experience.[17] This involvement heightened her awareness of the antisemitic and exclusionary policies of the Nazis who were in power in Germany. Significantly, she delighted in the fact that this union allowed her to take French citizenship. The press was just as thrilled: coverage of the marriage shows that journalists were almost as excited about gaining a compatriot as they were about the ceremony itself. The wedding, on 29 November 1937, was held in the town hall of Crèvecoeur-le-Grand, near Lion's family home, a vain effort to avoid the attentions that their wedding would attract in the capital. Just before taking their vows, under the terms of Article 8 of the 1927 French nationality law, Baker was asked by the mayor of the commune if she wanted to abandon her American nationality and be naturalised French. After her enthusiastically positive response, the ceremony could continue.[18] Marrying Lion had allowed Baker to become a French citizen with a French passport, something she valued deeply, particularly after her feeling of rejection by the US.

This was Baker's third marriage. While her marriage to Abatino had been illusory, Baker had actually been married twice before. At the time, it was quite usual across America – and particularly in the Southern States – to marry young. Marriage legitimised children who, born out of wedlock, would otherwise live with the stain of illegitimacy. Importantly, it also legally emancipated children, giving them access to their wages and enabling them to live apart from parents and to make their own decisions.[19] So, at the age of thirteen, Baker had married a boy called Willie Wells. Their union only lasted a few months.[20] She had married her second husband, Willie Baker, when she was fifteen and finally managed to acquire a divorce from him during the disastrous US trip, leaving her free to marry again. She kept his name as her stage name, despite their divorce. In an interview with a *Daily Mail* reporter on the day of her marriage to Lion, Baker announced, 'I am going to leave the stage in line with my husband's wishes' – but then immediately cast some doubt on this ambition.[21] Talking about her husband, in his presence, she told the reporter:

Well, now he says a woman can't be a wife and an actress as well. We shall see. I am going to England on December 12 for what my husband calls 'a farewell tour' ... We shall probably quarrel about it. It's the story of Napoleon and Josephine all over again.

The journalist reported that M. Lion responded in English with the declaration that there would be 'No more stage for Josephine when she has finished the London engagement.'[22] This insistence does not appear to have produced the results her new husband was hoping for: when interviewed again by the *Daily Mail* in Birmingham a few days later, Baker confirmed, 'I have stage contracts for the next 18 months, and I shall go on with them whatever he says.'[23] This assertion was doubtless behind the report in the paper the following day that 'Miss Josephine Baker has refused to retire from the stage following her recent marriage and that decision is a popular one in London.' She went on to explain how the land really lay with her husband: 'He asked me to be sure and go back [to Paris] in a few days – and ended up by promising to come over and join me here instead.'[24]

Baker relished playing out her private life in a public forum. She always had time for a chat with a journalist and would often confide in them, apparently sharing intimate information, well aware that the content of their conversations would appear in print. If indeed Baker had agreed to take a break from the stage, it was short-lived. In late 1938, she told the press that she was not retiring and was once again performing in shows. And in November, she went on tour in Scandinavia.[25]

The marriage was not a success. Whether this was because Baker was reluctant to swap her career for the role of a housewife, or because Lion was not prepared to play second fiddle to this accomplished international star, remains unclear. After a miscarriage,[26] it seems that Baker was quickly tempted back to the stage and to the world of the music hall that she so loved and where she was so adored. Even if the marriage was not destined to last, there were other positives for Baker. For example, Lion flew aeroplanes – an activity which she shared. She had started flying lessons in 1934 and passed her pilot exams in May 1937.[27] Her love of flying and her admiration for those who did would become very pertinent during the war, when she developed a personal affiliation to the French air force and maintained a longstanding identification with it.

Despite the couple's shared interests, the press reported that Baker had filed for divorce in February 1938, just fourteen months after the wedding.[28] Because of the war, their divorce would not be granted until 1941. The couple clearly remained on good terms in the intervening years and may have tried to make a go of things, since a year later there were reports in the press that 'Josephine Baker has no plans to divorce.'[29] Whatever his status, Lion remained a part of her close entourage, and they were regularly seen together in public.[30] In March 1939, *Ce soir* reported on the couple's decision to take an excursion flying together.[31] Lion also accompanied her to Bordeaux to see her off when she left for the South American tour in March 1939.[32] And on her return, in August 1939, she had even made a detour to visit the Lion family home in the Yonne, before appearing at her stage-managed arrival in Paris, where, as we have seen, Lion was present in her welcoming party.

After the festivities marking her return to the capital, and still glowing in the triumph of her South American trip, Baker took a break to recover before rehearsals began for the planned new show. She settled back into her splendid Villa Beau-Chêne located in Le Vésinet, a comfortable suburb to the west of Paris. Purchased with Abatino in 1929, the large stone house was set in lush parkland with a river running through it. Importantly, it offered plenty of space for Baker's menagerie. Her collection of animals was another way of generating publicity and reinforcing the colonial references that were associated with her.[33] Around the same time, she purchased a well-appointed Paris apartment building on Avenue Bugeaud in the 16th arrondissement. She rented out the apartments for income and only kept the top floor for private use. Owning these properties made her feel rooted in France.[34] This sense of belonging would prove a vital lifeline at a time when war was once again looming, despite the diplomatic efforts to placate Hitler at Munich the previous September. As Baker relaxed and recovered at the villa, events took a dramatic turn. Hitler, flouting all the agreements made at Munich, invaded Poland, forcing the hand of the British and French, who declared war on Germany on 3 September 1939. Men, aged between sixteen and thirty-five, were called up, including Baker's husband. Most were sent to the Maginot Line, the fortified border along the frontier with Germany that was at the heart of France's defence strategy. Amidst assurances that the Germans would be quickly defeated, everyone waited anxiously to see how the situation would develop.

The decision to stay

Virtually all the once thriving community of African American musicians and entertainers who had built careers in the French capital in the 1920s and 1930s had already returned to the US as war threatened in 1939. The coming of the Depression, which hit France later than elsewhere, had accelerated this trend. Apart from the economic considerations, African Americans were conscious of the dangers they faced from German racism and hostility, and this acted as a further spur to leave the continent. Many African Americans had established comfortable and prosperous lives for themselves in Europe. They had spent years away from the US, and for those who had been in Paris for ten or even fifteen years, America no longer seemed like home. Their original reasons for leaving in the first place had not gone away, and with segregation still very much in place it was not clear that the US had much to offer them. Nonetheless, reluctantly they came to understand that returning was probably safer than staying in Europe. They also recognised that they were particularly vulnerable both because they were Black and because they were representatives of liberal and democratic America. While Black people did not occupy a central role in Nazi ideology, it articulated a strong hostility towards jazz, which was seen as degenerate. Consequently, by the time war was declared, most African American performers had already weighed up the situation and deduced that returning to the US was in their best interests.[35] A few, like the singer Adelaide Hall, went to London,[36] and a handful of others made their way to cities elsewhere in Europe. Bricktop held out to the last possible moment, as France had become her home. Short of funds to pay for the journey back, she was reluctant to leave even when she knew she should. Returning to America had no appeal for her, but she finally relented when the American embassy explicitly called on all remaining Americans to depart in October 1939. It was then that she contacted her sister to lend her the money for the ticket.[37]

Baker had every reason to wish to avoid any contact with the Germans, and her decision to stay on in Paris was a rare exception to the widespread trend for Americans to return home. The *Afro-American* newspaper pointed this out to its readers soon after the outbreak of the war, with the headline 'Everybody but Jo'. Her decision was applauded: 'we can't help but admire Jo, France liked her in peace. She stands by France in War.'[38] Baker understood the threat represented by the Nazis. When she had visited Austria and Germany in 1929, while in Vienna, the first stop of her tour, the Nazis had demonstrated against her appearances. Pamphlets were circulated denouncing her as a 'Black Devil' and conservative groups petitioned the Vienna City Council to have her performances cancelled. During her stay, the conservatives continued to press their case and lobbied the Austrian parliament, which debated whether Baker's performances were a threat to public morals; but in the end, her shows went ahead. Despite her enthusiastic reception by audiences, Baker felt she had been effectively targeted.[39] Some months later, in Germany, Baker was unnerved by Nazi sympathisers heckling during her performances; her shows were cancelled in Munich, a Nazi stronghold, and she was forbidden from performing. The attitude of the National Socialists towards so-called 'degenerate' jazz musicians became more vocal after they took power in 1933. Baker herself was directly attacked in a brochure produced by Nazi propaganda minister Joseph Goebbels in 1937. Her picture – alongside those of other 'degenerate' artists, including Max Reinhardt, Siegfried Arno and Ernst Deutsch – was reproduced on the front of the brochure.[40] Thenceforth Baker knew that she was in the Nazis' sights. In addition, she was married to a Jewish man and was acutely aware of the dangers that Jews faced from Nazism. However, unlike most other African Americans in Paris, Baker felt that France was now her home and, as a French citizen, she should share in the misfortunes that befell her compatriots. She gambled on the fact that her French nationality would protect her, should she fall into Nazi hands. So she stayed. Like only a handful of others, her decision was marked by her feeling of integration into French life. She stayed as a Frenchwoman, not as a Black American.[41]

Despite the fears of the French people, the sky did not fall on their heads in the days and weeks that followed the declaration of war. The military was on high alert, but civilians were largely kept in the dark. No one really knew what this war would look like or how it was likely to develop. Reproducing First World War military strategy, French High Command had gambled on a defensive approach. It was convinced that the Maginot Line would hold and that those areas not covered by that line of defence, including the area of the Ardennes Forest on the Franco-Belgian border, would prove impossible for the German army to penetrate. When bomb attacks failed to materialise, mothers soon fetched their children home from evacuation locations. Parisians gradually began to adjust to the changed wartime circumstances. They became accustomed to the absence of loved ones, and did their best to carry on with their lives in the changed situations of the strange period of the phoney war. One of the most visible changes in the capital came with the blackout. Cafés, restaurants and cinemas reopened, but had to ensure that they had closed by nightfall. One American journalist explained how

Blackouts, have become a permanent nightly factor of Paris life. A flashlight and gas mask complete one's attire for circulating after dark. Curbs at all intersections, signal boxes, trees and posts are all painted in white, even traffic cops are draped in white cloaks and helmets for visibility to motorists who must drive in the darkness with dim-colored headlights.[42]

It was at this time, just weeks after the outbreak of the war, that Baker had her first meeting with Captain Jacques Abtey – a meeting that would launch her on an entirely new path.

Joining the French intelligence services

Abtey was a thirty-year-old from Alsace who since 1936 had been working in French military intelligence, in the department known as the Deuxième Bureau. In his role as deputy head of German military counterespionage, his first posting was in Nantes, under Captain Paul Paillole and Lieutenant Colonel Schlesser, head of counterespionage at Military High Command.[43] At the outbreak of war, in September 1939, Abtey was asked to become head of counterespionage in the Paris region. Throughout the 1930s, the French intelligence services had been struggling to keep track of the huge increase in the number of German agents in France, the 'Fifth Column' as it was known. With only modest means available to fight them, Abtey's limited funds meant he struggled to recruit enough French agents to be adequately informed about their whereabouts. He was therefore dependent on enlisting the help of a network of what were known as 'honourable correspondents' – people who were prepared to work for him voluntarily, out of patriotism.

Felix Marouani had been working as Baker's impresario since 1936. His older brother, Daniel Marouani, also an impresario, worked for Abtey as an honourable correspondent. Daniel, who also knew Baker very well, considered her to have many qualities that would make her very useful in this role. He held her in high esteem, considering her to be courageous, sincere and deeply grateful to France.[44] Aware of Abtey's financial constraints, Daniel recommended Baker to him and repeatedly pressed him to meet her, indicating that he could arrange for this to take place.[45]

Initially, Abtey rejected the suggestion. His judgement – and doubtless that of others in the French intelligence service – was influenced by the disastrous forays into the use of female spies during the previous war. He had Mata Hari in mind.[46] She had been executed by the French on 15 October 1917, having been found guilty of the war crime defined as 'espionage and intelligence with the enemy'. The French had believed that she was working as a double agent for them, but they became suspicious when it transpired that she was taking money from the Germans (though it remains unclear whether she actually passed on any sensitive information to them). Nonetheless, her exploits attracted press attention, and she became legendary.

For Abtey to have judged Baker's potential as a spy on the basis of this unfortunate experience was perhaps a little unfair. There were other female performers who had more success as spies. Mistinguett, for example, one of the best-known music-hall stars at that time, had collected vital wartime intelligence while working directly for General Gamelin, one of France's top generals during the Great War.[47] From his point of view, her most astonishing contribution was to discover from her former lover, the Prussian Prince Johannes zu Hohenlohe-Bartenstein, in June 1918 that the final German offensive would take place in Champagne, and not as expected on the Somme. This allowed the Allies to be well prepared and to thwart Germany's last hope of victory. However, Abtey was unlikely to have been aware of the significance of Mistinguett's activities, as Gamelin only revealed them in a secret report written the day after her death in 1956.[48]

Another aspect that made Abtey sceptical was the image he had of Baker gleaned from press coverage about her over the years, which presented her as a somewhat eccentric, if exceptional, artiste.[49] He eventually overcame his initial reticence, as his need was so great and Marouani was so insistent. After agreeing to meet Baker, he found himself becoming more curious about her. He recounts how he and Daniel Marouani went together to see her at her Le Vésinet home some weeks after the outbreak of the war. His story starts with his unexpected first sight of the star, very much at home in her garden collecting snails, dressed in a pair of old trousers and felt hat, and looking anything but the glamorous figure he was expecting. She greeted them warmly, addressing Abtey by the cover name she had been given, 'Monsieur Fox'. He was posing as a British captain. Baker, it seems, was just as astonished to meet this blond, athletic, dynamic man of her age.[50] She later confided to Abtey that she had been expecting the kind of detective who normally inhabits crime thrillers: an elderly gentleman wearing a traditional bowler hat, with a moustache and a cigar in his mouth; short, fat, his clothes reeking of cheap tobacco, with bushy eyebrows and piercing, shifty eyes.[51]

She had prepared herself, we are told, for someone dubious and mysterious, so when Abtey spoke to her, his German-sounding accent seemed to confirm her suspicions. He quickly explained that he was from the Alsace region, on the border with Germany, and the local accent was frequently mistaken for a German one. He reassured her that it was a common error. She led them to the house, where she arranged for them to be served champagne while they talked. During the conversation, Abtey was moved by the way she spoke about France. Despite his low expectations, Baker's commitment to France and her desire to return the debt she felt she owed her adopted country was obvious. She was keen to do all she could for the war effort. In a moving declaration, which may have lent itself to a bit of embellishment in the sources, she explained how Parisians had taken her to their hearts and that in exchange she was ready to give them her life.[52] 'France made me what I am. Today I am ready to give my life for my country.'[53] This probably paraphrases what she actually said, but it conveys the sentiment. Abtey's detailed description of this meeting, and its presentation of what they said, felt and thought on meeting one another, has the hallmark of hyperbole, a recurring characteristic of his account.

However, Abtey was impressed with Baker's commitment to France and her enthusiasm to play her part in defending the country, and decided to give her a try. What did he have to lose by seeing what she could achieve? He set her a task, asking her to work her connections at the Italian embassy to contact an attaché there who was of particular interest to the French intelligence services.[54] Baker's support for Italy's Abyssinia campaign in 1935 meant that she was still well regarded by the Italians, and this provided her with a convenient entrée to contrive a meeting with the attaché in question. Within a few days, she excitedly reported back to Abtey that she had contacted the individual concerned. They arranged to meet, so she could give him a full report. She came to collect Abtey in her luxury American Packard car. Once he had climbed in, she quickly and eagerly started telling him that she had been told that the Italians would probably join the Nazis in declaring war on the Allies – and indeed they did, but not until 10 June 1940. Her excitement at being able to relate this information was such that she took her eyes off the road, thereby attracting the attention of a policeman who blew on his whistle, thinking he had encountered a drunken driver. Baker's smile rapidly allayed his fears, and the officer sent them on their way. But the episode left Abtey wondering whether she really was cut out for espionage. Would he be capable of giving her the training she would clearly need to be effective at this kind of work?[55]

Once he realised what she had achieved on this initial trial mission, Abtey decided that Baker had more than proved herself. The intelligence she had succeeded in extracting from the unsuspecting diplomatic official corresponded exactly with other information that French counter-intelligence had already collected in these early months of the phoney war in relation to the wartime ambitions of the Italians. He decided that even if she did not fit with the traditional notions of the inconspicuous spy who blended into the background and passed unnoticed, Baker had something different to offer: she could hide in plain sight. So long as no one suspected her, her star power allowed her access to places and interactions with individuals that could prove very helpful. Abtey became convinced that she could be useful to the intelligence services, and he decided that he would act as her handler and set about preparing her for the challenges that she might need to contend with.[56] As he started training her in the art of spy-craft, he found her to be a fast learner and an alert apprentice.[57] She was soon able to build on this initial achievement. On friendly terms with the Japanese ambassador, Renzo Sawada, she invited herself to the embassy and used her contacts to acquire information about Japan's attitude to the conflict. She also supplied Abtey with essential information uncovering the identity of certain German agents in Paris.[58]

There was no doubting Baker's enthusiasm. But for her work as an honourable correspondent to be effective, it was vital for it to remain completely invisible to her unsuspecting admirers. Remarkably, and to some extent counterintuitively, Baker appears to have excelled at playing this 'double game' while still maintaining high visibility in her public persona. She was entirely credible. In her public life, she enthusiastically followed up on every possible opportunity to show her patriotic fervour to the people of her adopted country. The press frequently carried articles showing Baker writing to her numerous soldier *filleuls*, or godchildren, at the front,[59] or handing out toys to needy children in the capital.[60]

Throughout the early months of the war, Baker juggled a remarkably heavy timetable, integrating her intelligence work with her other activities. Along with all this, she was also rehearsing for a new show that had been created by Varna. This would be an opportunity for her to shore up the morale of Allied servicemen and play to what would become one of her most effective strengths.

At the Théâtre aux Armées: November 1939

In late October 1939, the newspapers announced that the following month Baker – along with Maurice Chevalier, France's most famous star – had plans to sing for the troops at the front before she returned to Paris to appear at the Casino de Paris.[61] Varna had been forced to shelve his plans for Baker's Brazilian-themed performance once the outbreak of war had become inevitable. Instead, he set about organising an alternative spectacle, designed to entertain the hundreds of off-duty French and British soldiers who, stationed in France since the declaration of war, came to Paris in search of amusement during their forty-eight hours of leave. Varna contacted Chevalier, another of his long-time collaborators, with a view to creating a patriotically imbued extravaganza that would appeal to both nationalities. Headlined by Chevalier and Baker, it also showcased Chevalier's lesser-known younger companion, Nita Raya.[62] Named 'Paris-London' to reflect that it was a celebration of the Franco-British alliance, the show included both French and English songs and performers. As advance publicity, and in line with the ambitions of the military to provide troops with entertainment, it had been agreed that in November 1939, Baker, Chevalier and Raya would take a few numbers from the show to venues in the Lorraine area, near the Maginot Line, as part of what was known as the Théâtre aux Armées.

Soldiers always had to combat extreme boredom on the front line, and even more so during this strange, phoney war, when nothing seemed to be progressing. Any entertainment that could help to pass the time and distract them was very welcome. Live performances for the troops had first been created by Émile Fabre, administrator of the Comédie-Française during the First World War. He had brought actors to the front to put on classic plays. In autumn 1939, the Théâtre aux Armées was relaunched under an agreement between the Military General Staff and the Ministry of Culture (Direction générale des Beaux-Arts). Front-line troops were promised 'first-class stars' and 'shows for which Parisians would pay good money'.[63] The first tour was launched on 7 November 1939 with these appearances by Baker and Chevalier.

Despite the aspirational promises made in these announcements, bringing such huge stars as Chevalier and Baker to the front was exceptional. It was doubtless another of Varna's publicity stunts, designed to draw attention to the Paris show; and the volume of the coverage of their visit suggests that his ambition paid off. The stars performed eight concerts between 7 and 10 November in venues in the areas around Metz, Thionville and other places, which were kept secret.[64] For days after their tour, the papers carried photographs of the pair posing in front of a venue, surrounded by a sea of delighted soldiers.[65] In one particularly memorable appearance, they were filmed for the army newsreel *Journal de Guerre*, which would have been widely shown to soldiers, and possibly also to civilians in cinemas across the country. One recording of Baker performing her most popular hit, 'J'ai deux amours', is particularly clear and gives a real sense of how she interacted with her audiences, involving them in a sing-along.[66]

Press reports describe the packed venues and rapturous welcome that both stars received from off-duty soldiers thirsty for entertainment and distraction. Baker was even made an honorary corporal of one of the regiments she entertained.[67] At one of the venues, when she was presented with a bouquet of golden dahlias by one of the soldiers, she carefully undid the bow and threw each flower into the audience. Then she left the stage to mingle with the soldiers, handing out cigarettes, shaking hands, signing autographs and embracing them.[68] When interviewed about the experience, both stars paid tribute to their audiences, explaining to one journalist that they were 'both delighted and moved by what they had seen'. Baker went on: 'I'm not going to talk about me, but about them, our precious soldiers. We just did our best to amuse them, and they listened to us intently with faces of angels.'[69]

Baker was not just the darling of the French soldiers at the front: thanks to the efforts of the Théâtre aux Armées, in coordination with its British counterpart ENSA, she also put on some exclusive performances for the British forces.[70] ENSA – affectionately dubbed by soldiers 'Every Night Something Awful' – had been founded by Basil Dean, a theatre entrepreneur who had long worked to put together what he called a 'Theatre of War'. In September 1939, he took up offices in the Theatre Royal, Drury Lane, and immediately started to arrange concerts for the troops at home, as well as sending out companies to entertain the British Expeditionary Forces stationed in France. Gracie Fields, a British music-hall star, was one of those he booked to feature in a performance at Drury Lane, topping the bill along with Maurice Chevalier. She also made a brief tour of France, giving a concert at Douai on 12 November 1939, followed by another in Arras.[71]

In one such event, probably also organised by ENSA, Baker proved a sensation with British airmen. A journalist from *Ce soir* recalled the evening in Reims, where she was welcomed with wild enthusiasm.[72] Reports also appeared in the *Royal Air Force Journal*[73] and the *RAF Weekly News Magazine*:

> Between battles, the British pilots often were able to snatch an hour or so to be entertained by visiting artistes sent out by ENSA. At one of these concerts, Josephine Baker was the big attraction. To those who had seen her on the stages of peace-time Paris she presented an unfamiliar appearance wearing a respectable amount of clothes. The house rose to her and she remarked that it was the first time for years that she had heard an audience whistle as a sign of enthusiasm. After she had sung a couple of songs, wearing a long, white evening dress, she said naively: 'I'm not used to singing in my clothes.' She had not long to wait for a reply. 'Then take 'em off' yelled the airmen in unison. She removed the frock, revealing a much scantier one which showed an expanse of bare brown back.[74]

Baker was still capitalising on her past in these troop performances, wearing revealing outfits even though she was, by this point, a well-established singer. In the early years of the war, teasing soldiers by taking off outer layers of her clothing continued to be a central facet of her appeal, and the troops loved it!

After three days of appearances, the stars returned to Paris for final rehearsals, and on 1 December 1940 the new show finally opened at the Casino de Paris. Opening night was a glitzy affair, with the stars each donating their share of the income to their chosen charities. For Baker, this was the Red Cross. The 'Paris set' (*Le tout Paris*) was there, including Mistinguett, the Duke and Duchess of Windsor and the Brazilian ambassador, M. Souza-Dantas, along with military generals from both the French and British armies to mark this celebration of the 'Entente Cordiale'. Advertised in both French and English, the show's audience comprised a mix of French and English civilians and military.[75] As well as its three headliners, other acts included a British troupe of sixteen 'Greasley Beauties', who performed what was described by *The Bystander* as a 'cymbal dance'. The photograph carried in the report shows the sixteen women in a chorus line, brandishing a small cymbal in each hand and dancing in formation.[76] *Variety* acknowledged that they contributed to the show's success.[77] Baker was star of the first half, while Chevalier and Raya dazzled in the second. Baker opened by performing some of her best-known tunes; then she appeared as some of the well-known characters she had made famous over the years in five large-scale tableaux, each recreating colonial and South American scenes. For her finale, she sang a new serenade written for her by Vincent Scotto, 'Mon cœur est un oiseau des îles' ('My Heart Is Like an Island Songbird').

Press reviews were unanimously positive and had a good word for all the performers. Baker was 'exquisite' for one reviewer;[78] and for another she was 'lively, playful and sentimental . . . Chevalier's worthy partner'.[79] For most reviewers, however, it was Chevalier who stole the show, as he 'had never been on such good form'[80] and 'has never been so perfect'.[81] *Mercure de France* agreed, with the assessment that 'Josephine is a big hit every night . . . but Maurice is a triumph'. It also noted that the stars performed separately, and acknowledged that this was 'doubtless . . . so that they would not be jealous of one another', hinting perhaps that there could have been problems between the two stars.[82] The British press was no less laudatory. *The Bystander* carried a very early review of the show, dedicating three full pages to it. The first was devoted to fifty-year-old Chevalier, who was probably better known to a British reader-ship at that time than Baker.[83] The production was described to readers in some detail:

> This huge factory of entertainment employing several hundred persons had lain idle since September until, soon after a deputa-tion of decorators, painters, costumiers, and so on had gone to Henri Varna to urge him to re-open, regulations and public demand made this possible. The revue, its guiding spirit the Entente Cordiale now blossomed into military alliance, bills Chevalier and Josephine Baker together for the first time. Third star is the young sensation of the last pre-war Casino revue, Nita Raya. The rest of the cast is strictly Franco-British, and many of their turns were shown first to the Army at a front-line concert broadcast to this country.[84]

The popular British photo-magazine *Picture Post* featured a photo reportage announcing the show as 'A Treat for Allied Airmen'. It carried a large image of Baker leaning over into the audience from the stage, giggling with some soldiers.[85] The article insisted that Baker's show was 'one of the things to see first in wartime Paris' for those on leave from the front. Rumours about her planned retirement – which seem to have taken a particular hold in Britain – were squashed:

> When she married M. Jean Lion, a wealthy French industrialist, there was talk of her retiring. But it was only talk. She has continued to hearten the world's pleasure-seekers and to startle ordinary folk by parading in public her monkeys, parrot, three dogs, twelve cats, her rabbits and canaries.[86]

The exact composition of Baker's ever-changing menagerie provided many column inches for journalists in both countries, and in 1939 this was lapped up by a readership eager for distraction from war news. The *Philadelphia Tribune* reported on her status as 'France's sweetheart' and extolled her 'beautifully rich and melodious voice . . . the fruit of her long relentless years of toil on the theatrical stage'.[87] For the entertainment journal *Variety*, Baker 'proves she's unique among Paris entertainers and that she has the quality of getting maximum effect out of old material. She charms with her friendly informal manner.'[88] This friendliness and skill at interacting with her spectators was often commented on by the press, and was seen as one of Baker's great assets as a performer.

Baker was much in demand and there was no doubting her popularity. She thrived on the attention. One press article described how, during the interval of her 'Paris-London' show, a 'throng of military and civilian visitors invaded Josephine's dressing room to greet her or ask for autographed photos'.[89] As well as her regular shows at the Casino de Paris, she was always game for putting on additional performances for soldiers at other venues. On one occasion, she joined the 'Greasley girls' on a trip 'somewhere in France' to help a group of mostly British soldiers celebrate Christmas.[90] She often carried out hospital visits to injured soldiers and encouraged them to join in with spontaneous sing-alongs if a piano could be found. In her role as wartime *marraine*, or godmother, to as many as 1,500 soldiers (according to one paper), she somehow found time to send Christmas parcels to every single one.[91] It was even reported that she had acted as a witness for one of them at his wedding.[92] She also became godmother to one of the French fighter squadrons, the Groupe de Chasse 1/2 'Les Cigognes' ('The Storks'), and there is a photograph of her visiting them in the winter of 1939–40.[93] She often appeared on the radio, singing and delivering comic sketches.[94] To this demanding programme of good works and regular appearances at the Casino de Paris and elsewhere, Baker added yet another commitment. In January 1940, she started shooting a new film.

Fausse Alerte: A film of overlooked importance for Baker

Fausse Alerte (*False Alarm*), a romantic comedy directed by Jacques de Baroncelli, is set during the phoney war in autumn 1939, the action taking place just a few months before the film was shot. It has loosely patriotic propaganda ambitions and satirises life in Parisian air-raid shelters. Baker plays a Parisian nightclub owner, Mlle Zazu Clairon, who, not unlike Baker herself, both owns a nightclub and performs in it. Baker sings three numbers in the film, dressed in outfits with plunging necklines and revealing a bare stomach – all very much in keeping with the role she plays, without being too provocative. Her exuberance while performing and her ability to engage come across strongly both in the dialogue and particularly in the scenes of the film where she takes the stage. The rather trivial plot is concentrated on a pair of star-crossed lovers, Claire and Bernard, who are aided by Baker's character in overcoming the hostility of their respective widowed parents, her mother and his father. Both they and their parents find each other by the film's end. However, the contrived plot is less important than the repartee between the characters and their environment. The story centres on an underground air-raid shelter in the cellar of a bourgeois apartment building in central Paris which serves to bring together a variety of characters from contrasting social backgrounds. Along with Baker and the two bourgeois families represented by the lovers and their parents, there is a local café owner and his wife, and a homeless man whom Mlle Zazu takes under her wing. The film sets out to offer a lesson on how these disparate members of French society pull together during this period of national difficulty, and to show that life and love can continue despite the adverse circumstances of the war.

The screenplay presents Baker in a very different light from the exotic colonial fantasy personas she played in her previous films *La Sirène des Tropiques* (1927), *Zouzou* (1934) and *Princesse Tam Tam* (1935). Those films were little more than vehicles for her celebrity, with Baker as the central character. In them, she explicitly adopted a colonial role in stories that set her apart from French metropolitan populations.[95] In *Fausse Alerte*, Baker's character also has 'colonial origins' (the implication being that she is from Martinique), but she is not presented as an outsider to the community. On the contrary, she is shown to be very much a part of the French nation in all its diversity, sharing the hardships of wartime along with others in her neighbourhood. Importantly, she moves from being cast as a romantic figure of unfulfilled desire who never gets her man, to a respected maternal figure with a full role to play in French society.

In what appears to have been a remarkably rapid production time, the film was already previewing in cinemas by early May 1940, when it was well received and attracted a good deal of coverage in the press. *Le Figaro* referred to it on 4 May as a 'cheerful comedy, inspired by the first months of the war'.[96] But as one astute journalist understood, the film had missed its moment. He commented that it had the 'feel of a very recent time which has already passed, when Paris, in its preparations for war, was still unaware of what war would bring'.[97] Despite gaining some advance publicity, by the time most reviews were published, public attention was focused elsewhere, as the events of the war took a dramatic turn. Few would get to see the film during its first, brief period of release in May 1940. While the propaganda message that *Fausse Alerte* promoted was a rather weak patriotic one, on their arrival in Paris the following month, the Germans required all screenings of the film to cease and compelled the new Vichy French authorities to seize all copies of it.[98]

The film was re-released after the war in France in 1945, and a heavily cut version with the English title *The French Way* surfaced in the US in 1952. By that time, its subject matter was even less relevant, and this doubtless contributed to the film being almost completely forgotten. Even Baker makes no reference to it in her autobiography, unlike her other films. For American reviewers, its main interest lay in Baker's participation, which was seen as the main selling point of the 'mildly entertaining French language picture',[99] a 'light farce ... [which] promises to stir up little or no excitement at the American Box Office' – although that particular reviewer conceded that 'Miss Baker does amazingly well in her slight role'.[100] Despite these lukewarm assessments, the film's importance from the point of view of Baker's story lies in its portrayal of Baker as a full member of the French national community.[101]

Meanwhile, events were taking a dramatic turn in the war. The encouraging headlines in the papers about the impressive perfor-mance of the French and British troops were not being borne out in practice, and it was becoming increasingly apparent that the Allied defences were not performing as effectively as had been promised. The Germans broke through the Allied lines with alarming speed. Refugees from Belgium, Luxembourg and the Netherlands had flooded into Paris, carrying with them a shocking message of mili-tary collapse. The numbers arriving in the French capital increased dramatically, and managing their plight became a major headache for the authorities, which worked hard to move them on to safety further south. The Red Cross fulfilled a major role in providing aid for these unfortunate populations. Baker wanted to play her part and, in line with her commitment to the air force, she decided to volunteer with one of its affiliated groups that was linked to the Red Cross, the Infirmières pilotes secouristes de l'air (IPSA). It has been suggested that she may have flown some missions for them at this point, but there is no evidence of this, and it seems unlikely, since it would have been very dangerous. However, in May 1940, under the aegis of this organisation, she regularly volunteered at a former shelter for homeless people in central Paris where the IPSA had arranged for the provision of support for destitute Belgian refugees.[102]

Many disparate individuals were present in these shelters, with only limited screening of their identities possible. All too well aware that they were unable to keep track of the growing number of German operatives in the capital, Abtey's intelligence services warned Baker to be on the alert for possible Abwehr agents who could be hiding among the refugees. One night, Baker phoned Abtey and asked him to come down to the shelter. When he arrived with a colleague, she pointed out a handful of individuals who she thought looked suspi-cious. One was the only young man in a group of elderly Belgians.

'Shouldn't he be fighting in uniform?' she asked. She then showed them another two 'suspects' in an adjacent room who were speaking in heavily accented French. 'If you carried out careful checks on these people, I'm sure you would be in for a few surprises.'[103] Subsequent investigations revealed nothing out of the ordinary: the three individuals were indeed Belgian nationals who, like all the others, had fled ahead of the German advance. Nonetheless, Abtey's service did decide to leave an agent at the shelter to keep an eye on the situation. A couple of days later, a man claiming to be a German 'deserter' was uncovered as a spy and arrested.[104] Baker's suspicions had not proved completely unfounded.

Remarkably, Baker managed to juggle her clandestine activities along with her multiple public commitments throughout this phoney-war period. She appeared to relish the demands being made on her and followed up on every request. As the influx of refugees into the capital increased, news filtered through of the desperate evacuation across the Channel of the Allied forces at Dunkirk, leaving the French feeling abandoned. By the end of May 1940, the Germans were proving unstoppable and looked likely to reach Paris within days. People began to wonder if they were being told the full story. Those who were able to leave and had the means to do so deserted the capital. Others began to wonder whether they, too, should consider making plans for departure. As the situation became increasingly worrying, Josephine's decision to throw in her lot with France was about to have serious consequences.

2

SERVING FRANCE
(1940–1941)

The bombardment of Paris on 3 June changed everything for the inhabitants of the city. It brought the perceived new normality of the phoney war to an abrupt end. Not only were 204 people killed and 906 injured, but it demonstrated that the Germans were confident enough to carry out a bombing raid in broad daylight. It alerted Parisians to their own vulnerability and the realisation that they were at personal risk. The trickle of initial departures now started to grow exponentially as fear of a German onslaught gripped the capital. The numbers of spectators attending the Casino de Paris dwindled significantly, as people were no longer inclined to attend music-hall shows. Varna called a meeting and advised everyone that he was closing the venue and wished them all luck.[1] In the days that followed, the situation only seemed to get worse. By 8 June, the German forces had reached Forges-les-Eaux, just 75 miles north of Paris. Ever since the start of the offensive on 10 May, the French government had insisted that it would stay in the capital whatever happened. When it was announced on the radio on 10 June that the government had left Paris for military reasons, it was clear to everyone that the arrival of the Germans in the city must be imminent. A hysterical panic broke out as everyone attempted to leave as swiftly as they could.

The success of the Nazi invasion brought Baker's decision to stay in France into stark relief. She knew that she risked more than just being a target of derision if the Germans found her in Paris. At the very least, she was likely to face internment, despite her French nationality. She therefore had more reason than most to get out of the city and make every effort to stay ahead of the conquering armies. Thousands of Parisians were leaving their homes by whatever means they could. They besieged railway stations; and when the last trains had departed, they took to the roads by bicycle or set off on foot if that was the only way. Desperate to escape the Germans, they joined the millions of fleeing refugees from Belgium, the Netherlands and Luxembourg. Some made for places they were familiar with; others just headed south and west, hoping that they would be able to find food and shelter along the way. Many ended up sleeping rough in barns or at the roadside as the towns of the south swelled and struggled to accommodate these now destitute arrivals.[2] Baker was lucky. She had a destination. Since 1938, she had been renting a property in Dordogne, the Château des Milandes, and she knew immediately that she should go there.

Escape from Paris

It is not clear exactly when Baker left Paris, but leave she did – probably in the days that followed the bombing of the capital. She packed up the Villa Beau-Chêne and left it in the hands of a reduced staff. She loaded as much as she could into her Packard – allegedly including a supply of petrol that she had collected in champagne bottles – and left with her maid, Paulette.

> I went, taking everything that I could in the car with me including a Belgian refugee couple, my faithful Paulette, and the animals that I didn't want to leave in the Le Vésinet house ... [The château] is a remote haven hidden away in a wilderness on the banks of the river Dordogne. In the past two years, I had only stayed there briefly between engagements, furnishing it little by little but secure in the knowledge that I would return there one day for a longer spell.[3]

She could not have ever imagined how useful the château would prove during the war, providing her with a haven when she most needed it.

She did well to leave the capital when she did. The Germans marched into Paris on 14 June, and in response the government moved from its first stop in the area around Tours further south, to Bordeaux. Marshal Philippe Pétain, an eighty-year-old hero of the First World War, was brought into government on 18 May and immediately began pressing for an armistice, believing that all was lost. By mid-June, the French army was withdrawing in disarray. The soldiers who were intermingled with the fleeing civilians – mainly women, children and the elderly – attracted the attention of German and Italian planes, whose indiscriminate machine-gun attacks intensified the panic. As members of the government argued vociferously about next steps, with some believing that the battle could continue from North Africa or even London, the consensus in the cabinet gradually shifted towards an acceptance of Pétain's view that requesting an armistice was the only way to save what was left of the country. There was little confidence in the British capacity to carry on the war against the Germans single-handedly. The Americans were unlikely to be able to come to their aid, apart from offering minimal air support. The assumption was that the British could only hold out for another few weeks before they, too, succumbed to Hitler's armies. Prime Minister Reynaud, who persistently pressed for a way to be found to carry on the fight, resigned in response to what he saw as a prevailing defeatism, and Pétain was immediately appointed in his place. The following day, 17 June, Pétain broadcast his intention to ask the Germans for an armistice, explaining to the French people: 'It is with a heavy heart that I have to tell you that the time has come to stop the fighting . . .'

The terms of the ensuing armistice agreement with Germany, which came into force three days after it was signed on 22 June 1940, were harsher than expected: 1.2 million French soldiers were taken prisoner and France was divided into zones. The largest of these was an 'occupied zone' in the industrial north, to be adminis-tered by the Germans. As Bordeaux fell within this zone, the government needed to find a new base in the unoccupied area, in the 'southern' or 'free' zone, which remained under the authority of the French. It alighted on the spa town of Vichy, whose multiple hotels could house the government ministries, and where the casino provided a place for the National Assembly to meet. The two zones were separated by a line of demarcation, which quickly functioned as a serious border. Overnight, the country was split into two and the Germans required everyone to have the appropriate papers to be allowed to cross from one side to the other. Fortunately for Baker, her château fell just inside the southern zone, beyond the area that came under direct German occupation. The property was located close to the demarcation line, which passed through the western edge of the *département* of Dordogne.

Dordogne: Summer 1940

Baker appears to have covered the 350 miles between Paris and her château without too much difficulty. This suggests that she probably left before the huge rush of departures, and was therefore spared the worst of the traumatic experiences suffered by those who fled at the last minute. Testimonies speak of the immense traffic jams that formed on overflowing roads packed with motor vehicles of all kinds, peasant carts, cyclists and pedestrians. Progress was painfully slow, and terror struck when these columns of fleeing civilians were machine-gunned by the Germans.[4] Léon Werth, for example, a writer who left Paris on 10 June 1940 to get to the family's second home in Saint-Amour in the Jura, wrote an account of their traumatic journey. A straightforward run which normally took them a few hours, ended up taking thirty-three days.[5]

In the weeks that followed Baker's arrival at the château, despite the disastrous turn of events for her adopted country, life appears to have carried on in relative peace. Situated on a hill above the river Dordogne, while not very visible from below, Baker's château overlooks the river valley. Its turrets and formal gardens give it a fairy-tale atmosphere. The fortified main building dominates a larger *domaine* with a chapel, stables and outhouses, as well as several other dwellings. The nearest tiny village of Castelnaud-Fayrac was a ten-minute drive away, and it took nearly half an hour to reach the local town of Sarlat. With her normal flourish for a good story, Baker recounts in her memoirs how she fell in love with the château straight away.[6] Its real name was the Château des Mirandes, but Baker could not pronounce this, so the property gradually became known as Château des Milandes – or Les Milandes. The story goes that she had met the owner on an ocean liner when crossing the Atlantic in 1935, and he had told her about the property. Then, when visiting the Périgord region in 1938 with her lover Jean Meunier, whom she was seeing after separating from Jean Lion, she remembered that conversation and decided that she would visit the château. It was then that she fell for the place and, with typical impetuousness, she made the immediate decision to rent it.

During the summer of 1940, Baker was not alone at the château. As well as the people she had brought with her, including the Belgian couple she had met at the shelter where she volunteered in Paris, it seems likely that her husband's family were also with her.[7] She was, after all, still married, and she was very fond of them.[8] Lion himself was not present, as he had been called up to fight. As Jews, the arrival of the Germans in the country meant that their situation had become very precarious, and anxieties would have been running high. For the Lion family, the remoteness of the château was an advantage, and they must have hoped to avoid attracting the attention of the authorities. At worst, it would buy them some time while they planned their next steps. In these early days of the Occupation, it was not clear how the French government would react to events.

The day after Pétain's announcement from Bordeaux that he was requesting an armistice from the Germans, a little-known general named Charles de Gaulle issued an *appel* – appeal – to the French military on the BBC, urging them to carry on the battle and join him in London. It is not clear whether Baker heard his broadcast on 18 June 1940. Most French people did not, and there was no reason why she should have. At the time, the focus of public interest was very much on Pétain. Many had received his announcement with relief: displaced from their homes and separated from loved ones, the French people craved normality. They wanted the nightmare to end, enabling them to go home and be reunited with their families. Pétain seemed to offer them that outcome. Those who chose to reject the armistice, like de Gaulle, were extremely few and far between. The French people believed in and trusted Pétain. A hero of the First World War, he seemed to be offering a viable way forward when the country was in an unprecedented state of crisis. Like most French people, Baker probably came to have knowledge of de Gaulle's appeal only subsequently. It was repeated several times on the radio. It seems most likely that she learnt of it from Abtey, who turned up at the château some weeks later.[9] He, on the other hand, moved in military circles and there were structural reasons why he would have been informed about de Gaulle's whereabouts and the steps he had taken to broadcast his appeal. Abtey had also left Paris and was caught up in the floods of people who had fled in haste just hours before the arrival of the Germans.[10]

The French intelligence services in the face of defeat

When reports began circulating that the Germans would soon reach the capital, the main concern of the French intelligence services was to protect their records and archives and stop them from falling into enemy hands. These files held sensitive information about their network of informers, some of whom might be of use to them in the future. The head of the intelligence services, Colonel Louis Rivet, agreed that Abtey and his team should leave Paris, taking 35 tonnes of archives with them. Trucks were organised and the paperwork was loaded up for departure. At first, as was the case for most of the French population who had taken to the roads, they had little idea of where they might end up. Like the French government and most fleeing civilians, they headed for the Loire river.[11] Initially there was a widespread belief that all was not lost, and that the army might still be able to stabilise the front in the Loire Valley. When this did not come about, in the absence of further orders from High Command, Abtey's party was forced to improvise as best it could. They decided to head for the military camp of Courtine in the Creuse region, near the town of Ussel and halfway between Limoges and Clermont-Ferrand.[12] There they were able to assemble with Rivet and other colleagues on 21 June. Together they vowed to make every attempt to leave the country, in order to carry on their work from abroad; but if they failed, they agreed that 'we'll have no other solution than to continue our fight clandestinely'.[13] It was there that both Paillole and Abtey claim to have first heard of the appeal made by de Gaulle from London.[14] The following day, the services reconvened at the seminary of Bon-Encontre, near Moissac. Under the terms of the armistice, the French intelligence services were to be formally dissolved and all actions against the invaders would have to stop. At a ceremony on 25 June, as the armistice with Italy was signed, Rivet spoke to his men saying 'we must continue to fight against the invaders'. Paillole writes that 'We all swore to do so.'[15] He later conceded that de Gaulle's appeal was not a significant consideration in their planning at the time.[16] However, they needed to find a way of taking this commitment forward. The solution they chose was a complex one.

Article IV of the armistice agreement allowed for the existence of a small French army stationed across the unoccupied zone and in the French colonial empire overseas. This armistice army offered an opening for the intelligence services and, in particular, the Deuxième Bureau, the counter-intelligence arm, to pursue its espionage activities. To achieve this, Paillole explains, the service created two separate entities. One was defensive and its role was to protect the army against anti-national subversion. It was overt and officially approved by Vichy. This entity acted as a cover for another – secret – wing, which was offensive, seeking to operate against Axis services in liaison with the Allies. Paillole became head of this clandestine side of the operation, which included responsibility for the archives – which had to be kept out of German hands at all costs. The view was that he had the contacts and the experience to pull this off.[17] Paillole therefore needed to find a cover for his operations, in order to deflect attention from his activities and avoid arousing the suspicions of the Germans, lest they discover that the French services were continuing to work against them.[18]

After a meeting with the sympathetic new head of the land engineering section in the Ministry of Agriculture, M. Préaud, it was agreed that Paillole's public face would be to lead a private company, whose mission it was to undertake rural works under the supervision of the ministry. The Société des Travaux Ruraux proved an ideal cover, because it allowed Paillole, as its director, under the name of Philippe Perrier, to place all his agents around the country as 'rural works engineers'.[19] So it was that the TR, *travaux ruraux*, was the name given to clandestine counterespionage until the Liberation of France. Paillole chose Marseille as his base, as he knew the city well and had many friends there – including, conveniently, the chief of police. It also had the advantage that it would be possible at any point to transfer everything to North Africa, should the need arise.

Storing the service's important archives was another headache to resolve. Paillole had ordered his men to burn the unimportant documents, notably those relating to lengthy discussions about comparatively trivial matters. This had reduced them from 35 to 30 tonnes, but a significant amount of paperwork remained. On 30 June, five trucks reached the cellars of a cheese manufacturer in Roquefort, and the archivists became cheese workers, so that they were well placed to watch over the papers.[20] Other archives were taken to the Château de Brax near Toulouse, and a final batch was sent to North Africa. Paillole would later bring all the archives still hidden in mainland France to his base in Marseille.

While Paillole set about salvaging what he could of his network of agents and establishing his new headquarters in Marseille, Abtey was allocated an office job in Toulouse, a major centre for the demobilisation of soldiers.[21] He hated his new position and his 'tawdry job as a paper pushing officer' and began considering his options. 'I kept mulling over the idea of going to England,' he later wrote.[22] It was with this in mind that he slipped away from his desk job unnoticed and surreptitiously made his way to Baker's château.

Hiding out at the château:
September–November 1940

Abtey arrived at Les Milandes in a new guise – as Jack Sanders, an American – with two other officers from the Deuxième Bureau. Their appearance caused considerable excitement on Baker's part.[23] 'Captain Fox died the day of the armistice,' explained Abtey, 'and the person that you have in front of you is both his double and his best friend . . . Jack Sanders at your service, Madame.'[24] As the British were considered by the Germans to be enemy aliens, Abtey had ditched his British cover and adopted a new identity as an American – a safer option, as America was a neutral country. It had been some weeks since Baker and Abtey had seen one another, and both had experienced considerable upheaval in the interim. Abtey briefed Baker about his ambitions to get to London to join de Gaulle, and she enthusiastically expressed a desire to go with him.[25] However, it was not immediately apparent how this could be achieved.

Throughout the summer of 1940, the Vichy authorities had worked with the Germans to ensure the repatriation of the majority of those who had left their homes during the exodus. Most had now returned, apart from those who were refused re-entry into the occupied zone – namely Black people, Jews and North Africans, whom the Germans barred from crossing the demarcation line. Movements around the country, and especially across frontiers, were closely monitored. Travel was difficult and various papers and visas were required to get through border controls. When Baker and Abtey learnt from one of Abtey's contacts that Paillole was now established in Marseille, they decided to approach him with their scheme to go to England and see what he could suggest.[26] At their meeting, Paillole was intrigued by the proposition and agreed to help them. His offer was not disinterested: Paillole's counter-intelligence organisation had managed to maintain a limited radio contact with British intelligence since the defeat, but he knew that he needed to re-establish more robust links with London if his agents were to operate properly and keep the British informed about German activities, in line with the ambitions of his services.[27]

Together, they hatched a plan for Baker and Abtey to go to Lisbon, on the pretext that Portugal would be the first leg of a concert tour to South America. In this way, Baker would provide cover for Abtey, who would travel with her. While in Lisbon, Paillole indicated that they should contact British intelligence via the British embassy located in the Portuguese capital. He proposed that they take with them the intelligence about the Germans in the occupied zone that his services had managed to collect since restarting his operation, and pass it on to the British as evidence of the good faith of the new clandestine Deuxième Bureau.[28] He instructed Abtey to ask the British to find a way of creating ongoing secure communication links, so that his operatives could exchange intelligence with their British counterparts in a regular way. He suggested that Abtey should mention the name of Bill Dunderdale, in particular, a leading figure in British intelligence who had been based in Paris throughout the 1930s.[29] Paillole and Abtey both had a close working relationship with Wilfred Dunderdale (known as both Bill and 'Biffy') who had been posted to Paris in 1926. He was a man of great charm and panache, who was well liked by his colleagues of all nationalities. Dunderdale and Paillole had joined forces in the 1930s to target Germany and share intelligence about the Nazi regime.[30] During the phoney war, Dunderdale's network had even closer links with the Deuxième Bureau under the direction of Paillole's superior, Colonel Rivet. After the outbreak of hostilities, Dunderdale was unable to run his own agents in France, due to 'insurmountable difficulties in travelling across frontiers' and across the country.[31] He was there-fore forced to depend almost entirely on information from Rivet's organisation during the winter of 1939–40. For his part, Paillole had almost completely lost contact with his British colleagues since the German offensive in mid-May 1940, when Dunderdale and his teams had been forced to evacuate to Britain.

Baker and Abtey's scheme, which offered Paillole the chance to rekindle connections with the British, was therefore crucial. Its success would depend on Baker's capacity to fool the Spanish and Portuguese authorities, not to mention the Abwehr spies who would circle her in Lisbon. That Paillole agreed to trust Baker with such a critical task may seem surprising. But, as we have seen, it was not without precedent in France for an entertainer to work with the military, aiding in the collection and transmission of intelligence. Mistinguett had been successful during the previous war, but when the Germans marched into Paris, she declared that at sixty-five she was 'too old' to take up espionage again. Marie Bell, an actress with the Comédie-Française, was another. Paillole claimed after the war that he had worked with her during the 1930s with considerable success. At a time when the French services needed as much intelligence as they could garner about what was going on in Germany, his colleague Schlesser had suggested approaching any French actors who travelled there regularly. In 1938, Paillole was made aware that highly placed Nazis like Goering and his wife both loved mixing with actors, as did Heydrich and Himmler. Bell agreed to collect intelligence for the services, using her role as an actor as cover. She passed on information about what she had learnt during her trips to Germany to the Deuxième Bureau under the code name 'Elizabeth'.[32] She continued to work as an agent during the war, acting as a TR and liaising with Colonel Gerard-Dubot in Paris to provide intelligence on the activities of the occupier, and especially on the organisation of Germany's propaganda services. She also sheltered some of those seeking to escape detection by the authorities in her own home. Bell's experience had shown Paillole that her position as an actor not only opened doors, allowing her to access key targets, but also provided her with an effective cover that enabled her to collect and transmit intelligence.[33] It therefore made sense that Paillole might agree to work with someone like Baker to support his services in a similar way.

Nonetheless it was a hazardous plan. Abtey would need a false passport, and he would have to travel in disguise. Lisbon was known to be teeming with German agents. There was a real possibility that he might be recognised by those who knew him from his days working at the Paris bureau before the war.[34] Importantly, the trip would also be a crucial test of their hunch that Josephine's fame would enable her to act as an effective cover for Abtey, allowing him to carry intelligence and travel unnoticed.[35] They all knew it was a gamble and potentially very dangerous for all concerned. Despite the risks involved, Abtey and Baker were keen to go, especially as there was a chance that British intelligence agents in Lisbon would be able to help them get to London. According to Abtey, who reiterates it repeatedly in his memoirs, it was this ambition to join de Gaulle in England which drove both him and Baker.[36] However, even once the decision was made, it would all take time to organise.

He and Baker returned to the château and lay low while they waited for news from Paillole and remained on alert for any unusual developments. Soon afterwards, in mid-September, a young man paid them a visit, claiming to have been sent by Father Dillard, a Jesuit who had escaped internment as a prisoner of war in Germany and had been sent to preach in Vichy. The young man's declaration that he had been advised by Dillard to bring them vital information to pass on to the British aroused their suspicions. Baker played dumb and Abtey, convinced that they were being set up, sent the young man unceremoniously on his way. The arrival of several heavily armed German soldiers at the château some hours later seemed to confirm his worst fears. The young man's visit had been a test of their loyalty.

After positioning themselves at all the entrances to the property, one of the soldiers rang the bell. Once she was sure that Abtey and the other residents who might be at risk from these uninvited visitors had safely placed themselves out of sight, Baker went to meet the officer who had requested an interview with the mistress of the house. 'Madame,' he asserted, clicking his heels, 'I am an officer of the armistice commission with special responsibility for controlling stocks of arms in the unoccupied zone.' Baker led him into the library and away from her companions as he complimented her on the beauty of the château. 'I've been told that you are hiding arms in your château! What do you think of that?' Going into full celebrity mode, Baker retorted, 'Sir, you can't possibly be serious! What on earth can you be thinking?' She kept him talking for a full ten minutes, and by the time he resolved to leave, he had been completely won over by her attentions. Baker's cover had held good, and the Germans had behaved appropriately. However, despite Abtey's confusion and his suspicion that Baker was somehow being tested, it later transpired that the original caller had brought genuine intelligence for them to pass on to the British.[37]

Abtey's accounts of these visits are difficult to verify. While Father Dillard did later become involved in anti-German activities (for which he gave his life, perishing in Dachau in February 1945), it seems unlikely that he commenced such activities as early as September 1940, and there is certainly no record that he did so. How news of Baker and Abtey reached him in Vichy is also left unexplained. The alleged German visit to the château is similarly perplexing: on the face of it, there is no reason why the Germans would have been present in the unoccupied zone, and there is no record of them in the *département* at this time.[38] Officers who were members of the armistice commission, as this German claimed to be, had the power to oversee French territory, but they were required to inform the French of their intention to visit a particular site, and their soldiers had to be accompanied by a French liaison officer when they did so. This meant that the French could take advantage of advance knowledge of these visits to hide anything that might be an infringement of the terms of the armistice.[39] Therefore, while it seems unlikely that this group of German soldiers would have turned up unannounced, it is not impossible that Abtey omitted to mention that there were also a couple of French officers in the party, even if the overall impression was that it was a German operation.[40]

Although some of the details relating to these visits appear historically implausible, the visit by the Nazi officers is included in Baker's citation for a Légion d'honneur: 'Suspected by the Germans of hiding weapons, she showed remarkable courage and composure while a search was carried out on her property.'[41] It nonetheless remains peculiar that Baker's presence at Les Milandes appears to have gone unnoticed by the local police, who would normally have kept a close eye on all the comings and goings in this period.[42] It would have been hard for Baker to pass unnoticed even in remote Dordogne, and it seems odd that she was not even recorded as a person of interest. Is the absence of any mention about her in the archives because she was being deliberately protected? It is impossible to know; but at the very least, she must have kept a very low profile while she was at the château to avoid drawing the attention of the authorities to the presence of those she was sheltering. While it would certainly be premature to talk of resistance at this time in the Dordogne, and there is no evidence of any such activities taking place, it is entirely possible that, aside from the Lions, Baker took in other refugees who were at risk, and provided them with a roof over their heads in the autumn of 1940. Government changes over the summer of 1940 would not have been reassuring for those taking refuge at Les Milandes, and the dangers they faced from the French authorities were ramping up.

In July, the deputies of the French National Assembly had been summoned to Vichy, and at a session held in the casino on 10 July 1940, those present voted full powers to Pétain, a move which brought the Third Republic to an end. The new Vichy government almost immediately set about introducing its own agenda, passing laws of exclusion and promoting its National Revolution. It blamed the disastrous defeat of France on the decadence of the previous governments, and sought to reform the country and bring about a return to traditional values. It also identified certain members of French society who were defined as 'undesirables': these included freemasons and Jews. The early measures of the Vichy government sought to target these groups, and in October 1940 an anti-Jewish statute was passed, which would be the first in a series of such laws that the French government introduced independently of the Germans. These measures would impact directly on the Lion family and others in their position. Later that month, Pétain was photographed with Hitler at a meeting in Montoire, and on 30 October he announced that France was 'entering the path of collaboration' with Germany. Despite this ominous sign, large numbers of French people liked to believe that Pétain was playing a double game and was secretly still dealing with the British. They would be sadly disappointed. In a bid to control the movement of men and prevent them from leaving the country, the government introduced travel restrictions for anyone aged under forty. This meant that Abtey's disguise for the trip to Lisbon needed to make him look older than his actual thirty-four years, in order to avoid drawing unwanted attention to himself. Paillole therefore arranged for the preparation of a false passport in the name of Jacques-François Hébert, born in Marseille on 16 September 1899, a dramatic artist living in Toulouse. For the photo, Abtey had donned a moustache and glasses, which changed his appearance effectively.[43]

When Baker and Abtey met again with Paillole to collect Abtey's new passport, Paillole delivered very clear instructions. The stakes were high. Paillole was acutely conscious that rebuilding links with the British was vital if his services were to develop effective counterespionage tactics against the Germans. He was aware that the intelligence he had collected from the occupied zone would be extremely valuable. It included information about the location of the main German divisions in western France, unit identifications, the size of the forces and equipment, their specialities, and the German agents who had been designated to be sent to England. The package also contained a complete summary of auxiliary airfields, the types and numbers of aircraft spotted and details of parachute formations. A further document was of exceptional value: 'a series of photographs of a landing craft that the Germans planned to use to attack the English coast'.[44] This intelligence would provide vital insights, as the British sought to defend themselves from a German offensive. Paillole had also added information pertaining to a possible attack on Gibraltar, as well as one on the Welsh coast in November 1940. He had uncovered information indicating that the Germans were supporting the Welsh and Scottish independence movements, in order to spark unrest. In what seems a very circuitous route, they were allegedly sending agents into the UK via Yugoslavia with a mission to bring this about.[45]

Once the intelligence they were to transmit had been secured from Paillole, all that remained for the journey to go ahead was for Baker and Abtey to procure the necessary travel visas to Spain and Portugal. This did not prove easy. Abtey's approaches to the Portuguese consulate in Nice elicited the response that a three-week wait would be required to secure the necessary permission from Lisbon.[46] In order to avoid this unwanted delay, Baker suggested that she might call on one of her many well-placed acquaintances – in this case, the Brazilian ambassador – to smooth their way to getting the authorisations they required. If she were able to obtain travel permits from him for a forthcoming proposed tour of the country, this would provide them with a pretext for needing transit visas through Portugal and Spain that would be difficult for the relevant authorities to refuse. The ruse worked magnificently, and within twenty-four hours the requisite visas had been stamped into their passports. To further reinforce Abtey's cover, Baker arranged for the words 'Accompanying Mme Josephine Baker' to be added to his Portuguese visa. This addition was decisive, in that it implicated Baker directly and she would face serious difficulty if Abtey's identity and the true reason for their trip were ever to be uncovered by the authorities.

Mission to Lisbon

The pair left Les Milandes by car for the train station early on 25 November 1940. Abtey was in full disguise as Baker's secretary. She was wrapped in a huge fur coat.[47] The intelligence they were carrying was well hidden. Paillole had instructed them to note down everything he had given them in code, using invisible ink.[48] Abtey therefore transcribed some of the most sensitive intelligence onto Baker's music scores using invisible ink and carried the sheets in his briefcase.[49] After a wearisome day of travelling by train, by nightfall they had reached Pau, in the southwest of the country. Abtey recounts how they were struck by the tragedy of those who lived in territories that had been annexed to the Reich and who had been expelled from their homes by the Germans:

> As we walked down the ramp to the station, we witnessed a heart-rending sight. A hundred or so people from Lorraine were shivering in the Siberian wind in a long queue to get into an encampment. There were old men and small children, no able-bodied men among them. They spoke the patois of the Thionville region. Jerry expelled them and they left with what they could

carry. They had just left the cattle cars that brought them to the Pyrenean border. Straw was still clinging to their clothes.[50]

After an overnight stop, they left Pau at 8 a.m. and commenced the spectacular journey to Canfranc. The relatively flat terrain of the Gave d'Aspe valley soon gave way to the foothills of the Pyrenees. There, the track started to climb steeply, often curving sharply until Somport, where it reached its maximum altitude (over 1,200 metres). It was a remarkable feat of engineering. The route took them over five viaducts and through fourteen tunnels before they arrived at their destination.[51]

Baker and Abtey were the only passengers to alight from the train on the deserted platform of this monumental international border train station. Known at the time as the 'Titanic of the mountains', it was designed to be the second largest railway building in Europe (after Leipzig station). Originally opened in July 1928, the grandiose 120-metre long, three storey, art deco main building, with 365 windows and 156 doors, had been intended as the new gateway to Spain. Despite its luxury hotel with lavish furnishings and marble staircases, since its inauguration, it had failed to generate the expected commercial and passenger traffic. From 1936 and the outbreak of the Spanish Civil War, General Franco's frequent extended periods of border closure had brought rail traffic to a standstill. Canfranc finally reopened in March 1940, but it remained relatively unknown and less frequented than the other border crossing points from France into Spain, like Cerbère and Hendaye. Baker and Abtey were banking on the fact that its remote mountainous location would mean that their presence might attract less attention, and that they would be able to dispense with border controls swiftly and unobserved.[52] There is no record of Abtey's and Baker's reactions to this unique and exceptional place, but as they disembarked and made their way down the lengthy platform to get to the border controls, they must have been struck by the décor of the station and the drama of its location, surrounded by 2,500-metre mountain peaks. Or perhaps their thoughts were elsewhere. Would they be found out at the border and prevented from continuing their journey?

As they presented their passports for inspection, Josephine's appearance, dressed as she was in her magnificent fur coat, had an immediate impact and threw everything into disarray.[53] Everyone rushed to speak to her. French customs officers, Spanish customs officers, French and Spanish border police, the stationmaster and all his staff, railway workers and officials – all mobbed the star. Some even ran to fetch their wives and children, so that they too could share in the excitement of her presence among them. Meanwhile, Abtey, keeping a respectful distance, as was appropriate to maintain his cover as her secretary, was able to pass through the controls completely unnoticed with the vital intelligence in his briefcase.[54] No one gave him a second glance.

Once the formalities had been completed, they were free to make their way to the Madrid train. As the Spanish railway gauge was broader than the French, their train left from a different platform to the one they had arrived at. They found seats and settled in for the journey, reaching the Spanish capital several hours later with no mishaps. In Madrid, there was no room on the fast train to Lisbon; fortunately, however, they were able to secure flights instead. There was a tense moment at the airport's passenger controls, when Abtey's name was checked by officials against a list of suspicious individuals. While he knew that the identity he was travelling under was a recent fabrication that had only been in existence for a matter of days, he still felt anxious. He noted that the border controls in Madrid were policed much more robustly than at Canfranc.[55] The Nazi presence was apparent everywhere, with several planes sporting swastikas parked on the airfield. He finally passed through without incident. Once again, Josephine's presence caused a stir; but despite a good deal of fuss, they soon boarded the flight and attempted to relax.

At Lisbon airport, they navigated the border controls without difficulty and took a car to the city. Baker was staying at the centrally located, glamorous, luxury Hotel Aviz (one-time residence of kings Carol II of Romania and Umberto II of Italy), whose rich interiors offered a temporary home to the wealthiest refugees and celebrity visitors to the city. Abtey took a room further down the city's main avenue, at the somewhat more modest Avenida Palace, more fitting to his secretarial role. The establishment would later become well known for the central role it would play in espionage activities.

The outbreak of the war had totally transformed the fortunes of Portugal's capital city. The country's dictator Dr Oliveira Salazar was keen to stay out of the fray and remain neutral. This had led to a huge influx of Allied and Axis agents, all keen to convert the Portuguese to their cause. When France fell, Lisbon became 'a centre of wartime activities and intrigues'.[56] It had acted as a huge transit centre for the countless refugees who had fled in the wake of the Nazi armies. Many still filled the city's hotels, waiting and hoping for the visas they needed to continue their journeys to safety and away from Occupied Europe. These refugees competed for hotel rooms with the ever growing number of spies, and the city became more and more crowded. In the evenings, its bars and cafés bustled with a clientele of foreign refugees, jostling with intelligence agents of different nationalities, all eyeing one another with suspicion and cautiously keeping to their own circles of contacts.

Lisbon was one of the few European cities in which both the Allies and the Axis powers could operate openly. In a bid to win foreign support for his New State regime, Salazar authorised the creation of a novel form of tourism. This offering was branded the 'Costa do Sol' ('Sunny Coast') and mainly comprised the areas covering São Pedro do Estoril, São João do Estoril and Santo António do Estoril. In these areas, access routes

> had been improved tremendously so the poorest and most degraded areas located a little further from the coast would not be identified by those touring either on-board the comfortable Sud-Express trains that travelled from Paris to Santo António do Estoril, or along a recently constructed coastal road which linked Lisbon to this Costa do Sol. The accommodation catering for these foreigners differed from the facilities dedicated to national tourists. In fact, palace hotels and similar chic lodging houses hosted not only these travellers, but also refugees and spies.[57]

Elite travellers fleeing the war would be greeted in Costa do Sol by an environment that allowed them to resume the round of parties, movies and music concerts, social habits they had been forced to abandon. 'Under the Estoril sun, on the beaches, yachts and the golf club, in the terraces and bars of the cosmopolitan hotels, and in the casino at night under the watchful eyes of the croupiers, the high society serenely enjoyed its privileges.'[58] Lisbon became a rather comfortable (if temporary) home both for exiled European royalty and for refugees who were seeking passage to the North and South American continents.

It was in this atmosphere that Baker and Abtey circulated freely during their visit. They knew that many Abwehr agents were present in the city, but it was nonetheless a more relaxed and less ominous atmosphere than in Vichy France. The German agents were power-less to do anything other than observe. Undeterred by their presence, Josephine played her role to perfection. She smiled and chatted to the journalists, who were keen to know more about her plans and the reasons for her presence in the city:

> Yes, she was stopping over in Lisbon en route to Rio, where she had a commitment. Yes, she had performed at the front . . . She had seen some tragic situations . . . No she had not been back to Paris since the beginning of the Occupation . . . No, she did not like the Germans . . .[59]

Her photo adorned the front pages of the national daily papers, and she put on a thoroughly convincing show of being the star that she undoubtedly was. Wartime Lisbon offered her the perfect stage, and she was feted across the city, including at the Belgian and British embassies. She mingled with the great and the good who were sheltering there or passing through, including King Carol of Romania.[60] Importantly, she kept her distance from Abtey, as it would have been disastrous for the German agents to have seen them together, in case he was recognised.

While Baker enjoyed the attentions of the various celebrities and diplomatic officials who flanked her wherever she went, Abtey took steps to progress their mission. He recognised several of the agents operating in the city, both German and British, and approached one of the latter, who he thought might help him gain access to British intelligence. He chose well. The agent secured him an appointment with the British air attaché at the British embassy on 28 November 1940. At the meeting, Abtey explained the nature of his mission with Baker and passed on Paillole's considerable intelligence dossiers.[61] In the discussions, he placed particular emphasis on their desire to get to London to join de Gaulle.[62] His British interlocuter promised to convey the dossiers and the substance of their exchange to London, and asked him to return to the embassy in a few days, once the diplomat had spoken to the relevant parties.

Working with British intelligence

At his second meeting at the Lisbon embassy some four days later, Abtey was told that the news from London was very positive. British intelligence was keen to renew its working relations with him and Paillole. However, rather than invite Abtey and Baker to continue to London – as they had been anticipating – the attaché indicated that London would prefer it if they returned to France and collaborated with Paillole's team, to put in place an underground network to collect and transmit information. British intelligence was working out the precise details of this plan and would communicate it to him within a fortnight.

From the point of view of the British, Paillole's proposal must have seemed like a godsend. Since their withdrawal from Paris to London in May 1940, they had only one secure wireless link with their French contacts, which had been arranged at the last minute just before they left.[63] Throughout summer and autumn 1940, intelligence returns from Occupied France remained disappointing for the British, deprived as they were of access to their former contacts in French military intelligence. All their habitual connections, including Rivet and Paillole, were now out of bounds, as they were considered to be serving the Vichy regime. Relations between Vichy and the British had gone progressively from bad to worse. Some 1,300 French servicemen had been killed when the British bombed the French navy at the North African port of Mers-El-Kébir in July 1940 to prevent it from falling into the hands of the Germans. This had not gone down at all well in Vichy and fed a strong anti-British sentiment there. The working relationship between French and British intelligence had been marked by effective cooperation and trust; but since the emergence of the Vichy regime, the British had no way of knowing how their former Allies positioned themselves. They had no idea whether their French opposite numbers were still sympathetic to the British or whether they had any freedom of action independent of the Germans.

Despite these uncertainties, under extreme pressure from the government to acquire intelligence from Occupied France, Stewart Menzies, head of British intelligence, instructed Dunderdale that he should foster contacts with his former colleagues in the French intelligence services, now working under the aegis of Vichy. To assist him in achieving this, two separate departments were created to deal with France. Dunderdale was appointed head of a new department known as A4 to deal with the Vichy agencies, including the Deuxième Bureau. A separate department, A5, with a different chief and a different network of agents, was deployed to work with de Gaulle's Free French army corps in London, which was starting to develop its own intelligence service under Colonel Passy, the Bureau central de renseignements et d'action (BCRA).[64] The British were therefore running two separate sets of agents to work with the two French networks. It was of the utmost importance that Dunderdale's department take care to ensure that their interactions with Paillole and his Deuxième Bureau were kept a secret from the Gaullist services, which would be horrified if they ever discovered that the British were dealing with Vichy government agents. This dual approach to France's intelligence services was not ideal; but from the British point of view, it was a pragmatic solution to the complicated French context. It would underpin all the dealings between the British and French intelligence services until these distinct branches were eventually brought together in 1943.

But in 1940, that was a long way off. While Baker and Abtey may have believed (or hoped) that they were working to the advantage of de Gaulle, as they claim in their memoirs,[65] by working with Paillole, who had direct links to Vichy, they were necessarily considered by the British as falling into a category that was separate from British operations with the Gaullists. From the time of this very first mission – doubtless unwittingly at this point – they had therefore become players in the intricate landscape of the underground war that had developed since the defeat of France.

This landscape – and the need to keep their activities secret – probably explains the British decision not to bring Baker and Abtey to London to join de Gaulle. Abtey was almost certainly disappointed that they would not be able to proceed to England, but he must also have grasped the importance of the role that he and Baker were being asked to play. He swiftly conveyed the news to Baker, and they agreed that she should return to France to inform Paillole of their successful interactions and the substance of the British plan. Abtey would remain in Lisbon and follow her once he had been fully briefed about how the proposed intelligence network would operate. After she had completed her Lisbon performances, Baker immediately set off for France on a visa obtained from Nicolás Franco, Spanish ambassador in Lisbon and brother of the dictator.[66] She took a flight from Lisbon to Barcelona, and from there made her way along the coast by train.

Marseille

When Baker arrived in Marseille on 5 December 1940, the city was still reeling from the excitement of a visit by Marshal Philippe Pétain.[67] The head of state was touring the major cities of the free zone to make himself known in person to the people. The carefully orchestrated visit had been a huge success, with residents turning out in droves to see their new leader and wish him well.[68] It was a welcome distraction for many who were struggling with wartime conditions, but it had caused major disruption. Marseille was a bustling Mediterranean port city that had become a key destination for those fleeing the German armies the previous spring. Most of the thousands of Belgians and French people who had ended up there had been repatriated throughout the summer of 1940. Those who still remained in December 1940 had been unable to return to their homes either because they had been forbidden to do so or because they felt targeted and hoped to find a place on a ship and leave Occupied Europe.[69] A large number of these foreigners and those who had been singled out as 'undesirables' by Vichy had been rounded up in advance of Pétain's visit, in order to prevent any possible unrest or interference that might draw attention to their presence in the city.

As Marseille returned to normal, Baker checked into the prestigious, but crumbling, Hôtel de Noailles on the Canebière, the main commercial street. She sought out Paillole, who had established himself in offices in Villa Eole, outside the centre.[70] She updated him on the outcome of Abtey's meetings with the British in Lisbon. Paillole was delighted and they agreed that she should remain in the city until Abtey returned. Marseille presented itself as a reasonably safe place for her to hole up: it was in the free zone, there were regular ships to North Africa should she need to make a quick getaway, and she was close to Paillole. Baker was not alone in biding her time in Marseille. The Hôtel de Noailles had become a temporary base for some of those who were trapped in the city, seeking to escape the French mainland. When her impresario Daniel Marouani came to visit her from Nice, where he was staying, he introduced her to his friends Rudolph Salmsen and Charles Smadja, who were also residents there. Their cinema production business in Paris had thrived in the 1930s, but when the war broke out they had been forced to cease their activities and had both ended up trapped in Marseille, on the run from the Nazis without passports or the necessary exit visas that would make it possible for them to leave. Salmsen, a Jew, had left Germany for Paris in 1933 to escape the Nazis and had set up the business with Smadja, who was from Tunisia. He had joined the Foreign Legion to escape the round-ups of foreigners, but since France's defeat he had been demobbed and was now trying to find a way to join his family in Peru. Like most of the refugees in the city, he had done the rounds of the consuls and had even befriended some of them, but he had not been able to secure the papers he needed. They all quickly became firm friends and Baker promised to do what she could to help them.[71]

Baker's funds were running short, and the winter was taking its toll. The Vichy government had introduced rationing in September 1940 and supplies in the city were patchy. Deliveries often failed to arrive.[72] Baker moved into a more modest, unheated room in a hotel in a run-down neighbourhood, near the St Charles station, which she claimed was 'filled to the gills with whores'.[73] She even wore her overcoat in bed to combat the cold. She would have to find a way of generating an income if she was to survive, and she also needed to find a way to justify her presence in the city. A chance meeting with a former dance partner, Frédéric Rey, pointed her towards a solution. Like her new friends, he had come to Marseille because he was in an 'irregular situation', having been in the Foreign Legion. He, too, was hoping to find a way to leave the country.[74] Baker promised to help him; but in the meantime, she persuaded him to participate in a new project she had dreamt up. With Rey's help and Paillole's approval, she would stage a revival of her 1934 performance of Offenbach's operetta *La Créole*.

Baker had vowed never to perform in Occupied France. 'As long as there is a German in France,' she had allegedly declared, 'Josephine won't sing.'[75] However, she was in the free zone, the Germans were not much in evidence, and she urgently needed a financial solution to her situation. Despite a newspaper report on 1 September 1940 that the Vichy government had decided that there would be no more '*nègres*' (negroes) on any stage in France and that 'it no longer wants to see or hear the charming Josephine Baker',[76] the directors of the municipal theatre in Marseille jumped at the opportunity to put on her proposed show. The production was soon being advertised and no questions were raised about Baker's right to appear. In the notices in the local press, reporters revelled in the fact that Marseille had been chosen as the venue for the revival of the operetta and celebrated the return of '*l'oiseau des îles*' to the stage. Baker and Rey threw themselves into their task with complete dedication. It was an ambitious plan and would prove to be a considerable undertaking, as Baker revealed in a press interview published the day before the opening. 'People only see the polished performance! But we must go through hard labour before it is fit for the public to see.' Remarkably, in the light of the constrained wartime conditions, the directors went all out to guarantee the success of the production. As Baker promised:

No expense has been spared to ensure the quality of the staging, including beautiful white satin draped on the walls. They even bought the original costumes from the Marigny theatre in Paris and the furniture is from the best antique dealers in Marseille. The troupe is excellent, and everyone is fired up. It's going to be as impressive as it was in Paris.[77]

Offenbach's *La Créole* had first been staged in 1875 and had been adapted considerably by Albert Willemetz and Georges Delance for Baker to perform in 1934. Its plot was relatively lightweight, telling of two couples forced into amorous deceit. As well as importing some songs and swapping around others, they made the piece substantially longer and added a new first section that focused attention immediately on Baker's interpretation of Dora, the female lead.[78] The changes made to the original were designed to embellish Baker's contribution, and Baker herself was particularly proud of her role, as it represented her graduation from music hall to opera.[79] She had initially been reticent to take the part on, as light opera was a new direction for her; but during rehearsals she soon embraced the experience and made a huge success of it, cementing her reputation as a singer, as well as an actor and a dancer.[80] This would probably explain her willingness to perform it some six years after its first run. Importantly, it had marked a significant breakthrough, allowing her 'to craft a more dignified, respectable image',[81] and showcased the breadth of her talents, which went far beyond the suggestive dancing that had been the basis for her initial runaway success. It had been one of the highpoints of her career. Many critics also saw this performance as the seminal moment of Baker's transformation to 'becoming French'.[82] As such, it was the perfect choice for her to show her patriotic commitment to the country, while also providing a strong rationale for her presence in the city.

For the audiences who came to see her at the end of 1940, her performance must have seemed heaven sent. The critics for the local press in Marseille could hardly believe their luck. In the reviews that followed opening night, Josephine's performance was applauded, and the show was declared a huge hit. Baker charmed everyone present and received standing ovations. One reviewer wrote admiringly:

> Josephine's triumphant performance carried the show. The great music-hall star is also an accomplished musician and in a voice that the phonograph has popularised, imbues her songs with pleasing nuances. This artist has the gift of theatre: she acts well and animates the play with her lively and irrepressible drive. These gifts, together with acrobatic dances, have earned her well-deserved success.[83]

Baker had to remember her performance from several years before, and she appears to have done so with aplomb. The popular show and its star were much in demand, and the directors arranged for it to tour the local area, including dates in Béziers, among other locations. They were therefore appalled when Baker unexpectedly announced in early January that she would have to cancel the remaining performances. She needed to leave for Morocco at once.

~

After Baker left Lisbon, Abtey had continued to have meetings at the British embassy, where the air attaché put him in touch with a certain Major Bacon of the intelligence service. He explained to Abtey the details of how the exchanges between the two intelligence services would operate. Baker and Abtey were to base themselves in Casablanca, where they would receive the intelligence that would be conveyed to them by Paillole's Deuxième Bureau agents. They would then transmit this information to the British intelligence station in Lisbon via a sea link. It would be slow, but it would be secure; and that was the priority, given the nature of the intelligence involved.[84] London had decided to purchase a small commercial ship that would sail between Lisbon and Casablanca under the Portuguese flag. Abtey had stayed in Lisbon while the necessary agreements with the Admiralty were completed. But eventually, he was given the green light to return to Marseille to collect Baker.[85] Armed with a thousand pounds to cover the costs of their journey and their installation in Morocco, he arrived in Marseille in time to see the curtain go up on Baker's first performance of *La Créole* on Christmas Eve 1940.

When Paillole was briefed about the British plan, he was delighted. Baker and Abtey started planning to depart for North Africa as soon as Baker had completed her contracted run of performances. Baker sent for her animals to be brought from Les Milandes so that they, too, could make the journey.[86] By January 1941, the situation in the free zone was starting to look rather delicate, due to the falling-out between Pétain and his close Vichy ally Pierre Laval. Pétain had sacked Laval in mid-December 1940 because his policy of collaboration with the Germans did not seem to be bearing fruit and had cast Pétain in a bad light with the French population.[87] The Germans had retaliated by closing the demarcation line even to civil servants, and the fear was widespread that they might cross over into the southern zone and occupy the whole of France. Everyone was on tenterhooks.[88] Paillole's agents had suggested to him that this was a real prospect; and as these reports became increasingly insistent, he feared that Baker and Abtey might be in danger. He did not want to risk jeopardising this team, particularly now that it had proved that it could operate so effectively. He felt compelled to take action to protect them. He therefore ordered them to bring forward their departure. They were to leave without delay, taking with them the latest batch of information that his services had been able to collect.[89]

Baker did not want to leave so suddenly; and in particular she did not want to leave without Salmsen and Rey, who were at risk in the event of a German arrival. Smadja had managed to secure a visa to Tunisia by this point, and so he had a means of escape. Paillole's services responded that orders were orders and that they should leave as soon as they could. Everything possible would be done to organise passports for Salmsen and Rey, but they would have to be patient due to the chaotic circumstances of the moment.[90] Despite her reluctance, Baker set about preparing for her departure. The revised plan meant that Baker was forced to break her contract with the directors of the municipal theatre, which had stipulated that she would perform throughout January. When she and Abtey informed them that, regrettably, she was compelled to leave Marseille immediately due to health issues, the managers were understanding. Baker had a heavy cold and had already cancelled some rehearsals in Béziers.[91] They accepted the medical certificate that Baker supplied without hesitation. When she had been for an X-ray, the doctor had expressed concern about her chest, relieved that she was heading for a warmer climate.[92] So it was that Baker and Abtey boarded the *Gouverneur Général de Gueydon* on the French line to Algiers with the 'two white mice, three monkeys, and a Great Dane' recently arrived from Les Milandes.[93]

~

It is worth pausing here to consider the accuracy and credibility of Baker's and Abtey's accounts, which have largely informed the events described in the preceding pages. The French military archives are reasonably curt about their activities during this period; but overall, the official sources appear to corroborate the versions in their memoirs. There is no doubt that the ploy of using Baker as cover allowed Abtey to travel to Lisbon, a trip that would otherwise have been impossible for him to undertake; and it was this that laid the groundwork for Baker and Abtey's subsequent intelligence work for the Allied effort. It would not have been possible without Baker's commitment and her effectiveness as a facilitator, and it was not without extensive risk to herself. While they both express disappointment at not being able to reach London to join de Gaulle, as they had originally intended, they quickly adjusted to the scenario that was presented to them. They both later asserted their belief that their adherence to the Free French dated from this time. Baker explained: 'Now I was no longer a volunteer agent, but a regular member of the military with retrospective effect from November, without rank or pay.'[94]

Abtey reports in his memoir that, when corresponding with Paillole in 1943, Dunderdale acknowledged that it had been an error not to bring Baker and Abtey to London at this point, and that he had been 'misinformed' by his agents in Lisbon. He alleges that Dunderdale said that by the time he realised the value of the intelligence they had delivered, it was too late to change tack.[95] However, if indeed this conversation took place, it may have been more in the interests of ensuring good relations with Paillole than a true representation of British thinking. There were compelling reasons why the British would have chosen to keep Baker and Abtey at a distance from the Free French in London, deliberately flying in the face of their requests to join de Gaulle. As we have seen, the state of the French intelligence services at the time was confused, and the tensions between the British and the French in London over the status of de Gaulle and the Free French were ongoing and unresolved. It seems likely that British decision-making was driven by the view that Baker and Abtey could serve a more valuable role based in France or North Africa than in London. Such practical considerations – and the need to maximise their utility as agents, with the capacity to provide potentially crucial intelligence at a time when the British were starved of information about what was going on in Occupied France, or indeed North Africa – must certainly have carried more weight than Baker's and Abtey's personal wishes. Even if they were not in fact working directly for the Free French at this point, but acting on behalf of British intelligence under the aegis of the Deuxième Bureau, it is significant that, after the war, they both succeeded in gaining official recognition for this work as contributing to resistance – although not without some difficulty in the case of Abtey.[96]

The nature of the relationship between Baker and Abtey also merits consideration at this point. They obviously enjoyed one another's company. While their memoirs do not explicitly reveal that they were in a relationship, they were undoubtedly deeply committed to one another in ways that suggest they were. Most commentators have assumed that they were romantically involved by this point in their story. Paillole mentions this explicitly in a recorded interview.[97] Abtey was a married man, and that might explain his discretion.[98] Baker was married, too, but was estranged from Lion by this point – although, as already mentioned, her close relationships with members of his family had led her to offer them her protection at Les Milandes. Abtey's account of their exchanges reveals his adoration for Baker, and the teasing attitude she showed towards him also suggests a high degree of intimacy. Required to spend extended periods of time with one another for the purposes of their mission, they must have had a very deep relation of trust, since their lives depended on it, quite literally. In moving to North Africa, a new chapter was about to open for Baker, which would allow her to put into practice her multiple skills and profit from her remarkable capacity to adapt. As it turned out, despite Paillole's fears, full occupation of France by the Germans did not actually materialise in the winter of 1940–41. Nevertheless, it is understandable that he would seek to protect his precious agents from the potential danger of arrest. The logic of their relocation to Morocco was a compelling one: removing them to North Africa was in line with British requests; and as North Africa was part of France's empire, it allowed them to remain on French territory, while also distancing them from any immediate Nazi threat. It would be nearly four years before Baker would return to the French mainland.

3

AGENT BAKER IN MOROCCO
(1941–1942)

Baker was very relieved when they finally reached Algiers, for it had been a lively crossing, with storms at sea.[1] The port was busy when Baker and Abtey disembarked from their ship with her animals in tow. Baker did not travel light: she had brought twenty-eight pieces of luggage.[2] All her stage costumes and various accoutrements took up a good deal of space. They made for the prestigious Hotel Aletti, where all the cosmopolitan elites of the city resided; meanwhile its bar and terrace attracted a variety of uprooted people, including business adventurers, agents of all kinds, politicians on leave and police informers. It was where the most extraordinary rumours were conceived and circulated. And in the evening, at the casino, those gambling at the tables included the rich Algerian landowners who had managed to make their fortunes, sheltered by the French tricolour flag.[3] Baker's arrival in Algeria's coastal capital city made the front page of the local paper, which carried a picture of the glamorous star emerging from a car in her signature furs.[4] It was quickly followed up by announcements that the star, 'a sensational attraction', would be performing early the following month in a charity *Gala des Ailes* (Air Gala) to raise money for the Secours national, a Vichyite charity. Her cover was assured; the rationale for her presence was clear. Under Vichy rule, North Africa may not have appeared so obviously impacted by the war as mainland France; but just beneath the surface it was a hive of covert activity. North Africa in general – and Baker and Abtey's destination of Morocco, in particular – had become a dramatic clandestine theatre of war, with representatives of the Allied and Axis powers all scrutinising one another's every step, attempting to predict their next moves.

Vichy North Africa

Algeria held a special place in the hearts of the French, though their North African empire also included its smaller neighbours of Morocco and Tunisia. Having been conquered in 1830 and colonised intensively since, it was home to several generations of French Algerians. France and Algeria were so closely entwined that its three *départements* were administered directly by the French Ministry of Interior in the same way as the Haute-Vienne and all the other départements of mainland France. 'Algeria is France', French politicians were inclined to say. Indigenous Algerians had few rights and very little say in how their country was governed. During the 1930s, young, educated Algerians began to organise and call for more rights, though calls for independence were still few and far between.[5] The reality of the closeness of these two countries is illustrated by the economics of the relationship: in 1938, 75 per cent of Algerian imports came from France and 83 per cent of its exports went there.[6]

Hitler understood the deep intimacy of France's relationship with its North African empire and realised that retaining French sovereignty over these nations of the Maghreb was crucial to the new government. He had therefore been careful to ensure that the terms of the June 1940 armistice excluded any suggestion that French North Africa be dismantled, or its territories annexed. Though they needed to be harsh, the terms must not be impossible for the French to accept. His main concern was for these arrangements to be resolved rapidly, so that he could turn his attention to his new target – the invasion of Britain. To achieve this, he forced Mussolini to give up on his territorial ambitions in Tunisia, at least for the time being. Leaving the French in control also made sense, as it was the most effective means of neutralising the possibility of unrest among the North African populations that a change in colonial administration might trigger. With the armistice signed and the Vichy government established, North Africa came under direct Vichy rule, allowing the German leader to concentrate all his military resources on pursuing his efforts across the Channel.

However, by January 1941, when Baker arrived in North Africa, Hitler's attempts to invade Britain had come to nothing, despite the intensive bombing campaign that was the Blitz. Instead, the British now feared that the Axis powers would turn their attentions to North Africa and the Middle East, threatening their position there. The Germans were already supporting Mussolini, who had commenced damaging campaigns in Libya and Egypt that threatened British control of the Suez Canal, a vital supply line linking Britain to its empire. Germany might now team up with Spain for an Axis attack on Gibraltar, an essential strategic location and important base for the British navy. Concern that such an attack on the Rock might be in preparation had already been heightened by Spain's takeover of Tangier on 14 June 1940, the day the Germans marched into Paris. Tangier was a precious stronghold situated on the northernmost tip of the African continent, directly opposite the British colony of Gibraltar. Franco had taken advantage of the distraction provided by the fall of France to order 4,000 troops under Spanish command to occupy the city on the pretext of safeguarding Tangier's neutrality and to protect it from Italian or German invasion. For Franco's Spain, it was a step towards that country's imperial dream in Africa and extended its existing interests in Morocco.[7]

Spain had looked to territory in Morocco as a way of reviving its imperial fortunes and bolstering its claims to greatness, after losing its New World colonies at the end of the nineteenth century. Under a 1912 treaty between France and Spain, the Spanish had already been 'leased' a strip of territory in the north, which became the Spanish protectorate in Morocco, with Tétouan as its capital. Spain was also allocated a southern strip next to the Spanish Sahara. Due to its proximity to Gibraltar and British concerns for its security, Tangier had originally been left out of the 1912 arrangements. In

June 1925, it was finally agreed to create an international zone administered by a joint council of French, Spanish and British diplomats. It was this agreement that was effectively overruled by Franco's aggressive takeover in 1940.

All this added up to North Africa looking worryingly vulnerable to potential German invasion. Much now depended on how Franco decided to position himself and, from the British point of view, whether Vichy caved in to German demands. The British were, of course, unaware that the French were as suspicious about German ambitions in North Africa as they were. The Germans had long harboured aspirations in the region. They may have lost their colonial possessions in Africa at the end of the First World War, but they had not entirely given up their designs on the continent. Of the French territories in North Africa, it was Morocco that interested them most. Germany had longstanding connections there, established by entrepreneurs prior to the First World War, and by 1939 there were several German firms that had been present for many years.[8] The country was of obvious strategic value, with deep ports at Casablanca and a coastal line along the Atlantic; and importantly, it could supply the German armaments industry with certain crucial key minerals. Despite the obvious German interests in the area, however, the British were virtually powerless to monitor the situation. They had some access to information from agents who were based in Tangier, where their presence was tolerated by the Spanish authorities. But with the Vichy government in control, they struggled to collect intelligence for themselves in French Morocco, despite having a few well-placed informants who kept them updated on public opinion among Moroccans.[9] It had therefore been decided that Baker and Abtey should be sent to Casablanca, where they were to establish themselves and work with the Deuxième Bureau to convey information to the British about German activities in both Occupied France and French North Africa. This would afford the British a better understanding of German movements in the area and of Vichy responses to the situation on the ground.

Soon after their arrival in Algiers, Abtey set about acquiring the paperwork they would need to make the journey from the Algerian capital to Casablanca.[10] They were delighted when one evening, Salmsen and Rey turned up at the Aletti. Salmsen's spirits had been low after Baker and Abtey's departure from Marseille, and he had started to investigate possible escape by illegal means. However, on his return to the hotel some days later, he found a man waiting to see him. The stranger produced two passports – one for him and one for 'Miss Baker's other friend' – with instructions that they were to leave for Algiers on the next boat. With a passport in hand, Salmsen was able to acquire the visas he needed for Peru to join his wife and daughter. Two days later, he and Rey were on their way to Algiers. Smadja flew, and they were all reunited at the Hotel Aletti that evening. Salmsen immediately felt safer in Algeria, comforted by the knowledge that he was separated from the Germans by an ocean. He later acknowledged how grateful he was that Baker and Abtey had given him back his freedom and assured him a future.[11]

Once Abtey had secured entry papers for Morocco, still under the name of Hébert, he departed by plane, leaving Baker in Algiers to finalise the preparations for her gala performance. The plan was for him to meet the named contacts in Casablanca that he had been given by the British and to organise the necessary visas allowing him and Josephine to return to Lisbon, where Baker would honour the planned concert dates and he would pass on Paillole's intelligence that they had smuggled in with them. Days after Abtey's departure, however, Baker was stopped at her hotel by police, who demanded that she pay the outstanding sum of 4,000 francs that she owed the directors of the Marseille municipal theatre for breaking her contract. She was perplexed. When she had explained that her poor health was the reason she had to leave Marseille so suddenly – an excuse supported by a formal medical certificate – the directors had appeared to accept the decision. Nonetheless, they had evidently decided to follow up by claiming their legal rights to compensation, and Baker was instructed that she would not be allowed to leave the country until her outstanding debt was settled. She immediately notified Paillole, uncertain as to how to manage the situation, and focused her efforts on her imminent performance. The *Gala des Ailes* on 1 February 1941 proved a 'magnificent matinee' attended by 'the most prominent dignitaries in Algiers' and raised a total of 200,000 francs for the Secours national.[12] It would be the first of many shows that Baker would put on for soldiers in North Africa.

In a further setback to their plans, however, Baker heard from Abtey in Casablanca that all his efforts to secure visas from the Portuguese consulate for their trip to Lisbon had failed. Without these, their mission would be sabotaged. She would have to join him in Casablanca and hope that she would have more success with officials. Experience had taught them that her presence in person could be very persuasive. She would explain to the consul that she needed Abtey to accompany her to Portugal to finalise arrangements for her forthcoming tour of South America. But she was still constrained by the legal order not to leave Algeria. Fortunately, Paillole was able to pull strings, which allowed for the order to be lifted temporarily and Baker was given the green light to depart. Relieved that she had escaped the legal process, at least for the moment, Baker left Algiers for Casablanca, reassuring her friends that she and Abtey would send through visas allowing them to join the pair in Morocco. She insisted on travelling with a bevy of creatures in tow, asserting that this was a necessity, since 'Josephine without her animals would immediately look suspicious.'[13] She was wise to take steps to maintain her cover. While there had been some underground intelligence activity in the Algerian capital, the atmosphere in Morocco was thick with intrigue, with a hugely complex web of undercover agents concentrated there.

Vichy and the Germans in Morocco

The railway journey southwest from Algiers to Casablanca followed a route through the border town of Oujda, where Baker crossed into Morocco. Unlike Algeria, but like the more longstanding French colony of Tunisia, Morocco was a protectorate. Since 1912, it had been colonised by the French according to the vision of Resident-General Louis Hubert Lyautey. His somewhat romantic notion was that Morocco should neither be annexed to France nor considered a colony, but should remain sovereign and 'protected' until it was 'developed, civilised, living its autonomous life detached from the metropole'.[14] Although the French paid lip service to a façade of indirect rule and insisted that 'the source of all authority in Morocco' lay with the sultan, in practice a parallel French government had been established and held the reins of power. Moroccans were slowly subdued by a painful process of 'pacification', only finally completed in the mid-1930s.[15] Since 1927, Sidi Mohammed ben Youssef, born in 1909, had been sultan, installed by the French authorities when his father died, to the detriment of his two elder brothers.[16]

General Charles Noguès had been appointed resident-general of Morocco in 1936 by the Popular Front government. He had seriously considered taking a stand against the Germans in 1940, but in the end did not carry through, and from June 1940 obediently followed the orders of the Vichy government. He, like most French settlers in Morocco and across the rest of North Africa, was completely won over by Pétain and the ambitions of his National Revolution. The Moroccan population, however, was another matter, and Noguès was very worried that France's prestige had been considerably diminished by France's fall, as he made clear to Paillole in August 1940:

> Nothing will ever be the same in this country. We've offered the sight of a defeated France. We'll have a lot of trouble to keep our authority over the indigenous populations who are so sensitive to prestige and strength. Since June, Axis propaganda has been spreading and has a very easy time doing so.[17]

After a break of just a few weeks, German propaganda seeking to undermine the protectorate had resumed and was having considerable success. The Germans had every intention of pursuing their ambitions to win the hearts and minds of the Moroccans and infiltrate French administrations. It was a particularly noxious problem for the French, who struggled in their efforts to frustrate those ambitions.

Under the terms of the 1940 armistice, armistice commissions were established as the main instruments of the Axis presence in Morocco, Algeria and Tunisia. Initially, the Germans had been happy to let the Italians dominate membership of these agencies. But as Hitler's interest in North Africa increased, he sent more German operatives into the country and Germans acquired a stronger representation. This was largely to facilitate their drive to acquire raw materials, including cobalt for the German war industry. It was also a reaction to the appointment of General Weygand as delegate-general in French North Africa in September 1940. A former commander in chief of the French military forces during the 1939–40 hostilities, he was well known for his anti-German remarks, and the Germans feared he might be secretly plotting against them.[18]

The Germans had selected Casablanca, Morocco's economic centre on the Atlantic coast, as the location for their North African power base. The busy port, with its remarkable jetty over a mile long, was a site of intense shipping and trade activity having been transformed by Lyautey's modernisation. He believed that the city should have separate 'native' and European quarters, and his works included building a wall around the densely populated medina, the non-European part of the city, and its winding, uneven streets. A new city had since arisen outside the walls of the medina, and by 1939 the overall population of Casablanca had swelled to 350,000. The war brought a huge influx of refugees from the European mainland, who were stranded there while they contrived to find transport to safety in the Americas. To keep a close eye on these populations, scrutinise activities at the port and monitor any signs of a build-up of troops or military movements by the French, in December 1940 Theodore Auer, a high-ranking official formerly posted to the German embassy in Paris, was sent to Casablanca as a formal representative of the Reich, with a mission to report back on all Morocco affairs.

Taking action that went way beyond the terms of the original 1940 armistice agreement, Auer tasked his deputy, Klaube, with immediately setting about building a tight network of Abwehr agents and informers, radiating from Casablanca across the country under the aegis of the armistice commission based there.[19] Other less-official agents were recruited from the small number of German nationals among the various waves of refugees who had come out to North Africa since June 1940. They were extremely effective spies, as they evaded suspicion. There were also some North African soldiers and members of the French Foreign Legion who had been taken prisoner by the Germans in June 1940. Identified in the Stalags – the camps in Germany where they were being held – they were offered freedom and permission to return home, on condition that they worked for the Abwehr. After undergoing training in Germany, they were assigned a double mission. First, they were to spy on the French army in North Africa and report on any clandestine preparations. Second, they were to spread propaganda about Germany, asserting that the victory of the Reich would rid Morocco of French domination.[20]

In relation to the latter, Auer launched a concerted German campaign to encourage Arab nationalism and foster resentment against the French. Supporting their demands for independence was designed to undermine the protectorate from within. To achieve this, he and his agents aggressively courted local Moroccan dignitaries. Winning them over to the Nazis' cause could only further reinforce their propaganda campaign and bolster their influence with local Moroccan populations. By early 1941, the German armistice commission in Casablanca was established as Germany's stronghold in French North Africa. The intense German presence in the city attracted secret agents of multiple nationalities, who all worked furiously to track the activities of their opposite numbers and report back home.[21] It was in this context of heightened German presence and mounting espionage activity that Baker made her way to the city.

Her forty-eight-hour train journey across the 800 or so miles from Algiers to Casablanca would not have been an easy one in the best of circumstances. And it was not helped by the added challenge of travelling with her menagerie of animals. She struggled to control her massive dog Bonzo, who was on a lead, while also managing her two monkeys in their cage on the packed train.

'I hoped that convincing the Portuguese consul would be an easier task,' she later confided.[22] As soon as she reached her destination, she made straight for the consulate, where the consul immediately granted her a visa for the Lisbon trip, without any question; but she had no success in securing one for Abtey. 'I don't know what the problem was,' she reported, 'he wasn't having any of it. He gave me my visa without any hesitation, without even charging for it, but he was entirely unreceptive when I requested one for you.'[23] Her best efforts to charm the consul had proved hopeless. He had not been persuaded even when she asserted that without Abtey she would not be able to organise her tour. There was no other solution. Abtey reluctantly agreed that Baker would have to travel to Lisbon on her own. She would find their British contact and pass on Paillole's intelligence herself. Baker promised that she would attain a visa for Abtey on her arrival, so that he could join her. She had no doubt that she would be able to acquire the papers he needed once she was there.

Baker's first solo mission to Lisbon: March–April 1941

Despite some apparent trepidation on the part of Abtey, who feared for her safety, Baker set off confidently for Lisbon.[24] She took a couchette to Tangier, the first leg of the trip, the following evening, on 16 March 1941. The train which ran the Casablanca to Tangier route was old and rudimentary, 'long past its "bedtime" for retirement to the scrap heap,' recalled Stafford Reid, a US vice consul in Casablanca and undercover agent.

> The sleeper, a wooden relic of luxury travel, revarnished and upholstered to a thickness contributed by thirty years of overhauling, bumped along the rails in springless rhythm . . . Electric bulbs shared a place in ceiling lamps alongside old gas-jets as a reminder of progress.

Having arrived in Morocco soon after Baker, Reid took the route regularly, along with the other agents of multiple nationalities who

operated in Casablanca and who needed to report to their diplomatic missions located in consulates there. These journeys were
shrouded in an atmosphere of suspicion and secrecy. The majority
of the travellers would normally be French, but Reid explains that
passengers included 'important civilian and military members of
the German and Italian Armistice Commissions', and operatives
making the trip would

> tip questionable Spanish or French porters to obtain names of
> other occupants in adjoining compartments. The usual roll call
> would consist of a mixture of German, Japanese, Italian and
> American names ... Conversations whenever the train stopped,
> which was incessant, were immediately reduced to whispers
> followed by furtive glances exchanged in the passageway ...
> During the middle of the night the car was minutely searched
> each time it crossed or re-crossed the Hispano-Moroccan border.[25]

These operatives made sure they were always close to their hand
luggage, and carefully protected the diplomatic pouches they were
delivering into the hands of the relevant parties in Tangier. Baker,
too, was carrying valuable secret information. Her case was 'stuffed
with all kinds of papers' on which Paillole's intelligence for the
British was written in invisible ink.[26]

Baker had previously visited Tangier when she was filming the
outdoor scenes for *Princesse Tam Tam* in the mid-1930s. At that
time, she had made many friends there. Her fame gave her an entrée
with Moroccan elites, who liked to be seen with her, and she had
enjoyed their attentions and being invited to their splendid palaces.
Several had since come to Paris, where she had entertained them at
her club. She was, therefore, keen to look them up again on her
arrival in the city. However, Tangier in 1941, now in the hands of the
Spanish, was a very different place from 1935, when she had last
been there. After taking occupation in June 1940, Spain had at first
affirmed its neutrality and confirmed its commitment to preserving
the international governance of the city. However, in the interim,
the Spanish had gradually taken control of the police force and the

international corps of civil servants based there. Franco, confident of German support, had expelled the sultan's representative in Tangier (who was considered a French puppet) and replaced him with a pro-Spanish pasha. In addition, in a dramatic display of German power, the former palace where the sultan's representative had resided was being repurposed as the city's first German consulate.

These steps had triggered alarm in both French and British circles about the intentions of the Spanish and the Germans. Could this move be in preparation for a Hispano-German invasion of Morocco? Were British interests in Gibraltar now going to come under increased threat? Baker arrived on 17 March 1941, just in time to witness the ceremonial installation of the Germans in their new consular residence.[27] From an intelligence point of view, the timing was ideal: she was perfectly placed to witness at first hand what was taking place. Baker understood that she was at the centre of a developing situation that could have serious repercussions. It was a 'powder box disguised as a nest', as she put it.[28] She knew that the British and French had concerns about Spanish and German strategic intentions, and she was also aware of the lengths that the Germans were going to in their efforts to win over the Arabs as a way of directly undermining the French protectorate. Their propaganda was intense and now, with a stronghold in Tangier, they would have easier access to a wider range of Arab populations in Morocco. Conscious of the role she could play reporting what was happening on the ground, Baker took careful and detailed notes on everything she saw with a view to passing this information on to the British when she reached Lisbon.

While she was in the city, she was looked after by one of her former contacts, S.E. Bel Bachir, who, with his family, invited her to his property in nearby Spanish Morocco. There, in Tétouan, Bel Bachir threw a grand dinner party in her honour, attended by the brother of the local *khalifa* (the pasha's first lieutenant), who was a colonel in the Spanish air force, along with other officers of the Spanish High Command.[29] 'If they had known! I was listening! I missed nothing. The Spanish officers were chatty,' she later recounted.[30] They showered her with gifts, including a permanent transit visa for Spain that was issued to her immediately and would prove an invaluable bonus to her ability to travel freely – unlike Abtey, who remained stuck in Casablanca. Some days later, having kept a record of all her observations in Spanish Morocco and the content of her discussions with members of the Spanish military about Franco's ambitions, she returned to Tangier to take the boat to Lisbon.

The difference in atmosphere in the Portuguese capital, compared to both Casablanca and Tangier, was stark.[31] Despite the intense espionage activities taking place in all three cities, it was much more covert in Lisbon. The Portuguese capital still offered visitors a sense of freedom that was not present in Spanish or French Morocco. It felt less dangerous to Baker, and little had changed since her visit some months before. The capital was still packed with European refugees of all types. She soon managed to make contact with the British and handed over Paillole's intelligence to the British agent that she and Abtey knew as Bacon. He was particularly pleased to receive the notes she had made during her stops at Tangier and Tétouan in Spanish Morocco. However, her efforts to secure a visa for Abtey under his cover name of Hébert, during her visits to the various embassies in the city, met with no success. Paillole's intelligence contact in the city urged her to be patient, and Baker focused instead on her planned shows. It would be the first time she had performed in Lisbon. She had previously visited the Portuguese capital on her way to South America in March 1939, but had only spent a day there, barely enough time to visit the sights.

Baker's presence in Lisbon and the promise of her forthcoming shows were the focus of considerable excitement. Posters advertising her performances appeared across the city and she was widely feted in the press, described variously as the 'Queen of Paris', the 'Black Venus' or 'Princess of the World'. An edition of the celebrated newsreel *Jornal Português*, on 27 March 1941, reported on her visit, alongside those of other visiting celebrities, including Laurence Olivier and Vivien Leigh, who were in Lisbon for the premiere of their film *Rebecca*. Uncharacteristically, Baker appears alone at the airport, probably having just arrived, looking rather wistful. Perhaps she felt a little vulnerable, fearful of carrying the burden of this double life on her own for the first time. Nonetheless, she pulled it all off successfully, without arousing any suspicion. She completed her tour, which comprised performances at the Teatro da Trindade in Lisbon and the Teatro Sá da Bandeira in Porto. As soon as they were over, she left for Casablanca empty-handed. She had been unable to secure a visa for Abtey. Once again, despite all her efforts, none of the authorities concerned were prepared to provide him with the papers he required.[32]

Soon after her safe return to Casablanca, exhausted by the travelling, Baker decided that the climate further south would suit her better. She was experiencing ongoing problems with her chest, which had been troubling her since her illness in Marseille some weeks before, and she needed time to recuperate in peace. She chose Marrakech as her destination. It was a very different prospect from the modern port city of Casablanca. Situated inland, 150 miles due south, it enjoyed a reputation as a cultural centre, a meeting point for Morocco's diverse tribal communities and a sought-after venue for tourists to visit. Its appeal was later captured by the Americans who found themselves there. For US Vice Consul Kenneth Pendar,

> This orange-red city, built in a palm oasis at the foot of rocky snow-capped peaks rising with breath-taking majesty from the flat barren plain, lies like a 'desert flower thrown over the wall of the Atlas.' Scores of mosques rise above its extensive walls, but the greatest monument of all is the splendid rose-colored tower of the Koutoubiya Mosque, a masterpiece of the ancient glory of Islam. It dominates the town against the everchanging background of the mountains and serves as a symbol to the Arabs of the former grandeur of their civilization.[33]

This image was reiterated by the American journalist Kenneth Crawford, who wrote of it in 1943 as the most highly flavored of North African cities . . . [it was] a picturesque relic of medievalism and a modern city of extraordinary attraction . . . Its bazaars and public squares, meeting places for the Berbers out of the hills, are unique. The Arabian Nights atmosphere combined with the comforts of a modern resort city has made it for years a haven for the sophisticated traveler.[34]

Baker's circle in Marrakech

Baker's arrival did not go unnoticed. Hoping to escape the glare of public attention, she checked in to the luxury hotel Mamounia, which prided itself on guarding the privacy of its often-eminent guests. Set in glorious former royal gardens, situated a short distance from the city's bustling walled medina, it was 'a hotel which feels like a palace with its terraces overlooking gardens and the Atlas Mountains on the horizon'.[35] Frequented by affluent Europeans and Moroccans, the Marrakech-based members of the German armistice commission were also among the hotel's long-term residents. It was in these extravagant surroundings that Baker met several powerful Moroccan dignitaries who were based in the city and whom she would come to know well. One of these was Moulay Larbi El Alaoui, the sultan's first cousin and *khalifa* to the pasha of Marrakech. He was son of the sultan's former grand vizier and minister for education.[36] He, in turn, introduced Baker to his brother-in-law, Mohammed Menebhi. An affluent and well-connected man, he lived in his father's Marrakech palace in the middle of the medina. A devout Muslim and serious-minded man, he opened his home to both Baker and Abtey. He provided them with accommodation and hosted them regularly for sumptuous meals. He became a firm friend of Baker's and fell completely under her spell. Her enthusiasm for de Gaulle would lead him to convert to the Gaullist cause, and he would come to play a key role in Baker's undercover activities. Baker's friendship with these two men also brought her into the circle of the despotic pasha of Marrakech, Thami El Glaoui, a central figure in Moroccan politics, close to the sultan, ruler of the country.

Glaoui's rise to power had been a remarkable one. When his older brother, Madani El Glaoui, died in 1918, Thami, who had already made his French sympathies known, was nominated by Resident-General Lyautey to become head of the Glaoui family, bypassing by absolute decree the claims of his brother's sons. He took over his sibling's extensive territories, giving him inordinate power, which soon earned him the title of 'Second Sultan of Morocco'. Thami married his own niece to secure his position at the head of the family, and wed his eldest son to one of his great-nieces. His brother's harem was absorbed into his own, except for those women with sons of a mature age who represented a potential threat.[37] The Glaoui family enjoyed considerable power, in some ways more than the sultan himself, who, under the conventions of the protectorate, was deprived of almost all his ministers. He had no representatives abroad and his signature to French decrees was no more than a formality. The Glaoui family, on the other hand, enjoyed almost total freedom of action in the south, provided they continued France's 'work of pacification', at which they had proved themselves conspicuously, if not wholly disinterestedly, successful.[38]

In the early days of Thami's authority after succeeding his brother, he took care to cultivate Europeans, particularly courting the French.[39] He treated his European guests to lavish banquets and offered them expensive gifts. His manners were exquisite, his clothes a refinement of tradition. He understood even then that his status as second sultan in the south depended upon the French; but he was also aware that the French had no alternative but to depend utterly upon him. Before the outbreak of the war, he often visited Europe, accompanied by an extensive retinue, including members of his harem.[40]

Despite the presence of French institutions, the pasha of Marrakech had absolute control of all police functions and of all justice in the region.[41] As his status and responsibility grew, so did his need for money. From 1934, Thami interested himself increasingly in the mining concessions, and took a controlling interest in the Moroccan press. During the 1930s, he gained control of four out of the five French-owned Moroccan dailies – *Le Petit Marocain*, *La*

Vigie Marocaine, Le Courrier du Maroc and *L'Echo du Maroc.* This combination of power and absolute press control put him in a pivotal position in the country.[42] To successfully administer the enormous area over which he now ruled, Glaoui ran a highly efficient intelligence system. He distrusted his servants and his functionaries (bar a handful of intimates), fearing (often quite rightly) that they were in the pay of the French. His spy network was enormous and costly, but it kept him informed in advance of any complaints made about him to the resident-general or the sultan.[43]

After the outbreak of the war, Glaoui pledged his support to the French and continued to back them when the protectorate came under Vichy governance. His own network of informers meant that he had knowledge of every aspect of Moroccan life. His dictatorial methods may not have been appreciated by those he ruled, but his attitudes and public pronouncements in relation to the Allied and Axis powers could be very influential. The French worried that he might withdraw support for the protectorate and join with the sultan, who was showing signs of a growing conviction that it was time for Morocco to further its ambitions for independence. Soon after her arrival in the city, Baker quickly became a member of Thami El Glaoui's inner circle, frequently attending the extravagant dinner parties held at his opulent Marrakech palace; Glaoui, for his part, was very taken with Baker. Educated in Paris, he was fascinated by Western culture and knew of her fame. He had most probably visited her nightclub before the war. Once she was established in his circle, she was ideally placed to observe her Moroccan friends at close quarters and keep tabs on their movements, reporting to the French on what she saw and heard.

After a short period at the Mamounia hotel, Baker realised that it was too expensive to reside there and decided that she wanted to adopt a Moroccan way of life. She found a house in the medina, near the famous Koutoubia Mosque. 'Most Europeans hated the area,' Baker later explained, 'with its small roads strangled by high walls. Josephine's little world, well protected from indiscretions, was located behind a dead end, with access through a hammered door.'[44] Baker loved the privacy it could offer her. The shaded vestibule opened out onto a patio, with a fountain surrounded by orange trees.[45] She would visit the nearby *souk* (market) incognito, in Arab dress. 'I would shop in the souks among the crowds. I was dressed as a Moroccan, but without a veil over my mouth. At first locals were scandalised, then they would call me "the little sister".'[46] For a spell, Baker enjoyed a brief respite from the worries of the war and lived comfortably with her animals. Marrakech would remain her base until she eventually left North Africa in 1944. 'I lived such wonderful days there and painful ones, too. Wherever I went in Africa, I always came back. For four years, I would take refuge there when I was weary, too weary to carry on.'[47]

In Casablanca, Abtey continued his battle to acquire the papers that would make it possible for him to travel to meet the British in Lisbon. He was so disheartened when all his efforts came to nothing, that he decided to give up. Accompanied by Salmsen and Rey, who by this point had arrived in Morocco, he determined that they should all join Baker at her residence in Marrakech.[48] Salmsen found the city to be extraordinarily beautiful, but Baker's choice of 'traditional Moroccan' accommodation was not to his taste. Plagued by the mosquitoes that came into the house from the patio at night, he also never worked out how to wash. Fortunately, he discovered a friend from Paris who was living in a hotel in the city. He would arrange to play golf with him every day and then make use of his bathroom.[49] After a few weeks, they all realised that this peaceful interlude could not last and, since Baker and Abtey were uncertain about what their subsequent movements would be, it was agreed that the time had come for Salmsen to be reunited with his family in South America. With Abtey's help, Salmsen acquired from Rabat, the Moroccan capital, the visas he needed for the trip to Peru. He would travel by boat to Martinique and then take the land route through the US. Smadja also left to join his family in Tunis.[50]

Not long after the departure of their friends, Moulay Larbi confided to Baker and Abtey that he was troubled by what he had heard about German ambitions in the country.[51] He had been told that Auer's activities in Casablanca were intensifying, and there were signs that German military action in Morocco was being prepared. There were unconfirmed reports that Hispano-German forces were being convened near Tétouan in Spanish Morocco, and that the Germans were reinforcing their presence in Spain. Baker and Abtey knew that the only way to discover what was really going on would be to see for themselves. But without papers, Abtey was confined to Morocco. Baker would have to risk another mission alone. After a few days mulling over her options in her secluded Marrakech dwelling, she decided that she was prepared to take a chance on a trip to Spain. After all, she had successfully made it to Lisbon and back on her own, and had not encountered any hitches. She could use her cover again to visit the country and report back to Abtey and her Moroccan friends on the situation. What could be more convincing than Josephine Baker deciding to do a tour in Spain? This time, however, it seems that only Abtey and Baker's immediate Marrakech circle were aware of the real reason for her trip.[52] There is no evidence to suggest that Paillole or any other Deuxième Bureau agents were put in the picture. Baker, with Abtey's approval, was undertaking a perilous mission and would be entirely dependent on her own resources, were her intelligence activities to be uncovered.

Mission to Spain: 1–21 May 1941

After a frenetic period of organisation, at the start of May 1941 Baker embarked on a three-week tour of Spain. She left Marrakech and travelled first to Casablanca with Abtey, and then on to Tangier by train, where she again looked up her friends and took stock of the situation there.[53] On her arrival in Madrid, she found herself being invited everywhere. 'It is very convenient to be Josephine Baker,' she opined. 'As soon as I'm announced in a city, invitations to my hotel rain down.'[54] It was the same at her other stops across the country. During her residence at the Teatro de la Zarzuela in Madrid, the American press somewhat delightedly caught up with her. Unaware of the real reasons for her presence, they remarked instead on her performances. They noted her distinct change of style, which came as something of a disappointment for some members of the audience. Playing on her former image, she teased them, declaring that she had 'eaten her bananas so was obliged to put on a dress'. A *Variety* journalist explained that

> the morality laws in Madrid are much stricter and would not approve of the costumes that the dusky comedienne wore in her successful appearances at the Casino de Paris in the good old days ... She announces that she is going to strip, but unlike Paris, the shedding consists of the removal of an outer gown ... She sings, she jokes and adlibs for one hour and completely runs away with all honours.

In what had become a trademark of her performances, Baker went 'among the audience distributing cigarettes and picking on the boys with hairless pates – and they love it'.[55] She also made it clear to reporters that performing in occupied Paris was a compromising step that she was not prepared to consider.[56]

Fortunately, during the trip, she found no evidence that the feared invasion of Morocco was in preparation. However, conscious that her every move was doubtless being monitored by German agents and that the information she had collected might seem suspicious if it fell into the wrong hands, on her journey back to Morocco she kept her notes safe on her person, attached with a safety pin to the inside of her clothes.[57] This was a method she had employed for some time as a way of storing her important personal information. In the early months of the war, rather surprisingly, Baker explained her inventive technique to a journalist, who took delight in revealing her methods to his readers:

> [Baker] has found an almost infallible mnemonic system. All her appointments for the day are written down separately on small sheets of paper that she pins to the lapel of her coat: 'They're my reminders,' she says. Sometimes these bundles are positioned artistically, reminiscent of a lace ruffle; Baker's ways are often extravagant and surprising to those who are not in the know.[58]

It was an effective ploy. As Baker made her way back to Morocco, unsuspecting border guards and customs officers were full of smiles for the star. No one thought to check for little pockets that contained the notes that she had hidden in her clothes. Fortunately for her, her cover proved no less effective during this second important solo mission. She soon reached Casablanca safely and was pleased to be able to inform Abtey and her Moroccan friends that there was no immediate prospect of a German invasion.

Enter the Americans

Baker's return to Morocco coincided with the arrival of a signifi-cant new player in the murky underworld of wartime North Africa. Since France's defeat in 1940, American public opinion had been predominantly hostile to joining the war in Europe. Although the country was technically neutral, President Roosevelt was sympathetic to the plight of the British, and believed that US involvement in the conflict was inevitable. He saw North Africa as an ideal location to spearhead an offensive against the Germans, if only the French Vichy government could be persuaded to support the Allies. To achieve this, in December 1940 he sent Robert Murphy, an American diplomat who had served in Paris for ten years, as his personal envoy to North and West Africa to investigate the situation. Murphy's secret mission was to attempt to persuade Weygand to defy Vichy and organise France's North Africa armies against the Germans and Italians. Weygand was steadfast in his opposition to the Germans, but refused to defy Vichy. He was, however, prepared to cooperate on a reciprocal trade agreement. The terms of the Murphy–Weygand accords, which were signed in February–March 1941, allowed for French assets in the US to be unfrozen for the purchase of essential consumer goods to feed struggling North African populations. The war had brought economic difficulties, which hit the local Arab populations hardest. Weygand knew that their misery was a threat to the stability of French North Africa and could be exploited by those seeking to gain support for independence from French rule.[59] For its part, the US hoped that the aid would entice North Africa to resist the Germans.

In implementing the accords, Murphy secured permission for US officials to be allowed to supervise deliveries at ports across North Africa, despite German opposition. This paved the way for Murphy to send twelve 'vice consuls', who, under cover of overseeing the reception of these consumer goods, were tasked with carrying out intelligence work. Around half were based in Morocco (mainly in Casablanca), while the others were allocated to Algeria.[60] Known in American diplomatic circles as non-career vice consuls (to distinguish them from those who were present in North Africa in an official capacity, rather than as spies), vitally they had access to protected diplomatic communications. The Germans were not duped by the American presence, but initially wrote them off as amateurs. The Gestapo reported to Hitler that these agents would give them no trouble, as they were lacking in methods, organisation and discipline.

The vice consuls who arrived in Casablanca in May and June 1941 were well-educated men, who had been selected for this role mainly on the basis of their knowledge of France and their ability to communicate fluently. Frank Canfield, for example, had worked as a lawyer in Paris and 'spoke French like a Frenchman'.[61] Kenneth Pendar, another vice consul who worked closely with Canfield, had been in France from 1937 to 1940 and saw this role as a chance to do something for the anti-Nazi cause – 'for my own country and for France'.[62] Pendar went on to explain their multiple tasks:

> Our more publicized job was to keep an eye on American shipments, check them at the port of entry, and follow them into every little Arab bazaar to their ultimate customer. We were also to make sure that no similar goods were shipped out of North Africa. Our secret job was a more dramatic one. We were to be undercover American agents acting as observers and organizers for the Army and the Navy. We were to appraise the military and political situation, make friends with the Arab chiefs and French officers, and set up contacts that might be useful to American defense.[63]

Pendar and his colleagues would send the intelligence they uncovered in secure diplomatic pouches to a Major Bentley, based in Tangier. He 'classified this material, made an overall summary, an analysis of the various reports' and conveyed them to Washington.[64] The Germans feared (rightly as it transpired) that the emissaries would not limit their activities to aid and might engage in military preparations in the area. These men were the trailblazers of what would become the Office of Strategic Services (OSS) and later the basis for the modern Central Intelligence Agency (CIA). Their role would be to lay the important groundwork for the Allied invasion of North Africa, which would take place some eighteen months after their arrival there.

Abtey claims to have been introduced to Vice Consul Frank Canfield in Casablanca, while Baker was still in Spain.[65] Canfield, however, only arrived in Casablanca in June 1942, some weeks after Baker had returned.[66] Nonetheless, it seems likely that they did meet. According to Abtey, Canfield promised to help him interact with his British contacts in Lisbon. The American knew Dunderdale, whom he had met in Paris before the war at the American embassy. After confirmation from London, it was agreed that henceforth they would work together. Canfield would take responsibility for forwarding the intelligence that Baker and Abtey collected to Washington.[67] Baker and Abtey were valuable contacts for the vice consuls. Not only could they supply intelligence directly, but they were also well placed to support the vice consuls in one of their main tasks in Casablanca – to identify and monitor the activities of German agents. The vice consuls needed this support, as their own capacity to operate was impaired by strict instructions from the French to avoid drawing attention to themselves, for fear that their presence might aggravate the Germans and jeopardise the status quo.[68]

Still very new to the field, Canfield was enthused by the intelligence that Baker had collected about the presence of the Germans in Spain and their activities in the Spanish Moroccan territories. Fears about German ambitions to invade Morocco were diminishing, however. The German attack on Russia on 22 June 1941 revealed that the Germans had cleverly played the French and

Allied intelligence communities, by seeding multiple rumours of a planned Moroccan invasion in order to distract from their real ambitions on the Eastern Front. With ideas for a possible landing in North Africa taking shape as a realistic possibility for the future, the vice consuls continued their important work of collecting as much intelligence as they could to help strategists at home gain a detailed picture of the Moroccan military, social and physical land-scape. For this they needed information about the allegiances of the diverse components of the population and their attitudes to France (Vichy and de Gaulle) and the Allied powers. Baker and Abtey, with their intimate involvement in Moroccan circles, were ideally placed to help their American partners collect the necessary intelligence. But just as this collaboration was getting underway, their activities were brought to an abrupt halt. In early July 1941, after returning home to Marrakech following a few shows at the Colisée in Algiers, without warning Baker collapsed.[69]

Baker falls ill

Seeing Josephine suddenly crippled by terrible pains in her abdomen, Abtey immediately called for a doctor. Fearing the worst, the doctor advised her removal to a clinic in Casablanca for treat-ment. In a panic, Abtey transported her by ambulance, hoping that the clinic would be equipped to manage her illness. It was not clear what was wrong with her or what had caused it; but the severity of the illness was not in doubt, and all those around her were extremely concerned. Baker's own version was that she acquired an infection following an intervention by a doctor she had visited in Casablanca, on her way home from Spain to Marrakech. She had been keen to check the state of her lungs, which had never fully recovered since her problems in Marseille,[70] and also whether there was anything preventing her from conceiving.[71] She had supposedly taken advan-tage of her time in Casablanca to have some X-rays taken of her chest. In a move that seems to confirm that she must have been in a relationship with Abtey at this point, once she had been given the all-clear, she had asked the radiographer to take further X-rays, in the hope that it might reveal details of why she was unable to conceive. He administered the necessary injection to take an X-ray of her abdomen (which revealed no abnormalities). However, it was her contention that the injection was carried out with a dirty needle, which caused the infection that then led to a serious case of sepsis. Baker underwent numerous operations, but despite short spells of improvement, she often suffered setbacks. She was close to death for an extended period, at least until late 1941. She continued to need sustained care and was confined to the clinic for months afterwards.

Abtey's devotion leaves little doubt about the nature of their relationship. During the early and most dangerous stages of Baker's illness, he supported her constantly. He spent most of his time at the clinic and slept on a camp bed beside her in her room. With Baker out of action, and Abtey by her bedside, the vice consuls carried on with their intelligence collection without their help. Throughout autumn 1941, they continued to compile information that allowed them to map the German presence in the country in some detail. They needed to uncover the full workings of Auer's network across the country. The German armistice commission was a key focus of their efforts. They recorded the names of all the members, and identified some Axis representatives whose diplomatic status was less official. It was more difficult for the Americans (and indeed the French) to track down those who were informers, acting as German agents. In July 1941, they reported that

> 91 members of the German armistice commission are in Casablanca and 8 in Marrakesh at the Hotel Mamounia. 194 members in all of Morocco. The Commission keeps certain men at specified places in the area, and the greater majority of them are continually on the move by automobile, train, etc studying the entire situation in all of Morocco.[72]

Pendar adds that 'their official function was to check on all French military installations, equipment, and personnel, and to see that the North African army made no attempt to rearm'.[73]

Vice Consul Stafford Reid and Vice Consul David King discovered that in Morocco, and elsewhere in North Africa, a vast network of French and Axis agents were trafficking in strategic materials and food, which was depriving locals. Goods were sneaked onto French ships, labelled for transfer to France, and were then diverted to Italian and German ports. Morocco was rich in metals, including zinc, copper and aluminium. The Germans also needed cobalt, which they used in electronics and to make synthetic fuel and metals to harden the steel armour of their tanks. Reid uncovered German specialists who were secretly working in mines in southern Morocco, supervising the production of cobalt. They held special military visas to enter and leave these forbidden militarised areas that had been allocated to them by Vichy, eager to gain concessions from Nazi Germany so as to free French soldiers from German prisoner-of-war camps and spare the lives of hostages.[74] Added to these incidents of cooperation between the French and German officials, Pendar found French army and civilian officials to be 'passionately loyal to Marshal Pétain' and 'anti-British'.[75] The military was strongly Anglophobe, unforgiving about the attacks the British had mounted on the French navy in Mers-El-Kébir in July 1940 (see above). This episode had been further aggravated in their eyes by the events in the summer of 1941, when British forces invaded Syria, a Vichy French colonial sphere of influence: they were enraged when control of the country was then ceded to their sworn enemies, the Gaullist Free French. Pendar did not find the anti-Vichy, pro-Gaullist underground in Morocco that the Americans were hoping for, but he did find that the French were 'patriotic, anti-Nazi and largely willing and even anxious to cooperate with us'.[76]

A further important brief of the vice consuls was to find out 'what the Arabs really thought about the Axis and the democratic nations'.[77] Murphy teamed Pendar up with Canfield and sent the pair of them to southern Morocco, to work in the territory of the 'powerful clan of the Glaoui'.[78] Their task was to discover 'what sort of propaganda swayed [the Arabs], how much the Axis infiltrated and corrupted the Arab world, and how receptive that world would be if American action were ever necessary in Africa'.[79] In addressing this assignment, Pendar describes how they 'crossed and recrossed the path of the German armistice commission and tried to elude the watchful eyes of the Vichy secret service'.[80] He took a very orientalist view of the Arab world, perceiving it to be 'quite separate from . . . the French one. Slow, secret and persistent, it led its own life in *souk* and shadowy streets, undisturbed, except economically, by the troubles of its European partners.'[81] Pendar reports that 'through our Arab contacts . . . we could learn much about Axis operations in North Africa'.[82] He soon had many 'Arab friends' and was developing a large network of contacts – including Glaoui, who appeared to offer support. 'Other chieftains did not give me the same impression that [he] did of belief in our cause, or at least in our victory.' As we shall see, this friend of Baker's remained a central figure of interest in all the American intelligence up until the end of the war. He was an astute player, who sought to remain of relevance to all the parties involved in the complex Moroccan wartime landscape.

While Baker was hospitalised in the clinic throughout the autumn of 1941, fighting infection after infection, Hitler's desert war against the British continued to rage. Rommel's German Afrika Korps battled for control of Libya and parts of Egypt. The successes of each side fluctuated in what proved to be a frustratingly long engagement. The dramatic Japanese bombardment of Pearl Harbor on 7 December 1941 finally brought the US openly into the war, and immediately boosted the British war effort. Roosevelt accelerated plans for Bill Donovan to construct a spy agency, of which Murphy's vice consuls were a component part. Colonel Bill Eddy was assigned the task of building the spy network in North Africa to prepare for 'sabotage, guerrilla warfare, and organized armed resistance' against the Axis.[83] He would work with Murphy to push forward with coordinating the work of the vice consuls, whose role was considerably stepped up.

But even with American involvement, the situation looked bleak for the Allies. Fears once again ran high that an attack on Morocco could be imminent and that American participation in the conflict could be the trigger for Hitler to finally convince Franco to join him in the battle for North Africa. Worrying intelligence reports indicated that Moroccans doubted whether the Allies had the resources to win, and were turning towards the Germans, who held a commanding position. Rommel was looking strong, and Weygand, who had been seen as a discreet ally for the Americans, had been recalled from North Africa. Resident-General Noguès, for his part, appeared to be ever more prepared to bow to German pressure, and agreed to monitor the actions of the vice consuls more closely. At the same time, more serious plans were being hatched for a potential Allied landing in North Africa as the basis for the conquest of the European continent. To aid in the elaboration of this strategy, the Americans needed the vice consuls to collect information about the geographical landscapes they would encounter, and in particular to offer insights into how both the French military and the various components of the Moroccan population would position themselves in the event of an American invasion. In addition, the vice consuls intensified their work of fostering the local Resistance groups that were beginning to take shape on the ground. These needed to be encouraged if they were to be in a position to offer the Allies the support they would need in the event of a landing. All this was vastly complicated by the need to stay out of sight of both French agents who were reporting to the resident-general and the plethora of German agents roaming the country. It was in this context that Baker and Abtey were brought back in to contribute to the work of the Allied cause.

Baker's bedside as a cover for meetings

By early 1942, although she was still experiencing severe relapses, Baker also had long spells of more cheerful convalescence. Abtey explains that during her better periods, he found time to meet the American vice consuls based in Casablanca. One was Sidney Bartlett, a new vice consul, who had replaced Canfield when he was sent home in December 1941. Bartlett requested that Abtey re-establish contact with Paillole's agents, indicating that Abtey could act as an intermediary for them to work together with the Deuxième

Bureau. Paillole responded enthusiastically to the suggestion.[84] To support this work further, during a period when Baker was in better health Abtey decided to make a trip to France to reconnect with some of his former colleagues in the French intelligence services. During the boat crossing from Algiers to Marseille, he became friendly with the man who was sharing his cabin, a certain Fernand Zimmer. He, like Abtey, hailed from the Alsace region of France, and Abtey decided to recruit him.[85] Zimmer subsequently visited Casablanca, where he met Baker at the clinic.[86] Described by Baker as 'a tall man with piercing eyes',[87] he soon became part of Abtey and Baker's network of contacts.

Since Baker's Lisbon trip the previous March, Abtey had been so preoccupied with Josephine's illness that he had not been in communication with their French intelligence contacts and Paillole's organisation. It is therefore plausible that the Americans might have prodded Abtey to get back in touch with Paillole, and that he in turn encouraged Baker and Abtey to cooperate with the Americans. The attitudes of the Deuxième Bureau towards both the British and particularly the Gaullists (whom they regarded as being in the hands of the British) was at best ambivalent. But like the French military in general and the men of Vichy, they had a much more positive attitude towards the Americans.[88] In June 1942, Paillole explained to his subordinates that they should not be overly worried about the Americans. 'Their activity is not primarily directed against France or the Empire. The Americans are mainly looking for information on the Axis.'[89]

By spring 1942, Baker was well enough to receive visitors, and Vice Consul Bartlett started going to see her on a regular basis. He suggested to her that the clinic she was at could function as an 'extraordinary meeting place', as no one would be suspicious when he called to see a former American citizen who had been seriously unwell.[90] Soon, this desire to visit and have news of the star's progress became a cover for the vice consuls to hold meetings with a series of different contacts without arousing the suspicions of the German and Vichy officials who were observing their every move. Baker and Abtey introduced the Americans to their French intelligence contacts, who came to the clinic on the pretext of visiting Baker. Deuxième Bureau agent Gilbert Guillaume claims in his memoirs to have been in contact with both Baker and Abtey in Casablanca before and after the Allied landings.[91] Abtey also mentions the involvement of certain individuals in the French military, including General Augustin Xavier Richert, who had sympathies for the Americans and was described by Vice Consul Bartlett as 'a very close intimate friend ... [who] would be of greatest value to our North African Occupation in the service of Franco-American collaboration'.[92]

Baker's Moroccan circles of friends were also regular visitors, and this allowed the Americans to have meetings with Moroccan dignitaries like Menebhi and Moulay Larbi, who were both close to Glaoui, a continued focus of interest.[93] Menebhi made regular trips to Tangier and Spanish Morocco, and could also pass on valuable information about the attitudes of the populations in these locations and the military situation there. Baker's clinic bedroom therefore became a secret hub for information exchange, and potentially even aided in the building of local Resistance networks. With the invasion of North Africa finally decided by the Allies in July 1942, these meetings became even more vital, as detailed plans were laid for what would be Operation Torch.

The occurrence of these gatherings sounds feasible, if a touch romantic; unfortunately, however, the dates cited by Abtey are blatantly out of kilter with the dates when the vice consuls were present in Casablanca. Canfield, Pendar and Bartlett were each transferred or sent home, one after the other, having compromised their positions for different reasons. Canfield was partnered with Kenneth Pendar on his mission to cultivate the leaders in southern Morocco and find out their allegiances, and the pair had settled in Marrakech, where they rented a famous villa, La Saadia, and became known for their raucous parties.[94] Canfield proved an inveterate card player and gambler, and the serving of alcohol to devout Muslims did not sit well with the Vichy protectorate authorities, who made frequent complaints.[95] He was the first to be sent home in late 1941 for his 'indiscretions and undue exuberance', having proved a liability. But he was not alone in being transferred: Pendar was also the target for complaints by Resident-General Noguès, who asserted that he was 'making Protectorate relationships with the Moslems more difficult by his propaganda and efforts to drive a wedge between France and native ties'.[96] Nonetheless, Reid later pointed out Pendar's 'unique role' as 'self-appointed Ambassador to South Morocco', and asserted that his champagne receptions were a small price to pay for the Americans gaining access to French officers, caids (local administrators) and pashas.[97] Pendar's success in this mission earned him the right to stay on in North Africa, but in June 1942 Murphy moved him away from Morocco and Noguès to join the team in Algiers.[98] Bartlett's departure occurred around the same time. His transgression had been to fall in love with a Vichy-German spy. Although he may have been set up by the Gestapo, he had become a security risk and was duly sent back to Washington.[99] So it was that neither Pendar nor Bartlett was in Casablanca during September and October 1942, when Abtey and Baker both claim to have met them.[100]

Stafford Reid and Dave King, on the other hand, were both in Casablanca at that time, and it is entirely possible that they met Abtey and Baker. Frustratingly, however, there is no reference to any such meetings in any of the surviving intelligence reports made by the vice consuls or any other agents. There are various possible reasons for this. First, agents and informers were almost never named in reports: mention is only made of their reliability, and in this they were ranked on a scale from A1–D1, an annotation that was included in all reports. Secondly, the intelligence agency of which the vice consuls were a part, the OSS, was still in its infancy and its filing systems were less than perfect. It may well be that records were made of Baker's meetings with the vice consuls and that they have been either mislaid or lost. While neither Baker nor Abtey is named, there is, however, other evidence confirming that the Americans did work closely with the Deuxième Bureau in Casablanca during this period. In a report dated 25 July 1942, Vice Consul King refers to working with 'a small efficient group of the remnants of the old French SR [Service Renseignements – intelligence service]'. This could potentially be a reference to Abtey and his circle. His description of their precise links with the government at Vichy seems to tally with Abtey's position:

> According to the terms of the Armistice in 1940, the French military and naval intelligence services were disbanded. Some of these men left France and came to Morocco where they formed a secret intelligence service. Some of them actually managed things so as to come out in the service of and with the authority of the Vichy government and they have been working here for us since then under that cover.[101]

While former SR agents like Abtey may have been using the Deuxième Bureau as a cover for their 'Gaullist' activities, it also seems likely that the Vichy authorities were aware of the anti-German activities they were engaged in and tolerated them. In so far as Vichy's ambitions were to protect France's interests against the Germans, particularly in North Africa, counterespionage was essential if this was to be achieved. It therefore made sense to allow (or at least turn a blind eye to) those activities that were intrinsic to the work of the Deuxième Bureau. King's report therefore sheds valuable light on how agents like Abtey continued to have an affiliation with the Deuxième Bureau, while at the same time distancing themselves from Vichy. King again stressed the value of these contacts in 1943, asserting that the Deuxième Bureau furnished 'very valuable intelligence on France, not only to the British Intelligence ... but also to the American Army'. He goes on to explain that the Deuxième Bureau had representatives abroad, including attachés in the Madrid and Lisbon legations, and special mention is made of 'Colonel Rivet's representatives in North Africa [who] were protecting and assisting Dave King and the other American consuls and OSS representatives in Northern Africa'.[102] Was this a reference to Baker and Abtey and their work in helping the OSS to identify German agents and to prepare the American landings? It seems a reasonable assumption, but the evidence remains patchy.

That is not to say that the meetings in Baker's hospital did not take place, or that Baker and Abtey did not play a significant role in supporting preparations for the Allied landings. It is just that the evidence base does not conclusively support their version of events. Compelling and dramatic evidence does exist that Baker offered extremely valuable input to the Americans in the immediate aftermath of their arrival in Morocco in November 1942 (though in this case not to the vice consuls). But this is to jump ahead a little. Before all that, Baker – still in convalescence – had other problems to deal with that were closer to home. The legal claims against her had not gone away. She was tried in absentia at the Marseille Tribunal, sued by the directors of the municipal theatre in Marseille for breach of the contract valid from 24 December 1940 to 23 January 1941, according to which they had paid 200,000 francs. The directors claimed that she had left for Algiers with her impresario, her chambermaid and her luggage about a week before the contract was due to expire. The court sentenced Baker to pay 50,000 francs and some additional compensation. Her lawyers did their best to appeal against this decision, but when the case was heard at the Court of Appeal in Aix-en-Provence in June 1942, the original judgment was upheld and the directors were awarded a further 50,000 francs in damages.[103]

Some weeks after this, in October 1942, Baker's death was widely reported in the French, British and American press.[104] It is not entirely clear how the story originated, but Baker and Abtey both blamed Maurice Chevalier. Baker read an article in which Chevalier claimed to have seen her 'dying and destitute in a Casablanca hospital', and his description quickly spread.[105] It probably sowed the idea of her imminent demise, as rumours of her death started to circulate soon after.[106] By the time the American papers got wind of the news, it had already been refuted in the French press, which announced that she was in fact doing much better.[107] However, the momentum was difficult to stop in the US, and obituaries started to appear in African American newspapers, including one in the *Chicago Defender* by Langston Hughes, a writer who had known Baker in Paris before the war. He referred to her as a

child of charm, dusky Cinderella-girl, ambassadress of beauty from negro America to the world, buried now on foreign soil – as much a victim of Hitler as the soldiers who fall today in Africa fighting his armies. The Aryans drove Josephine away from her beloved Paris. At her death she was again just a little colored girl from St Louis who didn't rate in Fascist Europe.[108]

Thus it was that, just as detailed reports started to reach the American public of the Allied landings in North Africa, it also learnt of Baker's supposed death, when in fact she was out of danger, though still confined to her clinic.

It was there that Baker waited impatiently, aware of the frenetic activity involved in preparations for the American arrival. The great unknown was how the French military would respond to the invasion. The hope was that – when the crunch came – the Vichy army would stop short of fighting the Allies. The events in Syria in 1941, when the Vichy armies had offered stiff resistance to the British and the Gaullist Free French forces, did not set a very promising precedent. Despite Vichy's ultimate defeat, few French soldiers had gone over to the Allies and joined the Gaullists. Loyalty to Pétain remained strong in the military, and the troops were also subject to persistent German anti-Allied propaganda.

The vice consuls had been working to bolster local resistance in the area, but it was not clear how effective these cells would be. Much would depend on how Noguès reacted to the invasion and how he instructed the Vichy army to respond. The Americans also needed to ensure that the attack came as a surprise. To achieve this, the vice consuls ensured that their meetings were conducted with the utmost secrecy and that their network of contacts was left in the dark about the exact timing of the operation – right up until the last minute. In the light of this, later reports that Baker and Abtey were aware of the date of Operation Torch seem unlikely.[109] Nonetheless, Baker certainly understood that the arrival of the American armies was imminent, and she was proud that they would soon be there to liberate North Africa. Her relationship with her former country was about to grow and deepen in ways she could never have anticipated.

4

BAKER AND THE AMERICANS IN NORTH AFRICA
(1943)

In the early morning of 8 November 1942, Baker leapt out of bed, roused by the sounds of battle. 'I rushed out onto the terrace barefoot, in my pyjamas and an old jumper, when I heard the cannon fire, General Noguès' anti-aircraft guns ... were firing at the American planes ... The battle of Casablanca was underway.'[1] Determined to soak in the atmosphere, she ignored the entreaties of the medical staff inside who feared she would be hit with shrapnel. 'I told you so!' Baker exclaimed excitedly. 'The Americans are here at last! Europe has no idea how strong and determined they are. You will soon see what they are capable of.'[2] The terrace was awash with leaflets that had been dropped in the early hours bearing the American flag and a photograph of President Roosevelt. They carried an announcement from General Dwight Eisenhower on behalf of the president, in French on one side and Arabic on the other. He assured the reader of American friendship and explained that they were engaged in a battle to protect the future of the people. 'We come to liberate you from those conquerors who wished to take your freedom and your right to live out your lives in peace.' The message finished with a commitment to leave as soon as the threat from Germany and Italy had been lifted, and it called for cooperation in the accomplishment of this project.[3] Operation Torch was underway. Casablanca was one of the three coastal cities, along with Oran and Algiers in Algeria, targeted by the Anglo-American forces in their three-pronged assault on North Africa.

Roosevelt's appeal was designed to solicit the support of the French and Moroccan people for the invasion. Much had hinged on the hope that the groundwork laid by the local Resistance would come good, and when faced with the strength of the American army, the French military would realise it was a fait accompli, and bloodshed could be avoided.[4] But much to the disappointment of the Americans, secret plans to bring the French army over to the Allies fell apart, and General Noguès chose to follow Vichy orders to repel the invasion. He instructed the French military to do everything in its power to battle against the Americans: they were not going to give up Casablanca without a fight. Anti-aircraft batteries in the harbour therefore greeted the American battleships as they moved to neutralise the shore batteries and prevent the French navy from leaving the harbour.[5] A direct attack on Casablanca was impossible because of its naval and shore defences, so the Americans landed troops in the north, at Fedala and Port Lyautey, and in the south at Safi. The plan was for the different detachments all to converge on Casablanca. French defences could not hold out for long against the mighty force of the American navy, and despite loss of life on both sides, in the end the battle of Casablanca was short. By the afternoon of 10 November, Noguès understood that he would have to relinquish Morocco to the Americans, and after Vichy confirmation, at 6 p.m. French commanders received orders by radio to stop fighting. On 11 November, at the Hotel Miramar in Fedala, Noguès signed an armistice with General Patton, head of the Western Task Force charged with taking Casablanca and securing Morocco.

While Baker observed events from the roof of her clinic, Abtey had managed to reach the Americans during the fighting. He had hoped to offer his services, but by the time he arrived, the ceasefire had already been declared.[6] After that, American forces swiftly took occupation of Casablanca and set about securing the area. It fell to the Counter Intelligence corps (CIC) to flush out German agents,[7] and they had Auer's spy network in their sights. After landing with the assault troops and participating in the encirclement of Casablanca, they set about hunting down the Germans as soon as they had access to the city. The landings had taken Auer and the members of the German armistice commission by surprise, but they were alerted to the American arrival by Roosevelt's (rather premature) broadcast some hours previously. As a result, they had been able to make their getaway and escape to the Spanish Zone before the troops reached the city.[8] The CIC discovered a mass of documents that the Germans had left behind in their hotel. Among these papers were lists of French Axis sympathisers, as well as a complete Italian intelligence service list of French intelligence service members. These operatives were immediately replaced by agents unknown to the Germans. CIC agents were deployed to cities across Morocco, where they worked closely with French intelligence agencies, as was stipulated by the armistice agreement between the Allies and the French, and took responsibility for counter-intelligence activity.[9]

Lieutenant Paul Jensen was the CIC officer who led the unit that was dispatched to Marrakech to administer the station there. He later described the role that Baker played in supporting him and his men during these crucial weeks. Drawing on her intimate knowledge of the situation in Marrakech, under her guidance and with the intelligence she was able to provide, his unit was able to 'vitiate the subversive efforts' of the members of the German armistice commission in the city.[10] Baker's input made it possible for the CIC officers to curtail enemy communications in the occupied areas. She also offered vital advice to the combat troops who were securing vital infrastructure in the area. Baker, Jensen reported, 'was our No.1 contact in French Morocco'. She supported our mission 'at great risk to her own life – and I mean that literally . . . We would have been helpless without her, for we were the only American intelligence unit south of Casablanca in Morocco.'[11] Baker provided Jensen with the names of Nazi espionage agents in hiding, who could have incited an armed revolt among the Arabs against the exposed southern flank of the American troops but whom, 'through information obtained by Miss Baker, we were able to apprehend in time'. In a further remarkable development, Baker helped Jensen 'make friends with the Arabs' by putting him in touch with Muslim leaders like Moulay Larbi. Their relations with local tribesmen in the area gave Jensen access to crucial intelligence that enabled his unit 'to capture Hermannus Van Ruyn, a German general and a fort at Oualidia where he arrested between 400–600 enemy agents'.[12] Baker's input was therefore critical to the success of American military activities in southern Morocco. Once again, her network of contacts with influential Moroccans facilitated her undercover work and made it possible for her to assist the Americans at this crucial time. Jensen's actions in Oualidia led him to be awarded the Silver Star, and one of his fellow officers was awarded the Legion of Merit.

This aspect of Baker's contribution to Allied landings, as described by Jensen, has not previously been documented, and neither Baker nor Abtey refers to it. Yet the military archives in Washington confirm the existence of a CIC officer, Lt Jensen, posted to Marrakech in 1942–43.[13] His intelligence reports make no direct reference to Baker, but, as we have seen, the Americans were careful not to name their informants. Perhaps more surprising is the fact that the incident relating to the coastal town of Oualidia is also not mentioned. The actions described by Jensen fall within the remit of the CIC, and Jensen's work with Baker would appear to reflect the close collaboration between the corps and the French intelligence services reported in its official history.[14] This account of the CIC and its activities in North Africa during this period also acknowledges that 'for their heroism under fire, many of its members received decorations', including both the Silver Star and the Legion of Merit award.[15] At the time that Baker's involvement in this mission was revealed to reporters – in 1951 – Jensen backed up his claims with official documents, though the full details of these medal citations do not appear to have survived. Nonetheless, Jensen's testimonial seems plausible – and importantly, it sheds new light on Baker's work with the Americans and adds considerably to our understanding of the role she played in their activities.[16]

In establishing a strategic foothold in North Africa, Operation Torch represented an important turning point in the fortunes of the Allies in the war. It laid the way for the Mediterranean to become a second front and act as the trampoline for the Liberation of mainland France. But the immediate problem facing the Americans was to resolve the question of how the region was to be administered. In advance of the landings, the Americans had set their sights on General Henri Giraud to command in North Africa. He had famously escaped from a German prisoner-of-war camp in April 1942 and, while he supported Pétain, he was strongly anti-German. This profile suited the Americans, who needed a leader who would keep the French army on side. However, during discussions in Algiers it became clear that he did not have the confidence of the Vichyite generals of the army, who refused to rally behind him. A rapid solution needed to be found, so that the American military could turn its attentions to assisting the beleaguered British forces in Tunisia, where Rommel and his Afrika Korps were proving increasingly menacing. In a move that surprised Allied sympathisers, the Americans turned to Admiral Darlan, commander in chief of all the Vichy French armed forces, who happened to be in Algiers when the Americans arrived there. He eventually agreed to switch sides and, under the terms of what became known as the 'Darlan Deal', assumed authority over French North Africa 'in the name of Marshal Pétain', on the understanding that all officials were to remain in their posts and continue to exercise their duties. In response to this step, the Germans immediately moved to occupy the whole of the French mainland, billeting their soldiers throughout the formerly unoccupied areas of the south.

Under the terms that were finally reached, Darlan would serve as 'high commissioner' for French North Africa, while Giraud commanded the French troops, which would now join the Allies in the fight against the Germans. In Morocco, Noguès remained in post as resident-general. All this resulted in a considerable degree of continuity in the protectorate's administration. The appointment of Darlan, renowned for collaborating with the Germans in the Vichy government, caused consternation on the part of the British. De Gaulle, who had not been briefed about the American plans for Operation Torch until it was well under way and was completely excluded from participating in the operation itself, was appalled at his nomination. Eisenhower, however, batted off the widespread criticism, justifying the move as a military expediency and explaining that, if they did not work with Darlan, any chance of the Allies defeating Rommel in Tunisia would be lost.

The ceasefire had come soon enough for Casablanca to survive the landings relatively unscathed, and its port became an important supply hub for the American troops. The arrival of the Western Task Force led to the injection of over 33,000 men into French Morocco, and the city was overrun with thousands of American soldiers and sailors. They pitched tents in parks and squares, and their huge camps appeared around the perimeter of the city.[17] Officers requisitioned attractive houses and apartments on Anfa Hill, a residential quarter on the outskirts.[18] Patton moved into the Villa Maas, the very same residence that had been used by Auer.[19] American supplies were unloaded in the port. They included what were seen as delights by the Moroccan locals, who were seduced by the new, intriguing American presence. Essentials that had been difficult to find for two years – like flour, matches and pharmaceuticals – flooded in. Most exciting for young Moroccans were Coca-Cola bottles, which rapidly became prized possessions.[20]

All this excitement coincided with Baker's return to better health. She left the clinic in Casablanca on 1 December 1942, nearly eighteen months after she had first been admitted.[21] She immediately made for Marrakech, where Menebhi once again arranged for her to be looked after, this time in a guest wing of his palace in the medina.[22] Soon after settling in, however, Baker once again became unwell, this time with a less serious, but nonetheless debilitating, illness – paratyphoid. She decided to move out of the medina to enjoy the comforts of the Mamounia Hotel, where she was soon joined by Abtey. They spent Christmas there while she recovered.

'Too busy to die'

During her stay at the Mamounia, Baker was gradually getting back on her feet when she encountered Ollie Stewart, a reporter for the newspaper *Afro-American*. By chance, he was also staying in the hotel and was amazed to hear of her presence in the establishment. Struggling with an upset stomach triggered by the local food, he was told by the Mamounia's staff that Baker was also unwell and that he would need to be careful not to catch the same illness. He excitedly sought her out and she agreed to an interview. This was a major front-page scoop for the paper, which headlined the article with Baker's assertion that she was 'Too busy to die'. 'Josephine Baker emphatically denies that she is dead!' he wrote.

> The St Louis-born entertainer who was the toast of Paris for years is very much alive and vivacious as ever. 'There has been a slight exaggeration,' she said with a gay smile and a French accent. 'I am much too busy to die ... I am practically well now and will soon be as good as new ... but I hate so much that I was not able to welcome our boys to North Africa, nor to put on a show for them since they have been here. But you can tell them that Josephine Baker will soon be singing again – for all of them.'[23]

Ollie Stewart was one of the first Black journalists to be sent into the theatre of war. He would be the first of a growing corps of African American war correspondents, and the first war correspondent for the *Afro-American* newspaper.[24] Treated as a celebrity by the paper for managing to get accreditation from the War Department, he was sent to England in September 1942. On the night of 9 November 1942, shortly after the first Allied landings in North Africa had been announced, Stewart was included in a group of correspondents headed for Morocco in a convoy of ships. Since they were on a British merchant ship converted for military use, US segregation rules did not apply. Fellow American journalist Ernie Pyle wrote:

We were officially assigned together, and we stuck together throughout the trip. Ollie Stewart was a Negro, the only American Negro correspondent then accredited to the European theatre. He was well-educated, conducted himself well, and had traveled quite a bit in foreign countries. We all grew to like him very much on the trip. He lived in one of the two cabins with us, ate with us, played handball on deck with officers, everyone was friendly to him, and there was no 'problem'.[25]

Although Stewart has been widely credited with breaking the news to America of Baker's survival, it had in fact already been reported in the *Philadelphia Tribune* earlier in January, when reporters had got wind of Baker's efforts to find her mother. She had wired a consultant at the city's hospital to inquire after the whereabouts of her mother, and the paper produced these communications as authentic proof refuting her death.[26] The following week, the paper took the lead in a search for Baker's mother, asking readers to come forward with her mother's name. Baker made a similar appeal to Stewart and her mother was later found.

Americans boost Moroccan independence aspirations

On 24 December 1942, Darlan was assassinated. His death relieved the Americans of the embarrassment of dealing with a collaborator and allowed them to break their ties with Vichy. But they were exercised by the question of his replacement. They were not at all convinced about de Gaulle, who was disliked by Roosevelt. They chose instead to revert to their original plan of nominating General Giraud to act as head of French North Africa, despite the ongoing intense hostility of many Vichy sympathisers in the military, who saw him as a traitor. There began a complex period of ongoing tensions in the French military camp, as French North Africans gradually transferred their allegiances away from Pétain and Vichy, but now found themselves torn between following Giraud's military leadership or supporting the Gaullist Fighting French. With an eye on this turmoil, in January 1943, Roosevelt and Churchill arrived in Casablanca for a major conference at the Anfa Hotel. While the main topic on the agenda was planning the next steps in the war strategy once the Germans had been driven out of North Africa, the leaders also proposed attempting to resolve the tensions between Giraud and de Gaulle. They needed to reach a workable political deal between the two men that would allow a merger of the Free French forces led by de Gaulle and the French troops in North Africa led by Giraud. Under extreme pressure, de Gaulle eventually agreed to a tentative alliance with Giraud.

The sultan, meanwhile, was keen to meet Roosevelt, and an introduction was duly arranged as one of the courtesies expected of the Allies in recognition of Morocco's role in hosting the conference. Controversy surrounds the exact content of the exchanges between the sultan and the president during their conversations at dinner, but the American president evidently let it be understood that he was sympathetic to the idea of Moroccan independence. His son Elliott Roosevelt, who was present, noted down his father's words:

> Why does Morocco, inhabited by Moroccans, belong to France? Anything must be better than to live under French colonial rule. Should a land belong to France? By what logic and by what custom and by what historical rule? . . . When we've won the war, I will work with all my might and main to see that the United States is not wheedled into the position of accepting any plan that will further France's imperialistic ambitions.[27]

Their encounter planted the idea in the Moroccan leader's mind that the US would support his country's aspirations for self-government, and the meeting is often cited as a crucial milestone in the trajectory of Moroccan independence.[28] The French authorities observed these developments with some concern. The American show of force during Operation Torch had impressed local populations and considerably reduced French prestige in Moroccan eyes. Roosevelt's announcing the launch of Operation Torch had seemed to hint at an end to protectorate rule. Like the rest of the Arab world, many Moroccans had warmly received the ideas of the Atlantic

Charter. Signed by Roosevelt and Churchill in 1941, this had stated that both the United States and Great Britain were committed to supporting the restoration of self-governments for all countries that had been occupied during the war, and allowing all peoples to choose their own form of government. Taken together with the well-known anti-colonial position held by the Americans, seen by many North Africans as a non-colonial country, it seemed likely that they might be supportive of their nationalist ambitions, and a potential ally against the residency. This concern preoccupied protectorate officials thenceforth.

By early January 1943, Baker was well enough to leave the Mamounia and return to her accommodation in the Menebhi palace. There is no record that she had any involvement in the events around the Anfa conference, or that she met the British or American leaders during their visit to Marrakech shortly afterwards, but Baker found herself at the centre of the new landscape of espionage which emerged from it. Operation Torch and the disbanding of the armistice commissions had diminished the intensity of the covert activities of the various intelligence services in the country, but it did not bring them to an end. The French, uncertain of America's long-term ambitions in the area and wary of its anti-colonial mindset, carefully monitored American activities, fearing that they posed a serious threat to France's hold on her North African empire, as the Germans had before the Allied invasion. They were concerned, not without reason, that the American presence might turn Moroccans against them, and were therefore attentive to any indication of growing unrest. They redoubled their surveillance of Moroccans, noting any changes in their allegiances or signs of agitation, and sometimes even intervened in an effort to prevent local populations from viewing the Americans sympathetically. One OSS agent later wrote: 'They would stop at nothing to discredit us with the natives and prevent the natives from developing close and friendly relations with us.'[29] The American military counter-intelligence similarly pumped resources into closely monitoring the situation, watching the French intelligence services watching them, as well as watching the Moroccans.

In southern Morocco, much of this espionage activity focused on the pasha, El Glaoui, who was considered by both the French and the American intelligence services to be a person of interest. Mixing in circles close to Glaoui, with her privileged position 'ornament[ing] the Pacha's circle', as journalist Kenneth Crawford put it, Baker was ideally placed to support French surveillance. One agent reported that Moulay Larbi, the pasha's *khalifa*, had been 'assiduously courting' Baker.[30] A later report confirms French awareness of the role she could play for their services: her patriotic credentials were seen to be watertight:

> Josephine Baker's national sentiments are without question. Her devotion is boundless and completely disinterested. With a quick and dynamic mind, Josephine is capable of rendering us great service in the study of the circles of the great Moroccan chiefs, a milieu where she could hardly be better accepted.[31]

These reports leave little doubt that the French were confident of Baker's loyalty, while they also acknowledged that Baker 'did not seem to be trusted by the American services'.[32] It seems likely that, with the intelligence landscape having moved into a different phase, the Americans had come to understand that her allegiances now lay exclusively with France.

Both the French and the American services acknowledged that the pasha and his acolytes had worked with the Germans before the November landings. The French recorded that Moulay Larbi was 'suspected of having German sympathies ... [and] is in contact with the Spanish consul in Marrakech'.[33] The Americans also saw the pasha as a devious figure, and were mindful that he had previously thrown his lot in with the Germans. In their intelligence reports they noted that, while the pasha had initially refused to receive any members of the German armistice commission who were present in Marrakech, as he became less certain about how events might turn out, he decided to play a double game. While ensuring that he was never seen with the Germans publicly, he started to deal with them secretly. Since the Allied invasion of

North Africa, the pasha was biding his time once again.[34] Conscious of the pasha's extraordinary hold over the local populations and his capacity to initiate unrest, the Americans kept him in their sights. Crawford noted: 'There is much calling and gift-giving back and forth between the headquarters brass hats in Casablanca and El Glaoui's retinue in Marrakesh.'[35]

The pasha enjoyed their attentions and revelled in the stories that were told about him. One anecdote that reached Crawford's ears recounted how an American in Glaoui's presence had apologised for the misbehaviour of a few American soldiers with Arab women, and remarked that the culprits ought to be castrated. 'That's been attended to,' Glaoui allegedly assured him.[36] The Americans were all too aware that they were being played by the pasha, and realised that he harboured hopes that they might help release Morocco from the shackles of the protectorate. They were aware that the 'Pacha feels like most natives and has lost all his respect for the French', and hoped that the Americans were planning to stay in Morocco for the long term. They reported that he was a bit perplexed when he realised that the Americans did not intend to involve themselves in relations between the French and the Moroccans, and that he would have to rely on the French, after all.[37]

The Americans were also acutely aware of the French interest in their interactions with Glaoui and were watching him carefully, fearing that he might transfer his loyalties in their direction. 'No efforts are spared by the French to find out what game the Americans are playing, and these agents get very excited each and every time an American calls on the Pacha.'[38] US officers who had called on the pasha or his advisors immediately found themselves interviewed by French secret agents, who wanted to find out why they had been there. The American operatives struggled to persuade the French that 'no US propositions have been made to His Excellency'.[39]

The Americans also acknowledged that the pasha had 'chosen on a new method of maneuvring', which was to encourage nationalist agitation, realising that it had the potential to enable him to advance his personal standing and maintain his position. In spring 1943, he acted as a messenger for the sultan, who sent him to the American and British consulates in Casablanca to state that he, the sultan, considered France no longer to be in a position to protect Morocco, meaning the protectorate was no longer valid; the sultan sought American and British support for a new multilateral international trusteeship for Morocco, with the participation of Britain, France, the US and perhaps Spain.[40] Later in the year, Glaoui and his *khalifa* again relayed a similar message to the American chargé d'affaires in Tangier, who reported that Glaoui was a strong Moroccan nationalist. These probings placed the American officials in an awkward position. They wanted to offend neither the French nor the Moroccans; so they did not take any action, but maintained contact with Glaoui and continued to closely observe the activities and concerns of ordinary Moroccans. Despite the worries of the French protectorate officials, the Americans did not intend to break French control.

Baker may have been well positioned to keep tabs on this situation, but to be able to carry out her espionage activities unsuspected, she needed to maintain her cover of performing. In January 1943, she occupied herself with making plans for a return to the stage, and was announced in the programme of the 1943 season at the Algiers Opera House.[41] She also aspired to honour her promise to sing for the American soldiers, and an opening arose some weeks later, in March 1943, when she was invited to perform in Casablanca. Against the advice of her doctor and her entourage, she agreed to the performance, even though her abdominal wound had not yet fully healed. She was determined not to let the opportunity pass.

Baker's gentle comeback

American servicemen, exhausted by the events of the invasion and conscious of the looming task ahead, which would require them to do battle with the Germans in Tunisia and Egypt, were keen to make the most of the pause in hostilities to recover. But Morocco provided very little for them to do in their spare time. To address this problem in Casablanca, the army instructed the American Red

Cross to arrange for four social clubs to be opened in the city. Of these, three were for the sole use of the US army; of these, just one, the Liberty Club, was designated for the use of Black soldiers, although white soldiers were also welcome. A fourth club was established to cater for all Allied soldiers – French and British, as well as Americans – and this was known as the Allied Club.[42]

It was deemed necessary to designate one of the clubs specifically for the use of Black soldiers, because segregation in the US army was strictly adhered to in Morocco, as it was wherever American soldiers were billeted. Black servicemen were forbidden to use the other clubs, and could only go to their own.[43] Baker had been invited to mark the opening of the Liberty Club by its director, Captain Sidney Williams.[44] The American army, navy and marine corps segregated African American soldiers, and the Black servicemen who landed on the Moroccan coast were in a minority compared to white soldiers. They were allocated separate tasks, serving in labour and supply units, rather than the more prestigious combat units. Their responsibilities revolved around cooking food, managing the canteens, digging ditches, dealing with the dead, unloading supplies from trucks and planes, serving white officers and washing laundry. They were also organised into units that built bridges, roads and runways, while others were mechanics responsible for repairing engines and radios.

On 21 March 1943, *Le Petit Marocain* reported mainly on the ceremony to mark the opening of the Allied Club, which brought together several French, British and American diplomats and officials. It was celebrated as an opportunity to mark the collaboration and friendship between the various parties involved, and the French authorities used the ceremony as a chance to smooth relations with the Americans and issue declarations of friendship.[45] The opening of the other clubs was a much more military affair, with General Mark Clark, deputy commander in chief of the American army ground forces, in attendance, along with a few other senior officers whose speeches extolled the virtues of the American Red Cross and the importance of its work in North Africa. After taking some refreshments, the personalities involved then moved on to the Liberty Club. More opening speeches were followed by a musical interlude. Then, Baker appeared and sang three of her most popular Parisian tunes to warm applause.[46] Crawford wrote: 'It was obvious after the first song that the old-time magnetism was still there. Supported by a red-hot Negro band, her act later became the hit of North Africa.'[47] *Variety*'s report was even more enthusiastic:

> ... what a performance – working with a pickup band of talented GIs! Her remark that she was still alive was hardly necessary. Her three numbers ... set the place afire, even though she was not in very good voice and wore a lengthy gown.[48]

Baker herself was aware of her limitations, but was determined to carry through on her promise:

> I couldn't get very far that night. Two American songs, a Black lullaby to prove to them that I hadn't forgotten my origins, a Gershwin tune to remind them that the American soul is beautiful, and then 'J'ai deux amours' to make them realize that I am now French and that France is the most beautiful country of freedom ... and that's why we have to give it back to the French![49]

Crawford's report of Baker's first public performance since the news had broken that she was alive was carried widely in the African American and entertainment press via the press pool.[50] In his article, Crawford stresses her fragility, but also celebrates the fact that, despite her worries – since she had not always felt appreciated by American audiences – she was very well received. She confided in him that 'I have to be as good as I can for these American soldiers. I hope they'll like me.'[51] She told him of 'her heartbreak at leaving beautiful Paris, which had been so good to her, and of the unbelievable victory of the Nazi barbarians'.

> Close up, Miss Baker, thin and lively and loquacious, seemed younger than her 36 years but she said she felt every one of them. What her morale required was a new Paris gown to replace the well-worn blue polka-dot leftover she was wearing. When I

caught her act about two months later in Fez she was still wearing it and wise cracks about its antiquity had become a part of her routine.[52]

After her performance, she was invited by Clark to join a celebratory evening reception with 300 guests at the nearby Anfa Hotel. She was escorted by her Moroccan entourage, including Mohammed Menebhi and Moulay Larbi, as well as Abtey and Zimmer, who had both come to Casablanca for the occasion. Referring to this event as her comeback, even though she was not yet back to full form, Baker wrote:

How funny: it feels as if nothing has changed. The clothes, the evening gowns, the jewels and the decorations shine in the way they did at those social evenings I knew so well before the war. And for the first time, as before the war, I do what I used to do so well: make an entrance. The world's press is here. No one will be able to say that I am dead, or half dead, anymore.[53]

For Abtey, she was a 'Star among the stars, this night she was reborn to life, to her life, to her life as a star.'[54]

Baker plays intermediary between the Americans and the Moroccans

Baker was a reassuring and familiar figure for American servicemen, many of whom had found their introduction to Morocco and its customs perplexing and at times bewildering. Crawford's description of Casablanca on his arrival in March 1943 reveals what many soldiers must also have felt:

[It] ... was the first native city I had seen and I was only half convinced that it was real, not just a curiosity maintained by subsidy for the benefit of western tourists. It simply couldn't be true that these narrow alleys, these stalls, these plaster houses which suggested Biblical times and, at their most modern, the

Middle Ages, could survive unchanged within an electric-lighted, mechanized, reasonably sanitary modern city.[55]

Crawford did not hesitate to adopt a judgemental and somewhat negative tone when he wrote, 'Everywhere in Morocco, even in Casablanca, one feels that the veneer of civilized restraint is so thin that it could be scratched away with a hairpin.' American soldiers had to try and make sense of a complex pattern of different Arab and Berber tribes, whose reactions to them ranged widely from the friendly, to tolerant, to outright hostile. They were frequently dependent on French officials to act as interpreters, guides and go-betweens of all kinds. In this context, Baker had a valuable part to play. She found herself invited to a series of social events, dinners and parties which brought the Americans together with the French and the Moroccan elites. Her presence was a reassuring one for all concerned. She could facilitate conversation with her fluent French and draw on her well-established friendships and familiarity with Moroccan traditions in ways that helped smooth over any difficulties brought about by the differences between the national cultural traditions of the guests.

Soon after the Liberty Club opening, she, Moulay Larbi and Menebhi went to a dinner at the Saadia, the residence of the American consulate in Marrakech.[56] The Moroccans soon reciprocated by inviting the Americans back to a 'grand soiree' at Menebhi's palace, described by Sidney Williams as 'strictly out of Arabian nights. I have never seen such a place. Josephine has a whole part of the palace to herself.'[57] The dinner was a huge success, with lavish food and dancing, and made a lasting impression on those who were present.[58] Pendar, on a passing visit to Marrakech, was also invited to this 'party-to-end-all-parties'.[59] 'Practically every American in North Africa, including most of the generals, received printed, gilt-edged invitations to dinner "to meet Miss Baker"', and 'at least a hundred guests' attended. The palace had been

jazzed up a bit for the occasion by Josephine Baker, with calla lilies and jungle-like decorations, Berber and Arab dancers, singers, American Negro Red Cross workers, white officers, civilians, women war correspondents, and Moors ranging from pure white to pure chocolate brown – all had a magnificent time. It would have done some American politicians a great deal of good to see how free, how gay, natural and simple an atmosphere was created amidst the fusion of races. From the roof tops, as always, the white-clad veiled Arab women looked down into the courtyard to watch the party. It was certainly the binding element of Islam that made this racial fusion, not only possible, but delightful. And the fusion of races was nothing to the fusion of oriental music and jazz, and the babel of languages – everyone from Vincent Sheean, Archie Roosevelt and Inez Robb to obscure Arab palace politicians conversing in a jumble of English, French and faltering Arabic.[60]

While his account of this event may seem romanticised, it represents how he – and several other Americans who were present, including Crawford – experienced the evening.

In considering these events retrospectively, Baker highlights the importance of her role as a facilitator not without a tinge of self-congratulation. The evening – which brought together Colonel Roosevelt, son of the president, with Sidney Williams, as well as with several French and British officers – was, she relates, a chance for everyone to forget their differences and allow 'Arabs, Blacks and whites to celebrate together'.[61] Tensions arose when the Moroccans discovered that the Black Americans among the Allied troops were being subjected to unequal treatment. Segregation made little sense to them. Fatima Mernissi, who was born in a harem in Fez in 1940, explains the stories she heard growing up:

...we could not figure out why, unlike the Arabs, white and black Americans did not mix and become just brown skinned, which is what usually happened when a population of whites and blacks lived together ... Instead, they kept the races apart ... We had a good laugh about that ... anyone who wanted to separate people according to their skin colour in Morocco was going to run into severe difficulties. People had mixed together so much that they came in hues of honey, almond, café au lait, and so many, many shades of chocolate.[62]

Baker also remarked to Abtey that many of her Moroccan friends were unimpressed by the way the American army differentiated between Black and white soldiers. Furthermore, incidents involving American soldiers and Arabs had led her friends to believe that they might be regarded in the same way as Black Americans, and were quick to note the hypocrisy of the situation. 'How can the US honestly present us with the Atlantic Charter when their policies towards their own nationals are so obviously based on old racist prejudices?' they would ask. Baker and Abtey found themselves unable to respond.[63]

Excited by the success of her performance at the opening of the Liberty Club, even though she was still recuperating, Baker made it known that she would be prepared to make more appearances to entertain American troops.[64] American shows were the responsibility of the United Service Organizations (USO), formed in April 1941 with the aim of bolstering troop morale and providing a 'home away from home'. Its Camp Shows Division was founded in October 1941 with the mission to bring live entertainment to the troops. But USO did not send many shows to North Africa in the first half of 1943, and there was a dearth of entertainment in Algiers and its surroundings. The local entertainment services director, Colonel Meyer, was therefore quick to follow up on Baker's offer, and soon secured her for a North African tour of all the American military camps in the area throughout spring 1943. It was agreed that Zimmer would organise the tour, in collaboration with Meyer.[65]

Baker insisted that she did not want any payment – simply to have their transport costs covered and to take meals in camp kitchens when they were in remote areas.[66] Her performances would play an important role in boosting the morale of the vast numbers of troops stationed in the Allied military camps across the region.

Touring the American camps in North Africa: April–June 1943

From Menebhi's palace in Marrakech's medina, Baker excitedly launched herself into preparations for her new tour with Frédéric Rey, her former dance partner, who had come from Algiers to support her. He said:

> My view was that Josephine was taking up her activities again far too soon. But there was no point in telling her that. She only ever did what she wanted and what she believed was the right thing. The Allies were in Africa, and she intended to carry on the war in her own unique way and continue to serve.[67]

Costumes had to be conjured up that would suitably hide her fragile limbs. They also needed to be cut to hide the strapping she needed to wear around her middle to support the healing process. New dresses were created to add to those that could be rescued and repaired from her old, rather moth-eaten wardrobe of concert outfits. Everyone in the palace household joined in and applied themselves to the task, including Menebhi's own daughters. From the outset of the North African tours, Baker, with Rey's support, introduced a new format to her shows – one that she would continue to adopt for the rest of her career. With his help – and she preferred it when she had help for her costume changes, as they would then go more rapidly – she would wear a different outfit for each of her songs, reflecting the atmosphere and content of the number. An orchestra would play an air to cover the time she was offstage.[68] Thus, she would wear a Brazilian-style outfit for the samba, a Breton look for 'Dans mon village', and an Asiatic one for 'La petite Tonkinoise'. For 'J'ai deux amours' she was draped in a blue-and-red crepe dress with long sleeves that were gathered at the cuffs; the colours of Paris enhanced the emotional impact of her delivery of the song. Before commencing the tour, as her finances were very low, a series of fundraising shows was arranged at the Rialto in Casablanca from 9–14 April 1943. Zimmer had arranged impressive staging, using French flags to decorate the theatre. This show represented Josephine's public relaunch, and was attended by many locals who had heard of her illness and were curious to see if she was fully back to form and able to make a success of her performance. More technically, in terms of presentation and repertoire, Baker planned to use these performances as a dry run for the tour. The show proved a huge success, and her earnings gave her some financial security to fall back on until the end of the war.[69]

The American camp tour proper kicked off in Oran, on the northwest coast of Algeria. The first night was not without its challenges, however. Rey was due to dance and had been included on the programme, but it was not clear whether he would be able to do so: his papers were deemed not to be in order by the Americans, so he had been refused permission to leave Morocco and placed in a holding camp.[70] Fortunately, Zimmer managed to blag it so that Rey could travel to Algeria, and he arrived just in time for the first show. Accompanied by a military African American orchestra, Baker made a huge impact. The Oran run culminated in an evening at the municipal theatre, before the show moved on to multiple military camps around Algiers. They were all situated within 20 miles of the city, where around 300,000 men were stationed.[71] Baker appeared several times a day, visiting camp after camp, often performing in the open air, on makeshift stages with a tent as a dressing room. She built on the skills she had learnt during her tour to the front in November 1939, and her interactions with soldiers during her subsequent performances at the Casino de Paris.

Baker understood the importance of entertainment for troop morale, and the inclusion of a group sing-along to directly involve her audiences had become one of the hallmarks of her performances. Every show finished with a rendition of the national anthems of the Allied countries. She also used comedy very effectively, engaging in banter with her audiences and obviously thriving on her contact with them. Her personable approach was noted by those who attended her shows. One American serviceman reported, 'She asked us to write the folks back home and tell them she is very much alive. Boy! You bet she is!'[72]

The tour attracted detailed coverage by the African American press. She told their reporters: 'I go out to the army camps whenever there are American boys . . . They seem to like what I am doing, and I am glad to "do my bit for our country".'[73] Baker knew how to flatter her audience, asserting that until after the war, 'her heart belongs to the American army'.[74] But despite these declarations designed to appeal to the Americans, there is nothing to suggest that her loyalties towards France were in any way diminished. Journalists commented on the changes in the way she performed, noting that she was not as provocative as in the past:

> The old Josephine Baker of the Folies Bergere days, when three small diamond clusters did full duty for clothing, has disappeared. She is very fully clothed now, but changes between each number. She says, and rightly, that the boys like costumes and a bit of color.

Baker rose to the occasion again and again, always receiving rapturous applause:

> I try to give the doughboys plenty of 'omph' but these days I wear an evening gown because the rough-and-ready stages I perform on are drafty and anyway the Yanks prefer me to sing them the old songs like 'Tipperary', 'Over There' and 'The Only Girl in the World'.[75]

With hostilities taking place close by, the tour was not without danger. One evening performance was interrupted by German planes, and the audience was thrown into darkness. As the ack-ack guns tried to defend the camp, the air-raid warning sounded and Baker, along with the audience, dived onto the floor. 'It still makes me laugh when I think about it,' Baker later recalled. 'I can see myself lying on my front in my lovely 1900-style Parisian outfit among soldiers from Missouri and Ohio; it must have been a remarkably comic sight particularly since I was still eating the lovely ice cream they had given me.'[76]

Published letters attest to her bravery. One serviceman described her show at a huge US camp, where her performance went ahead despite an air raid that had taken place nearby the previous evening. An 'improvised' stage was erected and the soldiers sat themselves on the ground awaiting her arrival, listening to the music that was broadcast on a 'tinny' gramophone, while her backing band tuned up. Baker donned her costume in a nearby tent, and finally her arrival was announced. The audience was informed that

> Miss Baker . . . had been very ill for a year and a half . . . The moment she was well she insisted, against her doctor's advice, on making an extended tour of all the American camps in North Africa, donating her services to the cause of entertaining the troops. 'So let's give Josephine a great big hand.'

Baker appeared

> in a flamboyant costume of vertical purple and red stripes, with a flowing skirt and puffed sleeves. She swept on to the stage and up to the mic. She looked the audience over, smiled mischievously, gave an impudent wiggle, kicked a foot in the air, disclosing a shapely leg through a slit in the skirt; then, as a gasp of pleasure rippled through the audience, she stood delightedly waving at 'the boys'. The 'boys', needless to say, roared their approval.[77]

As she entertained the thrilled audience with her now well-established camp repertoire, a soldier who had seen her perform in the Casino de Paris in the 1920s observed that she appeared no older,

> no less dexterous in putting over a song, in punctuating every line with an appropriate twist of her body – standing them up in the aisles (literally and to roars of disapproval from the soldiers seated in the rear) and holding the audience with as much ease as if both she and they had all the facilities of a comfortable theatre at their disposal.

He comments on 'her evident enjoyment of the furore she was creating', which 'was as infectious as the lilt of her strident voice and the brazen strut with which she sidled about the stage'. Just as she was about to embark on her encore, an air-raid siren sounded, interrupting the performance. Everyone was instructed to disperse into the surrounding fields. Undeterred, as soon as the all-clear sounded, Baker returned to the stage and, without hesitation, took up where she had left off.[78]

Baker's tour made for wonderful copy, and she enjoyed the attention she attracted from reporters. Published articles included photographs of her in glamorous outfits, surrounded by soldiers.[79] One serviceman appealed for more Black entertainers to visit them. He explained that artists like Josephine Baker acted as a 'great morale builder' and described her performance with feeling. When

> the lights dimmed ... not a sound was heard. Mingled with the music, a lovely being seemingly floated across the stage and her enchanting voice filled the theatre in a superb manner ... [Her renditions] had us eating out of her hands. After the concert we got her autograph and had pictures made with her, after which each soldier went his way a happier man. Speaking for myself, I was filled with an uncontrollable emotion and all the ugly, black marks of war had completely vanished from my mind. I uttered a prayer thanking God that all the hazards of this campaign had left me unscarred, and I had been able to witness such an affair.[80]

Baker never hesitated to come down off the stage, and genuinely enjoyed mingling with the troops. That she took the time to meet them after the shows only added to her appeal. One journalist conceded that

> Josephine Baker's tremendous favor with European theatre audiences has never been understood very well in the US ... when you see her in action, even under unfavorable circumstances such as an improvised, open-air stage and an audience of British and American soldiers sitting uncomfortably on the

ground, you begin to appreciate the charm and personality that make her still one of the foremost comediennes of our times.[81]

For those American soldiers who were struggling to process certain aspects of North African culture, her presence as a familiar figure was particularly welcomed. She was referred to as the 'Most American civilian in Oran' by one serviceman, in a letter that his sister must have passed on to the journalist. The soldier explains:

Our greatest need here is for something American – the morning paper, especially the comics; beautiful girls without veils over their faces; the good old home-like smiles and handshakes; a hot-dog and Coca-Cola at the corner store. You can readily see why we liked Miss Baker.

The article then goes on to contextualise his letter for readers, by explaining the Moroccan traditions that made the social life of the soldiers different from what they were used to at home:

Moslem men do not make companions of their women. A man's wife attends to the home, bears children, and may do work in the fields but she is in the position of a chattel … It is not conventional for men and women to make dates. Should a respectable woman be found conversing with a man not of the family, the scandal would lead to sudden death to one or both parties.[82]

Soldiers were under strict orders to carry themselves appropriately, and the numbers allowed on leave in the city were limited to 5 per cent of a unit at any given time. They were supplied with a fifty-page pamphlet containing guidance on how to behave. It was forbidden for them to socialise with local women. They were instructed to 'never stare at a Moslem woman. Never jostle her in a crowd. Never speak to her in public. Never try to remove the veil.'[83]

Press reports on Baker's activities in North Africa had a further, important, but perhaps less obvious dimension. American coverage of the North African campaigns in the major newspapers had left Moroccans almost completely out of the picture. Articles about these events, especially those destined for a white readership, tended to avoid mentioning the local North African populations, and journalists shied away from commenting on their colonial status in relation to France.[84] This rather deliberate oversight is also evident in the famous film *Casablanca*. It is almost devoid of Moroccan characters, except for a doorman who appears at the very start. Moroccan figures are excluded from the action and are considered irrelevant to the main narrative of the story. The African American press, on the other hand, as soon as it had been confirmed that there were African American troops involved in the landings, took a different approach, emphasising the links between African Americans and the peoples of the Maghreb, highlighting the sense of fraternity that Blacks could have with these Arab cultures. The editors of the *Chicago Defender*, for example, saw the landing of African American troops in North Africa as a heroic return to the continent. Cartoons were published which made the alliance between African Americans, North Africans and sub-Saharan Africans clear. Columnists also drew direct comparisons between Africans colonised by Axis and Allied powers and African Americans.[85]

Before the war, Baker had contributed to the idea that African Americans had a special involvement with North Africa. Her 1935 film *Princesse Tam Tam* had been shot in Tunisia, and she had played a Tunisian goatherd. When it was discovered that Baker was not dead, but alive and well in Morocco, the *Chicago Defender* was pleased to publish a photo of her entertaining the troops somewhere in North Africa. It was headlined 'First Picture of Jo Baker in North Africa', and the fact that she and five uniformed African American servicemen surrounding her were in North Africa was an occasion for pride.[86] In terms that seem surprising to us now, African Americans expressed their feelings of kinship with the Moroccans. Crawford cites Sidney Williams commenting on racial 'mixing' in relation to the success of the Liberty Club in Casablanca, which he ran:

The club that Williams opened is for Negro troops but is open to white soldiers also and Williams said more than half of his customers were whites. They preferred the Negro club, he said, because the natural sympathy existing between Negro troops and North African natives made it possible for him to get superior equipment on the local market. He said he found Moulay Larbi, like many other rich natives, extremely conscious of the Negro admixture in their race.[87]

We might question this notion, but it seems Williams conceived it to be the function of Black troops in the area to bridge the gap between white Americans and North Africans. He encouraged them all to make use of the Liberty Club.[88]

African American soldiers were not allowed to engage in combat until the final stages of the war, so journalists were not easily able to report on their military activities – and nor would such reports have made it past the censor.[89] Human-interest stories therefore tended to dominate in articles that appeared in the African American press about the progress of the war. Ollie Stewart's articles, for example, were known for his style of reporting: he would write as if he were sending letters home describing daily life and shortages in the country. He would include poignant, evocative details that his audiences could relate to. Baker's activities in North Africa provided correspondents with valuable copy. Not only did they celebrate her role in bringing people together, but also, by presenting the details of the events she was involved in, they could incorporate contextual information about Morocco and comment on its cultural traditions.

Thomas Young, correspondent for the *New Journal and Guide*, exemplifies this approach. He accompanied Baker in May 1943, and was very struck by a post-performance meal held 'in the palace of Mohamed Sebti, a wealthy Moslem leader and business magnate', at which Baker was the guest of honour. The event made the front page, under the headline 'Officers, Moslems meet at party for Jo Baker'. The newspaper carried a large photo of the beaming star, the only woman, seated with nine men, white and Black high-ranking army officers dressed in uniforms, and Moroccans in traditional Arab dress.[90] Young details their lavish spread:

> All the food is eaten from a common dish placed in the center. No knives or forks, or other silver is used, but the food is taken with the fingers of the right hand. It is in utter bad taste to use the left hand for eating, according to the custom, because that hand is employed in answering a call of nature.

On the menu was a squab pie, made of baby pigeons, and a 'huge roast of mutton' that had to be eaten

> without aid of a carving knife. Pulling it apart with the hands might have been not too difficult had it not been so very hot. When we had a lot of trouble the host would graciously tear a piece from it with his fingers and hand it to us. It would have been impolite to refuse it.

After two dessert courses, tea was served once the tables had been cleared. When the guests had eaten their fill, there was a large amount of leftover food:

> We ate hardly 15 per cent of the food placed before us. I keep wondering what became of that which was taken back . . . One of the guests explained that it was taken from our room to one where the men of the second class were gathered – these were the junior males of the family and their friends who were not permitted to dine with the elders. After they had taken their portions, the food was then taken to the women. What was left over, if anything, went next to the servants and the remainder to beggars and hangers-on at the back door.[91]

Having observed that the women were only allowed to eat the leftovers, Young pointed out that 'women play a subordinate role' and do not help entertain. In doing so, he highlights Baker's remarkable status: the only woman present, apart from the female servants.

During the after-dinner conversation, Baker excused herself and went to the room where the women were gathered and was allowed to talk to them. Baker, Young observed,

> speaks French fluently and most upper-class Arabs also speak French. As for the rest of the guests there was little conversation between the Americans and the Moslems except through one of Sebti's brothers who was a linguist rattling off French, Arabic and English with equal facility.[92]

Baker's 'charm and personality' clearly allowed her to play a role in facilitating and reassuring American soldiers, and to mingle with Moroccans and gain access to all areas of their society – including, remarkably, to the women, who were carefully separated from the male guests. This capacity to slip into different social groupings – even those that would normally have been forbidden to outsiders, not to mention foreigners – put her in an extraordinary position. Not only did it allow her to serve her ambitions to bring people together, but it also gave her access to intelligence.[93]

Baker extols the African American contribution to the war effort

The African American press made a point of stressing that during her troop shows Baker performed to racially mixed audiences, as, for example, at the opening of the Liberty Club earlier that year, when she had 'received a rousing reception from both white and Negro audiences'.[94] Another of her cited audiences comprised 'British and American air force units and a company of colored engineers stationed near an airport in Morocco'.[95] Playing to unsegregated audiences was unusual in a context where USO organisers normally 'followed the lead of the army in its practice of segregation'. Black performers were often excluded from playing for troops, and for much of the war, strict segregation was practised in the organisation of shows between those for 'All-Negro' units and shows for other units.[96] It seems probable that the absence of the

USO from North Africa until later in 1943 opened the way for Baker to ignore the rules of segregation during this period. While her camp tour operated on a relatively small scale, her actions were amplified due to the platform she had as a celebrity and the extent of the newspaper coverage it enabled her to attract.

She later related this intense period of troop entertaining to her long-time friend Stephen Papich, who published a book about her soon after her death.[97] She recalled that at the performances of other American entertainers, 'it was the white soldiers who took the seats in front' and 'the blacks stood at the back'. After their shows, the entertainers would take some time to meet their audiences, but 'never quite made it to the blacks in the rear'. Baker was determined to do things differently. When she performed, if there were any seats available at the front, she insisted that Black and white soldiers should have equal access to them, and after the shows 'she headed right to the black troops' to spend time with them. Baker would also write to as many of their parents as she could. When he travelled with her in the US – long after the war – Papich recounts that Black parents would come backstage to see her, bringing with them the letters she had written to them thirty years before. 'Sometimes there were tears when Josephine learned of a soldier who had never returned.'[98]

The tour brought Baker into close touch with African American servicemen and forced her to face the realities of segregation. In the years leading up to the outbreak of the war, Baker's negative experiences of the US had led her to distance herself from her home country, and she had also moved away from the African American community she had known in Paris, immersing herself rather in her French entourage. Wartime press reports map Baker's increasing preparedness to speak out about her race. In her interviews, she spoke quite freely and openly about how her experiences on the camp tour made her feel. She commented to one reporter that she was

so proud and thrilled at the great advancement my race is making in this war ... That advancement is so evident and I see it so plainly in my appearances in Red Cross club theatres and in all my performances . . . throughout North Africa . . . I think the Red Cross are doing a wonderful and marvelous job especially for my race. I have found through my contact with the troops . . . that all of America is not prejudiced against the Negroes. I have found that those who can are helping my people in their improvement.[99]

When interviewers asked about Baker's motivations to perform, she was clear:

First, I want to do what I can to win the war and thus perform whatever duty I can for my native land. Second, I want to help those of my own race. I am doing all I can to help win the war effort and to make people generally more appreciative and kinder to my race.

The journalist himself then goes on to explain the significance of her entertainment work:

It isn't just her appearances before audiences of her own people helping build morale and to provide much needed entertainment for war weary Negro troops, that is helping to build good will and tolerance for her race, but it is her performances before soldiers and sailors of all the allied nations. There is hardly an audience that thrills to her singing and her personal charm that isn't sprinkled with troops of almost all the nationals fighting on the side of the allies in this war.

She is upheld as a 'real trouper' for bravery in dealing with air-raid sirens and continuing her performances, even when she was 'scared plenty'. This added

much weight to the mounting respect she was building up for her race . . . She revels in the reception she receives from both white and Negro audiences. She has a simple philosophy. She thinks the war has made a lot of people understand a lot of things. And she thinks they will understand a lot more after the victory.[100]

In one of the versions of this article, a final sentence is attributed to her: 'After all, when you get on the battlefield, God don't care whether you are black, white or yellow.'[101]

In her autobiography, Baker represents the Liberty Club opening as being the first manifestation of a new conviction: 'I had the idea of what I could do with my limited resources from now on. Faced with the Nazis, there should only be one Allied force, with no regard for colour or race.'[102] She thought that she could perhaps have an influence on 'unifying the black and white troops'.[103] These comments show how pivotal her troop tour was in bringing about an evolution in Baker's understanding of her own identity. They reveal her growing awareness of how she could mobilise her performances to draw attention to the achievements of her 'race'. Thriving in this role, she was developing an awareness of the possibilities offered by her celebrity platform to promote the case for equality, and potentially bring about change.

Baker returned from her concert tour to ongoing French in-fighting between the Gaullists and the Giraudists. De Gaulle had finally arrived in Algeria and agreed to work with Giraud. The price he wished to exact for this union, which was so earnestly desired by the British and the Americans, was a purge of Giraud's North Africa team, to try and move the administration on from Vichy. Resident-General Noguès headed the list of those to be removed.[104] Together, de Gaulle and Giraud founded the Comité français de libération nationale (CFLN) on 3 June 1943 under their joint leadership.[105] This committee would be the basis for the emerging French state-in-waiting that was taking shape in Algiers, and intended to position itself to take over from Vichy once the French mainland had been liberated. Giraud, still favoured by the Americans, took the title of 'commander in chief of the army', but efforts to merge the Free French army with the former Vichyite (now Giraudist) Army of Africa was proving challenging, and confusion reigned.[106] The situation was aggravated by the fact that de Gaulle had no intention of maintaining the status quo, and was diligently strengthening his own power base in Algiers, with the ambition of ousting Giraud just as soon as that could be achieved.

Baker and Abtey took advantage of their presence in Algiers – ahead of Baker's planned appearance in a gala on 11 June 1943 – to meet Paillole and Rivet who were now based there.[107] The two men had escaped from Occupied France in November 1942 and had reached North Africa, placing themselves under the orders of first Darlan and then Giraud. They were put to work by the Giraudist authorities, which set them up under Colonel Ronin, who headed the Direction des services spéciaux (Directorate of Special Services – DSS). Rivet was put in command of the Direction des services de renseignement et de sécurité militaire (Directorate of Military Intelligence and Security – DSR-SM). At the beginning of 1943, Paillole took over the Direction de la sécurité militaire (Directorate of Military Security – DSM), which was responsible for counterespionage within the DSR-SM. Well-seasoned professionals in a long-established tradition of French secret warfare against Germany, they promoted themselves in Algiers as having been among the first Resistance fighters, citing the fact that they had not always had the whole-hearted support of Vichy to pursue their activities and continue their counter-intelligence work against the Third Reich. Relations were tense between the men of the former Deuxième Bureau and the equivalent service run from London by the Gaullists, the BCRA, led by Colonel Passy. The agents of the Gaullist BCRA viewed them as reactionary interlopers, stained by their strong links to Vichy.[108]

Abtey was now caught between the different allegiances of the intelligence services, whose internecine competition was paralysing processes. Having offered his services, he was waiting to be allocated a mission. Frustrated with the Giraudists around him, he redoubled his efforts to join the Gaullists in London.[109] Part of his problem may have been that the officers in charge were not convinced of his principles or his commitment. He, like Baker, was being closely monitored by the Gaullists, who had expressed certain reservations about him. A report dated April 1943 noted that

Abtey and Zimmer seem very devoted to our cause, but they are first and foremost wheeler dealers. They are involved in currency trafficking and were involved in regularising the situation of certain Jews whom they sent to England for a large sum of money. Abtey seems to regret following de Gaulle and would be ready to take orders from General Giraud. While his national sentiments are almost certain, his morality seems more dubious.[110]

It is not clear whether Abtey was aware of these unfavourable evaluations of his character, but he did understand that there were forces working against him.[111] This was in stark contrast to Baker, who does not seem to have been tarnished by Abtey's less-than-wholesome reputation and was, as we have seen, regarded by French intelligence in the most positive light regarding both her commitment and her patriotism. Having completed her planned tour for the Americans, she now wanted to focus her energies on building the morale of the French forces battling in Tunisia and Libya. However, her formal request was refused on the grounds that the Free French forces were off limits and their precise location remained unknown. She was made to understand that Giraud's High Command did not regard the entertainment of troops as a high priority.[112] So when Baker was approached with a request to undertake a four-week tour of British camps in the Middle East, she was free to assent and accepted gladly. Little did she know that she would soon discover a whole new undercover mission that she was ideally suited to take on.

5

BAKER IN THE
MIDDLE EAST
(1943)

In May 1943, Baker was in the middle of her American camp tour, appearing at the Colisée Theatre in Algiers, when she first encountered Second Lieutenant Henry Hurford Janes, a British officer who would become a lifelong friend.[1] Janes had been instructed by his boss, Basil Dean, the director of ENSA, to 'Find Josephine Baker and get her for the British and American troops.' Janes tracked her down, and the following morning, 2 May 1943, at 9 a.m. he knocked on the door of the top-floor room in the rather shabby Hotel Regina, where she was staying. Baker would not ask him in: 'I am in the nude, sir,' she told him. Instead, she suggested that he should come and find her in her dressing room at the theatre before her 9 p.m. show.

When they met that evening, Janes put it to her that she might do a series of performances for ENSA to entertain Allied troops in the Middle East. She was immediately enthusiastic and explained that she would be 'honoured', as she had the greatest admiration for Britain 'going on alone'. But before committing herself, she wanted to be sure that Janes thought her show was going to be suitable for 'English soldiers'. She therefore arranged for him to attend a performance. As her theatre shows were all fully booked, one evening subsequently, she placed a camp stool in the central aisle especially for him, and they agreed to meet to discuss her performance afterwards, once he had decided whether he felt it would be appropriate. If so, they could then go on to explore the practical arrangements necessary for a tour. Janes invited a couple of fellow officers he had bumped into in the audience to go along with him to meet Baker and express their enthusiasm about the show they had seen. An agreement was soon reached and, a few days later, Janes cabled Dean that he had obtained the consent of both Baker and the French authorities for her to appear at several venues. The tour would take her to Constantine, Sétif, Tunis, Tripoli and on through the British Middle East Command.

ENSA had been forced to adjust its mission to entertain in line with the exigencies of war and the movement of troops. After their evacuation from France during the German invasion of 1940, ENSA entertainers had mainly performed at home. But as British troops were sent to fight in campaigns across North Africa and the Middle East, so ENSA gradually gained permission to work there. It started doing shows in Cairo from 1941: among the performers who were engaged was the French actress Alice Delysia, who toured the Middle East in exhausting engagements at desert camps and hospitals.[2] She and other performers often found themselves in potentially dangerous areas. In early 1942, when it looked as if the Germans might overrun Egypt, the army had issued an order forbidding the evacuation of civilians, fearing that they would jam the roads. But an exception was made for ENSA artists. In order to facilitate their evacuation to the relative safety of Palestine, it was decided that those in the region should all be incorporated into the army. They were therefore sworn in and issued with uniforms.[3]

Amid ongoing concerns about their security in war-torn areas, and fears that if any ENSA members were captured they might be shot as spies, Dean ordered that all performers overseas were henceforth to wear uniform. Not only was this safer for them, as a uniform demonstrated their military status, but it also allowed them to avoid the delays faced by civilians who had to produce their passports and permits at checkpoints and borders. This facilitated the transport of the entertainers, who often struggled to reach units that were constantly on the move. The uniform adopted by Dean consisted of a standard-issue battle dress, and the only insignia allowed were ENSA shoulder titles. Delysia, however, as she was French, had special dispensation to have 'her own uniform in a becoming shade of Blue, covered in Free French insignia'.[4] Baker would also adopt military dress, but she only started wearing it when she came under the direct instructions of the French military some weeks later.

When Baker was engaged by Janes for her ENSA tour of the Middle East in May 1943, the challenge of organising events for all the Allied troops present in the area was considerable. ENSA's potential audiences were dispersed over a huge geographical area that was administered by an assortment of nations. In 1943, ENSA entertainment bases in the British sector ran from Tunis to Cairo; Morocco and Algeria were under American and French command; while Syria was purely French. Acquiring the necessary authorisation, organising transport for performers and putting on shows therefore represented a logistical nightmare. As ENSA staff did their utmost to deal with the situation, in March 1943 Dean finally paid a visit to the Allied-occupied North African front. Soon after he reached Algiers, where ENSA had a small office for liaison with the Office of the Supreme Commander, General Eisenhower, Dean, realising that he needed more support to deal with the situation, contacted Janes in London and asked him to join him there. A private in the British Expeditionary Force, Janes had been allocated to Dean by the War Office soon after his evacuation from France in 1940. He had secretarial and theatrical qualifications, and the work required someone with military status: it would have been inappropriate to subject a civilian to the inevitable demands the job required. As Dean's personal assistant, Janes was initially based at ENSA's headquarters at the Drury Lane Theatre, where he was put to work helping the deputy director, Alex Rea. Almost as soon as Janes had arrived in Algiers, Dean left him (now commissioned as a second lieutenant) in virtual charge of arrangements, and proceeded with his own inspection tour of Tunis, Tripoli and on to Cairo to troubleshoot the problems that had arisen there.

Major Rex Newman, head of the overseas section of ENSA, had arrived in Cairo at the beginning of 1943 to sort out a dispute between the local entertainments officer and Delysia, who had threatened to return to England and reveal the chaos and incompetence of ENSA in Egypt.[5] Some of the more assertive artistes seemed to be organising shows in the absence of any leadership from the somewhat faint-hearted local ENSA staff. They were also reluctant to leave Cairo for the desert. Far from home and compelled to stay longer than contracted to, they were 'sucked into the vortex of café-idleness, cocktail bars and their allurements'.[6]

Since the defeat of Rommel's forces in May 1943, the Egyptian capital was out of all danger, and it had become possible to organise larger shows outside the city at other venues.[7] The onus was on ENSA to supply stars, and Baker's invitation had been issued to meet that demand. Not only was she appreciated as a performer, but she was close at hand at a time when there was some reluctance on the part of British entertainers to go abroad. In addition, ENSA was not universally appreciated. Noël Coward, for example, was keen in principle to put on a series of troop and hospital concerts, but was dismissive of performing under the banner of ENSA. He found the whole concept of actors entertaining in uniform 'somehow ludicrous' and was critical of the organisation.[8] He did, however, eventually agree to an ENSA tour of the Middle East for several months, and met Baker while he was there.

Touring the British camps: June–July 1943

Baker set off with Janes, who personally accompanied her with a staff sergeant and an Arab driver, on the first stage of her ENSA tour. But after a while, Janes was called away: his presence was urgently required in Cairo to help deal with the situation there. He left instructions with various British army officers to look after Josephine from Tunis onwards, directing them to support and facilitate her movements eastwards until she reached Egypt.[9] Her tour started off in Tripoli, then she moved on to a huge aerodrome near to the structure that the British had christened Marble Arch (formally, the Arch of the Philaeni), put up by Mussolini between Ras Lanuf and Al Uqaylah. Next, she flew by light plane to Benghazi and made several stops along the coast. From there she went to Tobruk, then to Alexandria and on to Cairo,[10] the most westernised, glamorous and wealthy city in the Middle East. The British had longstanding colonial interests in Egypt and used it as a base for their colonial troops and operations throughout the region. Despite a widespread belief that the British were no longer welcome, and that the time was ripe for full independence, that summer the capital was celebrating the Allied victory over Rommel and there was a strong desire to party.[11]

Baker was based at Shepheard's Hotel, where many ENSA performers enjoyed a pre-war lifestyle.[12] Noël Coward commented:

> Sitting on the terrace at Shepheard's ... I observed that the restrictions of war-time were unknown; people sat there sipping gin slings and cocktails, and chatting and gossiping, while waiters glided about wearing fezzes and inscrutable Egyptian expressions ... all the fripperies of pre-war luxury living were still in existence. Rich people, idle people, cocktail parties, dinner-parties, jewels and evening dress; Rolls Royces came purring up to the terrace steps ... here these people had stayed, floating about lazily in their humid backwater, for four long years ... it seemed old-fashioned and rather lacking in taste.[13]

Baker was a star attraction and there was no respite from the public, who demanded her attention even after a hard day of entertainment in the desert. As one midwestern journalist recounted:

> She came up the stairs to the terrace of the hotel surrounded by civilians and military officials of the Allied forces whom we would see were listening intently to something she was saying, and the force of her personality made itself felt to the cosmopolitan crowd on the terrace and in the garden. She has been out to the camps in the desert entertaining American troops practically all day and they had cheered her to an echo from the Sphinx to the Pyramids. Here she was late in the day entering Shepheard's hotel as composed and chic as though she had just come from a

beauty salon ... She accepted the magnolia blossom I offered her with a beautiful gesture of simple graciousness ... Be sure and tell the people in Chicago that the Negro men in the Mid-East are fine soldiers and I am proud to see them perform their work so ably.[14]

Baker never missed an opportunity to promote her fellow African Americans when speaking to the press.

From the Egyptian capital, Baker 'radiated in the desert, singing in all the camps, for half an hour in each, at a rate of four or five a day'.[15] She also sang in nearby camp hospitals, where she met many men who had been recently injured on the battlefields of El-Alamein and Tobruk. 'The desert hospitals were remarkable, all things considered,' wrote Noël Coward.

Most of the wards were merely tents and the ingenuity of the staff was extraordinary; they had thought of so many little ways of making the men as comfortable as possible. The nursing sisters all contrived to look as though they had spent at least two hours on their toilettes; their uniforms were always spotless and looked cool and pleasant. They achieved this in circumstances that would drive ordinary women dotty; the sanitation was usually primitive, the heat terrific and the glare and sand and flies appalling.[16]

Touring the hospitals could be uphill work. Joyce Grenfell, the British singer and actress, highlighted the 'danger of being overwhelmed by what we saw' until 'compassion took the place of personal distress'.[17] Coward went 'with great solicitude to every bed, commiserating and attempting to cheer the patients',[18] while Grenfell acknowledged that it was 'sometimes obvious that ... injured servicemen didn't want entertainers in the wards'.[19] Baker faced it all with good humour and never balked at the difficult conditions.

She was performing for ENSA during the Allied invasion of Sicily in July–August 1943. Senior officers frequently called for entertainers when they knew that they were about to go into battle. As Baker wrote:

> For 21 days I went around the camps, sleeping in tents with the honour of being with the soldiers on the eve of the landing in Sicily in which they would be engaged. They did not know . . . but I knew that the operation was imminent. Seeing them like this, full of life, magnificent with enthusiasm, when many of them were already marked by death, left an impression on me that will never fade.[20]

Henry Janes confirms her account, describing the stops on her tour: 'Tunis, Tripoli, Cairo – back again to entertain the troops in sealed camps leaving at dawn to invade Sicily – Tunis again, Constantine, Algiers, Oran.'[21]

One of Baker's performances was written up for the *United Services Review* in an edition entitled 'How ENSA went to war'. She had set off, as guest star, with three other ENSA parties: 'On the way the lorry broke down and the generator was damaged. The hot wind blew sand into their faces and down their necks. At last, tired and uncomfortable they arrived more than an hour late to find 3,000 troops awaiting them.' The soldiers had improvised with a few boards placed to act as a stage and a couple of tents as dressing rooms:

> When Josephine appeared, the men went wild. She held them in the hollow of her hand as she sang the songs they wanted to hear: 'J'attendrai', 'J'ai deux amours'. Those who did not understand French followed the songs perfectly. Then she sang some English songs and the men joined in. In the middle the lights went out. Everyone laughed. 'C'est la guerre,' said Josephine and carried on. The evening ended with them all singing together the songs of the last war . . . It was, everyone said afterwards, such an emotional experience as only comes once in a lifetime.[22]

If Baker knew there were French soldiers in her audience, she would tweak her performance, as the dancer and contortionist Maisie Griffiths, who worked with Baker in Egypt, recounts:

I came back to Cairo at the end of 1943 when [Baker] was looking for specialty acts to join her revue for French troops. I joined the company and on the opening night at some outpost in the desert she asked me to assist her during the act. She wanted me to stand in the wings and pick up her two white stoles as she threw them off stage. The first time I caught them I looked back at her and to my surprise she was standing there, poised, with nothing on from the waist up. She told me afterwards that whenever she played to French soldiers, it was not only usual but they always expected it.[23]

The rudimentary circumstances often forced Baker to make do with makeshift, improvised stages. If there was nowhere to change, making frequent costume changes was not an option; or costumes might be dispensed with entirely and the shows performed as if they were radio broadcasts. In the desert, Baker was resourceful in finding ingenious solutions to her dressing room and lighting predicaments. On visiting one unit in the Alexandria area, the sector was particularly inhospitable, with no dressing room, no stage, no lighting:

Summoning 23 officers, Josephine got them to form a circle facing outwards. This was her dressing room. Meanwhile, lorries which could be spared came racing across the camp to spotlight with their headlights the lively figure of the international stage celebrity.[24]

Baker was relatively low-key about the discomforts she faced and the demands of repeatedly performing for tired, homesick soldiers. It is notable that Noël Coward is much franker about his experiences and often dwells on the challenges of the 'violent heat', the presence of insects, especially flies, not to mention his own nerves going on stage. At times, dealing with soldiers who were boisterous and drunk – 'sticky audiences', as he called them – could be especially challenging, with 'unreliable microphones' and 'eccentric lighting'.[25]

Baker did later reveal the relentlessness of troop entertaining: 'Many was the time I got up feeling violently ill but still went on to perform so as not to disappoint a group of men waiting for a show.'[26] Janes admired her resilience. He later wrote:

> Through the desert she worked tirelessly, four or five perfor-mances every day, scorning air priorities or staff care; lorries and jeeps, or more locally, the corridors or trucks of trains were her transport. There were nights when for lack of a stage or lighting, she would give a 'floor-show' by the light of hurricane lamps to thousands of men who had arranged themselves in a natural basin of sand.[27]

As Baker's tour continued, Janes found it increasingly difficult to juggle the demands of managing Dean's affairs, as well as his own. Neither he nor his colleague Newman could find the time to personally supervise all of Baker's many appearances. Without any dedicated escorts to accompany her, difficulties occasionally arose, with some soldiers behaving badly towards her during and after her performances. Forced to take steps to protect herself, Baker contacted the French authorities in Cairo. Janes recorded what happened: 'Unfortunately, following certain offences suffered owing to the stupidity of some Colonel Blimps, a complaint was lodged by the French ambassador with the British ambassador, Sir Miles Lampson'. Baker 'stipulated that she could not and would not give her services to British forces unless she was personally accom-panied by Lieutenant Janes who she felt would prevent any further offences mainly due to her colour'.[28]

It has been suggested that the British South Africans were the main culprits, but it is not clear whether offence was caused on one occasion or on several.[29] In any case, the situation had assumed serious proportions, and at the request of the British ambassador, Dean was obliged to release Janes from his duties, so that he could be free to accompany Baker on the remainder of her tour. Janes affirms that his presence did serve to prevent several further racist incidents from causing Baker offence – not because they did not happen, but because he was able to keep them from her. At one American camp, he discovered the words '"Special appearance tonight – the famous American n****r" chalked on a blackboard, which I had removed before she saw it.' He asserts that such ignorance and thoughtlessness would have 'meant no show' on her part. He refers to 'innumerable other instances' of racist slights she suffered. On one occasion, 'she was sent for refreshment to the Sergeants' Mess while supporting artists ... were honoured at dinner by the area Commander'. Baker appears to have weathered this persistent racism, but it must have cut deep. Janes was able to offer her support and shield her from the worst of these attacks when he was around, but he could not be there all the time. Ultimately, it seems likely that events like these precipitated Baker's early departure from the tour.[30]

Baker realises the position of France is under threat

When she returned to Cairo, Baker experienced a rather awkward interaction with King Farouk of Egypt.[31] Crowned when he was aged just eighteen, in July 1937, King Farouk was over-indulged, poorly educated and used to getting his own way. As a result, the various celebrities who passed through Cairo were expected to socialise with the king at his convenience. Baker was enjoying a rare free evening at one of Egypt's sought after nightspots when she was approached by the manager with a request from the king, who was also present at the venue that evening, that she should sing. She immediately responded in the negative and repeated her refusal to the king's secretary when he reiterated the royal request in the most forceful of terms, explaining that it should be taken as an order. Refusing to be intimidated, Baker answered that she was flattered to be told of the king's wishes, and that she would be happy to sing on another occasion, should His Majesty care to organise an event at his palace. Believing the incident to be over, she went to dance with the British officer who had accompanied her to the venue. The sovereign, unused to being openly disobeyed in this fashion, immediately ordered the orchestra to stop playing, and a police inspector directed Baker to leave the premises. She was furious. In ordinary circumstances, she would have been accommodating, and she normally acceded to such requests. However, on this occasion she had her reasons for refusing, and could not understand why the officials had made no effort to ask why she did not wish to sing.

Baker had been discomforted by the French community she found in Cairo: the Vichy presence having only ceased a short time before, the sympathies of most people still lay with Pétain.[32] In addition, de Gaulle and the Free French seemed little known; moreover, since they were seen only in terms of their association with the British, they appeared tainted by the colonial policies associated with the latter. As Baker saw it, this rendered them unattractive to the Egyptians.[33] It was explained to the king the following morning that the reason she had refused to perform was that, as a supporter of the Free French, she had felt compromised by Egypt's lack of public recognition for de Gaulle and the new CFLN based in Algiers. Keen to appease Baker and make amends for this oversight, Farouk agreed to the organisation of a gala to celebrate Franco-Egyptian friendship and promote de Gaulle. She would perform, and he would personally preside over the event.[34] Baker saw this as a major propaganda coup. She was keen to raise it with her military contacts on her return to Algeria and make plans to come back to Cairo to put on the show.

Delighted to have secured this commitment to the Free French, Baker prepared to return to Algiers. However, it seems her departure was not a happy one. For on his return from taking her to her 5 a.m. flight to Tripoli on 16 July, Janes wrote to Baker, addressing her formally as 'My dear Miss Josephine Baker'. He went on:

I am sorry that our very happy association as 'brothers-in-arms' should have come to such an untimely end, the more so since I feel that many of the heartburns and headaches could have been vanquished by good humour and understanding.

He indicated that his countrymen in Cairo were not fully 'in the war'. He went on to explain, 'Often we offend without the knowledge of doing so' and asked her to 'forgive anything and everything which was not meant'. He also expressed his bitter disappointment that the outcome of certain (unspecified) events was that she no longer felt able to come and perform in England. For his part, he would 'never forget the nights in the desert' and her 'never failing kindness and fine spirit', and he thanked her for her 'most valued and very real friendship'.[35] He wrote again at the end of the month saying that 'I feel sure I speak for the Director when I say that he would wish anything done that might atone for the unfortunate incidents during the time you were appearing for ENSA in the Middle East.'[36] Reading between the lines, it seems likely that Baker had been subject to further racist attacks and had left in disgust at this treatment. Baker and Janes, having been thrown together during the tour, had clearly come to appreciate one another's company. Janes' correspondence reveals a deep respect and a heartfelt concern that these unpleasant experiences might have an impact on future prospects for her further involvement with ENSA.

So he was delighted when he contacted Baker soon afterwards to find that the tensions surrounding their last encounter appeared to have dissipated. He had been instructed by Dean to find Baker and 'enlist her services for entertainment in the UK for home-based troops and factory workers'.[37] Janes soon located Baker in Marrakech, where she was recovering from the exertions of their tour. She invited him to visit her in person in early August 1943, and immediately agreed to his suggestion that she should come to England, provided the French authorities concurred. Baker's first loyalty always lay with the French, though naturally Janes knew nothing of Baker's undercover role and was unaware that she was also in discussions with her contacts in Algiers to embark on a new mission that would necessitate her return to the Middle East.

While Janes awaited the response of the French authorities, he was entertained by Baker's ever-generous Moroccan friend Menebhi, who, on 4 August 1943, organised a banquet at his palace in the British officer's honour, in the presence of Robert Murphy, Abtey and other French officers and civilians. 'This gesture was made by my host,' wrote Janes, 'as I was the first English subject to enter that house since the war started.' It left a lasting impression. 'I have told many people about his [Menebhi's] wonderful town and the incredible experiences I enjoyed there in so short a time. As for the banquet ... I still cannot believe those "dancing girls".'[38] Janes was unable to secure a definite commitment for Baker to visit the UK, so he left with an undertaking on both sides that they would try and make it happen at the earliest opportunity.

A new mission beckons

Baker had returned to Algiers after her four-week ENSA tour anxious at what she had seen and full of ideas about what needed to be done to promote the cause of France in general, and the Free French in particular.[39] Baker feared that France was losing ground to the British. During the tour, she had made a flying trip to Lebanon, where she had done her best to alleviate the tense atmosphere between the British and the French. Since the events of June 1941, when the British forces had cooperated with Free French troops to oust the Vichy regime from control of the Levant, relations between the Gaullists and the British had been extremely strained. The Gaullists feared that despite promises to the contrary, the British had ambitions in the area and were seeking to overthrow French influence. Baker found little improvement in their relations, and a British army officer, Major Dunstan, confided in her: 'The French seem to think we want to replace them; we thought if you could bring them together at your performance that might calm things down.'[40]

The experience in Lebanon left her worried about France's position there, and the lack of acknowledgement of de Gaulle in Egypt left her concerned about the future of its colonial presence in the region. She vented her frustration to Abtey, bemoaning the inaction she had observed on the part of the French. 'You are all here, with your hands in your pockets, swatting flies, while events are being prepared in Syria, Lebanon and Egypt that the French don't even seem aware of! ... It is time to act!'[41] She was amazed that developments in the Middle East were not a burning topic of discussion within the French intelligence services. She could not understand why no action was being taken by the Gaullists to ensure that the CFLN and de Gaulle's central role in France's liberation was not better known, supported and recognised across the Middle East.[42] Publicising the existence and the work of the Free French Forces (FFL) and presenting themselves as the official representatives of France was a key challenge facing the Gaullists, and Baker knew she could provide valuable support in the pursuit of that objective.

France's colonial authority seemed to be under threat on all fronts. Fear of German influence may have waned in North Africa, but it had been replaced by fear of the Americans, who were increasingly seen by the Arab populations as potential allies in their efforts to cast off colonial rule. The French had long been suspicious of British ambitions in the Middle East, and the British now appeared to be encouraging pan-Arab nationalism. Meanwhile the Cairo-based Arab Union was gaining momentum. These actions on the part of the British appeared to blatantly threaten the French position, although the British were in fact operating a policy of fostering and controlling, with the intention of moderating the tide of Arab nationalism and maintaining some influence over it to protect their own colonial possessions in Palestine.

Baker and Abtey had observed the growing level of support for nationalist movements in Arab circles. They had noticed that their ambitions to seek independence from the European powers were becoming increasingly insistent. In Baker's eyes, however, independence would pose a direct threat to the French colonial empire, and she was very suspicious of the encouragement the nationalists appeared to be getting from the British. The French were missing a trick, she believed. She had been warned during her trip that colonial issues would become a major concern, once the distractions of the war had subsided. The British had cottoned onto this and were taking pre-emptive action. France needed to shore up its presence, regain popularity in the region and rectify the confusion that dominated perceptions of France not just in relation to Vichy, but also surrounding the conflict between the Giraudists and the Gaullists. The country needed to act decisively, if it was going to win back the support of the Arab people for its colonial projects; and it needed to work hard to secure its position amidst the jostling for power that was already underway, as the Allies sought to establish spheres of influence that would mark the post-war order.

When she had left Algiers some weeks before, French in-fighting had reached its peak. Under the joint leadership, tensions continued between those who followed Giraud and those who supported de Gaulle. The intelligence services were still in a chaotic state, and the stakes were high. The Deuxième Bureau had a strong presence in Algiers, operating under Giraud; meanwhile de Gaulle's intelligence service, the BCRA, was still working mainly from London. Although there had been some tentative discussions about merging the two organisations, initial contact had revealed the extent of the gulf between them. Rivet's men of the former Deuxième Bureau were condescending towards the BCRA operatives, considering themselves to be superior and more experienced in every way. They criticised the Gaullists for playing politics, rather than focusing on waging war as effectively as possible. For their part, Passy and his men worried that the Giraudists of the Deuxième Bureau were no more than thinly disguised Vichyites, and that handing over power would result in the restoration of Vichy's intelligence services in North Africa; accordingly, they refused to relinquish their control of activities on the French mainland. The inevitable merger of the services was delayed by this wrangling over who would control the resulting fused intelligence service. The Giraudists called for the intelligence services to be attached to the military authorities, in keeping with tradition; the Gaullists argued for them to be placed directly under the control of the head of government – a step that was completely unheard-of in France.[43]

Amidst this upheaval and distrust within the intelligence services, Abtey had put himself at the disposal of the BCRA, as part of his ongoing efforts to find a way of getting to England. The apparent uncertainty surrounding his allegiances as a former member of the Deuxième Bureau probably explains why he was unable to secure a mission that would allow him to get there. Nonetheless, he was determined to support Baker's ambitions to bolster France's profile in the Middle East. In contact with de Gaulle's military command now present in the Algerian capital, Abtey arranged for her to meet de Gaulle's head of staff, Colonel Pierre Billotte, inform him directly of her experiences during her recent visit and voice her concerns about what she had observed.[44] At the meeting, Baker set out the situation she had found and explained what she believed she could do to promote and protect France. She could use her celebrity platform to introduce people to the Gaullist cause and generate respect for it. Although it was probably not made explicit at the time, the fact that Baker was African American added to her credibility in this propaganda role: her devotion to the cause of the Free French offered tangible evidence of Gaullist respect for people of colour, and would play well with local Arab populations, who were turning away from French colonial rule. Every effort needed to be made to persuade them that the Arab peoples were central to France's wider mission for the future.

Promoting the Fighting French

Billotte was very receptive to Baker's suggestions about the role she could play in promoting public recognition of de Gaulle. During Baker's ENSA tour, on 13 July 1942, the Free French movement had been renamed the Fighting French to symbolise its unification with the French Resistance and the fact that it represented all French people fighting Vichy and the German occupiers. A propaganda tour promoting its work across North Africa and the Middle East was therefore timely. The plan that was eventually elaborated, agreed with Billotte and authorised by de Gaulle was that Baker should return to the places that she had just visited under the aegis of ENSA and, in particular, to put on the gala in Cairo that she had agreed with King Farouk; but this time she would be accompanied by Abtey and Zimmer. The official aim of the mission would be to carry out a propaganda tour promoting the cause of the Fighting French that would provide a cover for the team to investigate the attitudes, allegiances and ambitions of the local populations in the area. The mission would be overseen by Major Amédée Brousset, former director of the Deuxième Bureau of the FFL High Command at Tunis. He was well qualified for this role, having been an administrator in North Africa before the war, so that he was regarded as an expert in matters of 'empire' and 'Moslem affairs'.[45] Along with their task of reporting on the activities of the British in the region and their popularity in Arab circles, their brief probably also included a remit to observe and report on American and British attitudes to de Gaulle.[46]

To finance the trip, the tour would be launched on 13 August 1943 with a spectacular gala at the municipal theatre of Algiers in aid of the Free French forces. To celebrate the first ever event of its kind in North Africa, de Gaulle himself agreed to preside over the entertainments.[47] Abtey was nominated to lead the mission and Zimmer was made responsible for all the practical arrangements. The paperwork set out their mission as a 'propaganda' tour of shows across the Middle East, to raise funds under the patronage of de Gaulle for the mainland French Resistance movement, which was gaining traction as the true extent of the Vichy collaboration with the Germans became increasingly apparent.

On 5 August 1943, Abtey went by jeep to fetch Baker from Marrakech, where she had returned for a short rest. The plan was that this would allow a driver to transport her bulky concert-tour luggage by land, while they took a flight to Algiers. He found Baker enjoying Menebhi's hospitality and socialising with her circle of Moroccan friends. Realising that Menebhi could play a valuable role in furthering the objectives of their trip, they took the decision to invite him to join them. From a well-established Moroccan family, he was widely known in Arab circles across the continent and could act as a valuable entrée for them: he could 'open doors' to circles that would otherwise be closed to them.[48] In addition, Baker and Abtey had carefully cultivated Menebhi during the time they had spent together, and he had been completely won over to supporting de Gaulle. Swayed by the general's undertaking to improve the lives of Arabs in countries under French tutelage,

Menebhi's conviction that Arabs should place their trust in de Gaulle would carry weight with influential elites across the Middle East. He could help Baker and Abtey promote their cause in these circles and further the ambitions of their mission to bring Arab populations over to Gaullism.

Menebhi accepted their proposal – with the caveat that permission would have to be sought from Abtey's superiors; and he would need assurances that those superiors were amenable to his participation in the mission. He agreed to accompany them to Algiers to discuss the plan with the relevant parties. Acquiring the visas necessary for Menebhi to fly proved too lengthy a process, and instead Abtey registered him as a 'soldier-interpreter', whose role was to accompany him and Baker on their own mission. This provided sufficient paperwork to allow him through the border checkpoints if they travelled by road. And so it was that the three of them ended up covering the thousand-odd miles between Marrakech and Algiers by jeep.

Now under the orders of the French military, both Baker and Menebhi adopted military dress for the journey. This consisted of a shirt, shorts and a police cap. Menebhi would still wear his normal white Arab robes, known as a *djellaba*, whenever appropriate; but they were less practical for travelling in a open jeep.[49] It took them three days to reach Algiers, including a stopover in Fez with Menebhi's uncle, who was pasha there, and a further overnight in Tlemcen. In the Algerian capital, they met up with Billotte, who strongly approved of Menebhi's participation, even arranging for him to meet de Gaulle in person, since he was the 'first Moroccan to join the Free French'.[50] According to Abtey, de Gaulle received Menebhi very graciously and offered him a small brooch in the form of the Cross of Lorraine, the Free French symbol, as a gift.[51] Menebhi was delighted, and told Baker and Abtey after the meeting that the general was 'an extraordinary man and I now understand everything that you do and why you do it. This man will be good for Islam.'[52] It was a significant step for Menebhi, who had been brought up as a British protégé, to shift his allegiances to support the French. With the final formalities in place for Menebhi to join the mission, their work could begin. But first, there was a gala to attend. And it would be Baker's turn to meet the leader of the Fighting French for the first time.

Meeting de Gaulle at last

The 'Grand Gala in Aid of the Free French Forces', which took place in Algiers on 13 August 1943, was a celebratory affair. De Gaulle was riding a wave of public enthusiasm, and the gala was ideally timed to channel and promote this. He had returned, just two days before, from a triumphant tour of Morocco. The excitement provoked by his visit and his effusive reception was reported in detail in the *Écho d'Algier*.[53] Crowds of Moroccans and Europeans alike had turned out in huge numbers to celebrate his presence.[54] De Gaulle's visit to the medina in Fez, which had left him 'visibly moved by his reception', appeared to have cemented his commitment to the Arabs in ways that chimed with the ambitions of Baker's mission across North Africa and the Middle East. In addition, while the Americans continued to be sceptical about de Gaulle's motives, an intelligence report on his visit to Casablanca remarked very positively on his reception and his capacity to bring the population together:

> The ovations tendered by other visiting dignitaries ... most certainly suffer by comparison ... [The] demonstration left the impression with this agent that the French nation can really be united again only under the leadership of de Gaulle ... he has captured the imagination and the hearts of the common citizen.[55]

This was just the kind of response that the Gaullists were hoping for in their campaign to promote de Gaulle's legitimacy as France's rightful leader.

The gala – the first public celebration of (and benefit concert for) the Free French forces – was transmitted live across North Africa by Radio France, to capitalise on de Gaulle's successful and growing public profile in Algiers.[56] Baker secured a sixty-strong band of Black American servicemen, who played the first half of the show;

her own act came in the second half, when she was accompanied by the André Farrugia band according to press reports. Aside from de Gaulle, who presided at the event along with his wife, all the Allied countries were represented: Harold Macmillan was there as the British resident minister in Algiers; Robert Murphy represented Roosevelt; and even the USSR sent a representative. Baker's act included her normal favourites, such as 'Tipperary', while the audience joined her for the chorus of the French First World War song 'Madelon'. She also sang a Russian song to acknowledge the presence of the USSR among the Allies. Dressed in an understated blue-and-red dress, the colours of Paris, Baker's repertoire of French songs provoked considerable emotion in the audience.[57]

Alla Dumesnil, Baker's later military superior, was also present that night. She recalled the evening, which had left a strong impression on her:

> [Josephine] had a lovely dress made of blue-and-red jersey decorated with white musical notes . . . At some point, Josephine started to sing 'J'ai deux amours, mon pays et Paris' and she broke down in tears. She fell onto her knees on stage. She reached her arms out towards the general's box: 'I can't sing. He is here.'[58]

In the interval, Baker was invited to the box where de Gaulle was sitting with his wife.[59] During their conversation, Yvonne de Gaulle teased Baker, calling her a 'sale petite gaulliste' – a 'naughty little Gaullist' – a diminutive nickname which Baker often later used to sign her letters in her post-war correspondence with the couple.[60] De Gaulle had a small Cross of Lorraine made of gold sent to her after their meeting, as a gesture of his appreciation. At the culmination of her performance, as she sang the French national anthem, a huge tricolour flag with a 6-metre-wide Cross of Lorraine on it dropped down dramatically behind her.[61] Baker had tasked a team of local seamstresses with producing it. According to Rey, 'the whole auditorium was overcome with enthusiasm and emotion. This was Baker's gift to General de Gaulle.'[62] It was a breathtaking moment, and the flag would accompany them throughout their forthcoming tour, providing a memorable conclusion to Baker's performances wherever circumstances allowed.

Baker's extreme reaction at seeing de Gaulle for the first time was a manifestation of her unshakeable Gaullist conviction. Whether it was the emotion of the event that prevented her from singing, or exhaustion from the demands of the numerous concerts she had recently put on is impossible to know.[63] But it certainly added to the drama of the occasion. By the time the party set off for its next engagement in Tunis, the emotions of the evening had subsided. They all knew that they faced a tough journey.

A taxing journey through the desert

They left Algiers one evening at 6 p.m.[64] According to Rey, who was in the party, Baker no longer conducted herself as a star of the stage: now she was 'just soldier Baker, in field dress . . . her face hidden under a military cap, wrapped in a soft padded jacket for the difficult night we were going to spend bumping along the rough roads'.[65] Abtey described Josephine as looking like the cartoon character 'Felix the Cat' in the black police hat that she liked to wear: its flaps folded down over the nape of her neck and protected her better than any other headgear, but its tips protruded above her ears, giving her a feline air.[66] The group travelled mainly at night to avoid the extreme heat.[67] From Algiers to Tunis, they decided to drive all night and make the trip in one go. They crossed the Kabylia mountains and navigated through the debris of the ravages of recent battle. Neither of their vehicles could manage the rough terrain: they had to be towed for the last 30 miles of the journey to Tunis.

There was little time to recover, as Baker's gala was the day after their arrival. Brousset had arranged for a troupe of thirty Tahitian singers and dancers to come from Tripoli to perform that evening. These volunteers from the Pacific Battalion proved to be gifted artists and shared the billing with Baker on her two subsequent evenings. The first two performances had been organised specifically for French troops only, but on the third night British military

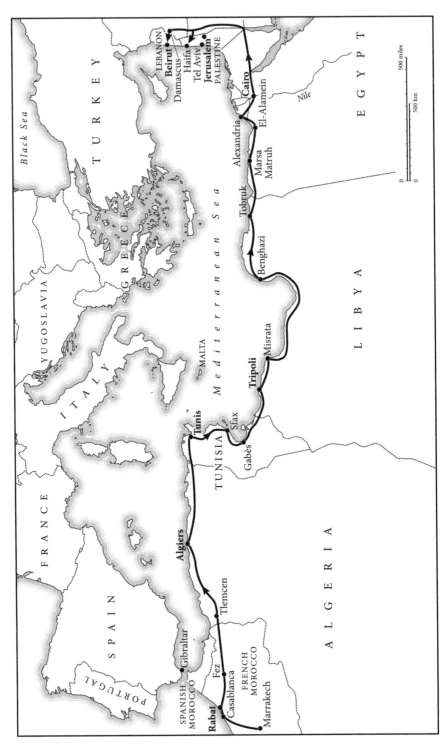

were also invited to attend.[68] Keen to repair the bad feeling that Baker may have harboured towards the British after the unfortunate end to her ENSA tour, Janes made determined efforts to ensure that she had a positive reception, explaining to the local ENSA team in Tripoli that 'owing to operational reasons, things did not go too well towards the end of her Middle East tour and anything we can do to help will be to the good'.[69]

Despite his efforts, tensions between the British and French soldiers threatened to ruin the evening. Baker, however, with typical aplomb, smoothed everything over, and the evening was heralded as a great success. Baker's diplomatic skills were increasingly well honed; however, throughout their trip encounters with the British proved unpredictable, ranging widely from friendly support to the kind of hostility they experienced that evening. The problem for Baker and her team – regardless of the strained relations between the British and the French military at this time – was that the practicalities of their mission would be largely dependent on the good will of the British present in the region. The Free French troops were not as widespread and had no organised entertainment network like the American USO or the British ENSA to escort them to their destinations.[70] The party then made a return trip from Tunis to Sfax for two performances on 24 and 25 August 1943.[71] After a final show in the Tunisian capital, the group was immediately confronted with a fresh practical challenge: how to get to Egypt.

Brousset had done his best to arrange all the formalities for Menebhi to participate in the mission, granting him the title of lieutenant-interpreter.[72] However, flights in and out of the Egyptian capital were operated by British and American companies, which were sticklers for paperwork. Organising the necessary visas and permissions would be time consuming. In the end, it was agreed that having come thus far by jeep, they may as well carry on.[73] They would make their way to Cairo along the coastal route through Libya. After eventually securing two jeeps that they hoped would be robust enough to cope with the demanding – almost 2,000 mile – journey, they were ready to depart. Along with Baker, Menebhi, Abtey and the dancer Rey, the party included two drivers allocated to them by Brousset: a sergeant and a young marine.[74] Travelling such a huge distance by jeep was certainly not ideal, particularly as the vehicles were not in tip-top condition. They would be very vulnerable to the vagaries of the weather and the demands of the rough desert terrain, and they would have to improvise stops to sleep and recover, depending on the circumstances they encountered. It was a very different prospect from the relative comfort that Baker had enjoyed travelling with Janes and his ENSA team of British army escorts.

They embarked on what would be a long, often monotonous, journey through mainly desert regions, following the line of the coast. This took them through uninviting desert areas, some of which were heavily mined. The stony, arid terrain was unrelenting, with small, stunted bushes and rocks scattered across its surface in a desiccated landscape that extended as far as the eye could see. They followed the track roads (such as they were), but even these posed danger for the vehicles: the drivers of the two jeeps had to keep their eyes firmly on the dusty road, in order to dodge the sharp rocks that threatened to rip the tyres and the boulders that could buckle a wheel in seconds.[75] There was very little rain, and the weather hardly varied. Travelling in high summer, they faced temperatures of 20–60 degrees Celsius in the shade, and they tried to avoid travelling during the afternoon, when temperatures were at their highest. They had to be careful not to get dehydrated, and they wore motorcycle goggles to protect their eyes from the sun and the sand. Whenever a vehicle went by, sand and dust would rise up in choking clouds. It was even worse when a strong wind or a sandstorm blew up. Then they would have to pull over and take shelter as best they could until it passed. The brown sand would find its way into everything, scratching their faces, arms and knees and leaving them red and sore. With water in short supply, washing was a rare luxury, and it was almost impossible to rinse out their dust-engrained clothes while they were on the road.

Baker whiled the hours away knitting, and they took every opportunity they could to make the best of the stops along the way. At the Tunisian coastal town of Gabès, for example, they swam in an oasis.

In the days that followed, they continued their journey along the coast southeast, crossing into Libya and on to Tripoli. Noël Coward, who would visit the city a few weeks later, described its crumbling pretentiousness in his diary. 'The coloured plaster is already peeling from the angular self-conscious architecture and the streets are dusty and woebegone. The whole place was obviously never intended to withstand bombardment and conquest.'[76]

When Baker's party arrived in the city in late August 1943, it was around 11 p.m. on the second day of their journey from Tunis. Finding no food or lodgings, they eventually managed to persuade a British officer to allocate a hotel room to Baker.[77] The rest of the group simply slept rough in the hotel courtyard. Conscious that this was their last opportunity to stock up, they managed to secure enough rations from the British to last them for the seven days it would take to complete the journey to Cairo. Loaded with stocks of corned beef, tinned tuna, sardines, vegetables and pineapple, tea, bread rolls and biscuits, they left the city the following morning. Along the coast, they stopped at the Roman town of Khoms; but when they arrived at the charming Italian seaside town of Misrata they had to be very wary of mines. The battle-damaged roads rendered progress painfully slow.[78] When they were too exhausted to go any further, they camped out in the open with the equipment they had purchased in Tripoli. Morale was low, and they took it in turns to keep watch throughout the night, having been warned to be on the lookout for desert robbers. As they continued their journey, the detritus of war that surrounded them added to their sense of dejection:

Wrecked planes, tanks and armoured vehicles of all kinds, broken or burnt out, soldiers' equipment, clothing, ammunition, all scattered in the most indescribable disorder, such was the infernal vision that our journey afforded us, with the exception of a few rare sectors.[79]

Late in the evening of the third day, while looking for somewhere suitable to make camp and rest, they were pulled over by a detachment of British military police who had inspected their papers some

40 miles earlier. Overtaking them on the road, the British officers insisted that they stop immediately and warned them not to leave the road on any account, as the surrounding areas were heavily mined. There was a safe route through the minefield, but it was too dark for them to see the signposts clearly enough to find their way: they would have to wait until morning to continue their journey. Concerned about leaving them on the open road, where they would be vulnerable, the British officers insisted on taking everyone back to their own camp, where they would be able to pass the night safely. Delighted to have some company for once in this remote corner of the desert, these kindly men from Hampshire turned the camp upside down in their efforts to uncover the best that they had of their stores and rations to share with their unexpected visitors. Getting to the camp had forced Baker's party to retrace part of its route; but the generous welcome they met there made up for the frustration.[80]

The next day, the party safely navigated the minefield to reach 'Marble Arch', the massive British air force camp where Baker had entertained the troops in more comfortable circumstances during her ENSA tour of a month before. In the baking heat, they continued along the coast to Benghazi, then through Derna, Tobruk, Bardiyah and across the border into Egypt. They steered their way through the ruins of the recent battlefields of the Western Desert campaign, where the British had defeated Rommel's Afrika Korps at El-Alamein just days before the Allied landings in North Africa.

Abtey, as leader of the mission, decided when and where they should rest, and it fell to him to ensure that everyone's needs were met, and to maintain morale. At one point, it became clear that the marine who was driving was visibly struggling with the physical demands of the trip. He eventually approached Abtey to ask if he could be released from the mission and return to Tunis; Abtey gently, but firmly, told him to pull himself together and reminded him that he had volunteered to join them in the knowledge that it would be tough.[81] The marine evidently buckled down, as he made no more complaints.

For her part, Baker seems to have been remarkably resilient. On one occasion, however, while they were in the Libyan mountains,

Abtey relates that she did lose her temper, provoked by some comment he had made. In her rage, Baker got the bit between her teeth and decided she was going to take over the driving. She grabbed the jeep's steering wheel, while Abtey was still on the road beside the vehicle, and sped off up the mountain. Abtey was forced to follow in the other car, racing after her and shouting instructions, as she had never driven a jeep before. Fearing that she would run into trouble on the windy road, he raced at breakneck speed to keep up with her, as she dodged boulders and flew over holes for more than 12 miles. At the end of this particularly tortuous stretch, Baker finally slowed down and continued at a more moderate pace. It turned out that it was Menebhi, in the car with her, who had finally managed to calm her down. The poor man had been terrified. 'I had my heart in my mouth,' he said to Abtey. 'The more I begged her to slow down, the more she accelerated.' Fortunately for the long-suffering Menebhi, such eruptions on Baker's part were rare. Most of the time, the company tolerated the challenges of the journey in calm companionship.[82]

However, further along the coast, past Sidi Barrani and Marsa Matruh, and about 40 miles from Alexandria, one of the jeeps hit something in the road and flipped over, killing the young marine instantly. The sergeant who was driving (having only recently taken over from Baker) was seriously injured. Josephine had a lucky escape, as she had just returned to travel in the other jeep with Abtey and Menebhi. Rey, who was also in the damaged vehicle, fortunately escaped unharmed.[83] British military police who happened to be in the area immediately took control of the situation. Menebhi and Rey accompanied the body of the marine to Alexandria in a military command car, while the injured driver was taken to the nearest camp hospital, 30 miles away. Baker and Abtey followed along behind. After assuring themselves that the sergeant was in good hands, they continued on to Alexandria. Since Abtey had Menebhi's and Rey's papers, which he had been looking after, he and Baker were sent by the police to the military hospital, where they eventually tracked down the two men.[84] They organised the burial of the young marine at the military cemetery, where he was laid to rest alongside other soldiers killed in the service of the Free French forces two days later.[85]

Just before leaving Alexandria, Menebhi was contacted by His Highness Prince Mohammed Ali, a former guest at the Menebhi family's palace in Tangier, who had learnt of his presence in the city from press reports. Menebhi played his role as an ambassador for de Gaulle to perfection. He explained to his host that his mission was to convey the French leader's friendly greetings to his Arab brothers. The prince had much to say about the current political situation:

France currently has a major role to play in the Middle East. The various political demands that are being formulated, are being openly favoured and controlled by certain Western powers. If France fails to take an interest in this issue, it will almost certainly lose out, although I do not believe that a Union of Arab Peoples is a reality just yet.

He urged Menebhi to inform de Gaulle that France needed to participate actively in the current political developments relating to the Arab peoples, if it wanted to prevent itself from being eliminated from the Middle East. He went on:

French people who are well versed in the matter should immediately set about defending France's interests, interests which are so closely linked with our own, whatever some of our politicians think – and he smiled wryly – who imagine that they have found brilliant innovation in the notion of independence. We need and will always need France in the Middle East, if only for the sake of balance.[86]

Some hours later, still shocked and saddened to have lost the young man, in whose company they had spent so long, the remaining members of the party continued on their way, and some nine days after leaving Tunis, on the evening of 6 September, they gratefully checked into Shepheard's Hotel, having completed the final leg of their route to Cairo.

The journey proved to be a testing, sometimes frightening, and physically extremely demanding experience for all involved. Abtey's account (on which this description has depended for the details of their experiences) probably plays down the full extent of the struggles they faced. Before Baker, Alice Delysia had also travelled around the desert; and while she may have been more directly exposed to dangers near the front line, she was always shielded by the weight of the resources of the British army. That Baker undertook such a venture, travelling such a distance across dangerous terrain while accompanied by so few people, bears testimony to the tenacity of her commitment, particularly in view of her tendency to struggle with her health. While they took some time to enjoy the rarefied atmosphere of British colonial Cairo, as they recovered from the demands of the strenuous journey, Baker, Abtey and Menebhi readied themselves to embark on the mission proper. Their propaganda assignment had already borne fruit in Alexandria, vindicating their decision to bring Menebhi along with them.

Egypt

The three of them remained in the Egyptian capital for a few days, finalising arrangements for the gala – which, it was agreed, would be held a few weeks later. Despite some uneasiness about the plan in French consular circles, it was widely acknowledged that if King Farouk presided at the gala, it would be a diplomatic triumph for the Fighting French. However, the French representatives did not favour Baker's use of the massive Cross of Lorraine flag that had become the mainstay of her performances. Abtey suggests that this reluctance reflected the fact that these French diplomats did not fully embrace de Gaulle and wanted to avoid such an overt promotion of the Gaullist Fighting French, which could have provoked reactions from the British authorities, as well as the king himself.[87] Baker, however, was determined not to allow their timidity to undermine her plans, and she dismissed consular warnings that propagandising on behalf of de Gaulle would be ill-advised.

Abtey, meanwhile, liaised with the representative of the Fighting French, Monsieur de Benoist, and put him in the picture about the nature of their mission. De Benoist welcomed the party and threw a lavish banquet in Baker's honour at the Auberge des Pyramides.[88] On this occasion, Baker offered to sing for the king, having had a reassurance that he was supportive of their leader. The king was delighted. The magnificent venue had opened quite recently and had quickly become a favourite with Cairo's cohort of British officers and the cosmopolitan elite intent on having as much fun as possible.[89] It soon became the site of some of the most glorious social gatherings given during the war by members of the royal family:

> It had a large open-air courtyard with a dance floor in the middle and was judged the most pleasant night spot in Cairo, becoming a frequent venue for charity galas and . . . a favourite haunt of the King's [Farouk].[90]

Any Egyptian escorting a beautiful woman shunned the Auberge – and indeed any of Farouk's favourite haunts – for fear that the king might take a fancy to the wife or girlfriend and create a most embarrassing situation, for he was well known for his wrath when refused the companionship of a woman he coveted. Farouk's arrival invariably provoked a precipitous exodus of the pashas and their partners.

The nightclub was also regularly frequented by the British ambassador, the recently ennobled Lord Killearn (Sir Miles Lampson, as was). Killearn brought Noël Coward to the Auberge during his visit to Cairo in summer 1943. They were led to a table next to that of the monarch. Killearn introduced Coward to the king, who left early, after having paid their bill. 'Coward rather regretted having ordered a beer and two packets of Gold Flake.'[91] It was during this visit to Cairo that Baker herself bumped into Noël Coward at her hotel. She had heard the soldiers talk of him and knew how much he was adored by them.[92] Coward wrote in his diary, in an entry for 8 September 1943, that

we ran into Josephine Baker looking really the last word in 'chic'
and as bright as a button . . . She is doing a wonderful job for the
troops and refuses to appear anywhere where admission is
charged or where civilians are present. She says firmly that
entertaining the fighting services is her self-appointed war effort
and she has no intention of being side-tracked from it for any
reason whatsoever.[93]

During a visit to the US a few months later, he made a point of
telling journalists what a great job Baker was doing: 'One of the
most popular stars in North Africa – if not the most popular – is
Josephine Baker who is giving daily concerts and is going over sock
with the men.'[94] The two stars of music hall performed across the
area throughout the early autumn.

While Baker and Abtey were preoccupied with arranging
her performances, Menebhi set about carrying out his part in the
mission. In line with his new-found enthusiastic support for France,
he politely turned down an invitation from the British statesman
Sir Anthony Eden, who was in Cairo, and instead spent time with
eminent Egyptian personalities, including a government minister.[95]
He was received by the grand mufti of Islam and was invited to the
University of Al-Azhar by a delegation of Moroccan professors.[96]
The Arabic Egyptian press was full of praise for this well-connected
Moroccan, who proudly wore the Cross of Lorraine on his white
djellaba.[97]

The Levant

With preparations for the gala in hand, Baker's party – including
Menebhi, whose papers now allowed it – flew up to Beirut, aware of
rumours about French and British squabbles in relation to the
forthcoming elections there. They were welcomed by the Gaullist
French 'delegate-general', Monsieur Helleu. The plan was to
organise a series of performances across the Levant with the intention of promoting de Gaulle, but their presence coincided with a
growing sense of crisis in French diplomatic circles: they appeared

to be losing control of the political situation that was unfolding. During her visit there some weeks before, Baker had already picked up on the growing tensions between the British and the French, as they battled over their competing interests in the Levant. These tensions stemmed from the independence ambitions of Syria and Lebanon, and de Gaulle's promises, made in 1941, to grant meaningful independence – but only once they had reached an agreement that would preserve France's interests.[98]

In December 1942, the CFLN had finally agreed to hold national elections in Lebanon. It was this much-postponed event that had become the battleground for intense Franco-British rivalry. The outcome of the legislative elections, held in August 1943, were inconclusive. Baker and her party reached Beirut just days before the presidential elections on 21 September 1943, which would determine the final composition of Lebanon's new government and decide France's future in the area. The French had been confident that their favoured presidential candidate, Émile Eddé, would win; but the British, led by General Spears, who headed up the British legation in the Levant, considered him a reactionary, and instead threw British weight behind his opponent, Bishara al-Khoury, a nationalist with ambitions gradually to emancipate the country from French control. He had the support of many local British residents, both civilian and military, who were keen to remove the French presence in the area, despite the formal British policy of friendship with the French. Efforts by the Foreign Office to impose this position and control what was happening on the ground were largely ineffective. Spears was a law unto himself, and his unilateral actions infuriated Whitehall, but he was protected by his personal friendship with Churchill. Previously a committed Francophile, Spears had turned violently against de Gaulle during the events in the Levant in 1941, on account of the differences that had surfaced between them.[99] Since then, he had become almost obsessive in his anti-Gaullist positioning. The Gaullists, for their part, were determined to preserve France's longstanding ties to the Levant – a region that was bound up with ideas of national prestige, power and the 'French civilising mission'. The battlelines were now drawn as the British and French vied for political control of the area. The policies of the British were also formulated with an eye not just to maintaining local support in the Levant, but to distract from their own difficulties in neighbouring Palestine. Both powers were acutely aware that their actions and the outcome of the elections would have reputational repercussions across the Arab world.

Baker's first event, at the Grand Sofar Hotel, just outside the Lebanese capital, up in the mountains, took place on the very night of the elections. The outgoing Lebanese president, along with royal guests and other dignitaries, were the guests of honour of the French ambassador.[100] As well as her programme of songs, to animate the evening Baker decided the time – and the audience – was right to put the gold Cross of Lorraine that she had been gifted by de Gaulle before she left Algiers up for auction, in aid of Resistance organisations on the French mainland.[101] She was able to raise a remarkable 350,000 francs for it, as Syrian and Lebanese members of the audience each tried to outbid one another.[102]

Meanwhile, much to the disappointment and frustration of the French contingent, the British-backed presidential candidate, Khoury, emerged as the winner of the election. He quickly took up his position as president in the new government. French prestige had suffered a heavy blow. To Abtey, it seemed to be the first nail in the coffin for France's future in the Middle East.[103] Unable to contribute anything further to the situation, Baker's party left for Syria. They spent the following two nights in Damascus, and Baker gave a memorable open-air performance in the lush gardens of the city's military hospital on 27 September 1943.[104]

Photographs of the event show Baker singing on a large stage – draped in the British, Syrian, French and Gaullist flags – that had been erected across the façade of the building. Flags also decorated the front of the stage. Three rows of injured soldiers – their stretchers carefully balanced on benches – were lined up right at the front, and there were several rows of soldiers seated behind them. At the very back, the more able-bodied stood, some on an elevated platform.[105] The beds of those who were too ill to be moved were brought to the window, so that they could see the stage and participate from a distance. After the performance, Baker went into the hospital to greet them all individually.

It seems likely that in Damascus, most of the audience was French. When Baker sang for French soldiers, her hold was particularly strong. A *Variety* reporter remarked that she symbolised all that reminded them of France:

> When her audience is a French one the applause is more, deeper, nearer the heart, than just that accorded a popular artist. The French audience's reaction is interesting. The fact is that Josephine Baker, the unknown colored girl from St Louis, who made good at the Folies Bergère, who is not a Frenchwoman except by marriage *symbolizes* Paris for thousands of Frenchmen in Africa and the Middle East. Paris to a Frenchman is the almost magic word signifying the heart of France, his sweetheart, mother, and a lot of other things all rolled in to one. No other capital in the world means to its nationals quite what Paris means to a Frenchman.[106]

Palestine

In another propaganda coup, before their departure from Syria, Menebhi was received by the recently elected new president of the Syrian Republic, allowing him to make the case for de Gaulle. From Syria, the party made its way south to Jerusalem by car. Baker had not visited the British mandate of Palestine during her previous tour and was deeply moved by the cultural heritage of the historical sights she went to there. They stayed at the King David Hotel, where Baker performed, as well as in Haifa and Tel Aviv. Her performance in late September in Jerusalem in aid of the 'Fighting French War Fund' (as it was described in a local newspaper) was a consummate propaganda event. Her appearance was preceded by a newsreel which set out the achievements of de Gaulle's Fighting French. As the journalist pointed out, Baker's songs brought back 'memories of the Paris that meant so much not only to Frenchmen but to all who loved the city on the Seine'. While, in the old days at the Casino de Paris, she had been a dancer 'clothed in little else but her smile', she was now showing herself to be chiefly a singer:

> To her song she brings the incomparable beauty of her shoulders, arms, and hands, her flashing eyes and smile and her rhythmic gestures and movements. Even after 15 years she is still as graceful as a ballet dancer. Her Wardrobe is exquisite and her rapid change from one magnificent gown to another was the wonder of her audience.

Describing her rendition of 'J'ai deux amours', which was 'sung against the headground of a gigantic Fighting French flag, she put all the nostalgia of the Frenchman bereft of those loves, and in her emotion appeared a veritable Joan of Arc'.[107] Baker was able to evoke the very essence of France and its culture among all those present, reminding them forcefully of her country's importance and its powerful past, and to equate it directly with the Gaullist cause.

Even when not performing, Baker maintained her ambassadorial role and never dropped her guard. She visited the local sights of Jerusalem with a journalist in tow, who reported in detail on her every move and reproduced her comments. On a visit to the Western Wall, she prayed for the family of her former husband Jean Lion, and explained to the journalist that she was glad to have married a Jew: 'It is a great thing thus to belong to both of the persecuted races.' This comment highlights the strength of Baker's sense of her Jewish identity, which in this interview she put on a par with her African American one. The journalist goes on to report that she was visibly moved at the Western Wall:

> The congregation . . . view the tall dark-brown lady with some astonishment. Readily they make room when, praying, she places her hands on the age-old stones, smoothed by uncounted generations. As Josephine steps back from the wall, tears roll down her cheeks.

During the time it took for her to reach the Dead Sea, where she planned to take a swim, she recounted the work she had done for the Americans after the landings:

> 'There I had to sing again, though I could hardly stand. After all I am American and French at the same time. I can help them understand each other. And now I have to go with the soldiers – every success I have counts for my coloured brothers in America.' . . . She regards it as her duty to cheer up the fighting men, and, like Marion [sic] Anderson, whom she admires, to foster understanding for the coloured race.[108]

Baker outlines to the journalist her own personal mission. In referencing the singer Marian Anderson, who was known for her insistence on performing to integrated crowds in the US in 1939, she highlights her own, now more crystallised sense of her commitment to promoting the cause of equality.

Perhaps one of Baker's most remarkable achievements was the way in which her audiences brought together all the key players in the local communities they visited, allowing her to convey her Gaullist message across a diverse range of people. Baker's performance at the Casino Bat Galim in Haifa on 3 October 1943, offers a telling example of this. Described as 'A unique demonstration of Anglo-French solidarity' by 'the French Consul . . . under whose auspices the function was held', it brought together the Haifa district commissioner, members of the consular corps, the mayor of Haifa, senior officers of the Allied forces (presumably mainly British) and Haifa's president of the Committee of Friends of Fighting France. At all these events, Baker and her colleagues promoted the work of the Fighting French with a particular emphasis on raising money for the Resistance. According to Abtey, their cause was clearly necessary, as the Jewish journalists they met claimed both that the CFLN had made no effort to communicate with them and that the French governing classes seemed to be curiously absent from complex developments that were currently playing out in the Middle East.[109]

Cairo

Baker and her party returned to Cairo in good time for the much-anticipated gala at the Opera House on 24 October 1943. French consular officials continued to insist that de Gaulle and the Fighting French should not be mentioned, and were prescriptive about the sketches that could be included. Baker, however, flouted their demands that the Gaullist flag featuring the Cross of Lorraine should not be used, and Abtey went ahead with his planned programme. Although the event was hugely successful, in the end it proved to be of only limited value as a propaganda coup for de Gaulle.[110] At the insistence of de Benoist, rather than overtly mention de Gaulle, the emphasis of the evening was placed on the cultivation of Franco-Egyptian relations and the money raised went to the children of France. This was reflected in the way the event was reported by the French photo-journal *Images*, which described it as headlining the inauguration of the Cairo season. According to this article, several dignitaries were present, including the king of Yugoslavia; but in the end, King Farouk did not attend in person. Instead, the head of his royal cabinet represented him. It was a splendid affair, reminiscent of pre-war occasions, and the audience included 'ladies in all their finery, men in dinner jackets and officers' uniforms, rarely has one seen such a beautiful setting. Some of the boxes look like jewellery shops.'[111] The king presumably shied away from appearing in person to publicly support the French amidst the ongoing tensions with the British. Egypt was, after all, technically a neutral country.

Baker's planned performances ended with a few days at the Ezbzkieh theatre in the city.[112] Demoralised, Baker, Abtey and Menebhi observed with concern the worsening situation in the Levant, convinced that the Arab Union based in Cairo, under the guidance of the British, in its first show of power, was actively seeking to eliminate the French from Syria and Lebanon.[113] The Arab Union appeared to be effective. The new Lebanese government had immediately started a campaign for the cessation of various interests and responsibilities that the French controlled.

The situation became increasingly fraught when, on 8 November, the new government took steps to abolish the French mandate and make Arabic the sole national language. Under the orders of Helleu, the Gaullist French delegate-general, local French officials responded swiftly: early on 11 November, the president, the prime minister, three ministers and one deputy were all arrested. They were interned, and the pro-French presidential candidate, Émile Eddé, was appointed as provisional president. When Eddé dissolved the Chamber of Deputies (the Lebanese parliament), violence erupted in the streets of Beirut and the French were forced to deploy troops to restore order. A clandestine meeting of the Chamber of Deputies issued a statement setting out its intention to arrange for a government of Lebanon to be convened. All dealings with the French were rejected, pending the reinstatement of the arrested leadership. The British and Americans sided against the French, demanding that the previous government be restored.

In response to these events, when anti-French demonstrations took place in Cairo, in mid-November 1943, Baker's party decided that they needed to return to Algiers urgently and present their findings directly to their hierarchies. The crisis only seemed to be escalating. Abtey was frustrated by the apparent lack of reaction to the intelligence reports he had been conscientiously filing for his superiors. The situation merited immediate action on the ground. Instead, however, Abtey feared that both the information they were sending to Algiers about the events they had witnessed and their concerns that the Gaullists were doing too little to protect France's interests in the area were being studiously ignored by those self-same individuals who had voiced scepticism about their mission in the first place.[114] In addition to the intelligence they had uncovered, they would return with the 3 million francs they had raised in aid for French Resistance groups.[115] However, the party's insistent requests for urgent transport to Algiers were ignored, forcing them to fall back on the only jeep they still had. Fortunately, at their first stop in Alexandria, they were able to retrieve their second jeep, as well as the injured sergeant, now sufficiently recovered to make the return journey.

1. Josephine Baker with her dance partner at the Folies Bergère in 1927 recreating a scene from the famous 'danse sauvage'. Her appearance caused a sensation when it was performed at the Théâtre des Champs-Élysées in 1925. Baker was carried onto the stage on her partner's back.

2. Baker in her iconic banana skirt from the Folies Bergère production of *Un Vent de folie* in 1927.

JOSÉPHINE BAKER dans "La Créole"

3. Baker in one of her costumes from Offenbach's comic opera *La Créole* in 1934. Her move into comic opera met critical acclaim. She organised and performed a revival of this opera in Marseille in December 1940 and January 1941.

4. Baker dancing with her husband Jean Lion at a charity benefit, a few days after their wedding held on 29 November 1937. The marriage allowed Baker to take French nationality. Although Baker initially announced that she would retire, she soon returned to the stage.

5. Baker and her co-star Maurice Chevalier are cheered by French soldiers as they arrive at the front in November 1939 to perform numbers from their forthcoming show 'Paris-London' at the Casino de Paris.

6. Baker performing in her section of the show 'Paris-London' at the Casino de Paris in December 1939.

7. Baker entertaining troops at the British Leave Club at the Hôtel Moderne in Paris in May 1940.

8. Baker playing nightclub owner and performer Mlle Zazu Clairon in the film *Fausse Alerte* (1945). In this scene she is surrounded by her women dancers in the basement air-raid shelter.

9. A 1940 portrait of Baker by Studio Harcourt, a Paris-based photography studio known for its black-and-white portraits of celebrities and film stars.

10. The Château des Milandes in Dordogne, rented by Baker from 1938 and purchased by her in 1947. After the defeat of France in May–June 1940, Josephine Baker left Paris and took shelter here for some months.

11. Baker performing on stage for an audience that includes a number of uniformed military personnel in Casablanca, French Morocco, on 14 April 1943.

12. Baker performing in May 1943 in Oran, Algeria, with a band of African American soldiers.

13. Baker during a troop tour for ENSA, on the steps of Shepheard's Hotel in Cairo in July 1943, with Lieutenant Lancaster, Basil Dean (head of ENSA), Colonel Dunstan and Colonel Haygarth.

14. Baker in military uniform with her superior officer Major Alla Dumesnil in 1944. This publicity photograph taken in Dumesnil's office in Algiers identifies Baker clearly as a member of the French air force and part of de Gaulle's Free French movement.

15. This extract from the diary of the operations of the French ministerial air liaison group for 6 June 1944 relates the air accident that occurred off the coast of Corsica, involving Baker. This page describing the accident was signed by Baker in 1946.

16. Baker performs in a villa in Algiers in the presence of General René Bouscat, chief of staff of the French air force, during the Youth Air Festival on 9 July 1944.

LA RECONNAISSEZ-VOUS ?
(Voir page 16)

HEBDOMADAIRE ILLUSTRÉ DU M.L.N. ⚓ = ADRESSE PROVISOIRE =
126, LA CANEBIÈRE MARSEILLE

17. V, the illustrated weekly magazine of the MLN (Mouvement de Libération Nationale), published this image of Baker on her arrival back in France from North Africa in October 1944, with the caption, 'Do you recognise her?'

18. Baker in military uniform rehearses with French composer Vincent Scotto, author of the song 'J'ai deux amours', in October 1944 in a Paris restaurant.

19. Baker performs on stage at an 'Air Gala' at the Paramount Theatre in Paris. In the background is the enormous flag representing the Cross of Lorraine which would drop at the culmination of her performances.

20. A still from a military film of Baker's visit to a barracks of French soldiers in Alsace in January 1945. She hands out cigarettes and giggles with the men.

21. Baker models a glamorous dress during a private preview of the gowns and hats she plans to wear during a forthcoming tour of England with ENSA. The event is held in Paris at Jean Dresses, her dressmaker, in March 1945.

22. A still from an army entertainment film, *Magazine récréatif*, showing Baker, dressed in her air force uniform, performing 'J'ai deux amours' to a studio audience of soldiers on 26 April 1945. Her performance is interwoven with a montage of images of Paris scenes and palm trees.

23. Baker performs at BBC Broadcasting House during her visit to London in April–May 1945.

24. Baker with a soldier she has brought on stage while entertaining the troops as part of the VE Day celebrations in London. The image was published by *Picture Post* in an article describing her visit, entitled 'Josephine Baker gives soldiers a victory song'.

25. Baker during her visit to the two French heavy bomber squadrons within RAF Bomber Command at RAF Elvington near York on 16 May 1945.

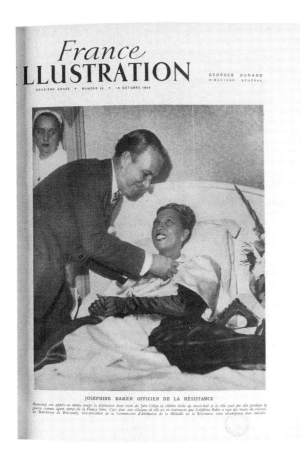

JOSÉPHINE BAKER OFFICIER DE LA RÉSISTANCE

26. The front page of the magazine *France-Illustration*, dated 19 October 1946, shows Baker being presented with her Resistance medal by Colonel de Boissoudy, vice president of the Awarding Committee, at a clinic in Neuilly, in October 1946. The caption reads: 'Josephine Baker Officer of the Resistance'.

27. A still from a military film shot at an official reception at the *Maison des équipages de l'air* in Paris, showing Baker with her close Moroccan friend Mohammed Menebhi, on 19 April 1947.

28. Baker and band leader Jo Bouillon just after their wedding ceremony at the chapel of the Château des Milandes, Dordogne, on 3 June 1947.

29. Baker with Henry Hurford Janes during a visit to London in 1948. Janes was her ENSA representative for her troop tour of North Africa and the Middle East in 1943. They subsequently became lifelong friends.

30. Dressed in her military uniform, Baker receives the Légion d'honneur and the Croix de Guerre medals from General Martial Valin of the French air force, in the courtyard of the Château des Milandes on 19 August 1961.

31. Baker poses with General Valin and the young children of her 'rainbow tribe' after the ceremony during which she was awarded the Légion d'honneur and the Croix de Guerre medals.

JOSIE-JEEP

32. Baker on stage during her last show, 'Joséphine à Bobino', on 25 March 1975 in Paris. In this scene, she sings while sitting on the 'Josie-Jeep' in a military-type uniform evoking her wartime troop entertainment tours in North Africa and the Middle East.

In the days that followed, they gradually made their way back across the desert, retracing their steps along the same demanding route that they had taken some weeks before. They suffered terribly from the cold and were taken aback at the sight of the rudimentary graves that had appeared along the roadside. Numerous unfortunate individuals had lost their lives in road accidents or from mines exploding when they had taken just a few steps off the road. The journey was punctuated by frequent stops along the way at camps and impromptu gatherings of soldiers they encountered on their route. And Baker was always game to perform.

On their arrival in Algiers in late November, they found the city packed and no accommodation available for them. During their absence, de Gaulle had finally managed to gain the upper hand over Giraud by means of the CFLN. Composed of delegates nominated by Resistance movements and pre-war parliamentarians who had not voted for Pétain in 1940, it was intended as a mouthpiece for French public opinion, in the absence of parliament. Gaullists dominated the CFLN, and when it first met, Giraud was attacked amidst demands for more Resistance representatives to be included.[116] Outvoted, and lacking the know-how to fight back, Giraud bowed to the inevitable and submitted his resignation from the co-presidency on 9 November 1943. He would gradually fade from the picture.

With Algiers now overfull, Baker, Abtey and Menebhi were forced to camp out in a doctor's surgery for a few nights. Abtey discovered that, as he had suspected, in the confusion of the Gaullist takeover his intelligence had been overlooked, and he felt that he was getting the brush-off. Adverse attitudes towards him had been aggravated by reports that had reached the hierarchy of the BCRA in Algiers about his disagreements with diplomats in Cairo in relation to Baker's gala there and his refusal to follow their recommendations.[117] Baker's outspokenness with certain French diplomats had also been noticed. Her tendency to reproach them if she felt they were not ardent enough in their support for de Gaulle or sensitive enough to the needs of the local Arab populations was not always appreciated.[118]

JOSEPHINE BAKER'S SECRET WAR

Nonetheless, Brousset was delighted with the achievements of their mission. He was particularly impressed by the impact of Menebhi's contribution. He and Abtey agreed that Menebhi had shown his potential and could continue to be a valuable asset for France, as a propaganda and intelligence agent in North African circles. With such a role for him in mind, Brousset wrote letters of introduction for Abtey to take to the local military authorities in Marrakech. In these letters he emphasised Menebhi's achievements on the trip, highlighting that '[t]hroughout the Islamic world, Menebhi was a skilful and enlightened propagandist for the cause of a free, strong and regenerated France' and asking for him to be shown good will by the local French authorities.[119] For his part, Menebhi, previously a British protégé, made a formal application for French protection, a gesture which confirmed his attachment to France.[120] With no further business in the Algerian capital and exhausted from the trip, Baker, Abtey and Menebhi decided to head back to Marrakech to recover.

Soon after their return in early December 1943, once both Baker and Abtey had settled back into Menebhi's palace in Marrakech, Paillole asked them to look after one François Mitterrand for a few days – the future French president, known then by the cover names 'Captain Monier' or 'Morland'.[121] Mitterrand had been taken prisoner in 1940 and had escaped to the southern zone of France, where he took up positions in Vichy, working to support POWs. However, he also began to organise a Resistance movement with escaped POWs and ex-soldiers, and left Vichy in January 1943 to continue this work clandestinely. Warned that he was in danger of arrest, in November 1943 he managed to get out of France and escape to London.

In a move orchestrated by Henri Frenay, leader of the Resistance movement Combat (and recently appointed 'minister for prisoners of war' by the CFLN), Mitterrand was ordered to Algiers to meet de Gaulle, in the hope that he could muster support for his Resistance activities.[122] De Gaulle, however, had plans for his nephew, Michel Cailliau, also a former POW operating with the code name 'Charrette' to lead this POW arm of the Resistance. The two men found themselves pitted against each other for the leadership of an overarching merged POW Resistance organisation. While Frenay was very taken with Mitterrand, Cailliau was suspicious of his Vichy past – and de Gaulle was sympathetic to his nephew's concerns, since Mitterrand was also reported to have Giraudist sympathies. The Gaullist intelligence services thus sought to keep Mitterrand in Algiers and prevent him from returning to France to carry on his Resistance work; however, their machinations were frustrated by Giraud's team, which secretly smuggled him to Morocco. There, under Paillole's orders, Baker and Abtey provided him with accommodation for several days in Menebhi's Marrakech palace in the medina, where they were staying.

Through their contacts with British intelligence, a place was found for him on an RAF plane to London (on which General Montgomery was also travelling).[123] From there, Mitterrand was able to make his way back to mainland France to carry on his Resistance work, and with Frenay's support would eventually take over the POW movement.[124] Baker's position and her links with French and British intelligence continued to serve her undercover needs throughout 1943. At some point during her stay in Morocco, her ex-husband Jean Lion came to see her. Their divorce had finally been granted in 1941 and he had moved to North Africa and joined the Resistance. Alarmed by the anti-Jewish legislation that was being introduced by Vichy, now based in Casablanca, he asked her to arrange papers for his family to get to safety in Brazil.[125] Her contacts with the French intelligence services evidently made it possible for her to do this.[126]

Since their return to Marrakech, Baker and Abtey had both noticed a step change in their friends' attitudes, which during their absence had grown increasingly strident. They were becoming increasingly focused on discussions around nationalism and the need for Moroccan independence.[127] Events in the Levant had taken the course that they had all feared, and it had become the first battlefield of decolonisation. France looked as if it was increasingly being outmanoeuvred, hurtling towards the loss of one of its most treasured colonial possessions. As 1943 drew to a close, Abtey sent

Brousset reports insisting that French administrators were allowing themselves to be misled into believing that the Americans had reduced their intelligence and propaganda activities in the area. To the contrary, he cautioned that the Americans were still promoting anti-French propaganda behind the scenes, with the complicity of the British. He also voiced his concern that events in Lebanon were fuelling independence aspirations.[128] Moroccans had drawn two key lessons from that episode. First, that France had been incapable of maintaining the status quo and had been obliged to bring in an Allied foreign power, to which the CFLN had been forced to defer. Secondly, it was now clear that the Moroccan nationalists would not necessarily have to wait until the end of the war to press their demands for independence, and that these demands were likely to be supported by the British and the Americans.[129] If the British, who had less of a presence in North Africa than in the Middle East, did not come through for them in Morocco, the nationalists had their eye on another foreign power that had led them to believe it might be helpful: America.

An important aspect of Baker's travels across North Africa and the Middle East is that they reveal how her affiliation with de Gaulle and her support for France necessarily placed her firmly in opposition to the ambitions of the Arab nationalists, who were seeking independence. Her commitment to France, as well as her Gaullist sympathies, therefore placed her in a pro-colonial nexus. While Abtey's account conveys a strength of feeling about the need to protect France's interests in the Middle East, such expressions are less evident in Baker's autobiography. It is, however, clear that Baker did not position herself on the side of the nationalists. For all the efforts of Abtey and Baker to counsel patience, they witnessed a growing militancy among the Moroccan members of their entourage, and support for de Gaulle was not guaranteed.

Abtey reported to Brousset that Menebhi had been well received by Glaoui on his first meeting after their return. Glaoui had congratulated him on his successful trip and applauded his support for the French. Menebhi related his firm conviction that the pasha had gone back to being 'very French'. Glaoui's son Brahim, on the other hand, had shown no hesitation in voicing his criticism of the French and appeared very anglophile. When he caught sight of the Cross of Lorraine pinned to Menebhi's robes, he said contemptuously: 'So now you've also turned into one of those Gaullists.'[130]

Baker and Abtey knew that if their influential contacts at the palace were won over to the nationalist cause and publicly threw their support behind it, the movement would be legitimised in the eyes of hundreds of others. Encouraged by the momentum that nationalism was gaining across the country, that same month, December 1943, three Moroccan nationalists announced the launch of the independence party Hizb al-Istiqlal.[131] The situation was coming to a head, and confrontation with the protectorate authorities would be inevitable.

6

LIEUTENANT BAKER
(1944–1945)

Over Christmas 1943, Baker and Abtey ensconced themselves in the comfort of their Marrakech residence. They were still recovering from the immense demands of their trip to the Middle East. Every time they socialised with their Moroccan friends, they were drawn into heated discussions about the country's future and the need for Moroccans to have more control over their country's destiny. Baker did her best to defuse their resentment against the protectorate authorities and told them that they should have confidence in de Gaulle, who would take their needs into account. She knew her friends trusted her judgement and she advised caution: 'You have to understand that the country is not yet ready for independence. The time will come, but it will take years to prepare.'[1] The insistent calls for independence that had been building across the Arab world were now pervasive in French North Africa. Moroccan nationalists, like those in the Middle Eastern nations, could sense that the colonial order was shifting, and they wanted to seize their moment.

The uncompromising position taken by the new Gaullist resident-general in Morocco, Gabriel Puaux, had contributed to the emergence of the militant stance of the nationalists, which had gained traction across the country. Formerly high commissioner in Syria and Lebanon, Puaux had been nominated by the CFLN to replace Noguès in June 1943, and since then had consistently taken a firm line with the nationalists. He had been dismissive about their demonstrations in Rabat in September 1943, and reported to the CFLN that they were no more than a reaction to the difficulties of food supply and were of no political importance. General Georges Catroux on the other hand, who was both general governor of Algeria and the CFLN's 'commissioner for Moslem affairs', was alert to the growth of Moroccan nationalism. He urged de Gaulle to start negotiations with the sultan to allow Moroccans a greater role in administration. Puaux, however, maintained his position: hostile to any political reform, he was prepared to use force, if necessary, to keep order and ensure that French authority was respected.[2]

Now in control, de Gaulle made it clear that one of the key priorities for the French government-in-waiting was to protect and maintain French power in the colonies. Baker's Moroccan circle now realised that, despite Baker's reassuring words, the Gaullists would not readily grant Moroccans more involvement in the administration of the protectorate, and certainly had no intention of considering independence. Baker and Abtey understood that they were fighting a losing battle in their attempts to keep their friends onside. Despite their best efforts, it had become increasingly clear that the independence movement was going to take dramatic steps to press its demands. Trouble was brewing, and Baker's calls for prudence fell on deaf ears amidst the growing wave of nationalist fervour that swept Morocco. The situation exploded early in 1944.

On 11 January, the new nationalist movement Hizb al-Istiqlal, emboldened by an apparent surge in support for it, and confident of tacit support from the sultan, decided to make its manifesto for independence public. With explicit reference to the Atlantic Charter, it demanded Moroccan independence and the installation of a democratic regime in agreement with the sultan. This move triggered a wave of unrest among Moroccans across the country. Puaux acted decisively. He delivered to the sultan a 'frankly worded note' from de Gaulle, and at a meeting with the sultan on 14 January made it clear that no change to the protectorate agreements would be countenanced. The joint communiqué issued on 17 January cited the sultan's wish that 'Morocco's future should develop in the

context of French friendship and with respect to the existing trea-
ties'.[3] René Massigli, the commissioner of foreign affairs for the
CFLN, also met the sultan at the end of the month and explained
that, while the CFLN was sympathetic to the aspirations of the
Moroccan people, any unilateral challenge to the protectorate
treaty, especially while the country was still at war, would be
rejected. The belief in French circles was that the nationalists had
been encouraged to take this action by German agents – at least,
this was the public line.

The following day, several leading members of the Hizb al-Istiqlal
were arrested by the security services on charges of collaboration
with the Germans. Riots ensued at Rabat, Salé and Fez, along with
demonstrations. French troops fired on the crowds, killing several
men and some children. The sultan, fearing unnecessary bloodshed,
decided to distance himself from Hizb al-Istiqlal. Although his belief
in the necessity for independence never wavered, he shied away
from offering Hizb al-Istiqlal his support openly in a way that would
legitimise the nationalist movement in the eyes of the Moroccan
people.[4] Moroccan independence claims were kept in check for the
time being; and by blaming the Germans, attention had been shifted
away from the Americans, who assured the French that they were
'hostile to any disturbances that might damage the war effort'.[5]

The exact role played by Baker is not entirely clear, but she
evidently worked her contacts and attempted to restrain the most
extreme elements within the nationalist movement, amidst fears
that the situation might lead to violence. Alla Dumesnil later paid
tribute to her activity during this period: 'Her action in Morocco
during the turbulent period end of 1943, early 1944 was officially
recognised as having powerfully supported the very precarious
situation of France.'[6] She stressed that Baker

> had a very important political role in North Africa, very impor-
> tant. Particularly in Morocco where she operated with the
> Glaouis, the pashas, all the important Arabs and the Americans.
> Morocco owes a lot to Josephine, French Morocco as it was at
> that time.[7]

Paillole also commended Baker's role, suggesting that, had she not been absent from Morocco during the run-up to these unfortunate events, they may have been prevented:

> I think that if Josephine, who was very active in Arab circles, had been there, we would have avoided the major nationalist incidents ... She would have saved lives. As fate would have it, Josephine was once again put out of action by illness.[8]

So it was that, while these dramatic events played out, Baker was taken suddenly and seriously ill in Marrakech while Menebhi was walking with her in the gardens of the Mamounia.[9] Deeply worried about her as she lay suffering in her quarters at his palace, and in an effort to alleviate her pain, Menebhi paid for some of the poverty-stricken residents of the medina to pray for her, and even sacrificed a sheep in a desperate quest to ensure her recovery. Baker heard the prayers coming through her window. However, once she was taken to hospital, it was discovered that she required immediate surgery for an intestinal blockage. Although the intervention was serious, on this occasion Baker rallied more quickly than the doctors had anticipated and was soon back on her feet.[10]

In Algiers, de Gaulle's ascendancy was now complete, and the more coherent power structures that came into operation gradually extended to the intelligence services. On 20 November 1943, the two competing intelligence services had been merged to form a new General Directorate of Special Services, which was entrusted to Jacques Soustelle, a civilian and a committed Gaullist. Abtey's expertise in North African politics was finally recognised: his weeks of waiting were rewarded when he was assigned an undercover mission to report on the activities of the Moroccan independence movement. His familiarity with the Moroccan political context meant that he was well placed to take it on. Thanks to Baker, he had access to several individuals in the nationalist movement, including their friend Moulay Larbi, who had fully embraced the cause.[11]

Baker in uniform

Once she had fully recovered, Baker left Abtey in Morocco to carry out his mission to report on the activities of the nationalists and moved to Algiers, where she started working in a more formal military capacity. In recognition of her effectiveness at promoting the Fighting French, on 23 May she was officially enlisted as a second lieutenant propaganda officer in the auxiliary services of the Women's Air Force (Forces féminines de l'Air, FFA).[12] This was appropriate, as it played to Baker's abilities as a pilot and her personal respect for the air force. The American military newspaper *Stars and Stripes* later reported in its London edition that Baker had pointed to the wings on her crisp blue uniform and said: 'You don't get these for singing. When I joined up you had to have at least 50 hours flying time.'[13]

Most importantly, Baker was now able to gain official recognition of her visible entertainment duties as part of her work as a 'soldier' operating in the interests of France. Her final contract included a formal request by her to forfeit her pay,[14] and she was also given official dispensation to wear civilian clothes.[15]

The formation of French female volunteers to the air force to which Baker was assigned was a branch of the Corps féminin des transmissions (CFT), the equivalent of the Women's Signal Corps, founded in December 1942 by Colonel Lucien Merlin. In March 1944, there were 400 women members of the air force – known, along with those from other forces, as Merlinettes. The women were trained in Algiers at a school directed by Major Alla Dumesnil, who had been responsible for the female volunteers to the air force since April 1941.[16] The daughter of an admiral, Dumesnil had been born in Russia and, as the child of a naval officer, had travelled around the world as her father was posted from one place to another. As a young adult, she had divided her time between Paris and London, and had homes in both cities. Finding herself in London at the outbreak of the war, she had stayed there, initially working as an interpreter in hospitals treating injured French soldiers. She had heard de Gaulle's June 1940 appeal and decided to join the Free French, rather than return to her family in France. She became part of the women's auxiliary forces based in London, the 'formations féminines'.[17] She was keen from the outset to create a section dedicated to the air force (to reflect her love of aviation), but initially failed to secure support from the British: they were not disposed to fund separate strands of the women's auxiliary forces, preferring in the early days to stay with one female grouping. Undeterred, she had continued to push hard and eventually managed to grow her air force section little by little. Once she had recruited sixty women, she was able to secure separate barracks.

In 1943, when the Gaullist army was sent to Algeria, Dumesnil relocated, accompanied by her women, and they were united with others that General Bouscat, head of the French air force, had recruited locally. She was promoted to the French rank of commandant (the British equivalent being major or squadron leader),[18] thus becoming, at the age of thirty, the youngest commandant in the French army.[19] In the Algerian capital, Dumesnil set up a series of education centres to train the volunteers in those functions that were needed to support the work of the air force. These included specialist secretaries for military headquarters, interpreters, drivers, communications specialists, health care operatives and social workers.[20]

For the rest of the war, until she was decommissioned in September 1945, Baker would invariably appear wearing the official uniform. This uniform was described by General Martial Valin at the time as

> khaki, like that of their sisters in the territorial army or the navy, but they wear the distinctive signs of the French air force. These are the black tie and the dark blue police cap adorned with the air force eagle insignia, which also appears on the shoulder tabs of the jacket with, on the right breast, the badge of FAFL [*Forces aériennes françaises libres*, the Free French Air Forces], consisting of the tricolour with the Cross of Lorraine topped by the winged star.[21]

Over the two previous years, Baker had already taken to adopting varying degrees of military attire, as we have seen. This was symbolic of her own sense of military engagement, in a bid to show that she had a role that went beyond that of a mere entertainer. Now dressed in full French air force uniform, she impressed those who saw her with the weight of her changed image. A *Daily Mail* reporter commented:

> Josephine Baker in uniform. Who would have thought that even a world war could have wrought such a transformation? But I saw the glamorous coffee-coloured star striding with easy grace into my little hotel the other day wearing a very smart dark blue uniform with gold buttons and a dark blue side cap on her ebony hair. She looked as young and as lovely as ever. Recent stories of her demise have greatly amused her. She has been singing for ENSA and for the French Army in camps all over the Middle East and North Africa. Hence the uniform.[22]

Others like *The Tatler and Bystander*, for example, could not resist poking fun, teasing that she was in a uniform because of the banana shortage.[23]

The uniform had its desired effect in conveying that Baker's image had changed. This was something that she would capitalise on. For example, after the war, in chronicling her experiences, the magazine *Point de vue* would later reflect on the importance of this step: 'She's in uniform now. She's no longer the vivacious, high-spirited Josephine of the Paris stage. She is wearing the austere uniform of an air force officer.'[24] For commentators outside the military, Baker's uniform seemed to make her the epitome of seriousness, compared to her earlier pre-war image; but there were those in the army who saw her in a somewhat different light. While not doubting the sincerity of her commitment, Dumesnil also acknowledged that Baker had another, more trivial side, in line with her celebrity persona. This frivolity, she explained, surfaced in Baker's attitude to her uniform:

> Josephine was – and remained until the end – very beautiful, very upright, very well built, and in an air force uniform you

don't wear a belt or a harness. And one morning, she came into my office and started her normal patter. 'My little Commander Cherie.' So, I said to her. 'What on earth are you wearing?' She had put on the leather double crossing over both her shoulders, and she was belted. She said, 'It's prettier, you can see me better like this.' And I said to her, 'But what are those campaign medals, Josephine?' And she was wearing them right across from her shoulder to her wrist. And she says: 'They're not campaigns, they look like a Christmas tree.' But if we calculated it, she was wearing the equivalent of 80 years of campaigns. So, then we had to find a way to persuade her to take them all off.[25]

With the CFLN in Algiers operating as a full-fledged French provisional government, encompassing many of the trappings of the French state, putting Baker in uniform only served to increase her impact and aid their cause. It shifted her persona from promoting the Gaullist cause to reflecting Gaullism's wider importance; in uniform, she was now working on behalf of the French nation.

A propaganda photograph of Baker dressed in her air force uniform, posing with Dumesnil, had already been circulating widely in the press.[26] The image is perfectly staged. It places the women in an office, looking up at the camera, which is apparently distracting them from their duties. A framed photograph of de Gaulle hangs to their left, and a poster over Baker's head affiliates their activities with those of the French Resistance. Baker is standing, while Dumesnil is seated at her desk. Both women look off camera. The same scene is replicated in a propaganda film, *Filles de France*, designed to encourage recruitment. The film follows the women volunteers in the Free French Air Forces from their training centre in North Africa through to their various (mainly female) activities, including working as secretaries, interpreters, nurses and ambulance drivers. In a short scene, a lively and enthusiastic Baker joins Dumesnil in her office, vigorously gesticulating while a voice off screen explains in French: 'And here is Josephine, yes Lieutenant

Josephine Baker, bringing back a cheque for four and a half million francs for the Resistance from a tour of Egypt.'[27] It was obviously a publicity stunt designed for the propaganda photo shoot and French newsreels, as the tour had in fact been completed months before. However, it demonstrates that Baker had become central to a propaganda strategy on the part of the French air force that was directed at promoting the importance of its contribution to the liberation of the French people.[28] The question of the role of the air force was a particularly topical one at a time when the French mainland was suffering the intense Allied bombing. The French air force was also struggling with an image that had been seriously undermined by its failure to defeat the German attacks in May–June 1940, and needed any boost to its image that Baker could provide.[29]

Les Filles de l'Air

Baker was billeted in barracks in Algiers and Oran, along with the other women she was serving with, and she undertook her military duties without question. According to Dumesnil, 'She would always join in without the slightest discussion, doing all the chores we had to do, the parades, getting up at dawn. [She was] not at all the big star of the screen or the music hall. She was really very straightforward.'[30] Nonetheless, she would regularly be granted leave to appear at fundraising galas and to deliver performances. She was never subject to the disciplinary rules of the air force, as from the time of her inclusion she undertook theatrical tours for active units (troops) and participated in galas in aid of troops, prisoners and deportees.[31] Dumesnil would later be a vocal backer of Baker's wartime activities, supporting her later claims for more robust recognition of her work.[32] One of the only women in the surviving sources to discuss Baker, Dumesnil's evaluation of her personality and achievements carries particular weight. She refers to Baker as being one of the 'most courageous and the most colourful' individuals she had under her.[33] When talking about her experiences, Baker explained:

There were eighty of us living in barracks in Oran, with links by car and by plane within a radius of several hundred kilometres . . . Now I only act on orders. Living in a communal environment, with discipline, risk and often danger, is something new and extraordinary for me.[34]

She also later told journalists in Paris and in London that her 'main job has been ambulance driving and aiding the wounded'.[35]

In a 1943 radio broadcast, General Valin christened the women 'les Filles de l'Air'. He makes a point of emphasising that they were valued by the military, explaining that the women were 'a genuine part of the Air Force' with

the 'inflated' mentality of the aviator. I am often obliged to moderate their ambitions – no, they don't seek promotion, but they do want to learn to fly, become parachutists and most of them wish to remain in the air force after the war in an operational capacity . . . the women originate from all social classes and marital statuses and serve in a wide range of capacities in the services linked to aviation . . . little by little, we are training these auxiliaries to take over the positions hitherto occupied by men, excluding combat.

Referencing Dumesnil, he explains that 'the officer in charge of these auxiliaries is attached to my Military Cabinet and is regarded as a real General Staff officer'.[36] Valin's words 'genuine' and 'real' reveal his efforts to ensure that the women were taken seriously as part of the military. In a similar way, in introducing Baker's role, the editorial of the internal forces paper, Les Ailes, was at pains to underline the sincerity of her commitment and justify her appointment. Readers were reassured that

It's not an honorary rank, but a function that she fulfils conscientiously; she has genuinely been mobilised . . . However, when an army has an artist in its ranks, it takes every opportunity to exploit her talents. At concerts organised by the Ministry of the

Air in aid of its social causes, Lieutenant Baker makes way for Josephine Baker. As an officer she must obviously bow to the orders of her superiors. As an artist, she quite simply bends to the will of her own generous nature.[37]

All the while, Baker continued to perform – especially in Algiers, where the Military High Command frequently mobilised her presence for celebrations or asked her to perform at air force benefits. A *Gala des Ailes*, for example, held on 20 May 1944, was noted for Baker's contribution. She 'crown[ed] the evening's success. Always beautiful and exciting, passionate to her very core, singing with exquisite humour and a deep passion, a repertoire that is worthy only of her, the great star enchanted the audience.'[38] Baker did not sing exclusively for French troops. Donald Wyatt (area field director of welfare workers) arranged for Baker to entertain the American officers and men of an infantry regiment in North Africa in a context where the soldiers had complained of the lack of entertainment.[39]

Mission to Corsica

On the one occasion that Baker left North Africa, to visit Corsica, she had quite an adventure. The trip was initiated by the mayor of Ajaccio, who approached Baker to do a propaganda tour of Corsica in support of the Fighting French. He indicated a strong show of support for de Gaulle highlighting the involvement of the Free French forces in the invasion would provide the Americans (who were still ambivalent about the general) with clear evidence of his popularity. Baker's superiors approved the idea, and it was agreed that both Zimmer and Abtey should join the mission. The date was set for 6 June 1944. Early that morning, as the group convened at the Algiers home of General Bouscat, where Baker was a regular guest,[40] Zimmer arrived with the exciting news of the Normandy landings, which he had heard from the British war correspondents staying in his hotel. None of them had been aware that it was imminent – not even Bouscat in his role as commander of the French air force – and they celebrated the moment.

Baker and her party made their way to the airfield in two cars to accommodate their luggage. They were joined by Bouscat and his wife, who had come to see them off. They were a little nervous when they saw their aircraft, a Caudron C440 Goéland known as a 'Seagull', but Bouscat reassured them that it was a sturdy machine. So they loaded up and took their seats, despite their uneasiness at its apparent fragility, dismissing from their thoughts the stories that had reached them of its recent failings. They settled themselves in, said their farewells and the plane prepared for take-off. Baker was looking forward to being back in mainland France, albeit on an island, for the first time in four years. Despite seeming to struggle to get off the ground, the heavily loaded plane made it into the air, and they were soon soaring above the Kabylia mountains. Baker's thoughts returned to the events in Normandy. 'What a magnificent day,' Abtey recalled her saying. 'How good it is to be alive at a time like this.'[41] They crossed the Mediterranean safely without encountering any signs of the enemy – which was just as well, as they had no way of defending themselves. They had just flown over the Sardinian coast when a violent vibration shook the aircraft. Something was wrong. One of the engines seemed to be failing, and after a loud banging noise, the propeller blade came to a complete halt. They anxiously waited to see what would happen, but the plane carried on towards the coast of Corsica, which they could now make out in the distance. Progress was slow, but the pilot was confident he would still get them to their destination on just one engine.

The aircraft continued to lose altitude and the pilot steered them into a creek, in an effort to clear the fast-approaching head-land. The plane lurched worryingly as the cliffside loomed straight in front of them. They shut their eyes as they saw the wall of granite coming at them, anticipating the shock of a direct impact. Somehow the plane pulled up just in time – only for the one functioning engine to burst into flames, due to the heat generated by the manoeuvre. The plane was now making a rapid descent towards the sea below. 'Hold on tight!' shouted the pilot. Before they hit the water, Zimmer somehow found time to gather up the huge Cross of Lorraine flag from the floor of the cabin and place it around Baker.

Then he threw himself in front of her to protect her from the worst effects of the crash.

Miraculously, the pilot managed to carry out a sea landing and no one was injured, even though the main body of the aircraft split. Water poured through the cabin windows smashed by the mechanic, and they were all completely soaked, as was their luggage. With the plane at a standstill, they climbed onto one of the wings as the 'Seagull' floated towards the coast. 'To our amazement, we saw a group of Black men on the beach calling out to us as they threw themselves into the water and started to swim towards us.'[42] The entry in the military logbook explained that a

> detachment of Senegalese riflemen . . . pushed the plane to the shore and then carried the shipwrecked passengers to the beach on their broad shoulders, with Josephine Baker in the lead. It must be said that they didn't have any swimming trunks![43]

Baker later remarked:

> And so I arrived on French soil, on a man's shoulders, draped in our Cross of Lorraine flag. How's that for a theatrical entrance and I really didn't do it on purpose . . . My African heritage would have led me to kiss the ground in gratitude if I hadn't been in uniform.[44]

Less than an hour later, they were all safely reunited at the aviators' mess, toasting their good fortune over a bottle of wine.

During this tour of Corsica, Baker agreed exceptionally that she would sing for civilians, as well as soldiers. Stages were erected in public squares in towns and villages across the island. The day after her performance in Ajaccio, the party flew to Sardinia where, at the airbase in Cagliari, Baker sang exclusively for the Free French airmen, who were readying themselves for their next sortie in the coming hours:

> She sang with an emotion she had never felt before, because from her stage, under the bright glare of the headlights of the

lorries, she could see hundreds of men in boiler suits ready to take off in a massive formation for Occupied France . . . 'I wanted them to take with them a vision of Paris, the spirit of the capital, the soul of France.'[45]

The following morning, when she looked across to the row of 'Marauders' bearing the Cross of Lorraine lined up next to the airfield, she was saddened to see the gaps left by those who had not returned from their night operation. Their eight-day mission complete, they flew back to Algeria.

Baker returns to mainland France

Paris was liberated in August 1944, but it was October by the time Baker finally reached the French mainland. Before her departure from North Africa, she made a last visit to the Liberty Club in Casablanca.[46] With her to Europe went the little dog she had adopted and christened 'Mitraillette' ('Machine-gun' in English): 'I called him Mitraillette, because he would pee all the time, little sharp bursts, tinkle, tinkle, tinkle, five or six drops as he lifted his paw.'[47] She took the animal in while she was impatiently awaiting her repatriation, 'with a group of sixty women' in a nun's convent in Guyotville, which had been transformed into a centre for the 'Women's Air Corps'.[48] The dog soon became the mascot of her unit. When their orders to leave finally came through, they were taken by military train 'in field uniform, with our rucksacks, water bottles and sponge bags with us',[49] to embark on a Liberty ship at the port of Mers-El-Kébir. Animals were not allowed on board, so Baker hid the dog in her coat:[50]

All my other animals had disappeared in Africa. I didn't want to leave Mitraillette behind. He was passed around from bag to bag until the storage man took care of him. And I disembarked with Mitraillette in Marseille.[51]

Her arrival was captured in a large photograph carried on the back page of the Marseille-based Gaullist *Hebdomadaire Illustré du*

M.L.N. (*Mouvement de Libération Nationale*) with the caption 'Do you recognise her?'[52] With her air force cap cocked to one side, dressed in fatigues belted at the waist, her satchel slung over her shoulder, she grins at the photographer. Needing no introduction to her readers, she must have been a heart-warming sight.

From there, Baker was taken to Paris by car. Her arrival in the capital led to a blaze of carefully staged publicity, and she capitalised on this press attention to promote stories of her wartime activities and demonstrate her commitment to France. The French public learnt from these interviews not only that Baker was alive, but also that she had been a patriot and a Gaullist. She made a point of emphasising her identity as a soldier in articles like the one which appeared in *Défense de la France* on 11 October 1944.[53]

Baker's photograph on the front page shows her dressed in a heavy army uniform overcoat, striding down the Champs-Élysées. She looks confident and happy, visibly delighted to be back in her beloved city comfortably sporting this very different persona. The photo is placed under the striking headline, '*Je ne suis qu'un soldat*' – 'I am just a soldier'. The article immediately kicks off with a reference to 'J'ai deux amours':

> Josephine Baker was believed dead, considered lost, but when you have two loves, you don't die at 30, you don't succeed in losing Paris.

Conveying her identity and the importance of her ongoing role as a soldier was important to her: 'Until the war is over, I'll remain a soldier and I can say no more than that . . .' Explaining that she was in the air force, she continues: 'A soldier never talks about the tasks they perform' – but she does reveal that 'I carry out missions, but I also sing.' The exact nature of these missions is not explained, but we are to understand from this that she is not just involved in entertainment.

Baker enjoyed being courted by the press, and such articles were doubtless designed to function as propaganda, promoting Baker's role in the war effort. In underlining her military responsibilities, her interviews convey her patriotic commitment, but Baker holds back from revealing the full extent of what she did. Similarly, in a later article she also clearly hints that she is involved in more than she can say:

> Don't ask Josephine to tell you the whole story. A discreet secret closes her lips, which only open for words of friendship and hope, for songs, which are like professions of faith . . . A soldier like so many others in the huge and diverse 'war effort', Josephine Baker fought and then fell silent.[54]

Since her military duties were ongoing, reports acknowledged that she was still giving all her time to the French aviation corps. 'She is expected to remain in Paris for only a short time with a minimum of entertaining' – although there were a couple of luncheon parties held in her honour.[55] She was not carrying herself as a star. 'There is no fanfare for her arrival. She simply slipped into town like a good soldier and went to work.'[56] She explained to reporters that her greatest wish, if she were not in service, would be to appear at the Casino de Paris again, and that she considered 'her present exist-ence, in which community spirit, discipline, adventure and often danger replace the triumphs of the stage, a magnificent life'.[57]

While in Paris, Baker returned to see what had become of her beloved home in Le Vésinet. Occupied by German officers of the Kriegsmarine, the German navy, it had been used by them as a mess hall. They had left nothing but the bare walls.[58] The Americans had also spent time in the villa. While she set about the renovation work, Baker stayed in a hotel on the Avenue des Champs-Élysées and turned her attention to performing at a series of benefit concerts, raising funds largely for charities and organisations patronised by de Gaulle and the air force. A widely recognised pre-war figure, she was a reassuring presence for a French public coming to terms with the impact of the Occupation and a trans-formed political landscape. She inspired confidence in de Gaulle and the new elites who, unlike her, enjoyed virtually no visual recognition.

As part of her ongoing propaganda role, she appeared on the radio and in short films, including one entitled *Magazine récréatif*, aimed at an audience of soldiers.⁵⁹ These appearances demonstrate Baker's effectiveness as a propaganda tool and give a sense of how she must have come across during her benefit concerts. After being introduced, Baker goes straight into her signature anthem – 'J'ai deux amours'. Though she had been singing it for years, the song resonated more powerfully during the war. The lyrics evoke a longing for a homeland and a capital city, from which many of those listening were distanced. In addition, her performance is inter-spliced with shots of Paris, on the one hand, and an exotic location on the other, alluding to Baker's pre-war image, when she had become the perfect expression of the French colonial fantasy. At the same time, they also make a clear reference to the importance of the colonial territories, so central to the identity of the Free French forces. This editing therefore astutely merges Baker's past with her commitment to the Free French. Her uniform, the way she wears her hair – everything underlines the seriousness of her role and her status as a soldier. The film shows how Baker's fluid cosmopolitan identity was repurposed for contemporary propaganda purposes. As the camera pans round the audience, we understand her impact from the reactions of the soldiers, some of whom appear near to tears. Even in trousers – very unusual in images of Baker – and without the glamour of her normal ward-robe, Baker was a mesmerising presence, and her transition to a different performing style was complete, as an American reporter observed:

> Dressed in military uniform which modestly hides her Dietrich-rivalling stems [legs], she explained she has of neces-sity had to alter drastically her routine built around alternate French and American songs. Gone, for example, are those impudent wriggles of the derrière which used to cause beads of sweat to form on the front-row baldheads. 'Not dignified,' the actress who used to shock the puritanical murmured puritanically.⁶⁰

Enter Jo Bouillon

While planning her entertainment schedule, as the Théâtre aux Armées was no longer operational, Baker was tasked by senior military officers with putting together a troupe to perform a series of benefit shows for both soldiers and civilians in the devastated areas along the Mediterranean coast.[61] She needed to find an orchestra, and was advised to contact the band leader Jo Bouillon.[62] She was already acquainted with him. A violinist and graduate of the Paris Conservatoire, he had appeared with many orchestras and dance bands in the early 1930s and had accompanied famous Parisian stars. He was used to a tiring schedule of tours; but unlike Baker, he had stayed in Paris throughout the Occupation, playing in restaurants and theatres. In autumn 1944, Baker tracked him down to the popular venue Boeuf sur le Toit, where he was performing with his orchestra. As she was still in uniform, and nightclubs were strictly forbidden, she left him a message asking to meet him. He was hesitant when she put it to him that he and his orchestra might join her tour: they would have to abandon all their current engagements for an unknown length of time. However, a week later, he and his twenty-five musicians launched their participation at a benefit in Marseille in aid of the city's war victims.[63] While Baker continued to offer her services for free, in order to ensure the involvement of members of his orchestra with family responsibilities, their busy schedule included some paid radio broadcasts.[64] Baker would appear in the second part of the show to deliver a repertoire that included some new songs with ten costume changes designed to promote the Paris couturiers who were supporting the galas.[65]

Bouillon was fascinated by her double persona:

I study her every night . . . Out of uniform, carefully made up and coiffed, she gives it her all: her smile, her vitality, her joie de vivre. And then she is back to being Officer Baker, a bit boyish, unassuming, formal, anxious to do her duty. A dual personality, each one as captivating as the other.[66]

After Marseille, they toured along the coast to Monte Carlo, with stops at Toulon, Cannes and Nice. From there they made their way back to Paris. Back in the capital, Baker made frequent appearances on the Parisian stages, where the music-hall scene was gradually resurfacing, and where she was much in demand. She appeared with Noël Coward at the first major ENSA concert for Allied troops, on 15 November 1944 at the Marigny theatre, which Basil Dean succeeded in requisitioning.[67] Later in November, she did a show at the Paramount Cinema, under the aegis of the Ministry of Aviation.[68] On 2 December 1944, she performed at a grand fête held at the Vél d'Hiv, in the presence of the repatriated communist leader Maurice Thorez.[69] There were various other major dates throughout the month, and then in late December, she toured the Italian front with Edith Piaf.[70]

Subsequently, Baker and Bouillon were instructed to perform to the French First Army as it advanced eastwards:

I had passes like those carried by diplomats and an undated permanent military permit. We played and sang at random, on the occasional roadside, accompanied by a guitar, or in barns, by the light of a few paraffin lamps.[71]

At times, the weather was severe. In early 1945, they were in liberated Alsace. Film survives of Josephine visiting a camp in the snow. She laughs and jokes with the soldiers, wearing a heavy sheepskin coat and a scarf tied around her head. She hands out cigarettes and they look on as she struggles to get her jeep going and navigate it through the snow.[72]

Following the advance of the soldiers, from town to town, at Mulhouse, Nancy and Colmar, with the help of the local Resistance, we opened the theatres so the soldiers could come on their days off ... Wherever we went I looked for Black soldiers. I saw many poor Senegalese riflemen whose feet were frozen.[73]

From Alsace, in March 1945 they followed the French army into Germany, the first time Baker had been back in the country since 1929. When they arrived at the Buchenwald concentration camp, just days after survivors had been liberated, Baker volunteered to sing to

> the wretched dying deportees [who] were there, lying on the planks when I came. They were smiling all the same. They were trying … They had an armband with the Cross of Lorraine around their scrawny arm … I had to smile. I had to sing. I sang to them 'In My Village', as if I were singing for each of them, going from group to group, in the barracks.[74]

In Sigmaringen, where the Vichy government had fled in August 1944 during the Allied advance, Baker was received by French generals seated in the place of honour at the monumental dining table.[75] 'I was without doubt the first woman of colour to be admitted to the throne room, where the blinkered scoundrels who had served Hitler's madness had ruthlessly pursued their racist policies.'[76] Later that year, Harry Janes' constant efforts to bring Baker to England finally bore fruit.

England in April–May 1945

Ever since their last meeting in Marrakech in the summer of 1943, Janes and Baker had been in touch, trying to find a gap in her commitments that would allow her to visit England for an ENSA-sponsored series of performances. In their exchanges, they quickly moved from formality to warmth on both sides. Janes suggested that he might throw a party for her in his home during her proposed visit.[77] But despite genuine good will, their efforts to bring her over in 1944 had failed, due to her illness and the other demands on her time made by the French air force.[78] Their letters reveal a growing affection between the two. Their desire to maintain a friendship was mutual. Writing in May 1944, Baker asserted to Janes, 'We are good friends you and I, aren't we.'[79] The French authorities, however, did not take kindly to Baker's attempts to make plans directly with Janes. In late 1944, an official at the French Ministry of Aviation called ENSA with a message for the director, Basil Dean, complaining that Baker 'has no right whatsoever to enter into negotiations' and asserting that 'she is under military orders, and it is impossible for her to leave France again.'[80]

Eventually, in spring 1945, after several exchanges between the relevant British and French authorities, Josephine's availability for Allied purposes was agreed and gaps were identified in her busy schedule. General Valin's office, which oversaw all the arrangements, finally authorised dates for her visit. During the planning phase, Valin insisted that a trip to York be included in her programme, so that she could visit the Free French airmen stationed there; Janes, however, expressed doubt as to whether she could incorporate the long journey north, in addition to her other commitments.

In the end, to satisfy all the demands for her presence, it was agreed that she would make two trips in quick succession. For the first, in late April, she would fly to London from Lille. This initial, five-day visit would focus on visits to military camps and factory shows for workers involved in the war effort. Then she would go to Switzerland to honour engagements there, returning to England on 9 May for more hospital and camp visits. Her trip would culminate in a major fundraising gala under the aegis of ENSA, in aid of the Association des amis des volontaires français (AVF – Association of Friends of the French Volunteers) in central London on 14 May 1945.[81] Basil Dean agreed that Baker could stay at the Savoy in London during her visit, as she was performing free of charge, and Janes assured him that she had been very reasonable when they had put her up in Shepheard's in Cairo.[82]

During her first visit, from 25–29 April, Baker gave fifteen performances in the five days she was in the country. She delivered camp shows, including at Hodgemoor and Dropmoor camps, Shenley Hospital, and factory shows at the General Aircraft Company in Feltham, Middlesex[83] and Creed and Company in Croydon.[84] On her return visit, Janes met Baker at Croydon Airport on 9 May at

17.50. It was the day after Victory in Europe Day, and her performances now became a part of the widespread celebrations that were taking place in London and across the country. Baker was put to work as soon as she arrived:

> From 19.30 that same day, she entertained wounded and dying repatriated British prisoners-of-war in Shenley and other hospitals until 01.00 hrs on 10th May. Many of these did not live to see the dawn . . .[85]

Baker also made other impromptu appearances at hospitals where repatriated British former prisoners of war were being cared for. Her plans to model Paris fashion in a show in the run-up to her main gala performance had to be cancelled, even though Baker had already secured many of the outfits. Several reasons were behind this decision, including Board of Trade restrictions, competition from British dress-making firms, difficulties in finding a suitable setting and the possibility that the show might overshadow the success of the gala, which was the primary aim of the tour. In addition, 'the French Embassy did not consider it politic to arrange such a function which might give the wrong impression'.[86] Presumably there was a fear that it might look like a misplaced effort to promote French business. The embassy also refused to authorise Bouillon's permissions to accompany Baker, so she had to rely on a local orchestra.

After recording some radio sessions for the BBC,[87] her gala took place at the Cambridge Theatre in London's Seven Dials on 14 May. It was billed as Baker's first appearance in London since 1940, and the first indoor theatrical event following on from the open-air Victory Day celebrations in the British capital. Along with Baker, there were contributions from Sir Cedric Hardwicke, who acted out a scene from his successful show 'Yellow Sands', and from comics Naunton Wayne, Eddie Gray and Noël Coward. Coward had initially been approached to introduce Baker and had agreed. Janes was then requested by the organising committee to ask whether he might also contribute to the programme on his own behalf, which he also agreed to do.[88] His rendition of a French song –which revealed his impeccable French accent – was a great hit. Baker, for her part, *France* reported, had thrown 'the crowd into ecstasy with her dazzling dress collection while she sang her repertoire of old and new songs. Her prestige dating from the period between the wars made everyone feel 20 years younger!'[89]

Picture Post carried a single-page spread with photographs of one of her camp performances. The reporter focused on hopes for the changed post-war world, where entertainers like Baker might be better accepted. This was doubtless a reference to racism, and a dig at segregation:

> London was never unkind to her. Perhaps that is how the world, sobered by nearly six years of war, will take its Josephine Bakers now. It will not be prostrate before them, nor will it stone them with stones, but will find them charming or leave them to those who do.[90]

The *News Review* spoke of how 'Fabulous Josephine Baker floodlights an otherwise gloomy London show.'[91] Baker was keen to highlight that she did not only entertain soldiers: 'Please don't get the impression that entertaining is my sole Army occupation.' She explained that she was an ambulance driver helping the wounded, as well as working for the Free French as a liaison officer without expanding any further on the exact nature of her role.[92]

On 16 May, Baker made a visit to RAF Elvington in Yorkshire, in accordance with Valin's request. A military base for two French squadrons, 2,500 airmen, under the command of Colonel Gaston Venot. The village became known as 'La petite France' for two months. French airman Pierre-Célestin Delrieu would later recall the visit:

> Josephine Baker, yes, Josephine Baker came to surprise us one day, in all her charm. Proudly wearing the cap and uniform of the French Air Force, with two gold stripes, we saw Lieutenant Baker climb on an improvised stage inside the largest of the

hangars. All the Frenchmen of Elvington wanted to see and hear her. Her beaming smile, her grace, her simplicity, her talent – it must be said – all contributed to victory; because, everywhere she went, she gave confidence to the troops, uplifting their morale. It was a spectacular triumph. The climactic point was when she sang 'I have two loves: my country and Paris'. There were cheers, encores and tears on people's faces. That evening, Josephine dined in the Officers' Mess. Inside the lounge, she was mingling, from group to group, relaxed, friendly and informal. I was lucky to have her sit in front of me, for a few moments, and able to chat with her, moved by her presence, moved by everything she represented from France, our country freed nine months ago but still so far from us.[93]

Baker's personal touch could also be powerfully moving for those she comforted during her hospital visits, as Janes explained:

In the course of a single evening, she sang, accompanied only by a pianist with a mini-piano, in the wards of as many hospitals as time and medical needs permitted. 'I'm willing to go on all night' she said to me. And would have done. To a few, alas, the last words they ever heard were fragments of one of her songs of that time 'I'll be seeing you'. Judging her movements, gestures and timing with unique skill she would walk up and down the ward, pausing at the bedside of a painfully afflicted serviceman and sing that passage exclusively to him. For myself, who has seen her perform in a variety of settings over a long period of time – from a few boards slung down on the sands of the desert to form a stage and lit only by the headlamps of an army lorry to the glittering panoply of . . . the Summer Casino at Monte Carlo – the most moving experience I ever had and perhaps Josephine herself has had, was during those improvised and make-shift appearances in English hospitals when the unification of European peoples and of all peoples seemed at last a possibility.[94]

And, he went on, she 'confided to me on the way home [back to Paris] that she would never again experience the emotion of that evening or give such a performance'.[95]

'A servant of the State'

Baker had made this confidence to Janes as they travelled together to the French capital after her London visit. He was with her at the 'express wish of Miss Baker, the Director of ENSA and the Service authorities . . . in order to try and overcome difficulties Miss Baker was having to obtain leave to entertain [Allied] troops in Burma and India'.[96] Janes, in his role as secretary to ENSA, had been trying to arrange this trip since autumn 1943, when, having heard of her work for the British troops in the Middle East, the service authorities had officially requested a visit from Baker to India and the Far East. Janes had conveyed this request to Josephine. Highlighting how this would fit with her interest in acting as a cultural ambassador, he wrote, 'there is other most important international work you can do which will greatly improve relations with the coloured people as well as white people'.[97] His comments reflect their mutual understanding of her ability to bridge diverse populations and bring peoples together. He was concerned that

> there is a tendency . . . to forget these men and there has been a great deal of criticism in the Press . . . that most of our artists have gone to France when the entertainment is so sadly needed further afield. There will be new shows in Paris and I am sure the French people will not let you go willingly, even for a short time, but I have been with you in the desert and I know that you will not forget the men who have spent so many years of their lives in the Burma jungle without seeing a European woman let alone a star!

Baker was very keen to get to India and Burma before the end of the hostilities, in order to boost the morale of the troops, as she had in North Africa. She had persuaded Janes to come with her to Paris to make a personal approach to those responsible for making the decision and accompany her to see General de Gaulle's chief of staff, so that they could personally secure the necessary authorisations from him in writing.[98]

When Janes saw the most senior generals of the French air force – General Bouscat and General Valin – they assured him, off the record, that they saw no objection to the tour. Janes even offered to send a French-speaking English star to cover the period of Baker's absence. The generals informed him, however, that the final word would rest with M. Charles Tillon, the minister of aviation. Unable to secure an interview with the minister himself, Janes put in a formal request via his personal secretary. The negative reply that finally arrived in early June explained that Baker could not be spared from her valuable work in France, and that her presence was needed at home to boost the low morale of civilian populations. It was a bitter disappointment for both Baker and Janes, neither of whom had expected it. Baker had already announced the planned tour to the press during her visit to England, when it had been reported that 'Miss Baker is preparing to go to the Pacific. She recently was "alerted" she disclosed.'[99] She had told the journalist Ollie Stewart that she was scheduled to leave France on 15 July, bound for India to entertain Allied troops and visit Pacific installations for three months. 'Though my doctor and friends have advised against this trip, I am determined to make it.'[100]

In light of this advance publicity for a tour that would not now take place, Janes was anxious for the French refusal to be kept quiet. First, because ENSA had been struggling to persuade stars to visit the region, and he had hoped that Baker's enthusiasm for the trip might serve to stimulate others. And secondly, he feared that 'if it should become known in the press that this act of grace has been refused, there will be considerable ill feeling'. Baker was 'terribly distressed' by the refusal of the Ministry of Aviation, despite Janes' assurances that he would continue to put pressure on the French government at the highest possible levels.[101]

He also did his best to galvanise his own hierarchy, pointing out to his ENSA colleagues that they had received a letter from General

Lattre de Tassigny only that week thanking ENSA for all its assistance in providing entertainment for the French First Army. As they had done this to support the French, who had no entertainment organisation of their own and sorely needed their help, he suggested that this point might be made privately, behind the scenes, as leverage to secure agreement for Baker's trip.[102] Mary Newell, an ENSA employee and personal friend of the British ambassador to France, Alfred Duff Cooper, wrote asking if he would make a direct approach to Tillon, explaining that 'the experience of Josephine going [to India and Burma] would do boundless good and perhaps act as a spur to some of our artists there'.[103] However, Duff Cooper did not feel that the time was right to make such a request. 'As you have no doubt seen from the newspapers,' he wrote, 'our relations with France are not happy at the present moment, and so I hesitate to ask favours of the French Ministry and thereby give them the opportunity of not granting them.'[104]

Unfortunately for Baker, she was once again caught in the crossfire of worsening Anglo-French relations, and it was this that had sabotaged the proposed trip. By the spring of 1945, de Gaulle, who was working hard to rebuild France's status on the international stage, had become extremely hostile to the British, who seemed determined to frustrate his efforts. First of all, there were arguments around the French zone of occupation in Germany. De Gaulle was stung by having been left out of the milestone meeting in early February 1945 held at the Yalta conference, where Churchill, Roosevelt and Stalin met to discuss the post-war occupation of Germany. Originally, there were to be only three zones, with France excluded. In de Gaulle's view, France's honour could only be restored if it, too, participated in the occupation of Germany. In the end, the other powers agreed that France should be allocated some of the British and American areas; but when the final plans were laid in Potsdam in July–August 1945, France was again absent from the table. With its own plans for how the occupation should be organised, the French set about vetoing the arrangements that were planned by the Allies, insisting on a firmer line. De Gaulle demanded that Britain should accede to his request, but the Foreign Office prevaricated.[105]

The second, and most important issue was in relation to France's colonial possessions. De Gaulle had become convinced that the British were actively trying to sabotage and undermine French interests. It was the situation in the Levant that had brought relations between the powers to a head just at the time Duff Cooper had been asked to make an approach to the minister of aviation. France was making robust efforts to reinstate its position in Syria, and de Gaulle insisted that Britain should agree to France's 'special position' in the Middle East mandates of Syria and Lebanon. He had been enraged in mid-1945, when British troops intervened there to end armed clashes between French troops and the Arab population, which wanted independence from French rule. At one point the general even talked of war with Britain over this. French Indochina was another French colonial area where de Gaulle was suspicious of British intentions. As plans were laid to retake Vietnam, de Gaulle found himself reliant on British military support and therefore vulnerable to their potential ambitions. France's intentions to return to the international stage appeared to be repeatedly – and vindictively, in de Gaulle's eyes – frustrated by the British. De Gaulle's extreme mistrust of the British, along with his overarching fear of American influence, meant that the idea of Baker undertaking a celebratory tour of Allied troops in the Far East was unthinkable in the circumstances. Baker continued to talk to journalists about her planned trip to the Pacific until August 1945,[106] but the permission she needed to travel to India and the Far East was repeatedly refused.

Janes wrote to Baker to inform her of the situation, explaining that, as she was a military officer, nothing could be done:

> If you were a civilian, things would be different. On the other hand, you cannot be expected to give up your rank. I think it is a great shame that both you and the boys in the Far East should suffer because of politics . . . it is a case of being a servant of the State.[107]

Baker responded, 'I am longing to go to India, our poor men there so all alone, still fighting, still wanting someone to think of them. Oh, people disgust me.'[108] Janes knew that Baker had taken the news badly. He wrote to his contact in India: 'Josephine wants to jump into a plane and go even if they put her in prison when she gets back, but naturally ENSA cannot support such an action much as we might wish to.'[109] The weeks they spent together in England, and afterwards in Paris, along with their profound disappointment at being unable to get her to Burma, strengthened the connection that had developed between Baker and Janes. They held a deep affection for one another, and these shared experiences formed the basis of what Janes referred to after her death as a 'long and close friendship'.[110] While not romantically involved, they had much in common, and Baker confided to Janes that she always waited with impatience for his letters.[111] They often discussed how Baker might promote herself in the future, the songs she might sing and how Janes might be able to represent her in England after the war. They hatched a plan to get Noël Coward involved in writing something for her as part of her post-war relaunch. Although their correspondence was patchy at times, Janes increasingly became Baker's confidant. He acknowledged to others that she could occasionally be a handful, but he also considered her to be a rather lonely figure.

The sultan of Morocco's visit to Paris, June–July 1945

Despite her disappointment, Baker knew her duty, and as a servicewoman she was obliged to follow orders. Her final mission would be a more pleasant one from her point of view. With the war reaching its closing stages, the French provisional government had turned to wider planning for the reconstruction of France. Issues relating to its colonial empire surfaced as a priority, and the Gaullists once again turned to Baker for support. Recognition of the role she had played in Morocco in advocating a reasonable approach to the demands for independence made her a suitable choice to help the French navigate the complexities of the situation. Since she had left North Africa, the Arab Union, now well established, was providing impetus to the hopes of the Moroccan nationalists, with the apparent support of the sultan for their ambitions, along with the tacit encouragement of the Americans.

With the war reaching its final stages, expectations were high in Morocco that independence would be on France's political agenda. There was disagreement among French politicians and administrators as to how to tackle the issue, but de Gaulle favoured a direct approach and understood that winning the sultan over was key to France's future in Morocco.[112] He therefore invited the sultan to Paris for a state visit, hoping that he would be able to impress the Moroccan sovereign and make an ally of him, which would enable him to reach a personal understanding about Morocco's future and France's role within it.

At a time of heightened tension between the two countries, much was at stake from this visit, and Baker was brought into the picture for her diplomatic skills. She was an obvious choice in the light of the time she had spent in Morocco and her personal links to those involved. Her friends Glaoui and Moulay Larbi El Alaoui were both included in the Moroccan delegation.[113] As well informed as ever, it was the *Afro-American* that broke the news that Baker had been detailed to look after the sultan:

> Josephine Baker has recently been conscripted to do a bit of colonial work ... welding shall we say. During the visit of the Sultan of Morocco and his robed entourage to Paris, she was something of an officially appointed hostess to them ... Seems France had done some promising, too, during the less happier days and the Sultan was in Paris to talk things over. Miss Baker was nominated to make him feel good about everything.[114]

Given its political importance for de Gaulle, the sultan's visit was planned meticulously, and no effort was spared to make it a success. The sultan attended the prestigious 18 June parade on the Place de la Concorde, where, in a dignified ceremony, he was made a Compagnon de la Libération – this, de Gaulle's personal medal designed to recognise exceptional service, was rarely bestowed on foreigners. Then, between 21 and 29 June, he went to visit Moroccan troops stationed in Germany and Austria, where he was received by General Lattre de Tassigny, commander of the French First Army.

209

He then accompanied General de Gaulle on a visit to the Auvergne between 30 June and 1 July. De Gaulle wrote of the sultan in his memoirs that 'He is celebrated everywhere, which creates a favourable atmosphere for our personal talks.'[115]

The outcome of the visit appears to have been positive for both sides. They agreed that Morocco should take its place within the newly formed Union Française, the political entity that was created to replace the old colonial system of the French empire. Within this union, it could secure internal autonomy and then subsequently become independent. Baker also did her bit. To celebrate the sultan's visit, she organised an extravagant reception in her wonderful – and now restored – Le Vésinet villa. It was the last she ever gave there:

> Several orchestras were scattered around the park, whose groves are illuminated. The guests, ministers, ambassadors, artists, soldiers and the sultan himself arrived in magnificent American cars that cause a sensation in this quiet neighbourhood. When this dreamy night came to an end, it is over. The beautiful property falls asleep until Josephine leaves it.[116]

De Gaulle's departure from power in January 1946 prevented him from putting his promises into action. But the new government continued to call on Baker to play a diplomatic role when her friends were received formally. For example, in 1947 she was part of the welcoming committee for a visit to Paris by Menebhi, documented in film held on the website of the French Defence Archives,[117] and he was awarded a Légion d'honneur in 1949 for his wartime service.[118] However, amidst irreconcilable differences between the two countries, the Moroccan people had to wait until November 1955 for independence to be granted.[119]

Soon after the party in Le Vésinet, in September 1945, Baker was demobilised and released from her military commitments to the French state. Her contract had been valid for the length of the war plus three months so, strictly speaking, she should have stayed on until the end of 1945. Given Baker's particular circumstances and services rendered, a special measure was put in place allowing her to be discharged from the military to resume her artistic activities from the beginning of September 1945.[120]

Baker emerged from the war a very different performer. Her professional persona had undergone a considerable metamorphosis in the five years of the conflict. No stranger to change in terms of the style and dynamics of her performances, she had always been alert to her audiences and knew how to maximise her talents in order to appeal to them. During the war, as she had done all her professional life, Baker honed her art and learnt as she went along. She mobilised her experiences and reinvented herself, tailoring her performances to the circumstances and in line with whatever the situation permitted. She emerged as a more seasoned performer and became the forces' sweetheart for servicemen of various nationalities. The war had allowed her to completely reinvent herself. She emerged from the conflict very much empowered as a public figure. In 1945, Baker was nearly forty years old and was increasingly seen as an aging performer. No longer able to trade on her physical beauty in the same way as before, would her status as a war heroine suffice as the basis for her relaunch?

7

AFTER THE WAR
(1945–1975)

Any thoughts of retirement were far from Baker's mind when she was demobilised. Without a break, she immediately started touring in her own right. 'Once peace came,' she explained, 'it was back to work to win back my pre-war public.'[1] Released from the constraints of her military responsibilities, Baker was free to relaunch herself, her public persona strengthened by her wartime activities – although she was called on from time to time to be a guest at charity and fundraising galas. Her unblemished patriotic war record put her in a different category from many other entertainers who had gone on performing during the Occupation and were seen to have supported Vichy and the occupiers, however tacitly. The purge committees that were established to judge the conduct of those in entertainment did hand out severe penalties to some, but most actors and entertainers got off lightly. Many performers, including Tino Rossi and Maurice Chevalier, who were suspected of collaboration, were eventually cleared by the investigations. Baker's pre-war rivals Mistinguett and Cécile Sorel came in for much criticism, and Edith Piaf was cleared. Only a few performers were put on a blacklist, but this did not affect their careers for long. Baker, however, rose above them all. She was seen as a shining example of someone who made the right choices and took the right course of action.

Although the war was over, the implications of her wartime service and activities carried on for the rest of her life. But Baker's first task was to set the record straight in light of the widespread rumours of her death, which still had considerable purchase across Europe and the Americas. She also had to face the challenge that, for many, she was seen as a pre-war has-been who appealed to a different generation, with a different taste in music. To address this, she was determined to try and persuade Noël Coward to write her a musical comedy. Both she and Harry Janes had gone to considerable lengths to contact him with this suggestion. But although Noël Coward appears to have held Baker in high esteem, he did not bite, and nothing came of it. Instead, Baker enthusiastically launched her new world tour.[2]

'Winning back the public'

Baker chose Switzerland to be the first stop on her tour – allegedly because it was the only place in Europe where people still had the money to spend on theatre tickets, so her performances could be held in real theatres, not army camps.[3] In her preparations, Baker set about honing her performances, launching a new repertoire that was more suited to her age, presenting a more sophisticated, elegant, less suggestive image. She ordered numerous fashionable gowns in the style of the New Look trend of Paris haute couture and adopted a distinct outfit for each number. These extravagant costumes were designed to charm her audiences and perhaps compensate her public for her new, more fully clad image. The formula seems to have worked. She wrote to Janes about the 'wonderful success' of her shows and enclosed press cuttings testifying to her rapturous reception from Swiss audiences:[4]

> Her regal appearance, her graceful movements of unparalleled elegance, her costumes so splendid in both material and colour – all these combined to create an ensemble of rare perfection.[5]

Soon after the Swiss tour, and despite being plagued with ongoing health issues, in early 1946 she and Bouillon's orchestra united once again to return to Germany for a victory gala. In her detailed description of the visit, she commented that she was shocked by the ruined state of the defeated country.[6] Held in Berlin's Courts of Justice, this victory gala was the first, she recounted, to be presided over by generals from the four 'victorious' nations. Each nation was represented by its own artistic troupe, and they all competed with one another to be considered the best. Baker, accompanied by Bouillon and fellow artiste Colette Mars, represented France. They performed last, to a rapturous reception. After the gala, Baker and Bouillon stayed on for a further ten days. They found a small local cinema in the French quarter of the city and played to troop audiences of between 150 and 200 at each performance, every two hours throughout the day, from 10 a.m. to 11 p.m. After Berlin, they went on to other German cities, including Karlsruhe, Stuttgart and Hamburg.

Baker and Bouillon followed up their visit to Germany with a series of benefit shows in France. This became the pattern of their performances, accepting invitations to attend fundraisers for causes often linked to the military, as well as putting on shows on their own account. In 1946, they travelled with their 'Joséphine et Jo' tour through Belgium, Scandinavia and Italy. The text about them in the programme for the show highlighted Baker's wartime camp tour credentials and recounted to her public her 'patriotic conduct'. By contrast, Bouillon's war record is artfully glossed over, with the emphasis placed on his musical background and trajectory.[7] That summer, at the request of General Bouscat, Baker interrupted this comeback tour to return to North Africa for a two-week trip to perform to the air force troops stationed there. She wrote that it was an opportunity for her to visit her old haunts and introduce Bouillon to her Moroccan entourage, implying that they were a couple at this point.[8] But in an unfortunate repetition of history, Baker experienced acute pain in her abdomen once again and was transported from Casablanca to Rabat for surgery, and then urgently repatriated to a clinic in Paris on 9 July 1946.[9] Her close entourage flocked to her side as she battled against intestinal infection and septicaemia that followed the surgery.[10] Once again, she cheated death; but her convalescence would be a long one and the press made much of her collapse, a serious setback to her plans. In August 1946, *Claudine*, for example, alerted its readers to the news:

> Unfortunately, JOSEPHINE BAKER did not enjoy the joyous, triumphal return to which her heroic and discreet conduct over the last six years entitled her. She had to be flown back from Morocco. An operation had put her life in danger. In Paris, they had just enough time to give her a blood transfusion. But when will she be able to play again?[11]

Yet again, Baker was consigned to weeks of convalescence, forced to remain at the clinic in Neuilly and focus on her recovery. But there was one high spot. On 5 October 1946, she was awarded the French Resistance medal 'with rosette'. The Resistance medal had been introduced by General de Gaulle in February 1942 to recognise remarkable acts of loyalty and courage that contributed to the resistance of the French people. The official decree announcing Baker's award resulted from the deliberations of the awarding commission on 24 September 1946, but it does not set out the reasons for the decision.[12] Jacques Soustelle, who had taken over the merged French intelligence services, was on the awarding commission and wrote to Baker with unreserved congratulations: 'As a member of the Resistance Committee, I was delighted to join all my colleagues in proposing that you be awarded this well-deserved distinction.'[13] A ceremony was arranged in the clinic in Neuilly, and Baker was presented with the medal in her hospital bed, in the presence of a number of notables and members of the Resistance. Her photograph adorned the front page of *France-Illustration* with the caption 'Josephine Baker Officer of the Resistance'.[14] In the photo, Baker can be seen wearing, we are told, red and white. *France-soir* reproduced an image of her being congratulated by the clinic's chef, and it cited the impressive list of dignitaries and generals including General Bouscat and General Valin, who were present in her hospital room to celebrate recognition of her role as 'secret agent of the Resistance'.[15] De Gaulle was not present, but was represented by his daughter Élisabeth de

Boissieu. He sent her a message some days later: 'It is with full knowledge of the facts and with all my heart that I offer you my sincere congratulations on the high distinction of French Resistance that you have been awarded.'[16] Reports of the event which appeared in the *Afro-American* and the *Chicago Defender* were at pains to stress the exceptional honour it represented.[17]

Baker's war record revealed

This award did not come as a complete surprise to the French public, as Baker's wartime undercover work had already been trailed in various press and magazine articles since the beginning of the summer. The weekly magazine *Point de vue* carried a full-page revelatory interview with Baker about her war record, to coincide with the second anniversary of D-Day on 6 June 1946.[18] Abtey, under the name of 'Captain Apert', figures in the article; however, the emphasis is firmly on Baker's testimony, as demonstrated by the six images across the top of the article, which depict Baker in various poses, talking and gesticulating to the unseen journalist. The attention-grabbing headline under the images could not fail to attract the reader: 'Released from her oath of silence by victory, the Black spy shares her story with us.' After a short summary of her pre-war successes, the reader is informed that without giving it a second thought, Baker took on a new role as 'Mata Hari', a shorthand that readers could easily relate to.

The presentation of her wartime exploits in this account is surprisingly explicit about Baker and Abtey's allegiances when working under cover. The article explains that they were working for – or more exactly, perhaps, under the aegis of – Vichy, which 'without the Germans being aware of it . . . reconstituted its intelligence service'. Although, after discussions with the British in Lisbon, 'Apert' was immediately 'accepted into the ranks of the Free French forces'. In reality, this 'acceptance' would prove less straightforward than is presented here, as we shall see from Abtey's later efforts to claim recognition from the military authorities for his work during this period. Interestingly, when in Casablanca under the name of

Jacques-François Hébert, he is described in this article as working as a secret agent for the FFL, while still a member of the Vichy SR, and was 'therefore under its protection'. It is notable that at this early stage of recounting their wartime story, Abtey is explicitly presented as having had a double affiliation, acting as a double agent of sorts for both the Vichy intelligence services and the Free French. As in much of the media coverage, Baker's later adoption of a military uniform is seen as significant. Her comment that she prefers her uniform to the razzle-dazzle of the music hall is particularly notable. Bearing in mind Baker's penchant for embellishment and telling a good story, it seems likely that this account was a more honest one than some of those that came later.

Nonetheless, Baker's wartime heroism was without doubt, and she clearly anticipated the award of more significant military honours for her contribution than the civil award represented by the Resistance medal presented to her in the clinic. Just before her dramatic collapse in Morocco in 1946, she had told *Le Petit Marocain* that Abtey was preparing a book about their wartime actions, though she kept his name out of it:

> I can't reveal the name of the writer who is currently writing a book about my secret missions and my role in the Resistance. But I will soon be awarded a Légion d'honneur, not as a performer but by the War Ministry, for military activities.[19]

The emphasis she puts here on the fact that it is a *military* honour is crucial. The Légion d'honneur is the highest decoration that the French state can award to an individual (not necessarily French) for achievement in any field of activity. Admission into the Légion d'honneur for war services automatically includes award of the Croix de Guerre, the highest French military medal to reward feats of bravery. This was what Baker was referring to in this interview. She expected to be awarded the Légion d'honneur in recognition of her services to the French military, rather than the civil version, which was regularly awarded to other wartime entertainers. Marlene Dietrich, for example, would be given a Légion d'honneur in 1949 in recognition of the work she did performing for the Allied troops during the war. Unfortunately for Baker, however, initial efforts to secure the award on her behalf were not successful, and it has been suggested that she was overlooked at this point because of her sex and/or race.[20] The evidence shows that there was internal disagreement in military circles about whether she had done enough to merit the award, and this was the reason her candidature was turned down. It seems that her clandestine work in the intelligence services was not recorded or recognised by the appropriate official channels, leading to dissension on the awarding committee about the tangible value of what she had done. Although testimonials were subsequently submitted on her behalf by those she had worked with closely at the time, particularly after the first nomination failed, they did not carry sufficient weight during the initial discussions.

French ministers are responsible for nominating candidates for the Légion d'honneur, and in 1946 the then minister of the army, Edmond Michelet, put forward several members of the Forces féminines de l'Air (FFA) for this honour. Those he nominated included Baker, along with Major Alla Dumesnil and others she had worked with at the time. The Légion d'honneur he asked to be awarded to Baker was the *civil* version, in line with the nature of her activities during her time with the FFA, when she focused primarily on entertaining the troops. The supporting documentation did not therefore reference her undercover intelligence work. Baker (the submission explained) had taken her position very seriously and carried out the military role assigned to her with steadfast and ardent patriotism. She displayed outstanding dedication and commitment at innumerable events which were arranged for the benefit of welfare organisations and troops in operation or under occupation, and which helped maintain troop morale in North Africa, the Middle East, Corsica and Sardinia, Italy, Germany and mainland France.[21]

Despite this positive assessment of her wartime service with the FFA from 1944–45, and although other members of the FFA were awarded the Légion d'honneur, Baker's case was rejected at a meeting in early July 1946. This led General Bouscat, head of the air force at the time, to immediately request that her case be reconsidered.[22] In October 1946, he, along with Major Alla Dumesnil and General Billotte, wrote statements designed to persuade the committee that Baker's was a deserving case. In her letter, Dumesnil expressed dismay at the refusal and underlined her belief that Baker had acted as 'an admirable and patriotic French woman', highlighting the important missions she had carried out in North Africa and the considerable sums she had raised for the Resistance. She went on, 'for a year, General Billotte (then Chief of General de Gaulle's staff) charged Josephine with particularly delicate missions which she always carried out with devotion and intelligence which surprised our staff'.[23]

Bouscat seconded Dumesnil's comments in his cover letter to the minister, stating that

> it was abnormal that the proposal to award her the Légion d'honneur was not successful. Her military qualifications are at least on a par with those of her comrades who were decorated, and it should be stressed that her special qualifications, gained for the French intelligence services, are particularly commendable. Finally, it is worth adding that her wartime service compromised, perhaps definitively, her health. I therefore strongly recommend that Lieutenant Baker's case be re-examined and that a favourable response be given to my proposal.[24]

For his part, Billotte stated that her contribution had gone above and beyond serving the air force, and that she should also be recognised for the exceptional intelligence with which she had used her numerous international contacts to pass on valuable information to relevant bodies concerned with the interests of France's national defence.[25]

Despite the strength of all these additional arguments in her favour and the military standing of the individuals making them, the award of the Légion d'honneur was again refused unanimously on 30 June 1947. The awarding committee explained that it did 'not dispute the merits of the person concerned but considers that a civil non-military award would more legitimately reward her services'.[26] They may have been swayed by an undated memo from the Air Force General Staff's Air Security Service to Air Brigadier General Jean-Flaustin Plou which is included in Baker's file and which minimises the importance of her contribution to the work of the intelligence services: 'The former Head of Counterespionage [i.e. Abtey's previous superior, Louis Rivet] is very well aware of Josephine Baker's activities on behalf of the French Special Services.' The memo reports that, although Baker had been in contact with the French intelligence services in 1939,

> nothing positive had been achieved by the time of the 1940 debacle. After these tragic events, Josephine Baker declared that she would no longer sing abroad as long as France was occupied by the enemy. However, at the request of the French services, she agreed to organise a tour of Spain and Portugal; and among the staff of this tour was a representative of the French Special Services, whose mission was to make contact with the Allies.

This must be a reference to Abtey, but is factually incorrect as he did not accompany Baker on those trips in spring 1941. In an odd sequencing of events, the memo claims that 'Baker then fell ill and moved to North Africa'. But it is the final sentence that is the most damning: 'This, in all honesty, is the extent of her activities on behalf of the French Special Services.'[27] If members of the committee took this memo at face value, it is not surprising that they did not consider her to be deserving of the Légion d'honneur. Baker, however, continued to demand official recognition from the military authorities of her wartime service and acknowledgement of her status as a Free French combatant.[28]

Marriage to Bouillon

Meanwhile, Josephine was considering marrying again. She and Lion had divorced in 1941 but he had not given up without a fight.

Having been wounded in the head during the 1939–40 campaign, he had moved to North Africa and become commander of a Moroccan regiment that fought in the battle of Tunisia. He had continued to pursue Baker, frequently begging her to marry him again, overtures which she consistently refused.[29] Janes relates that when he was in Paris in June 1945 trying to secure permission for Baker to sing to the Pacific troops, he discovered that she used him 'as a decoy without [Lion's] knowledge at a dinner at Maxim's ... pretending she was in love with him' to throw off Lion.[30] However, Baker's choice of a new husband was not proving easy, and she prevaricated for months. She confided in Janes that she was 'toying with the idea of Jo Bouillon or Claude Meunier' as a future husband. Claude Meunier had a huge fortune and showered her with gifts. Baker had been engaged to his brother Jean before the war, but he had been killed at the front.[31]

Janes explains in his papers that he first met Bouillon during that same visit to Paris, in June 1945, at Baker's Avenue Bugeaud flat, where she was staying – presumably because the Le Vésinet house was still uninhabitable. Janes went back to France and visited Baker in Les Milandes in January 1946. He wrote, 'she confided her secrets to me. Offers of marriage, Jo Bouillon or Claude Meunier.'[32] After her death, Janes disclosed to Baker's close friend Harold Lars Sorensen that during his stay he had 'asked her why she was confiding in me. She answered, "Harry, you are a rock – my brother." Since then, she entered my heart and I have never betrayed her.'[33]

Janes was very worried by what he witnessed when he met Josephine in Brussels in February 1946. Baker was still very undecided about Bouillon. Janes had been invited there as Baker's guest to see 'Joséphine et Jo', to assess whether it might have potential for a British tour. He recounted that 'there were quarrels and one night after a furious row, Josephine asked me to spend the night with her. We were never lovers in the accepted sense, but "brother and sister".' He believed that this was another ploy on Baker's part, this time to make Bouillon jealous.[34] After his visit, Janes wrote to Baker commenting on these events, urging her not to pursue the engagement because she felt professionally bound to

Bouillon: 'You stood on your own feet years before he was heard of, and your name will be remembered centuries after his has been forgotten.' Janes felt that the idea of getting engaged was self-interested on Bouillon's part and that she should not pursue the idea.[35] Baker responded by telegram from Brussels on 19 February to say that things had got worse and she was following his advice.[36]

Eventually, in April 1946, Baker wrote to Janes from Copenhagen, explaining that she was planning to separate from Bouillon after their Scandinavian tour, at which point she and Claude would get engaged. She finished her letter exclaiming, 'Oh Harry, I am so happy.'[37] Janes expressed his relief and wrote that he was looking forward to meeting Claude.[38] In July, while touring in Morocco with Bouillon, Baker announced her engagement to Meunier to *Le Petit Marocain*, asserting that she would be giving up the stage and her planned trip to America to marry him.[39] One can only imagine what Bouillon – who was regularly performing with her – must have made of this. He was extremely attentive when she was taken ill and had to be rushed back to Paris, and in the ensuing months, Meunier seems to have faded out of the picture, becoming rather mysteriously ill and remaining in Switzerland. With him no longer on the scene, while Baker was still convalescing in Les Milandes, her engagement to Bouillon was announced to the press in December 1946.[40] Baker wrote to Janes explaining that she had finally agreed to marry Bouillon in mid-April 1947. 'I know you do not approve darling, but he has been so good to me during this time I have been ill throughout these long months. Claude has been ill for a year in Suisse, no one can see or hear from him.'[41] Janes responded reassuringly to her news and mentioned that he understood her decision and that he thought she was lonely.[42] His papers in fact divulge that 'the widowed mother of Claude was firmly against the marriage and her son was removed from Josephine's influence'.[43]

The relationship was a love match, although the way in which Bouillon describes their decision to marry suggests that they both stood to gain. From the point of view of the public, Baker told a convincing story, explaining that the special rapport between them had grown from the moment they teamed up for their 1945 army tours.[44] 'I got to know him as we rushed from place to place following the Victory army. Our love was born to the sound of violins, amid ruins, on improvised stages.'[45] From Bouillon's point of view, marriage to Baker, the war heroine, protected him from the stigma of having performed during the Occupation and helped him to re-establish his credentials.[46] Baker was candid about having found in Bouillon someone who was supportive and would fall in with her ambitions: 'Jo gave up part of his career to devote himself to mine and to our joint projects.'[47] She had time to study him and knew what she was getting herself into; but she could count on him to help engineer her return to the stage in her new guise.[48] She needed his help, as there were challenges. Her repeated ill-health had led many to believe that she was no longer in a condition to perform and that her career was over. When she was able to secure bookings, many promoters still wanted to see the 'old' Josephine, as Janes pointed out during their discussions when they were trying to plan for a possible tour of England.[49]

Bouillon's efforts to get Baker back onto the stage occupied so much time and effort that settling on a day for the wedding proved a challenge. The original April 1947 date had to be put back, as Bouillon was caught up in Mexico, negotiating Josephine's performance schedule.[50] Eventually, their marriage ceremony was held in the little chapel at the Château des Milandes on Baker's birthday in early June 1947. She allegedly presented Bouillon with the deeds of Les Milandes as a wedding gift, though other accounts suggest it was a wedding gift to herself.[51] Images of the couple in their rural idyll featured in newsreel reports and made the front pages of most of the French newspapers. Almost immediately afterwards, they left on honeymoon to continue Baker's comeback tour in South America.

La guerre secrète de Joséphine Baker

As we have seen, Baker knew that Abtey was preparing a book about their wartime activities that was to focus on her 'secret war'.[52] In early 1948, *Samedi Soir* announced the appearance of this book as if it were Baker that was going to

[p]ublish her adventures as a black Mata Hari ... It is a work which will make its heroine the most alluring star of the Deuxième Bureau ... Paris will soon learn the details of her exploits. 11,000 copies of the book have already been ordered.[53]

By April, Abtey's book was out and Baker was engaged in promoting it at the Club des Champs-Élysées, where she was performing at the time.[54] The publication presented a much fuller chronicle of Baker's wartime activities than had been made public until then. The handwritten two-page letter to Baker from de Gaulle announced on the book's cover, and reproduced at the beginning as a preface, gives the book an impression of authenticity. However, the letter had, in fact, been written to Baker two years previously, to congratulate her on the award of the Resistance medal, and did not therefore directly relate to Abtey's account. Yet its reproduction was designed to create the impression that de Gaulle had endorsed Abtey's version of events. This impression is replicated in her 1949 *Mémoires*, where Baker let it be understood that the letter was deliberately intended by de Gaulle as a preface for the book,[55] as was also advertised in the press.[56] De Gaulle must have agreed to its use in this way, though he makes no reference to it in their correspondence. It cannot be denied, however, that Baker's story was one which suited the Gaullists in their post-war efforts to promote the significance of their own role during the war. Baker's devotion to the Gaullist cause, and Abtey's presentation of it, provides a compelling story that appears to offer evidence of the unity of French Resistance behind de Gaulle. It also chronicles the Gaullists' political struggles to hold on to the colonies in North Africa and the Middle East in ways that played into their agenda.[57] Such an interpretation would go some way to explaining the presence of the letter to 'authenticate' the narrative.

Unfortunately, Baker and Abtey fell out over the publication rights of the book, as Baker explained to Janes:

The copyright belongs to Abtey and we are quarrelling he and I because the book is out with a big big success but he forgot to sign the contract with me. I had confidence in he [sic] and his editor but they both took advantage of it.[58]

In mid-March 1948, they were in dispute. However, Baker, a press article explained, had decided not to take Abtey to the civil courts to demand her 50 per cent share of the royalties: 'The secret war was enough for her, and she doesn't want to engage in a legal war now.' She had made it clear to the editors that if her adventures were to be made into a film, she would like to play herself and not be cheated again.[59]

The book appears to have sold well, though the reports that plans were 'underway to have [it] translated into English' never materialised.[60] Baker had understandably been keen that this should happen. Abtey does not appear to have taken this forward, but Bouillon and Janes had exchanged letters about the possibility of an English translation even before the book's appearance in France. Quite why Bouillon was dealing with this, rather than Abtey, is unclear; but his involvement suggests that Baker and Bouillon were keen that Baker's wartime activities should be made known to English-speaking audiences. In early March 1948, Janes arranged for Bouillon to meet several British newspaper editors, including the editor of the *Sunday Express*, with a view to the book's serialisation in a Sunday edition.[61] A translator was also found, but it was agreed 'that only condensed extracts of the highlights and the part [Baker] played for the British should be developed for English consumption', since translating the whole book would be too costly, given the paper shortages at the time. There was genuine interest on the part of the British press; however, for reasons that are not entirely clear, a copy of the book never actually reached Janes.[62] Despite his repeated requests and assurances that he would soon receive it, he was eventually forced to read it in the British Library reading room sometime later. He was disappointed with the account, and especially with the treatment of Baker's involvement with the British:

The war memories of Captain Abtey as far as my encounters with him are concerned are neither accurate nor complete and the only mention of Josephine's passionate Anglophile attitude is confined to a few days with ENSA in Syria (French) with Major Dunstan. There is no reference to her frustration in not being permitted by the French to entertain the Allied troops during the Japanese war. There is no reference to her work both for the Free French, and the British in London and in Brussels and Paris.[63]

These criticisms are not without substance. The book recounts Baker and Abtey's activities through Abtey's eyes, and he often puts himself at the centre of the story. The obvious factual errors already identified in this discussion point to the possibility that other details could have been embellished – or indeed may be incorrect. Abtey's main motive for publishing the book must have been his belief that it would be lucrative; but there is also a sense throughout the narrative that he had something to prove. He often dwells on the forces that were working against him. Despite his promotion from captain to major in August 1945, he was not universally appreciated by his peers (as the intelligence reports on his wartime behaviour indicated). Did Abtey believe that by linking his own wartime exploits to those of Baker, his tarnished reputation might be improved? It seems likely, and he did ultimately succeed in getting the recognition he sought. In the 1950s, he fought successfully and with some determination to have his work for the Free French forces recognised and backdated to June 1940.[64]

Despite her evident frustration with Abtey, Baker appears to have endorsed the account of her war service that he presents in the book and talked about it in interviews. A series of portraits of her posing in her air force uniform at the Harcourt studios appeared in 1948 – doubtless designed to promote both Abtey's book and the Sauvage *Mémoires* that followed closely on its heels. These publications cemented Baker's reputation as a Resistance heroine and placed her in a strong position to launch her new campaign.

Baker's anti-racist crusade

Baker's commitment to fight racism had been engendered by the war. 'I wanted to serve in the war against the Germans as best I could because of their racial policies,' she told Marcel Sauvage.[65] Years later, in December 1973, in an interview published in the magazine *Ebony*, Baker was uncharacteristically candid about this:

> Miss Baker says that few people know why she risked her life to help the Allied forces during the war years. 'Of course I wanted to do all I could to aid France, my adopted country,' she says, 'but an overriding consideration, the thing that drove me as strongly as did patriotism, was my violent hatred of discrimination in any form. The Nazis were racists. They were bigots. I despised that sort of thing and was determined that they must be defeated.'[66]

Baker had believed that the end of the war would bring a better outcome for the oppressed. 'Now the world will be a different place, pure and fair,' she exclaimed in May 1945, when peace was declared.[67] Of course, she was not alone in seeing in her wartime experiences hope for a better future for people of colour in the US, and an end to segregation. African American servicemen, particularly those who served overseas, were radically changed by the war, and this affected their civil rights struggles subsequently. Like Baker, journalist Ollie Stewart was hopeful that the wartime contribution made by Black servicemen would trigger a transformation in the lives of Black Americans after the war. Optimistic that American racial divides were being erased by 'common danger, the common foe and hardships of battle', he had written in 1943 that:

> Many lives will be lost before the final victory is achieved, but already our men are looking ahead toward their part in a postwar world. While statesmen study maps in anticipation of global control, these boys lie on the ground and swat flies and sweat on the docks to make this control possible, and all they want

to know is, will they be allowed to enjoy what they have fought for?[68]

Baker's contact with the American forces during her wartime tours in North Africa had rekindled her frustrations with segregation, and she had become increasingly outspoken. In 1946, when awarded her medal, in an interview with the *Afro-American* she was keen to emphasise her association with her 'race': 'I want my people to know in America that I'm very glad to have been decorated, for myself and for the whole race.'[69] Some days later, she set out her new mission: 'God has spared my life for some reason . . . and I believe that reason is for me to realize the greatest ambition of my life: To do a lot for race progress and elevation.' As a result, the article went on, 'Miss Baker has decided to devote her life and her resources to be a real champion of the cause.'[70] This cause was a continuation of her wartime commitment to free the world from racism.[71]

However, as during the war, her main critique was persistently focused on the US, and she refused to take on the French colonial legacy and did not comment publicly on the difficulties of decolonisation in North Africa, even as they were becoming particularly acute in her beloved Morocco. Before the war, white America, blinkered by segregation, had stubbornly refused to recognise her talents. Nonetheless, Baker longed to replicate her European successes in America and, encouraged by her reception during the war with the American troops, she resolved to persevere. Success in the US also promised to bring the financial gains she would need to underwrite her scheme to renovate the Château des Milandes. She and Bouillon were laying plans to make the château into a tourist business. Once achieved, this would allow her to reduce her artistic commitments and eventually retire from the stage and focus on the family she so longed for.

Initially she struggled to gain traction for her comeback in the US. In 1948, her show flopped in Boston. *France-soir* carried the uncomfortable headline: 'Josephine Baker disappoints the Americans'.[72] The audiences, it seems, were somehow expecting to experience the Josephine Baker that they had seen or heard about from the mid-1930s, and notably were disappointed to see her with so many clothes on. While they were sensitive to the charms of high Paris fashion, the reporter went on, acknowledging that Baker had transported her lavish wardrobe in thirteen suitcases, audiences were not keen on her transformation. The planned three-month revue closed after just three weeks.

To fill this unexpected vacuum of time, Baker went to see her family in St Louis. That trip brought home to her that racial prejudices were still deep seated, and that there appeared to be little willingness to bring about change. Arriving in New York soon afterwards, she rejoined Bouillon, and they struggled to find a hotel that would accept them. She spent the rest of the trip putting together articles which were printed by *France-soir* and reproduced in Sauvage's book the following year.[73] What she saw cemented her determination to act against segregation. In the short term, however, Baker returned home to France to focus her energies on Les Milandes.

Baker brought members of her family over to help on the property. Her mother, Carrie Hudson, accompanied by her youngest sister, Margaret Wallace, and her husband Elmo arrived in November 1948,[74] to be followed by her brother, Richard Martin. Along with the château, once fully completed the 'Village du Monde' consisted of a 700-acre farm, a luxury hotel, La Chartreuse, a water-side amusement park with a dance pavilion and two theatres (one open air and one indoors), a mini-golf course, numerous play areas and a J-shaped swimming pool. Several houses were refurbished to accommodate a restaurant (Le Tornoli), a museum that recounted Josephine's life (the Jorama), a post office, a *boulangerie* run by her sister Margaret and a petrol station run by her brother Richard. All in all, about 150 people were employed there.[75] The site was successfully inaugurated on 4 September 1949, in the presence of 6,000 guests,[76] and the following summer tourists flocked to the site.

Two years later, in 1951, Baker was on tour in Havana when she was engaged for a show in Copa City, Miami. French diplomatic officials kept tabs on her activities, having got wind of her determination to oppose segregation. They reported that a few minutes before going on stage in Florida, she declared that she would only agree to perform that evening and to sign a contract for a series of further appearances across the country if, wherever she was due to appear, audiences were mixed. To general surprise, her conditions were accepted and, for the first time in the history of American theatre, a contract was signed between a white impresario and a Black artist stipulating that 'spectators would be admitted without discrimination according to race, color or religion'. Signs to the effect that Black people were not admitted were removed from the entrances to other similar venues.[77] The impact of this event was extraordinary, according to the French consul, especially in Harlem, and her initial success inspired Baker to carry on. She was outspoken in support of Willie McGee, who had been condemned to death for a rape he had always denied. She had herself photographed with his wife, came to the aid of the family and later paid for his funeral. The night of his execution, she was playing a show in Chicago and, with her eyes full of tears, she declared to the mainly white audience, 'It is a tragic day for African Americans and for all Blacks in the world.'[78]

She followed up her successes in January 1951 with a series of live shows in cinemas across the continent, and people flocked to see her, particularly African Americans.[79] The shows were not in glamorous venues, but they were packed. She appeared between film shows for an hour's performance at a time, and, as was her style, as well as singing she chatted to her audiences. At every theatre she insisted that Black musicians were included in her orchestras and that there should be no discrimination in ticket sales. If this could not be guaranteed, she turned down the engagement.

When the New York branch of the National Association for the Advancement of Colored People (NAACP) proclaimed Josephine Baker Day on 20 May 1951, to be celebrated in Harlem, it really seemed as if the tide had turned, and that Baker had gained acceptance in her home country. Designed both to celebrate her extraordinary success as a Black performer and her championing of civil rights, the day included a luncheon, a motorcade, a cocktail *dansante*

and a dinner for stars of stage, screen, radio and television to celebrate Baker's achievements. The French ambassador in Washington
was invited, but he sent Roger Seydoux, the French consul in New
York, to represent him. Seydoux attended the evening dinner and
gave a short speech referring to Baker as 'his good friend' and referencing the importance of her war service.

In his full report to the ambassador, Seydoux surmised whether,
based on what he had witnessed that day, Baker might one day
become spokeswoman for the Black community of America. He
wondered whether she would be prepared to accept the role of
national heroine that certain people seemed to want to entrust her
with. He equated the events of the day organised in her honour with
the kind of reception that was normally reserved for foreign heads
of state or victorious generals and cited the tributes that were paid
to her during the speeches. He also mentioned that Baker responded
'with tact and kindness, demonstrating once again the qualities of
intelligence and compassion that our fellow countrymen appreciated, particularly at the time of the Liberation'.[80] At the age of forty-
five, Baker seemed at last to have achieved recognition in her country
of birth – the one great success that had eluded her until then.

Baker returned to Les Milandes in late August 1951 to finalise her
tourist project for the château, which included the establishment
of a restaurant, a hotel and a nightclub. Her recent anti-racist work
attracted the interest of the French press, and the weekly magazine
Femmes Françaises dedicated its front cover to her, with the headline 'Josephine Baker sings, dances and fights racism'. The edition
included a two-page article on her past and present activities, celebrating her recent successes in the US. In the interview, she focused
not just on her new-found success across the Atlantic, but explained
that her new calling to fight racism 'is the only thing that interests
me now'.[81]

Defending her war record

Some weeks later, Baker returned alone to America to pursue this
ambition. Soon after her arrival, on 16 October 1951, she visited one

of New York's go-to venues, the Stork Club, with some friends. Although they were able to gain access without question, Baker was outraged when her food order never arrived. She immediately determined to publicly expose the racism that she had experienced. The French consul in New York summarised the subsequent events in a series of telegrams to the French ambassador in Washington. He reported that the consulate had insisted that Baker, a French citizen, renounce her intentions of organising a demonstration in front of the club.[82]

In her rage, Baker confronted the popular radio personality and columnist Walter Winchell, who had also been present in the club. He had previously been a champion of hers, and she reproached him for not being more vocal in his support for her on the night. Deeply hurt by what he perceived as a public humiliation, and claiming that although he had been present in the club that night he had not been aware of what was going on, Winchell retaliated with a radio and press campaign against her. In an excoriating attack designed to undermine her, he made a rather confused set of accusations, including allegations that she was a communist, was antisemitic, had supported Mussolini (which she had, as we have seen) and had only joined the war effort after the Americans had invaded North Africa, once the outcome of the conflict had seemed certain:

> While our boys were over there stopping bullets, Jose-Phony Baker was living it up, making oodles of dough in Paris, wining and dining the Nazis and Mussolini's bigwig generals. Now she's over here trying the same thing with her pinko stories and trying to make a comeback and take our American dollars back to France to support her commie causes.[83]

Baker took this attack very seriously and was determined to defend herself. Some of the allegations were more difficult to deny than others. While her support for Mussolini in 1935 had been genuine, she rejected accusations that she was a communist or antisemitic, and stood up for her war record. In a remarkable development, one of the American officers she had worked with in Morocco in 1942, Lieutenant Paul H. Jensen of the military counter-intelligence corps, spoke out publicly in her defence. Baker was due to perform at the National Guard Armory in Washington, and Jensen was there to meet her train at Union Station on 31 October 1951. In the presence of Bouillon, who had flown in that morning to support his wife, Jensen made a statement to the waiting press. He explained that he was incensed at the treatment accorded Miss Baker at the Stork Club.[84] He told the press that he had come forward when he read Mr Winchell's column 'because of his personal acquaintance with Miss Baker in French Morocco', asserting that 'To impugn Miss Baker as being anything but a friend of the United States when I know she risked her life for us . . . is shocking.'[85] He went on to describe in detail the ways in which she had offered service to his intelligence unit when he was sent to Marrakech on 8 November 1942.[86] A report in the *Arizona Sun* went even further, indicating that Jensen 'credited Baker with being responsible for his winning the Silver Star and the man serving with him being awarded the French Legion of Merit for their exploits in North Africa'.[87] This testimonial is crucial not just in relation to the support it offered Baker at a time when her war record was under attack, but also, as was shown in Chapter 4, for what it reveals about Baker's activities in November 1942.[88]

Just a few days after Jensen's revealing testimony was reported, the *Afro-American* published further 'new light, refuting Winchell's diatribe on Baker's services in the Allied cause', which included 'more revelations of her heroism and self-sacrifice [provided] in a recently compiled survey of her war record written by Col. Jacques Abtey'.[89] It has not been possible to trace the original document, but its contents, as cited in the press, appear to have offered a somewhat embellished summary of Abtey's 1948 book. We learn that 'the famous star not only contributed her talent in entertaining Allied troops of all nations in North Africa but was one of the most trusted persons who participated in the planning of the Allied inva-sion of North Africa in 1942'. In addition, 'Miss Baker was one of the few persons privileged to know the date of the US invasion of North

Africa to the exact hour of D-Day'.[90] As we have seen, this was highly unlikely.[91] Whether or not this was part of Abtey's 'report' or the work of an enthusiastic reporter (who also promoted Abtey to colonel) cannot be verified. Regardless of this, between them Jensen and Abtey offered compelling evidence that Winchell's accusations were unfounded.

On her return to New York, Baker organised a press conference with her American lawyer, Arthur Garfield, to respond in full to Winchell's accusations. The star's publicist distributed a long declaration by Baker, in which she expressed her regret that Winchell had not checked in advance what he was writing: 'If he had done so, he would have learnt that I had worked for the French intelligence services and the Free French forces from 1940.' She then announced that her military chief, Colonel Abtey, intended to come to the US from Casablanca to reply to Winchell's accusations in person.[92]

On 21 December, Baker sued Winchell for libel and lost income. That evening and the two that followed, she discussed the accusations that had been made against her in radio interviews, with interventions from her supporters, including Abtey. Through an interpreter, he explained that he had travelled over 3,000 miles to 'defend the honour of a war heroine' and read aloud affidavits from two French generals.[93] Baker wanted to go further than refuting Winchell's spurious accusations: she wanted it to be known to the American public that during the war she had done more than entertain the troops, and that she had been actively engaged in resistance. Neither Abtey's 1948 book nor Sauvage's 1949 *Mémoires* had been translated into English, so this was the first time that full details of her war record were revealed to the Americans. However, the events of 1951 and her unfortunate spat with Winchell made Baker's ongoing presence in the US difficult. At Winchell's behest, the FBI started to investigate her activities, and the controversy led many of her performance dates to be cancelled. Baker ended her American tour in early 1952, when she left for Cuba. In Havana, she was arrested briefly and then released. She went on to Mexico, then Argentina, where she remained for the next six months. Inspired by her time in Latin America, on her return to France she laid plans for the new project that would dominate her life thenceforth.

A 'rainbow' family

In 1953, aged forty-seven, Baker announced to the press her plans to adopt a family of children from many ethnic backgrounds, who would come and live in France to be raised like brothers. They would be from countries around the world, but especially from the Global South, from Southeast Asia, North and West Africa, and Latin America. According to *Le Monde*, the political point that Baker wanted to make with the family was 'to show people of colour that not all whites are cruel and mean. I will prove that human beings can respect each other if given the chance.'[94] She wanted to demonstrate that it was possible for people to live in racial harmony.

She chose her first two 'orphans' – Korean Akio and Japanese Janot – during a visit to Japan.[95] She intended at first to have just four children, but ended up with twelve. Baker felt the first two were too similar, and she wanted more variety. Her family needed a diversity that could be easily seen and understood, which would forcefully carry her point about a common humanity and the roots of racism. She began to collect children during her tours as she travelled the world, bringing them back to be part of the family she was creating at Les Milandes. Jari (now Jarry) joined them from Finland and Luis from Colombia. In late 1955, two French boys, Jean-Claude and Moïse, arrived; they were followed by a French girl, Marianne, and then Brahim from Algeria in 1956. The following year, Koffi came from Côte d'Ivoire. In 1959, Mara came from Venezuela, and in the same year Noël – found on a rubbish heap at Christmas – also joined the family. Some years later, in 1964, Baker brought home Stellina, of Moroccan origin.[96] Baker ensured that the children came from a variety of ethnic backgrounds and brought them up according to the heritage and religions that she assigned to them.

Baker's 'rainbow family' became linked to the project to make the château into a tourist resort. Visitors were to be invited to 'meet' the children, observe them and experience this living experiment at first hand. It was a huge undertaking: the children had to be looked after and the estate had to be managed. While Bouillon proved a reasonably capable administrator, Baker had no real sense of what she was taking on. She was ill prepared to cater to the children's needs, and her aging mother and her sister were allocated to childcare. For a while, it looked as if the plan was going to be a success, as visitors came in their hundreds and thousands. But the numbers were not high enough to ensure the long-term profitability of the château.[97] In a triumphant return to the stage in 1956, Baker did what she knew best and went back to performing, not unwillingly, in a concerted effort to keep the project afloat. Ultimately, she would not succeed, and her frequent absences on tour, attempting to raise funds, also deprived the children of precious time spent with their mother.

At the same time as juggling her growing family and the tourist resort, Baker and Bouillon became increasingly engaged in anti-racist activities in France. Baker had been involved since 1938 as a member of the local Bergerac branch of the Ligue internationale contre le racisme et l'antisémitisme (LICRA), and after the war she took up the mantle even more forcefully. In 1953, she was appointed the organisation's ambassador for international propaganda. Her ability to appeal to spectators while performing lent itself well to speaking engagements, and she took pleasure in exposing her ideas to rapt audiences. In 1957, launched at an anti-racist conference at Les Milandes in May, she and Bouillon embarked on a major lecture tour of France, speaking in several cities across the country under the aegis of LICRA.

Her interventions were closely monitored by the Renseignements généraux (RG), the French security intelligence services, which were concerned at Baker's potential influence, particularly in relation to her alleged communism. Their reports reveal that Baker's talks were very well attended: she could draw up to 1,200 people, while women frequently made up over 60 per cent of the audience. They were doubtless attracted by the glamour of the star. Police reports acknowledge that her personal family stories about the children were particularly appreciated – though her talks generally were enthusiastically received. Baker was a skilled orator, who knew how to hold a room.[98] She liked giving speeches and attending conferences: they fit her model of 'performance politics', offering her a chance to play a public role and stage her political views for receptive live audiences.[99]

If Baker's fame was often the main reason that her audiences were attracted to these events, it was her race, as well as her war service, that underpinned her authority to speak on the topic. A talk she gave in Toulouse included representatives of the Deuxième Division Blindée – General Philippe Leclerc's Second Armoured Division – the French forces responsible for liberating Paris. In the opening statements that preceded her talk, they offered Baker their public thanks for her wartime service.[100]

Her addresses all took a similar form. She would first evoke the war and discuss how the Occupation had led men to the Nazi crematoriums for racial, religious and political reasons. Then she would relate her travels in America, drawing on many examples of discrimination and showing the ways in which African Americans were considered inferior. She illustrated her talk with dramatic and humorous examples, and made it clear that she did not want to 'attack the US, but American racism. Comparing it to motherly love which should not be blind to punishing their children's bad behaviour', as one police report stated. However,

> according to certain comments made at the end of the meeting and in the press, while Josephine Baker's criticism of the United States was generally accepted without reservation, she failed to mention the countries of the French Union, such as North Africa and Black Africa.[101]

As during the war, Baker always directed her comments across the Atlantic, adopting a deliberate blindness about the issue of race at home. She would frequently repeat during the event, 'I am proud to be French', underlining the difference between France and America in a way that doubtless reassured the security services.

Soon after this, in late 1957, Bouillon finally left her, moving first to Paris and then to Argentina, where four of the children would join him after Baker's death. The relationship had run into trouble after the adoption of the sixth child, and they fought over every subsequent child that Baker adopted.[102] Bouillon admired her generosity and appears to have genuinely loved the children, but was conscious of the financial and emotional commitment brought by each additional child. They disagreed about the running of the estate. He tired of being forced to manage everything, as well as of having to cater to the children's needs during her frequent absences. He felt that he made every effort to prioritise financial viability, only to be overruled by Baker, who was keen to experiment with every idea that occurred to her, without any consideration of its feasibility.

The Légion d'honneur at last: 1961

Since her return to France after the disasters of 1951, when doubt had been cast on her war service, Baker had redoubled her efforts to secure a Légion d'honneur, demanding recognition for her war service that went beyond the civil actions of entertainment, and which formally acknowledged the contribution she made to the work of the French secret services in her role as a combatant for the Free French. General Valin's second effort to make her case in 1949 had again been unsuccessful. The reservations towards Baker in military circles may have been linked to the doubts about Abtey's allegiance and the undocumented nature of work they did before November 1942. Abtey was also experiencing difficulty in convincing his hierarchy of the veracity of his own war record as a member of the Forces françaises libres (FFL).

At the time of his formal enlistment in Algiers on 8 June 1943, it had been specifically agreed by General Billotte that an annotation should be included, backdating his record to 25 June 1940, to account for his earlier work for 'Fighting France'.[103] However, Abtey's formal request to the Department of Military Personnel (Direction du personnel militaire) for recognition of his FFL service between 25 June 1940 and 8 June 1943 was refused in 1954. Abtey was forced to appeal and to document exactly what he had been doing in the three years between June 1940 and June 1943. He made the case that, from the time the armistice had been signed onwards, he had persistently made every effort to join de Gaulle, but had been prevented from doing so by the British and Americans, on the basis that 'they were absolutely determined to keep me in North Africa'. Each time, 'they (Bacon, Canfield, Bartlett) made it clear that since November 1940 my status was that of an FFL on mission'.[104] In 1955, a special hearing of the FFL Certification Commission agreed to support his case, but he was classed solely as having been in the service of the Resistance, without any formal attachment to a military corps or service.[105]

This resolution of the uncertainties relating to Abtey's war record may also have helped to remove the previous objections in relation to Baker. It opened the way in 1957 for Jacques Chaban-Delmas, in his role as minister of the armed forces and defence, to find a solution to Baker's award that satisfied all parties. It was agreed that Baker should be awarded the civilian Légion d'honneur, along with the Croix de Guerre avec palme, one of the highest military honours that can be bestowed by the French state. Chaban-Delmas had an additional, vested interest in finding a solution:[106] as well as being a minister, he was also mayor of Bordeaux, and his position included overseeing the district where Baker's château was located. He used to attend events there, and it seems likely that he regarded resolving the issue as part of his mayoral role; as minister, he happened to be ideally placed to achieve this.[107] The decree which announced Baker's award referred both to her work as an intelligence agent and to her position as a second lieutenant in the air force.[108]

Baker's formal award ceremony took place four years later, at the château, in 1961. It was carefully orchestrated both to showcase the property and to promote her 'rainbow tribe', as she called them. She insisted that the ceremony should take place at Les Milandes, rather than in Paris, as would have been customary.[109] While her project was in serious trouble and Bouillon was no longer on the scene, the medal ceremony on 18 August 1961 was nonetheless a significant high point for Baker and attracted international press interest. She had written to General de Gaulle in early 1958, asking him to pin the medal on her, but he had responded – cordially enough – that he did not do this for anyone.[110] Nor did he attend the ceremony in person, as she had hoped.[111] Many dignitaries and diplomats were present, however, including two generals, three colonels, the consuls from Bordeaux representing the US, Italy, Spain and Morocco, as well as locals and tourists. At noon, a helicopter brought the generals and senior officers to a site near the château, where they were greeted by Baker, dressed in her hastily repaired air force uniform. The ceremony took place in the courtyard of the complex's Hôtel de la Chartreuse. While those present listened to the 'Marseillaise', General Valin pinned the two medals on Josephine's uniform – first the Légion d'honneur, then the Croix de Guerre avec palme. Afterwards, Valin summarised the achievements that had merited her award, noting: 'As an artist, she was able to pass on many secret messages during the Occupation. After months of illness, she donned a uniform in 1943 and travelled the roads of the Liberation.'[112] He went on to underline that she had 'created a magnificent weapon against racism'. Visibly moved by his words, Baker asserted that she was 'proud to be French because this is the only place in the world where I can realise my dream'.[113]

The ceremony was timely publicity for her project and helped to remind potential French visitors of the château's existence. The images of the event showing her in her wartime uniform once again offered her up as a potent symbol of her commitment to and embrace of France.

The March on Washington: Summer 1963

Without Bouillon to oversee the business, the finances of the château and its related places of entertainment continued to decline, and by 1963 had become increasingly precarious. Baker was threatened with bankruptcy, and in June the compulsory sale of Les Milandes was on the cards. Fortunately, Baker was distracted by another timely opportunity which would, she hoped, allow her to promote her project, this time in the US. Wearing her French air force uniform, with all five of her bright, shiny medals on her left breast to remind everyone present of her heroic wartime service, she addressed the crowds at the Lincoln Memorial in Washington, DC. Her presence at this event was her crowning moment as an activist of the American civil rights movement, and we can draw a direct line from this to her engagement in Resistance activities during the war.

It had come about at the initiative of Jack Jordan, an African American performer turned producer and impresario, who had arranged for her to be offered a trip to the US. He was aware that a coalition of civil rights groups was planning a march on Washington, as a strategy to encourage the passage of the Civil Rights Bill that was before Congress.[114] He managed to secure bookings for a series of concerts at Carnegie Hall in the autumn and gained the approval of Martin Luther King Jr for Baker to be placed on the roster of speakers for the planned march. She was keen to participate in the event, as it would not only support civil rights causes, but also allow her to promote her multicultural experiment at Les Milandes – and perhaps even raise some very necessary funds. Baker, along with a few others, had slots to speak before Martin Luther King Jr gave his groundbreaking speech on the dream of equality and human dignity at the end of the day.

Baker cut a very different figure from the other activists present, and 'her foreign military attire contrasted strangely with the other civil rights activists'.[115] Her very popular speech, according to her account, lasted twenty minutes. She had not prepared anything formal, but as she did with her normal talks, she improvised, relating events from her own personal story. Her presentation was not widely disseminated, and the only record that survives is her own retelling to Stephen Papich.[116] She referred to France as a 'fairyland place', where she could 'go into any restaurant' she wanted to and 'drink water anyplace' she wanted, and which she compared with her experiences in America:

> I have walked into the palaces of kings and queens and into the houses of presidents ... But I could not walk into a hotel in America and get a cup of coffee, and that made me mad.

Baker took the opportunity to highlight, once again, the contrast she found between her personal experiences in America and in the other places she had visited.

Throughout this period when she was dedicated to denouncing segregation, at the March on Washington and as she toured the United States with her message, she continued to downplay any critique of France or to comment publicly on the issue of race in France.[117] Her selective blindness did not go unnoticed by other activists in the civil rights movement. In part this silence was a matter of loyalty. Her wartime dedication to de Gaulle remained steadfast and unwavering. Just days before departing for Washington, on 25 August 1963, she had participated in a Gaullist-imbued commemoration ceremony at Paris's Hôtel de Ville to mark the nineteenth anniversary of the Liberation of the capital. She performed on a stage late in the evening with the singer and actor Yves Montand.[118] The writer Langston Hughes happened to be there and found it thrilling to see how she sang in her army uniform with all her medals.[119] During de Gaulle's presidency, Baker made several public appearances lending her support, and most notably, demonstrating in his favour during the civil unrest of May 1968.

Une sale petite gaulliste

Baker's unswerving commitment to de Gaulle emerges from their post-war correspondence. It was a loyalty that was fed by her wartime service, and they both make frequent reference to it. Baker often signs her letters 'Sale petite gaulliste' – a 'naughty little Gaullist', the nickname originally accorded her by Yvonne de Gaulle at their first meeting in Algiers in 1943, when de Gaulle gifted Baker a gold Cross of Lorraine.[120] She wrote to General de Gaulle and his wife regularly after his letter of congratulations on her award of the Resistance medal in 1946. Baker's letters and telegrams were more frequent than the relatively short responses from the couple. She always made a point of sending de Gaulle a telegram on the anniversary of his *appel* on 18 June, along with regular good wishes on May Day, Easter and at New Year. She was careful to write when she

learnt that either of the couple had been taken ill. De Gaulle reciprocated with polite acknowledgements of all her communications,
often expressing how touched he was by her attentions and reiter-
ating his recognition of her loyalty that dated from 'the tough years
of our national resistance'.[121] Bearing in mind that de Gaulle tended
to remain aloof, was not given to emotional declarations and
shunned any kind of intimacy, the sustained nature of their
exchanges and his systematic responses probably points to a high
degree of affection on the part of the French leader. He must also
have struggled to know how to deal with the exuberant communications and boundless loyalty that Baker frequently expressed. He
often expressed a strict courteous formality in his responses. At
times, he would add a short handwritten note to the formal typed
responses, probably dictated to a secretary, and these do reveal a
closer association. For example, in 1949 Baker wrote congratulating
de Gaulle on giving a speech at an event where she had also
performed, exclaiming that 'you warmed the hearts of all in the
crowd . . . and more than ever I am proud to be a Gaullist'.[122] De
Gaulle's response was not dissimilar to his usual missives: 'I am
deeply touched by your loyalty.' But he had added in his own hand:
'I know how much pleasure you gave everyone that day and how
much you were applauded and celebrated.'[123]

During his presidency, de Gaulle tasked officials with thanking
Baker on his behalf. He sent flowers when she was ill and arranged
for a donation to Les Milandes during the appeal; but he also kept
his distance publicly.[124] It is not clear that they met very often
outside formal events. Baker was invited to receptions at the Élysée
on occasion, but both de Gaulle and his wife politely declined
Baker's frequent requests that they visit Les Milandes while he was
president.[125] Baker would send him pages of lengthy 'advice', offering
her very personal take on given political situations and asserting, 'I
will never abandon you.' And de Gaulle appears to have been genuinely appreciative of her concern.[126] Sometimes her letters even ran
to several pages. In one, she wrote about the attitudes towards him
that she had observed during her travels in South America, North
Africa and Scandinavia, informing him, for example, that he was

admired in Brazil, but in Copenhagen they feared his rapproche-ment with Germany.[127] He responded graciously to her efforts to alert him when she believed he was in political danger, but glossed over the (at times) conspiratorial – even hysterical – content of some of her letters. In September 1964, she wrote to warn him to be extremely careful in Latin America when he visited, asserting that the countries of that region were extremely dangerous for him, due to the presence of 'French devils' who were his number-one enemies.[128] Only once did an official pass on one of her letters with a cover note asserting that Baker seemed a little unhinged because she had written to him about one of her dreams.[129]

Baker also divulged in her letters that her loyalty to de Gaulle made her unpopular. In December 1963, she wrote: 'I have never told you how much I am harassed, attacked, humiliated and muzzled by every means in the region . . . all because of my ideas about you.'[130] After the general's death on 9 November 1970, she wrote to Yvonne de Gaulle explaining that her participation in the demonstrations in de Gaulle's favour in the Dordogne and on the Champs-Élysées in May 1968 had led to the defacement of the posters advertising her concert at the Olympia.[131] De Gaulle was not the only target of Baker's letter writing: she also had much to say to J.F. Kennedy, for example, and Janes reveals that she would 'send greetings to all of the British royal family and proudly display their replies'.[132] But while Baker would send missives to any public figure inside or outside France, she worshipped de Gaulle. After her death, Janes wrote that Baker had adored the French leader,[133] and her letters reveal a devotion that bordered on the obsessive in her later life.

Downward spiral

By 1964, the situation at Les Milandes had become so bad that the electricity, gas and even the water had been cut off, and the restaurant and bar on the complex had been forced to close. Baker made public appeals for help at home and even wrote to heads of state across the world, including Queen Elizabeth II. These had little impact until the film star Brigitte Bardot made a television appeal on her behalf. The money raised and Baker's ongoing performances helped stave off the creditors; but in early 1968, the château and its contents were compulsorily put up for sale. Baker tried to have the auction put off, determined to stay at Les Milandes, but it was sold. In September, she was given formal notice to quit the premises or face eviction, but was able to gain a further postponement, as it was illegal to carry out evictions in the winter. In March 1969, having already removed the children from the premises, Josephine barricaded herself in, in the faint hope that there would be a last-minute reprieve. Everything had been sold off by the bailiffs, so this was an orchestrated step, designed to draw public attention to her plight. In sight of the cameras, she camped out in the kitchen, where reporters gave her supplies. The new owners finally brought in a team of heavies to remove her. Soon after a photoshoot of her seated miserably on the steps outside the kitchen, she collapsed and was taken to a local hospital, where she was also photographed. 'They threw me out like a sack of potatoes,' she told local reporters.[134]

Nonetheless, Baker quickly recovered and was soon on the road again, battling to secure an income for her tribe. In an unexpected development, it was Princess Grace of Monaco who came to her aid. The two women met when Baker performed at the August 1969 Ball of the Sporting Club of Monaco. The princess was moved by Baker's plight. She had been present at the Stork Club when Baker was snubbed and had been impressed with her courage. She was also moved by Josephine's commitment to her rainbow tribe. She arranged for Baker to take possession of a house in Roquebrune, near Monaco, which allowed her to live in relative comfort with the family. Baker continued to give charity galas and some performances to help support her children. She continued to pull in audiences in the US, the UK and France in the early 1970s, despite bouts of ill-health, including a series of minor heart attacks and strokes. A retrospective review that she performed in Monte Carlo drew particular attention, and in 1975 backing was found for it to be transferred to the Bobino theatre in Paris. Baker rehearsed all winter for the demanding show, which required her to be on stage for over two hours.

The show consisted of a series of tableaux vivants drawn from Baker's life. It played on her new persona as a camp glamour diva, which had gone down very well with American gay audiences during her US shows in Carnegie Hall in 1973. In one of the scenes, referencing her wartime service, Baker made a dramatic entrance dressed in uniform and perched on the bonnet of a jeep. On 8 April, a gala performance of 'Josephine' attended by friends, colleagues and other stars was followed by a glamorous reception at the Le Bristol hotel, with 250 celebrity guests. Hailed as a huge success, it was equalled by the performance the following night; and once again, Baker celebrated into the early hours. The next day, she took a nap after lunch, from which she never awoke. She was found in bed amid piles of rapturous press clippings reviewing the show, but could not be roused. She was taken to Salpêtrière hospital, but all attempts to revive her from her coma over the next two days were unsuccessful. She was pronounced dead of a cerebral haemorrhage early on Saturday, 12 April 1975. She was sixty-eight years old.

Her funeral, held four days later, reflected her status as a holder of the Légion d'honneur and was given national television coverage. The cortège left the hospital, went past the Bobino theatre and made its way slowly through the Paris streets to the magnificent church La Madeleine. Onlookers came in their thousands to watch her pass by and gathered to pay their last respects. For her son Jean-Claude Baker, it was not like a funeral, but more like an opening night, with countless stars, photographers and television news reporters present. Others commented that, had it not been for her Bobino performance, she would have died virtually unnoticed.[135]

In keeping with her military status, she was given a twenty-one-gun salute, and twenty-four official tricolour flags were displayed at the ceremony. Distinguished veterans of the Resistance stood to attention by her coffin during the service. Certain of the wreaths and flowers that lined the pathway required several men for their transportation,[136] and afterwards they were laid across the capital at monuments and memorials to those who had died in France's wars.[137] Le Figaro described the scene:

The coffin, surrounded by a double layer of tricolour flags as well as an American flag, was covered in flowers: huge crosses of white roses, wreaths of lilacs, pink roses, lilies, delphiniums and orchids, in the middle of which was a cushion bearing the three decorations of the Croix de Guerre and the Croix de la Résistance awarded to the deceased.[138]

There was also a bouquet in the shape of the Star of David, but no one knew where it had come from.

A few days later, Princess Grace, having found the Paris event unseemly, organised a smaller and more dignified private funeral in Monaco.[139] A stream of mourners came to visit while Josephine's body lay in repose. The presence of veterans among them, 'dressed in their old regimental colours', impressed Jean-Claude Baker, who stood guard beside the coffin:

> Some could hardly stand, but were there to give Josephine a last military salute. 'She was one of us,' they said, as they walked past crying.[140]

Princess Grace prevaricated for weeks over her choice of marble for the stone, delaying the final interment. When it finally took place, on 2 October at the Cimetière de Monaco, most of the tribe were present, as was Bouillon. Jacques Abtey also joined the modest mourning party. Along with the large Christian cross engraved on her tombstone is a brass plaque in the shape of a feather, honouring her as a veteran of the Second World War and a member of the French Légion d'honneur.[141]

AFTERWORD

Josephine Baker had a good war. The course she chose was a unique one, and despite her extended period of life-threatening ill-health, she emerged from the experience with her public image boosted by her war record. Her decision to stay in France in September 1939 may have been risky, but she did not hesitate, and fortunately it did not lead to personal disaster. Of all the other African Americans who weighed up the dangers of staying in France at the outset of the war, Eugene Bullard's position was the most like Baker's. A boxer, he had settled in the country and had fought for France during the First World War. After the 1918 armistice, he stayed in Paris, finding work in jazz clubs. Soon he was managing several nightclubs of his own. In 1923, he married the daughter of a French countess, and they had two children, though their union did not last. A good businessman, he survived the economic crisis and, when the war broke out, like Baker he wanted to participate in the war effort to support his adopted country. Again, like Baker, he agreed to help the French intelligence services by collecting the intelligence that came his way from the numerous German nationals who frequented his clubs.[1] In spring 1940, when the Nazis invaded, Bullard was uncertain what to do. He finally opted to join the exodus of fleeing Parisians, leaving his two daughters behind. After signing up as an army volunteer for a regiment stationed in Orléans, he was wounded, but managed to reach Angoulême, where he collapsed in hospital. There a doctor recognised him, patched him up and sent him on his way. He reached Biarritz on 22 June 1940 and, via Lisbon, managed to secure passage on a liner bound for the US.[2] He would not return to Paris for another fourteen years.

Since America was neutral at the outset of the war, Americans who remained in mainland France during the phoney war, even after the Nazi Occupation, should not have been explicitly targeted. This proved to be the case for white Americans, who were mostly left in peace by the Germans until the US entered the war in December 1941. Even then, it was not until September 1942 that American women in France were arrested as enemy aliens, even if they were married to Frenchmen and had taken French nationality, as Baker had. Three hundred or so were taken to the Vittel internment camp, where they joined British women in similar circumstances who were being held there.[3] More American women arrived later, and some were joined by husbands and children. There is no record, however, of any African American women in the camp. The conditions at Vittel were at least not too harsh, and in terms of food supplies the inmates were sometimes better positioned than most French people during the Occupation.[4]

African Americans were less fortunate. On 24 June 1940, the Germans banned concerts by Black American musicians in an effort to eliminate what the Nazis called 'degenerate Jewish-Negro jazz'. The following month, the Germans ordered a census of all foreign nationals in the capital. African Americans were directed to report to the police, and were offered no protection by the American consulate.[5] The famous jazz trumpeter Arthur Briggs was sent in late June 1940 to a concentration camp in Saint-Denis, where he formed a classical orchestra with other Black musicians from America, Britain and the West Indies. The Germans detained many other African American performers, including Roberta Dodd Crawford from Chicago, a prominent singer. Celebrated pianist Henry Crowder was giving a concert in Belgium when the Nazis invaded. He managed to get a train to Paris, but it was bombed by the Luftwaffe and he was taken by the Germans as he attempted to complete his journey on foot.[6]

After the Liberation, the African Americans who had survived the war returned to the capital. The *Afro-American* reported the indignities they had suffered:

> Doreen Renner, a Brooklyn dancer who went over with Teddy Hill in 1934 and stayed, got spit on and called 'black she-dog' by the Nazis. Charlie Louis Fisk, graduate pianist, was interned. Arthur Briggs, trumpeter, was not permitted to maintain his band which was one of Paris's best.[7]

The jazz trumpeter Valaida Snow also chose to risk it and remain in Europe. She and her orchestra had already been caught in Vienna during the 1938 *Anschluss*, when two members had been captured and assassinated. Snow, however, made it to Paris and, in 1939, when the last Americans left, instead of returning to the US, she went to Scandinavia. Unable to leave following the Nazi occupation of Denmark, she remained in Copenhagen. Forced to live there under some form of house arrest from October 1941 until 15 March 1942, she was then moved to a prison for political prisoners in the city. Finally, in May 1942, a US-chartered ship was able to enter the waters controlled by the Axis powers to bring Snow and stranded US embassy workers to New York.[8]

In 1945, Baker explained to journalists that she had fled Paris when the Nazis arrived. She would have remained, she said, only her colour made her a marked woman.[9] But it was also the case, as she revealed to journalist Kenneth Crawford, when they met in Morocco, that she felt that she 'couldn't leave French territory . . . it would have been like leaving a sinking ship. I'm no rat.'[10] Operating in North Africa proved an effective compromise for Baker, and she not only refused to leave the country, but also refused to do what many of her colleagues in the entertainment industry finally did – cave in and perform in the occupied territories. In this, she stood out as having acted differently, an aspect that was remarked on at a relatively early stage. Baker was 'the only one of the Paris revue stars of pre-war Paris including Chevalier, Mistinguett and Lucienne Boyer, to steadfastly refuse to return to Paris and perform under the Vichy and Nazi banners,' reported *Billboard* in 1943.[11] Similarly, *Variety* informed its readers that

> Miss Baker from St Louis is one of the very few, if not the only one, among the Parisian stars who has escaped, has devoted herself to the cause of France, and against whom there is not even a hint of collaboration with the enemy. It may be that this is the reason she conjures up this magic [for French soldiers]; maybe that gay, warm and tremendously sincere personality has something to do with it too.[12]

Baker's unblemished war record – by comparison with other entertainers who were besmirched by their association with Vichy and the Nazis – left her well positioned to relaunch her career, unlike some others, whom she, for one, never forgave for their wartime stance.

The most notorious of these was Maurice Chevalier, who she felt keenly had been a traitor to the Allied cause. Longstanding tensions between the two artists came to a head during the war. Baker blamed Chevalier for revealing her illness in a magazine article in 1942, when he claimed that she was dying in an impoverished state.[13] They had also allegedly had a falling out during their 1939 visit to the Maginot Line, when Chevalier complained that she took up more than her allotted share of performance time, due to the repeated encores.[14] During her American camp tour in late May 1943, she denounced Chevalier as pro-Nazi and vented her rage against him to journalists:

> Chevalier is doing for the Germans what I am doing for United States soldiers. His type of propaganda, trying to put Nazism over to the French people is worse than a speech by Hitler ... he's helping Goebbels keep up Nazi morale. He even has performed in Berlin and other parts of Germany, to say nothing about all he has been doing on the radio and the music halls of occupied France for the Nazis.[15]

Baker's assertions must have been speculative, as she could not have been fully aware of all his wartime actions; yet her remarks were picked up by several British and American papers and did great damage to Chevalier's reputation. At the time, these comments passed unquestioned, but most of her accusations proved to be untrue. Chevalier had allowed his songs to be broadcast on Radio-Paris and had sung emotional odes to Pétain, but that was a long way removed from her claims that he had promoted the Nazis. He had made a rapid return trip to Berlin in late 1941 to entertain French prisoners of war at their camp in Altengrabow. This was exploited by Goebbels, who presented his visit as a concert tour of Germany.[16] Exonerated after the Liberation, he played a full part in the celebratory galas of 1944–45. Baker, however, never forgave him and continued to hold a grudge against Chevalier to the end of her life. Just three years before she died, she wrote to Harry Janes from Sweden:

> I saw a documentary film of Maurice Chevalier here. I was scandalised to see and hear him talk about the war when we know the truth about his scandalous conduct – no one is saying a word about all those lies. They even have the gall to show General de Gaulle with him.[17]

Baker was not the only female artist to take up the mantle in support of the Fighting French, as she had been careful to point out to journalists when she arrived back in the capital in October 1944. 'I don't just want to talk about the work I do, but about the collective work we all do together, my comrades and I: Françoise Rosay, Germaine Sablon and Alice Delysia, who are great Frenchwomen, true patriots.'[18] These female entertainers also contributed to the war effort as part of their patriotic commitment to France and de Gaulle. Françoise Rosay was a film actress, married to the Belgian-born film director Jacques Feyder in 1917. They made several films in both French and German, and so Rosay was well known in two countries. She spoke to German women on the radio during the phoney war in an anti-Nazi propaganda effort, and left France for

Switzerland in 1940, to escape the German invasion. After completing a film there, she moved to London, where she worked as a broadcaster for the Free French. By the end of the war, she had moved to North Africa to work as a director of Radio Algiers, in charge of cultural broadcasting – a position she held from 1944–47. She was awarded a Légion d'honneur in 1957.

Germaine Sablon's profile was closer to that of Baker. A singer and actress, she left Paris in 1940 for Saint-Raphaël, where she sheltered the author Joseph Kessel and his nephew Maurice Druon. During 1942–43, she performed in Switzerland, and when the Nazis marched into the southern zone in 1942, she escaped with Kessel and Druon over the Pyrenees, reaching London in February 1943 via Spain and Portugal. On 30 May, she first recorded the song written by Kessel that was adopted as the anthem of the Resistance, 'Le chant des partisans'.[19] Having joined the Free French, she became a nurse with the Hadfield-Spears Ambulance Unit, and after the Liberation she followed the 1st Division of the Free French through France and Italy. At the end of the war, she was awarded the Resistance medal and the Croix de Guerre, followed in May 1951 by the Légion d'honneur.

However, it was Alice Delysia, the singer, who had the closest professional trajectory to Baker's. Although French, she made her career in British music hall. Like Baker, as we have seen, she supported the Allied war effort by entertaining the troops.[20] Noted for her determination, she had battled to be allowed to go to the North African front, and as one soldier wrote,

> it took . . . months before she finally managed to overcome official objections and fears and play to us under fire. When she succeeded, we had a new General – Montgomery. Alice regarded her work for the fighting men as a crusade. No one and nothing was allowed to stand in her way . . . while German artillery did some desultory shelling in the afternoon heat, she gave us something of France that will always live, something of its sparkle and courage. To us Alice Delysia is the woman of the war.[21]

Again, like Baker, Delysia carried out lengthy tours thoughout the war years. For nearly three years she performed in the Middle East, undertaking a series of exhausting engagements, including in desert camps and hospitals. She was respected by other entertainers, including Noël Coward, who wrote of her when their paths crossed in 1943:

> For two years she had been back and forth across the desert, tirelessly entertaining the troops, frequently under conditions that would have driven artists of less stamina into nervous breakdowns. She had bounced about in lorries and trucks, been under fire and lost in sandstorms, and here she was, chic and cool in a pink linen tailleur, looking younger and more vital than I had ever seen her.[22]

Another said of her:

> She roughed it with the rest of us in the desert. She took to the stage in sandstorms, cloudbursts, and heat waves. She never once let us down. In the desert, the Luftwaffe bombed the area round the mobile stage, but Delysia kept on singing and the audience did not budge.[23]

Delysia and other wartime performers, including Baker, undertook extensive tours, despite the financial sacrifices, at a time when there was widespread reluctance among stars to travel to North Africa.[24] The limited number of entertainers performing overseas for the troops had been criticised amidst a sense that stage stars had 'let the fighting soldier down'. Gracie Fields, a well-known cinema and music-hall personality, was alleged to have been 'hurt and upset by the charge that she had left the troops . . . in the Middle East to fulfil commercial engagements in the United States'. She explained that she had honoured all the dates that she had been asked to perform by ENSA. Other 'stars' also defended themselves, explaining that the reason for their absence was not loss of salary (as most of it was taken in taxes anyway they explained); rather, they insisted, 'the reason why so few top liners are visiting our troops in the field is the reluctance of managements and agents to release them even temporarily from lucrative contracts'. ENSA's director, Basil Dean, tried to counter these accusations, pointing to Delysia, who 'has been out in the Middle East for two years at a tenth of the salary she could earn in the West End. She has refused offers to come home to play in the West End.'[25] The troops agreed: 'All glory to Alice Delysia, the only top liner to visit a desert camp.'[26] But loved and courageous as she was, often doing camp shows in dangerous locations close to the war zone, her contribution was confined to her stage performances. Her war work did not compare with that of Baker, whose role went beyond that of entertainment. A much more dynamic and outspoken ambassador for France and the Free French, Baker's espionage activities set her apart from all these other female artistes.

Nonetheless, Baker was as proud of her troop shows as she was of any of her intelligence missions, and its value in maintaining morale was recognised by the military hierarchies.[27] Her camp tours were never just a cover for her other activities: Baker revelled in the pleasures and comforts she could bring, even if it could be hazardous. As another female entertainer who performed in North Africa recalled, whatever the dangers, any risk was worthwhile: 'Once on stage, it was magic – we knew that we were making a difference and all that we cared about was making them laugh. A troop audience was the best in the world – you couldn't get better.'[28] Baker felt that she was 'not merely entertainer to the troops but a soldier cheering on her fellow soldiers in the fight to regain Paris'.[29] When this was recognised during her Middle East tour by a general of the Fighting French – who asserted after one of her shows, 'Madame vous êtes un soldat' – she was delighted.[30] Baker invariably took no money for her countless energetic performances – and if she did, it was only the basic military pay. Her lack of personal gain was widely recognised.[31] Most of the time, if she was not on a morale-boosting exercise for troops, she was involved in fund-raising, predominantly for Gaullist charities, promoting de Gaulle's Fighting French and the work of the internal French Resistance, and she successfully raised impressive sums.

Baker was dedicated, too, coping with demanding conditions in the hottest months in the desert, and repeatedly putting her health at risk. She had a reputation for being 'more concerned with entertaining audiences in isolated locations'.[32] She never lived ostentatiously. When in barracks, she did not hesitate to follow orders; and on her camp tours she would bed down in tents and sleep rough, as the situation required. Baker's commitment attracted comment: 'In all her shows she gives the impression of working harder and more selflessly than anyone else around.'[33] She lived with the soldiers in their camps and ate with them. On one occasion she even took the time to attend a softball game, screaming on the sidelines to encourage the teams.[34]

Baker excelled in her role and had 'a gift for "sensing" her soldier audiences, fitting her songs to their moods'.[35] This was particularly true when she sang her own personal anthem 'J'ai deux amours'. Langston Hughes wrote: 'She has made of [it] a kind of prayer that brings tears streaming down the faces of the men, women and children that remember Paris.'[36] For homesick soldiers, particularly French soldiers, she brought 'a little breath of home'.[37] The fact that Baker, an African American, was seen by the French military authorities 'as a living symbol of Paris – even France' was not lost on a Variety reporter, who commented that 'the French authorities thought so much of her effect on the newly forming French army' that they offered the 'colored girl from St Louis' every means to go on tour to build French morale.[38] Baker could draw on her knowledge of both French and American culture in ways that allowed her to promote a cross-national appeal, and she always made a point of acknowledging the nationalities of those who were present in her audiences. In referring to her as 'the reigning theatrical star of France-in-Exile', Hughes noted her enormous popularity 'among the French and North African peoples alike'.[39]

Her skill as an entertainer lay in her ability to reach out and convince members of her audiences that she was directing her attention to them alone.[40] She would pass round cigarettes, banter, clown around and ad-lib to interact with the soldiers in ways that fostered this informality. After the war, she confided on stage that

'Contact with the troops has served me well; it makes us more human, less artificial. You follow your impulses, your heart. I used to adopt an attitude, seek to create an effect; now I try to be myself.'[41] The war had revealed to Baker how to bridge the gap between herself and her audiences more effectively. In embedding her own recent experiences into her performances, she made people feel that they were sharing those experiences and seeing the real Josephine Baker. 'The great star has captured the hearts of the public with her natural charm and her personal, yet engaging performance, and she knows how to connect with them in the most intimate way,' wrote a Swiss journalist.[42] This sense of closeness, however, was an illusion; and creating it was a key component of her performative art. Her success in creating this public-private persona, a staged 'private' self,[43] allowed her to foster the sense of intimacy and accessibility that her audiences craved, particularly during wartime. Her remarkable ability to hide her own real identity, her capacity to keep her true self secret, was what made her such an effective spy.

Fighting for France and freedom

In February 1952, Baker explained that during the war she 'went in with all my heart and soul to fight for the freedom of those who were being tortured'.[44] She was determined to use her position to help those who were facing danger. In Marseille in 1940, she spent her time writing 'letters to various consuls for ... dispersed companions who were waiting in hiding for me to help them out'.[45] She saved her friends Salmsen and Rey, and later helped Lion and his family. These are the individuals we know about; there may well have been others. When it comes to her espionage activities, through her service for the Deuxième Bureau in the crucial years of 1941–42, she provided valuable assistance to the British, and probably also served the Americans in North Africa in the run-up to the Allied landings. British intelligence agent Donald Darling referred to her as a 'cherished agent of de Gaulle's government' in his 1977 account of his own wartime activities.[46] He revealed that MI6 was tracking her activities in 1943, and that British intelligence saw her as the 'pet lady agent' of the Free French.[47]

However, shadows remain, the details of Baker and Abtey's story have changed over time, and we will probably never know the full picture, particularly when it comes to Abtey. He emerges as something of a slippery, maverick figure, perhaps even an opportunist, who was not entirely trusted by many of those he worked with. While he repeatedly espoused his loyalty to the Gaullists in his post-war accounts and testimonials, the evidence shows that he was treated by them with some suspicion – even at times a notable lack of respect. Yet Baker appears to have admired him, trusted him implicitly and was prepared to follow his lead, seemingly unquestioningly. He was, after all, her superior officer. On some of her missions, notably to Spain, they virtually operated in a vacuum and were out on a limb, involved in tasks that neither the Deuxième Bureau nor the Gaullist FFL were fully aware of or overseeing. The irregularity of their situation, or at least its lack of clarity, could have spelt disaster. But they were saved by the strength of Baker's cover and her skilled use of it to disguise her intelligence work. After the American landings in North Africa in November 1942, Baker adopted a more ambassadorial approach – ostensibly for the French, but also supporting the Americans. She came to understand the importance of the overt role she could play: 'I had to sing again though I could hardly stand. After all I am American and French at the same time. I can help them understand each other.'[48]

When a reporter tried to get to the bottom of Baker's determination to engage in such a demanding programme of entertainment for the troops, she related how, after the collapse of France, her conviction of the need to act had been triggered by reading an announcement in the paper 'by the German military commander of Paris to the effect that all visitors were welcome . . . with the exception of Jews and dark-skinned people'. As Baker said, 'I am afraid that most people don't know what a calamity it would be if Hitler were to win the war.' Explaining how the situation haunted her at night, she went on:

I sometimes would awaken from my sleep after dreaming that prejudiced crowds of Germans and other prejudiced nationalities were breaking down my door to grab me. One night I made the resolve to sing to soldiers for the duration with this view of helping my race and my adopted country and furthering the progress of humanity. When soldiers applaud me, I like to believe they will never acquire a hatred for colored people because of the cheer I have brought them. It may be foolish, but it is the way I feel.[49]

Baker felt that gaining acceptance from the troops was key to promoting racial tolerance. 'Every success I have counts for my coloured brothers in America,' she exclaimed.[50] She later told Sauvage, 'I tried to unite people with fun and laughter.'[51] We may consider her assessment of the role she could play to be fanciful, even naïve, but her dedication and her will to act was genuine, and she undeniably had an impact.

Baker's awareness of her own power to advocate and bring about a change in attitudes grew throughout the war years. She was a superb ambassador not only for her 'race', as she put it, but for de Gaulle, Gaullism and indeed, for France.[52] She helped advance the cause of de Gaulle's Fighting French at a time when it was far from gaining widespread acceptance across the North African continent. For local North African populations, her very presence on the stage as an African American female star conveyed a clear message of French racial tolerance, even before she started to speak out in favour of de Gaulle. Baker may have found her voice to promote freedom and combat segregation, but her passionate commitment to Gaullism also put her in an ambiguous position in relation to French colonialism. In acting to protect French interests across France's North Africa empire and in the Middle East, she was also favouring French imperialist and colonialist ambitions, a position which sat uneasily with her opposition to American segregation and vocal defence of freedom. In supporting de Gaulle's Fighting French, she found herself caught in the complex relationship between freedom and colonial rule. Her wartime loyalty to France had also necessitated her support for the despotic rule of Glaoui and her other aristocratic friends in Morocco – contacts that proved vital to her undercover intelligence work, as we have seen.

Baker continued to come up against this same dynamic of complexities and competing interests for the rest of her life. It exposed her to criticism, especially when she was actively engaged in her civil rights campaigning, and at times made her anti-racist words seem a little empty. An article published in December of 1951, during the Stork Club debacle, pointed directly to this:

> Edith Sampson, noted Negro attorney of Chicago, said she is tired of hearing Jos. [sic] malign the US and praise France for its handling of race problems ... 'She should stop and consider what France is doing to some 45,000,000 in its African colonies, French colonialism is a blot on the world's conscience. Education and health facilities are meager. These people suffer much more than does Miss Baker in Atlanta or in New York. In the United States we are at least attempting to eradicate these barriers. When France tries to do at least one tenth as much in the colonies I will be willing to listen to Josephine Baker.'[53]

Yet in December 1953, Baker claimed: 'I fight racial, religious and social discrimination wherever I find it, because I am profoundly against it and I cannot remain insensitive to the misfortunes of those who cannot defend themselves in this area, even if I find it in France.'[54] Despite these fine words, as during the war, Baker knew that she had no place commenting on French colonialism. Journalist Gary Younge has acknowledged that at this time American exiles were 'free to write about racial atrocities in America, but not to comment on colonial atrocities committed by France at home or abroad'.[55] Concerns that her anti-racist campaigning might breach this edict probably explains the close police monitoring of her French lecture series for the LICRA in 1957. Baker made her peace with the unspoken pact which underscored her acceptance in the country, and this probably also influenced her decision to represent France in the most positive of terms in her address during the

March on Washington in 1963. Publicly, Baker chose to take French universalism at face value, allowing her to stay in favour with the French government and the public. Denouncing France's post-war colonial policies risked jeopardising her need for support in her battle for the survival of Les Milandes.

Tracking Baker's post-war life back to her wartime experiences allows us to identify how she came to understand that she could exploit her celebrity to promote her ideas. Instead of focusing on the frames of nostalgia and colonialism that have dominated work about her to date, it shifts us away from her pre-war representations as the 'Black Venus' and her success in performing tropes of women from the French colonies, and centres the analysis more squarely on her later political activism.[56] After the war, rather than simply relaunch her music-hall career bolstered by her impressive war record, Baker chose to use her position to protest. The war had taught her how to mobilise her performances as political statements, and she could work a crowd to perfection. When touring to promote the Free French during the war, her rousing enthusiasm for the cause would bring hundreds of soldiers and civilians to their feet to cheer loudly in support of de Gaulle.[57] In the 1950s, Baker drew on these wartime experiences to harness her celebrity and attack US racism. She saw the larger picture through the lens of her own life, rather than in terms of history and structural forces that shaped social conditions.[58] She applied what she had learnt, and performed politics by mobilising the armoury that she had perfected during the war to work towards her goal of fostering a harmonious society in which racial and cultural difference could thrive without prejudice.

Memorialisation

Nonetheless, Baker's war record was rarely the focus of the obituaries that appeared in the days following her death in 1975. Most were dominated by her remarkable comeback performance at the Bobino theatre and the dramatic circumstances of her sudden demise. Her war work was generally seen as secondary to the wider importance of her musical performances and her artistic contributions. Jacques Siclier's obituary in *Le Monde* is a telling example. His tribute to the 'legendary superstar' concentrates on her music-hall career and devotes only a brief paragraph to the war. He rather caustically targets Mistinguett, noting that 'Josephine disappeared [from Paris], while Mistinguett hung around carrying the torch for music hall and singing "La Tour Eiffel".' He acknowledges that Baker did great service for her husband Jean Lion, in helping him escape the Nazis, as well as for the officers of the Deuxième Bureau, to whom she transmitted valuable intelligence. He commented that she returned from Morocco

> in uniform, with the Free French Forces, and resumed her career. But the days of the Black Venus with a belt of feathers and bananas, of the island bird and the woman-as-object were over. In the revues, Josephine wore sumptuous costumes. Her voice was deeper and warmer.[59]

After briefly mentioning Baker's wartime actions, rather than celebrating her actual contribution to the war, Siclier cites the period as notable for the turning point it represented in her style of performing.

On the other hand, the popular weekend edition of *Ici Paris Hebdo* dedicated several pages to different aspects of Baker's life and included a full page on her wartime activities, featuring them in some detail, if not always accurately. The in-depth overview finishes with an account of her funeral, linking it directly to her wartime service:

> They were there, the veterans, clad in medals, brandishing tricolour flags, carrying her decorations on a cushion, the military Légion d'honneur, the Resistance medal, reminding us that this great star was also a 'great man' when circumstances required it. [The funeral] summed up Josephine Baker's whole life. A tribute from her public, a tribute from the artists, a military tribute to a woman with many faces and a big heart.[60]

It is notable that Baker's espionage activities are seen in gendered terms. Rather than presenting her as a remarkable woman who made a significant contribution to the cause of the Resistance, these activities are seen by the journalist as qualifying her as an honorary man.

To capture attention before Josephine faded from public consciousness, Bouillon hastily produced a biography of Baker, which appeared just fourteen months after her death. Designed first and foremost to make money – to 'ensure the survival of the Rainbow family'[61] – the book has been the most frequently quoted source about her life. This is largely on account of the inclusion in it of several first-person passages apparently authored by Baker herself. She had been gathering material for her autobiography throughout the 1960s and 1970s, perhaps with an eye to having a hand in her own memorialisation, and was looking for someone to co-author it.[62] When she died, Bouillon quickly saw an opportunity. He explains his approach in the introduction:

> We set to work, sorting through the famous boxes, digging out the memories, the declarations of intent, correspondence from the world's greatest figures, and those that were unsigned . . . Josephine wrote everywhere and anywhere: on stationery from international palaces visited during her tours, on paper tablecloths in bistros, on pages torn from a notebook, on sheets of paper that would eventually be typed. Little by little, it all came together, and we were able to reconstruct a fascinating, unpredictable, sometimes disconcerting human being . . . If there was a gap, I turned to her sister Margaret, our children, her friends or my own recollections to fill it.[63]

In line with Baker's earlier autobiographical collaborations with Sauvage, it was carefully crafted to preserve the public image that she was a past master at projecting. It emphasises her achievements as a dancer turned music-hall performer and then civil rights activist, rather than devoting detailed attention to her wartime activities. The narrative set the tone for most of the biographies that followed.[64]

A second book dedicated to Baker appeared in the same year, this time in English, authored by Stephen Papich, who was both a long-time friend of Baker's and director of her 1973 American tour. *Remembering Josephine* was based on their regular conversations in the last decade of her life. Papich concedes in the preface that 'many times Josephine confused dates and incidents'.[65] As a result, despite some passages where Baker seems to offer tangible insights into her life and motivations, overall the book is often inaccurate; at times it even seems fantastical. This is particularly true of the war period. Over several pages, Baker tells a nonsensical story of herself as a member of the French Resistance being tracked by the Gestapo for her espionage activities. The escape she recounts includes hiding in the Paris sewers and having to dodge Hermann Goering, chief of the Luftwaffe, when he attempted to poison her at her home.[66]

Harry Janes had also aspired to write Baker's biography. An experienced writer, he considered himself well qualified to produce something worthy of her memory, and could draw on his insider knowledge due to their longstanding friendship. She may even have suggested the project to him. He had already commenced the task of collecting notes and drafting a few passages when she died, and his exchanges with Baker's sister Margaret reveal that she had agreed to collaborate with him on the project. But Janes soon found himself unwittingly pitted against Bouillon, as they both prepared to write the first authoritative book about the star.[67] In the end, he could not compete.

'The Book of Bouillon', as Margaret called it, did not make money.[68] However, Bouillon did have more success in securing a lucrative deal selling exclusive worldwide rights to Baker's life story in July 1975, again just months after her death. During Baker's 1973 American tour, American talent agents Hank Kaufman and Eugene Lerner had started discussions with her about a film project. The initial plan was for a Broadway musical, but in the end Kaufman and Lerner failed to secure financial backing for it and it never came to fruition.[69] They had ambitions not just for a musical, but also for an 'official' documentary and a feature film, although neither of those plans materialised either. Lerner's research for these projects – held at Stanford University – reveals his serious efforts to build as accurate a representation of Baker's life as possible. In relation to her wartime activities, for example, he wrote to President Giscard d'Estaing in September 1975 asking for help, and was put in contact with the military archives. His collection includes many of the documents that have informed this book.[70]

Lerner also contacted Abtey, and their correspondence reveals that the latter pitched his authority as an informant with credentials, as

the man who, having supervised Josephine and spent some of the most exciting, and at times the most dangerous and dramatic hours of her life with her, is the person who in psychological terms knows the most about Josephine Baker.[71]

He suggested that Baker's

fiery, passionate life could be reconstructed exactly where it took place, with a thousand real-life anecdotes. This very private Arab world has kept all its secrets and its magic, its enchantment too ... The doors of the palaces and houses where Josephine lived are still open to Jacques Abtey [and] Josephine's life during this very particular period can be recreated in the very places where she lived.[72]

His short summary of 'Josephine's Secret and Artistic Double Life During the Second World War' includes some details that are not mentioned in his 1948 book. For example, he indicates that, at the time he recruited Baker, in November 1939, rather than going into the embassies for information, they installed microphones in her Le Vésinet villa, where she received important diplomatic personalities and made them talk. Abtey also refers to 'actions' they took both against the German armistice commission in Morocco and in relation to the German agents encountered working on 'missions in Spain', and names Abwehr officer Frigate Captain

Unterberg-Gibhardt as their nemesis.[73] Frustratingly, he does not offer any details of these 'actions', but as Baker went on just one mission to Spain alone, and probably without the knowledge of the Deuxième Bureau, it is hard to imagine exactly what 'actions' Abtey could be referring to. He was doubtless responding to Lerner's assertion that the film would not be a documentary, but 'an adaptation, a transposition, a cinematic theatrical invention. . .loyal to Josephine's spirit and heart, based on facts, events and experiences of her life . . . in the style of a "cinematic novel"'.

Lerner was grateful for Abtey's input, and in return expressed support for his ambitions to rework his 1948 book for an American audience. However, the publishers Lerner approached were hesitant, believing that the market was likely to be saturated, with Bouillon's book imminent and another by Papich on the way.[74] Abtey's new book project therefore never happened, and his 1948 book has never been translated. Some years after his death, his second wife, Jacqueline, whom he married just after the war, produced an exact reprint of the original, with a portrait of Josephine by Abtey on the front cover.[75]

Les Milandes – A *lieu de mémoire*?[76]

In 2001, the Château des Milandes was purchased by Henry and Claude de Labarre. It had fallen into serious disrepair and the couple set about having it thoroughly renovated. They tasked their daughter, Angélique de Labarre, with transforming the site into a tourist attraction and converting the central main château building into a museum to celebrate Baker's life. De Labarre refurnished its fourteen rooms, which had been completely emptied of Baker's belongings during the sale in 1969, and acquired extensive memorabilia to put on display, including one of Baker's famous banana skirts. In 2012, it was one of the first sites to be awarded the new title of a 'Maison des Illustres' by the French Ministry of Culture, highlighting its significance in the preservation of Baker's memory and affirming that she was seen by the state as someone who was distinguished in the political, social and cultural history of

France.[77] It has since become one of the key tourist attractions in the area, drawing around 200,000 visitors a year.

The centrepiece of the main exhibition presents several of her dramatic stage costumes, displayed on waxwork figures, recreating Baker's own former waxwork museum known as the Jorama. These iconic outfits – along with others shown elsewhere in the building, numerous vivid posters advertising Josephine's appearances over the years and photographs of her in her various costumes and personas – lead the visitor through her pre- and post-war music-hall appearances. Photographs of her 'rainbow tribe' of children in situ are poignantly displayed in several of the rooms where they lived. These images evoke their lives at the château and chronicle Baker's last unfortunate days there.

While Josephine's wartime life is mentioned, it is not the main emphasis of the overall display. A couple of attic rooms are dedicated to it. In the absence of the kinds of objects that are present in the other parts of the exhibition, Baker's wartime experiences are conveyed using a dramatic installation with lights to communicate her spying activities, and with a waxwork display of Baker receiving her Légion d'honneur medal from General Valin. A very worn blue air force uniform jacket is exhibited, along with a selection of books (including Abtey's) and photographs. Several documents hang on the walls, but overall these attic rooms, while effective, are some-what overshadowed by the beauty of the site itself and the other rooms of the château, including Baker's magnificent bathroom deco-rated in gold leaf and black tiles – allegedly chosen to match the bottle of her favourite perfume, Arpège.

Until recently, this kind of presentation of Baker's life, which places the emphasis clearly on her performative legacy, has been a key concern of her memorialisation. It is the legacy she celebrated herself and has been the focus of the existing scholarship about her life. Commentators point to her importance as an artist, and her impact on other, more contemporary performers, like Madonna and Beyoncé, is often evoked as proof of this. Beyoncé even went so far as to don a banana skirt in 2006 in tribute to Baker.[78] Scholars have therefore tended to be preoccupied with her dance and film performances, seeking to evaluate her cultural impact, while neglecting not just her wartime contribution, but also her later post-war activism and the overall political dimension of her activist work.[79] This lack of emphasis on Baker's wartime activities both in her memorialisation and in the existing scholarship may go some way to explaining why her wartime engagement and espionage work for the Free French forces was seen as a huge reveal in the run-up to the celebration of her life and the transfer of Baker's ashes to the Panthéon in November 2021.[80]

Panthéonisation

In April 2021, journalist and commentator Laurent Kupferman rekindled a campaign that had been initiated in 2013 by the philosopher and journalist Régis Debray in response to a public appeal from the then President François Hollande for suggestions of distinguished women who should be brought into the Panthéon, in order to start to redress the gender balance of those honoured there.[81] This process, which makes individuals into national heroes by transferring their ashes to the Panthéon, had previously been an almost exclusively male domain. The tradition of burial or reburial in this secular national site represents the highest distinction that can be paid to a French citizen. The pomp and ceremony surrounding these events is considerable and, most importantly, it serves to draw public attention to those whose lives are being celebrated. Debray's arguments for choosing Baker had centred on her achievements as being worthy of those of a man. This gendered understanding of Baker's case was designed to suggest that her contribution equalled that of the men who had already been honoured in this way. However, Debray's case did not meet with Hollande's approval, as he allegedly considered the idea '*farfelue*' – 'totally wacky'.[82] Instead, he chose two other very deserving women resisters, Geneviève de Gaulle-Anthonioz and Germaine Tillon, who were honoured in a ceremony in 2015. However, when Kupferman relaunched the campaign amidst intense media interest, it immediately took off, and a petition under the slogan '*Osez Joséphine Baker*

au Panthéon' ('Dare to choose Josephine Baker for the Panthéon')
quickly attracted signatures.

Kupferman put this enthusiastic public reaction down to Baker's
ongoing relevance, suggesting that she represented 'a powerful
symbol of national unity, of emancipation and of France's universalism'. The petition argued that

> She was a free woman and an activist, a feminist, a resistance
> fighter, and an activist against racism and antisemitism. In a
> world turned in on itself, where tribalism and racism are exacer-
> bated, her ideals resonate in people's hearts.[83]

The petition's almost 38,000 signatures allegedly convinced
President Macron to take the suggestion seriously: only the French
president can decide to induct someone into the Panthéon. On 23
August 2021, the announcement came that the ceremony to transfer
Baker's ashes to the Panthéon would be held on 30 November 2021,
to coincide with the eighty-fourth anniversary of Baker's wedding
to Lion and thus marking the date she took French citizenship.
Kupferman's campaign was timely, as it coincided with the end of
Macron's first term as president. With elections on the horizon, it
would be naïve to ignore the political opportunism that influenced
his decision to proceed with Baker's *panthéonisation*. Notably, it
allowed him to symbolically reach out to more diverse populations,
offering evidence of his 'commitment' to inclusivity. *Le Monde* celebrated his decision days after the announcement, stating: 'few
personalities incarnate the values of Republican France as bril-
liantly and as unassumingly as Josephine Baker'.[84] It was a remarkable development. For the first time, an American-born Black
woman would be inducted into the Panthéon. She was also the first
performer to be honoured there. Kupferman has emphasised the
importance of Baker's war record as a consideration in Macron's
decision.[85] It would allow him to project her as a heroic figure of the
Resistance, and he could stress her wartime humanism in a way
which rendered her politically appealing to a wide audience. Her
credentials were unassailable.

Her family did not wish her remains to be removed from where she was buried in Monaco, beside Bouillon and one of her children, and not far from Princess Grace. Her coffin was therefore symbolically filled with samples of soil from the four places that meant most to her (St Louis, her birthplace; Les Milandes; Monaco, with which she had had a strong affiliation in her later years; and Paris). The ceremony, which commenced at dusk on 30 November, was a moving and lively spectacle. Qualitatively different from past induction ceremonies, which were notably more sombre, daytime occasions, the darkness allowed for a theatrical lightshow of projections onto the front façade of the Panthéon, presenting scenes from Baker's life. Macron's wide-ranging twenty-minute speech, 'Ma France, ma Joséphine', detailed Baker's life and activities. He stated that: 'She was on the right side of history every time – she made the right choices, always distinguishing light from obscurity.' He hailed the comic genius of her Paris cabaret performances that 'ridiculed colonial prejudices'. He stated that during the Second World War she had served France 'without seeking glory' and that as a civil rights activist 'she defended equality for all above individual identity'. Though born American, Macron pronounced, 'no one was more French' than Baker; she was 'an exceptional figure who embodied the French spirit'. The dramatic event attracted the attention of the world's media, which delivered Baker's life and achievements to an international public.

Macron's description of Baker's wartime contribution, a lesser-known aspect of her life for contemporary audiences, was a revelation to many. In France, as we have seen, she was best known for her life as a music-hall star, whereas in America she was recognised as a civil rights activist. For Macron, Baker understood her acquisition of French nationality not as a right, but as a responsibility which necessitated the daily affirmation of her devotion to her new country and the defence of its values. It was this sense of responsibility that underpinned her motivation for her wartime actions. Macron then recounted these reasonably accurately, despite the odd embellishment. For example, he made reference to Les Milandes as a place of refuge for Jews and resistors. While Baker probably did shelter Lion's family, there is no evidence for the latter. In addition, his assertion that a radio transmitter was housed there does not hold up to historical scrutiny.[86]

Macron, like the Gaullists during the war, recognised in Baker her enormous symbolic potential to promote an 'idea of France'. Her race was as valuable to Macron in projecting a commitment to diversity and republicanism as it had been to de Gaulle in 1943–45, and this evidence of her civic commitment to the Republic operated as forcefully at the time of her *panthéonisation* as it had during the war. Both Macron and de Gaulle saw in Baker a valuable political icon, and both were able to capitalise on her transnational identity. *Panthéonisation* has completely transformed Baker's legacy both in France and overseas. Since the event, her son Brian Bouillon Baker, the nominated spokesperson for the family, has reported that requests for his presence at events to talk about his mother have reached 'tsunami levels'.[87] Visiting the Panthéon is a moving experience. It is striking to see Baker's tomb in the same area in the crypt as the communist resister Missak Manouchian and his wife Mélinée, who have been inducted since Baker. The vault is located near tombs and plaques honouring eighty-one other eminent figures who have marked France's history, including Émile Zola, Louis Braille and Jean Jaurès. Three Black men are honoured there. Félix Éboué, a colonial administrator and early supporter of the Free French, and author Alexandre Dumas are both interred in the crypt. The life of writer and politician Aimé Césaire is marked by a plaque and an inscription. Baker joins them and just a handful of other women, including the scientist Marie Curie, the philosopher Simone Weil, and resisters Geneviève de Gaulle-Anthonioz and Germaine Tillon. It is to be hoped that other women, and other people of colour, will follow. There are many suitable candidates.

It is fitting that Baker should have attracted France's highest national honour. Her wartime actions were driven more than anything by her conviction that France and its republican traditions had to be defended. France had offered her safety and opportunity, allowing her to thrive as an African American entertainer and to achieve a degree of success that would have been impossible in the context of America's racial divisions. Her attachment to France was visceral and she embraced France completely. Serving in the French military was her crowning moment, and she asserted that she preferred her uniform to her music-hall regalia.[88] She said of her promotion to second lieutenant: 'I was so happy . . . it seemed to me that I had thus begun to fulfil my contract with France. And in the end, it was the only contract that ever mattered to me.'[89] She inhabited her French citizenship, and she delighted in her wartime service. After the war, Baker commented that 'My life as a spy is the story of a Frenchwoman who loved her country.'[90] Full details of her intelligence work may not have been recorded in the archives, but we do know that Baker showed herself willing and risked her life. She volunteered to work for the French intelligence services, she was a fervent Gaullist, she enlisted and was deeply committed to the cause. In the Resistance, you did what you could and what you were told. You followed up on the opportunities that presented themselves to join the battle against Nazi Germany. What was Baker's contribution if it wasn't that? Hers was a unique and courageous story. She used her talents and her fame to play a full part in the Allied victory and helped to secure the future of her country.

NOTES

Author's Note

1. See Mike Laws, 'Why we capitalize "Black" (and not "white")', *Columbia Journalism Review*, 16 June 2020.

Introduction

1. Terri Simone Francis, *Josephine Baker's Cinematic Prism*, Indiana University Press, 2021, p. 47.
2. Bryan Hammond and Patrick O'Connor, *Josephine Baker*, Jonathan Cape, 1988, p. 41.
3. Bennetta Jules-Rosette, *Josephine Baker in Art and Life: The Icon and the Image*, University of Illinois Press, 2007, p. 53.
4. Phyllis Rose, *Jazz Cleopatra: Josephine Baker in Her Time*, Vintage, 1990, p. 132.
5. Tyler Stovall, *Paris Noir: African Americans in the City of Light*, Houghton Mifflin, 1996, p. 90.
6. Jules-Rosette, *Josephine Baker in Art and Life*, p. 174.
7. Jules-Rosette, *Josephine Baker in Art and Life*, p. 63.
8. Tyler Stovall, 'The new woman and the new empire: Josephine Baker and changing views of femininity in interwar France', in Kaiama L. Glover (ed.), *Josephine Baker: A Century in the Spotlight*, 6:1–2 (2007/2008), S&F Online.
9. Andy Fry, 'Du jazz hot à "La Créole": Josephine Baker sings Offenbach', *Cambridge Opera Journal*, 16:1 (2004), pp. 43–75.
10. Fry, 'Du jazz hot à "La Créole"', p. 58.
11. 'La métamorphose de Joséphine Baker', *Le Cri de Paris*, 21 December 1934, cited in Fry, 'Du jazz hot à "La Créole"', p. 58.
12. Fry, 'Du jazz hot à "La Créole"', p. 59; see also Jennifer Anne Boittin, *Colonial Metropolis: The Urban Grounds of Anti-Imperialism and Feminism in Interwar Paris*, University of Nebraska Press, 2010 on the significance of this discourse around the lightening of Baker's skin.

13. Rachel Gillett, *At Home in Our Sounds: Music, Race and Cultural Politics in Interwar Paris*, Oxford University Press, 2021, p. 203.
14. Hanna Diamond, *Women and the Second World War in France: Choices and Constraints*, Longman, 1999; Rod Kedward, *The Legacy of the French Resistance*, Bloomsbury, 2022.
15. Joséphine Baker with Marcel Sauvage, *Mémoires*, Phébus,1949, republished 2022, p. 280 (henceforth referenced as Sauvage, *Mémoires*).
16. 'Josephine Baker', *Guardian*, 26 August 1974, p. 6.
17. Jess Shahan, '"Don't keep mum": Critical approaches to the narratives of women intelligence professionals', *Intelligence and National Security*, 36:4 (2021), pp. 569–583.
18. Jacques Abtey, *La guerre secrète de Joséphine Baker*, Editions Sédoney, 1948.
19. Most of the existing biographies of Baker draw on it for their chapters dedicated to the war. The best of these is Rose, *Jazz Cleopatra*. Jean-Claude Baker, the last of Baker's adopted children, offers the most detailed biography, which draws on his contacts with her entourage: Jean-Claude Baker and Chris Chase, *Josephine: The Hungry Heart*, Random House, 1993, republished by Cooper Square Press, 2001 for references used here.
20. See chapter 7 for a fuller discussion of this book.
21. Joséphine Baker and Jo Bouillon, *Joséphine*, Robert Laffont-Opera Mundi, 1976.
22. See Terri Simone Francis on the relationship the American Black press had with Black artists in Paris, *Josephine Baker's Cinematic Prism*, pp. 50–55.
23. See Christopher Andrew and Julius Green, *Stars and Spies: Intelligence Operations and the Entertainment Business*, The Bodley Head, 2021.
24. Including works such as Michelle Perrot (ed.), *Une histoire des femmes est-elle possible?* Editions Rivages, 1984; M.R. Higonnet, J. Jenson, S. Michel and M.C. Weitz (eds), *Behind the Lines: Gender and Two World Wars*, Yale University Press, 1987; J.W. Scott, *Gender and the Politics of History*, Columbia University Press, 1988; Françoise Thébaud (ed.), *Résistances et Libérations: France 1940–1945*, Presses Universitaires du Mirail, 1995; Luc Capdevila, François Rouquet, Fabrice Virgili and Danièle Voldman (eds), *Hommes et Femmes dans la France en Guerre (1914–1945)*, Payot, 2003; Catherine Lacour-Astol, *Le genre de la Résistance*, Presses de Sciences-Po, 2015.
25. Robin Mitchell, *Vénus Noire: Black Women and Colonial Fantasies in Nineteenth Century France*, University of Georgia Press, 2020; T.D. Keaton, T. Deanean Sharpley-Whiting and T. Stovall (eds), *Black France/France Noire: The History and Politics of Blackness*, Duke University Press, 2012; F. Germain, S. Larcher and T. Denean Sharpley-Whiting, *Black French Women and the Struggle for Equality, 1848–2016*, University of Nebraska Press, 2018.
26. Richard Dyer, *Stars*, BFI, 1990; C. Gledhill (ed.), *Stardom: Industry of Desire*, Routledge, 1991; A. Chenu, 'Des sentiers de la gloire aux boulevards de la célébrité', *Revue Française de la Sociologie*, 1 (2008), pp. 3–52; D. Negra and S. Holmes (eds), *In the Limelight and Under the Microscope: Forms and Functions of Female Celebrity*, Continuum, 2011.
27. Len Scott and Peter Jackson, 'The study of intelligence in theory and practice', *Intelligence and National Security*, 19:2 (2004), pp. 139–169; Deirdre Osborne, '"I do not know about politics or governments . . . I am a housewife"': The female secret agent and the male war machine in Occupied France

(1942–5)', *Women: A Cultural Review*, 17:1 (2006), pp. 42–64; Hamilton Bean, 'Intelligence theory from the margins: Questions ignored and debates not had', *Intelligence and National Security*, 33:4 (2018), pp. 527–540; R.F. Toy and C. Smith, 'Women in the shadow war: Gender, class and MI5 in the Second World War', *Women's History Review*, 27:5 (2018), pp. 688–705.

Chapter 1

1. *Ce soir*, 8 August 1939, photo with caption cited, p. 1; see also Baker and Bouillon, *Joséphine*, p. 163.
2. 'Joséphine Baker est revenue à l'une de ses amours: Paris', *Ce soir*, 8 August 1939, p. 3.
3. *L'Intransigeant*, 8 August 1939; *Paris-Soir*, 8 August 1939; *Excelsior*, 8 August 1939; *Le Petit Parisien*, 8 August 1939.
4. 'Joséphine ne rentre pas seule', *L'Humanité*, 8 August 1939.
5. *Variety*, 30 August 1939; 'Tous les oiseaux des Iles de Joséphine Baker sauf un sont morts!', *Paris-soir*, 12 August 1939.
6. See Rose, *Jazz Cleopatra*, p. 143; Hammond and O'Connor, *Josephine Baker*, p. 86.
7. Stovall, *Paris Noir*, pp. 60, 90.
8. Matthew Pratt Guterl, *Josephine Baker and the Rainbow Tribe*, Harvard University Press, 2014, p. 35.
9. Gillett, *At Home in Our Sounds*, p. 52.
10. Jules-Rosette, *Josephine Baker in Art and Life*, p. 49.
11. Rose, *Jazz Cleopatra*, p. 148.
12. Boittin, *Colonial Metropolis*, p. 31.
13. Stovall, *Paris Noir*, p. 92.
14. Gillett, *At Home in Our Sounds*, p. 203.
15. Rose, *Jazz Cleopatra*, p. 176; Lynn Hanley, *Naked at the Feast: The Biography of Josephine Baker*, Robson Books, 1981, p. 206.
16. 'Josephine Baker quarrels and weds', *Daily Mail*, 1 December 1937, p. 13.
17. She may have made efforts to convert, though probably never actually completed the process: Melba Joyce Boyd, 'The unconquerable Josephine Baker waging war against fascism', in Sylvie Eve Blum-Reid (ed.), *Impressions from Paris: Women Creatives in Interwar Years in Paris*, Vernon Press, 2024, p. 11. Her son Brian Bouillon Baker confirms that while she began the process of conversion and was sympathetic to the religion, she never completed it. Presentation to 'Journée d'Etude sur Joséphine Baker', Petit Palais, 15 March 2024.
18. 'Joséphine s'est mariée avec un aviateur et devient française', *La Petite Gironde*, 1 December 1937.
19. Nicholas L. Syrett, *American Child Bride: A History of Minors and Marriage in the United States*, University of North Carolina Press, 2016, p. 145.
20. Hanley, *Naked at the Feast*, p. 25.
21. 'Joséphine Baker s'est mariée hier à Crèvecoeur-le-Grand', *Le Progrès de la Somme*, 1 December 1937.
22. 'Josephine Baker quarrels and weds', *Daily Mail*, 1 December 1937.
23. 'Josephine Baker minus husband', *Daily Mail*, 7 December 1937, p. 11.
24. 'Josephine Baker opens new season', *Daily Mail*, 14 December 1937, p. 9.

25. See, for example, 'Joséphine Baker ne quittera pas la scène', *Ce soir*, 22 October 1938.
26. Baker and Bouillon, *Joséphine*, p. 161.
27. 'Joséphine Baker aviatrice brevetée', *L'Intransigeant*, 29 May 1937; by her account, Lion forbade her from flying.
28. 'Joséphine va divorcer . . .', *Ce soir*, 2 February 1938.
29. 'Joséphine ne songe nullement à divorcer', *Excelsior*, 2 February 1939.
30. 'Une journée avec Joséphine Baker', *Pour vous*, 28 February 1940; in one of the images, she is reported as purchasing something for her husband, who had been called up – it looks like boots. There is also an image of 'tata Jo' having lunch 'en famille' and playing with the Lion family children.
31. 'Joséphine et son mari sont maintenant pilotes d'avion', *Ce soir*, 5 March 1939.
32. *Excelsior*, 15 March 1939.
33. See Boittin, *Colonial Metropolis*, p. 7.
34. Baker and Chase, *Josephine*, p. 169.
35. 'Few in war zone', *Afro-American*, 9 September 1939, p. 10.
36. I.C. Williams, *Underneath a Harlem Moon: The Harlem to Paris Years of Adelaide Hall*, Continuum, 2002.
37. Stovall, *Paris Noir*, p. 121; T. Denean Sharpley-Whiting, *Bricktop's Paris: African American Women in Paris between the Two World Wars*, State University of New York Press, 2015, p. 157.
38. 'Everybody but Jo', *Afro-American*, 18 November 1939, p. 4.
39. Ean Wood, *The Josephine Baker Story*, Sanctuary Publishing, 2000, p. 145.
40. Wood, *The Josephine Baker Story*, p. 206.
41. Stovall, *Paris Noir*, p. 119.
42. 'The Paris scene in wartime', *Philadelphia Tribune*, 18 April 1940, p. 14.
43. Abtey, *La guerre secrète*, p. 19.
44. Baker and Bouillon, *Joséphine*, p. 163.
45. Baker and Bouillon, *Joséphine*, p. 163.
46. Andrew and Green, *Stars and Spies*, pp. 184–188; Julie Wheelwright, *The Fatal Lover: Mata Hari and the Myth of Women in Espionage*, Collins and Brown, 1992; Bruno Fuligni (ed.), *Dans les archives inédites des services secrets: Un siècle d'espionnage français (1870–1989)*, Gallimard, 2014.
47. Andrew and Green, *Stars and Spies*, pp. 182–183.
48. Fuligni, *Dans les archives inédites*, pp. 158–160.
49. Abtey, *La guerre secrète*, p. 19.
50. Baker and Bouillon, *Joséphine*, p. 165.
51. Abtey, *La guerre secrète*, p. 20.
52. Abtey, *La guerre secrète*, p. 21.
53. Baker and Bouillon, *Joséphine*, p. 163.
54. Abtey, *La guerre secrète*, p. 22.
55. Abtey, *La guerre secrète*, p. 28.
56. Abtey became her *officier traitant*, officer in charge. Dossier de résistant GR 16 P 28445, Service historique de la Défense (henceforth SHD).
57. Abtey, *La guerre secrète*, p. 29.
58. Her acquisition of this information (without going into the specifics) is included in her citation for the Légion d'honneur, but none of the sources give any details about this. Dossier de résistant GR 16 P 28445, SHD.

59. 'Marraine de nombreux soldats, Joséphine Baker a préparé des colis pour ses filleuls', *Le Phare de la Loire*, 28 December 1939, photo with caption, p. 1; 'Belle et bonne', *Le Petit Provençal*, 30 December 1939 – the paper claims she sent a parcel to every one of her 1,500 *filleuls*.

60. 'Joséphine Baker sur la Zone', *Le Progrès de la Côte-d'Or*, 25 December 1939, photo with caption, p. 1; 'La célébre vedette Joséphine Baker est allée sur la "zone" où elle a distribué des jouets', *Le Midi socialist*, 25 December 1939, photo with caption, p. 1.

61. 'Maurice Chevalier et Joséphine Baker avant de faire leur rentrée à Paris iront chanter aux armées du front', *Paris-soir*, 30 October 1939.

62. Bernard Lonjon, *Maurice Chevalier: le Chéri des Dames*, Editions du Moment, 2012, p. 73.

63. 'Première du Théâtre aux Armées', *L'Intransigeant*, 4 November 1939.

64. Maude Williams and Bernard Wilkin, *French Soldier's Morale in the Phoney War*, Routledge, 2018, p. 73.

65. 'Première du Théâtre aux Armées', *L'Intransigeant*, 4 November 1939.

66. *Journal de Guerre*, no. 7, 11 November 1939, Reference J7, ECPAD - Images Défense https://imagesdefense.gouv.fr/fr/17920.html

67. *Variety*, 13 December 1939, p. 14.

68. 'MC et JB chantant pour les soldats', *Le Figaro*, 13 November 1939.

69. 'Maurice Chevalier et Joséphine Baker à leur retour du front nous content leurs souvenirs', *Le Journal*, 12 November 1939, p. 2; see also *Le Miroir*, 26 November 1939.

70. Andy Merriman, *Greasepaint and Cordite: How ENSA Entertained the Troops during World War II*, Aurum Press, 2013, p. xvi.

71. Merriman, *Greasepaint and Cordite*, p. 29.

72. 'En Egypte, au Maroc, en Syrie, les troupes alliées ont applaudi Joséphine Baker', *Ce soir*, 17 September 1944.

73. 'The American contingents', *Royal Air Force Journal*, 19 September 1942, pp. 3–4.

74. A.H. Narracott, air correspondent for *The Times*, stationed in France with the Advanced Air Striking Force, wrote in *Contact: RAF Weekly News Magazine*, vol. 1, No. 3, 18 April 1941, pp. 7, 14.

75. 'Au Casino de Paris', *Le Temps*, 8 February 1940, p. 3.

76. 'The Casino de Paris: First war revue joins Chevalier and Baker for first time', *Bystander*, 3 January 1940, p. 15.

77. 'Paris-London', *Variety*, 24 January 1940, p. 44.

78. 'Au Casino de Paris: Maurice Chevalier et Joséphine Baker', *Paris-soir*, 5 December 1939, p. 2.

79. 'Dimanche, soir de réveillon au Casino de Paris', *L'Intansigeant*, 28 December 1939, p. 2.

80. 'Au Casino de Paris', *Le Temps*, 8 February 1940, p. 3.

81. 'La rentrée de Maurice Chevalier et de Joséphine Baker au Casino de Paris', *L'Intransigeant*, 3 December 1939, p. 4.

82. 'Cirques, Cabarets, Concerts: La Revue des Variétés', *Mercure de France*, 1 February 1940.

83. 'The Casino de Paris: First war revue joins Chevalier and Baker for first time', *Bystander*, 3 January 1940, p. 14.

84. 'The Casino de Paris', *Bystander*, 3 January 1940, p. 14.

85. 'Josephine Baker steps down', *Picture Post*, 16 March 1940, p. 22.
86. 'Josephine Baker steps down', *Picture Post*, p. 22.
87. 'The Paris scene in wartime', *Philadelphia Tribune*, 18 April 1940, p. 14.
88. 'Paris-London', *Variety*, 24 January 1940, p. 44.
89. 'Une journée avec Joséphine Baker', *Pour vous*, 28 February 1940, p. 4.
90. 'Quand les girls du Casino de Paris sont aux armées pour retrouver avec Joséphine Baker des milliers de boys en kaki . . .', *L'Intransigeant*, 2 January 1940, p. 2.
91. *Le Petit Provençal*, 30 December 1939; 'Joséphine Baker répond à d'innombrables lettres. Elle veille aux distractions, envoie des jeux, des disques, des postes de T.S.F même, et ajoute chaque fois un petit arbre de Noël pliant', *Marie-Claire*, 22 December 1940.
92. *Pour vous*, 28 February 1940, p. 4.
93. Géraud Létang and Natalie Soutet, 'Feux de la rampe et "armée des ombres". A la recherche de l'expérience combattante de Joséphine Baker (1939–1945)', *Revue Historique des Armées*, 304:1 (2022), pp. 108–111.
94. *Pour vous*, 28 February 1940, p. 4.
95. There is a vibrant scholarship on these films, including excellent books by Elizabeth Ezra, *The Colonial Unconscious: Race and Culture in Interwar France*, Cornell University Press, 2000 and Jules-Rosette, *Josephine Baker in Art and Life*. But all the scholarship tends to overlook *Fausse Alerte*, which is mostly mentioned in a line as an afterthought. Jean-François Staszak, 'L'écran de l'exotisme. La place de Joséphine Baker dans le cinéma français: Géographie et cinéma', *Annales de Géographie*, 123:695/696 (2014), pp. 646–670, and Francis, *Josephine Baker's Cinematic Prism*, pp. 169–170 both dedicate a little more time to the film.
96. 'Petites Nouvelles', *Le Figaro*, 4 May 1940, p. 4; see also 'Un soir d'alerte', *Pour vous*, 27 March 1940, p. 9.
97. 'Un film nouveau. Ce que sera "Fausse Alerte"', *Pour vous*, 29 March 1940, p. 10.
98. 'Refugee seeks to start anew', *Motion Picture Herald*, 22 August 1942.
99. 'Feature reviews', *Box Office*, 20 September 1952, p. 1409.
100. 'Film reviews', *Variety*, 10 September 1952, p. 6.
101. Jacques Siclier would say in her obituary that 'Cinema used her but did not serve her well.' This was also true of her last film *Fausse Alerte*; 'Joséphine Baker est morte', *Le Monde*, 14 April 1975.
102. Baker and Bouillon, *Joséphine*, p. 166.
103. Abtey, *La guerre secrète*, pp. 31–32.
104. Abtey, *La guerre secrète*, p. 32.

Chapter 2

1. Wood, *The Josephine Baker Story*, p. 201.
2. Hanna Diamond, *Fleeing Hitler, France 1940*, Oxford University Press, 2007.
3. Baker and Bouillon, *Joséphine*, p. 167.
4. For more on these experiences, see Diamond, *Fleeing Hitler*.
5. Léon Werth, *33 Days: A Memoir*, Melville House Publishing, 2015.
6. Baker and Bouillon, *Joséphine*, p. 158.

7. Baker and Chase, *Josephine*, p. 230, though they include Jean 'convalescing from his war wounds', which seems unlikely at this early stage after the hostilities.
8. Sauvage, *Mémoires*, p. 266.
9. Even if she didn't hear de Gaulle's call at the time, she certainly made up for it by proclaiming her dedication to him as an ardent Gaullist for the rest of her life and contacting him every 18 June throughout the 1950s and 1960s. See chapter 7.
10. Abtey, *La guerre secrète*, p. 32.
11. Oral interview, Paul Paillole, GR 3 K 15 1, SHD
12. Paul Paillole, *Fighting the Nazis: French Intelligence and Counterintelligence, 1935–1945*, Enigma, 2003, p. 157.
13. Paillole, *Fighting the Nazis*, p. 158.
14. Paillole, *Fighting the Nazis*, p. 158; Abtey, *La guerre secrète*, p. 33.
15. Paillole, *Fighting the Nazis*, p. 160.
16. Oral interview, Paillole, SHD.
17. Paillole, *Fighting the Nazis*, p. 165.
18. Historians acknowledge that while Vichy collaborated with the Germans, the regime continued to have a policy of protection from German encroachment. See Simon Kitson, *The Hunt for Nazi Spies: Fighting Espionage in Vichy France*, University of Chicago Press, 2008.
19. Paillole, *Fighting the Nazis*, p. 170.
20. Paillole, *Fighting the Nazis*, p. 170.
21. Abtey, *La guerre secrète*, p. 33.
22. Abtey, *La guerre secrète*, p. 34.
23. These are named as Commandant Boué and Lieutenant de vaisseau Bayonne in an article about Baker which appeared in 1946 ('Déliée par la Victoire du Serment du Silence, L'Espionne Noire Raconte', *Point de vue*, 6 June 1946, p. 8). Abtey mentions that he went to Les Milandes with two unnamed colleagues from the Deuxième Bureau in a summary he prepared for Eugene Lerner held in the Stanford University Collection, 'La double vie de Joséphine', Undated, p. 1, Collection Number: M1297 Box 2, Folder 12, File 12, Josephine Baker correspondence: Captain Jacques Abtey. These two men are not mentioned in *La guerre secrète*, however, and their fate is never explained.
24. Abtey, *La guerre secrète*, p. 35.
25. Abtey, *La guerre secrète*, p. 35; Baker and Bouillon, *Joséphine*, p. 167.
26. Abtey, *La guerre secrète*, p. 39.
27. Paul Paillole interview, SHD.
28. Abtey, *La guerre secrète*, p. 39.
29. Keith Jeffrey, *MI6: The History of the Secret Intelligence Service, 1909–1949*, Bloomsbury, 2010, pp. 199–200.
30. Jeffrey, *MI6*, p. 291; Paillole, *Fighting the Nazis*, pp. 80–81.
31. Jeffrey, *MI6*, p. 389.
32. See article by Paul Paillole, 'Une Grande Dame – Une grande Française la Mort de Marie Bell', in Bulletin No. 127, Anciens des Services Spéciaux de la Défense Nationale (France), available at https://www.aassdn.org/xldd11271.htm; and Paillole, *Fighting the Nazis*, p. 59.
33. She was awarded the Légion d'honneur.
34. Baker and Bouillon, *Joséphine*, p. 168.

35. Abtey, *La guerre secrète*, p. 39.
36. It was important for them to emphasise this in their memoirs to offset accusations that they were working for the Vichy intelligence services – which in fact they were, though this context is tricky to unravel.
37. That he would have been aware of Baker and Abtey's activities seems very unlikely. For Abtey's account of these events see *La guerre secrète*, pp. 41–43.
38. With thanks to Simon Kitson for indicating that this should not be considered surprising.
39. Simon Kitson, *Police and Politics in Marseille, 1936–1945*, Brill, 2014, p. 125.
40. With thanks again to Simon Kitson for suggesting this explanation.
41. Extrait du décret en date du 9 décembre 1957 portant nominations dans l'ordre national de la Légion d'honneur, Dossier de résistant GR 16 P 28445, SHD.
42. An exhaustive search of police reports and Renseignements généraux records for this period found no reference to Baker. Archives départementales de la Dordogne (henceforth ADD).
43. Abtey, *La guerre secrète*, p. 51.
44. Abtey, *La guerre secrète*, p. 52.
45. That they would come via Yugoslavia seems a bit odd; Paillole cited in Baker and Bouillon, *Joséphine*, pp. 168–169.
46. Abtey, *La guerre secrète*, p. 53.
47. Abtey, *La guerre secrète*, p. 54.
48. Abtey, *La guerre secrète*, p. 52.
49. Baker and Bouillon, *Joséphine*, p. 169.
50. Abtey, *La guerre secrète*, p. 55.
51. One of these was the extraordinary spiral tunnel at Forges-d'Abel. A railway spiral rises on a steady curve until it has completed a loop, passing over itself as it gains height, allowing the railway to gain vertical elevation in a relatively short horizontal distance.
52. The station at Canfranc would later become known as the 'Casablanca of the Pyrenees' due to the role it played in providing a route to freedom for fleeing Jewish refugees and Allied pilots.
53. Abtey, *La guerre secrète*, p. 55.
54. Rémy, J.A.: *Episodes de la vie d'un agent S.R. et du contre-espionnage français*, Editions Gallic, 1961, p. 57.
55. Abtey, *La guerre secrète*, p. 57.
56. Neil Lochery, *Lisbon: War in the Shadows of the City of Light, 1939–1945*, Public Affairs, New York, p. 37.
57. Cândida Cadavez, 'Tourism in Portugal at the beginning of the Second World War', in Maria F. Rollo et al. (eds), *War and Propaganda in the XXth Century*, Lisbon, 2013, p. 210, cited in Pedro Cravinho, 'The "Black Angel" in Lisbon: Josephine Baker challenges Salazar live on television', available at https://roderic.uv.es/rest/api/core/bitstreams/e5740e45-17b1-44c5-9bd2-8b062a062af9/content
58. Bernardo Futscher Pereira, *Crepúsculo do Colonialismo: A Diplomacia do Estado Novo (1949–1961)*, Publicaçoes Dom Quixote, 2017, p. 20, cited in Cravinho, 'The "Black Angel" in Lisbon'.
59. Abtey, *La guerre secrète*, p. 60.
60. Abtey, *La guerre secrète*, p. 61.

61. Abtey claims this represented forty pieces of information on the German army: 'Exposé succinct des états de services du Commandant Abtey au titre de la Résistance de Juin 1940 à Juillet 1943', Dossier de Résistant, 16 P 2170, SHD.
62. Abtey, *La guerre secrète*, p. 60.
63. Jeffrey, *MI6*, p. 190.
64. Sébastian Albertelli, *Les services secrets du général de Gaulle: Le BCRA 1940–1944*, Perrin, 2009.
65. They believed that they were working for the Free French. Abtey, *La guerre secrète*, p. 73.
66. Baker and Bouillon, *Joséphine*, p. 169.
67. Wood, *The Josephine Baker Story*, p. 225; 1 December in Abtey, *La guerre secrète*, p. 62.
68. Pétain's visit to Marseille, 3–4 December 1940, covered in Robert Mencherini, *Vichy en Provence, Midi Rouge, ombres et lumières 2*, Editions Syllepse, 2009, pp. 209–220.
69. Mencherini, *Vichy en Provence*, p. 31.
70. Paillole, *Fighting the Nazis*, p. 172.
71. Rudolph Salmsen, 'The one who got away', p. 31, unpublished typescript in the Josephine Baker Collection (JBC), Eugene Lerner-Hank Kaufman correspondence with French government and army, 1955, M1297 Box 2, Folder 12, SU.
72. Mencherini, *Vichy en Provence*, pp. 79–82.
73. Hanley, *Naked at the Feast*, p. 222.
74. Baker and Bouillon, *Joséphine*, p. 170.
75. Wood, *The Josephine Baker Story*, p. 220.
76. *France*, 1 September 1940, p. 2.
77. 'Le retour de l'oiseau des Iles', *Le Jour*, 23 December 1940, p. 1.
78. Andy Fry, *Paris Blues: African American Music and French Popular Culture, 1920–1960*, University of Chicago Press, 2014, p. 127.
79. Rose, *Jazz Cleopatra*, p. 165.
80. Rose, *Jazz Cleopatra*, p. 164.
81. Stovall, *Paris Noir*, p. 90.
82. Fry, *Paris Blues*, p. 147.
83. *Le Sémaphore de Marseille*, 25 December 1940.
84. Abtey, *La guerre secrète*, p. 72.
85. Abtey, *La guerre secrète*, p. 73.
86. Baker and Bouillon, *Joséphine*, p. 172.
87. Julian Jackson, *France: The Dark Years, 1940–1944*, Oxford University Press, 2001, p. 175.
88. Salmsen, 'The one who got away', p. 31, SU.
89. Abtey, *La guerre secrète*, p. 85.
90. Baker and Abtey enrolled Salmsen on a reserve list to join a boat that was on stand-by to evacuate people from Marseille immediately in the event that the Germans crossed the demarcation line. Salmsen, 'The one who got away', p. 3, SU.
91. Note to director of the municipal theatre at Béziers explaining that she was unwell and promising a medical certificate would follow. Josephine Baker Collection 1940–1960 (JBC), JWJ MSS 108, Box 1, Beinecke Rare Book and Manuscript Library, Yale University (henceforth YU).

92. Sauvage, *Mémoires*, p. 228.
93. Baker and Bouillon, *Joséphine*, p. 172; Hammond and O'Connor, *Josephine Baker*, p. 152; Sauvage, *Mémoires*, pp. 227–228.
94. Sauvage, *Mémoires*, p. 227.
95. Abtey, *La guerre secrète*, p. 195.
96. Abtey made the following statement to the military authorities in 1955: 'Keen to ensure that my situation with the Free French Forces was regularised, I had made it a condition of my return to France that General de Gaulle would be informed of my mission and that I would be considered a member of the "Free French" from the day of my arrival in Portugal. Major Bacon gave me the most formal guarantee of this.' 16 P 2170, SHD. See chapter 7 for more discussion of this issue.
97. Interview with Paul Paillole, SHD.
98. He had married Emma Marie Kunst in Alsace in 1928. They had a son. 16 P 2170, SHD.

Chapter 3

1. Sauvage, *Mémoires*, p. 229.
2. Baker and Chase, *Josephine*, p. 238.
3. Pierre Guillemot, *Les 12 Vice-Consuls: Afrique du Nord 1942*, Oliver Orban, 1977, p. 158.
4. 'Joséphine Baker à Alger', *L'Echo d'Alger*, 19 January 1941, p. 1.
5. Chantal Metzger, *Le Maghreb dans la guerre, 1939–1945*, Armand Colin, 2018, p. 35.
6. Christine Lévisse-Touzé, *L'Afrique du Nord dans la guerre, 1939–1945*, Albin Michel, 1998, p. 48.
7. Sasha D. Pack, *The Deepest Border: The Strait of Gibraltar and the Making of the Modern Hispano-African Borderland*, Stanford University Press, 2018, p. 234.
8. Kitson, *The Hunt for Nazi Spies*, p. 14.
9. Michel Abitbol, *Histoire du Maroc*, Perrin, 2009, p. 490.
10. Baker and Bouillon, *Joséphine*, p. 173; Abtey, *La guerre secrète*, p. 92.
11. Salmsen, 'The one who got away', pp. 33–34, YU.
12. 'Le gala des Ailes réussite parfaite rapportera près de 200,000 fr au Secours national', *L' Écho d'Alger*, 2 February 1941, p. 1.
13. Baker and Bouillon, *Joséphine*, p. 174.
14. Susan Gibson, *A History of Modern Morocco*, Cambridge University Press, 2013, p. 90.
15. Gibson, *A History of Modern Morocco*, pp. 91–94.
16. Metzger, *Le Maghreb dans la guerre*, p. 28.
17. Paillole, *Fighting the Nazis*, p. 179.
18. Levisse-Touzé, *L'Afrique du Nord*, p. 97.
19. Levisse-Touzé, *L'Afrique du Nord*, p. 97.
20. Guillemot, *Les 12 Vice-Consuls*, pp. 40–41.
21. This mix of undercover operatives was dramatically depicted in the Michael Curtiz 1942 film *Casablanca*.
22. Baker and Bouillon, *Joséphine*, p. 174.
23. Abtey, *La guerre secrète*, p. 96.
24. Baker and Bouillon, *Joséphine*, p. 175.

25. Report by Stafford Reid, 'Personal Experience in French North Africa from April 1941 through the Armistice 11 November 1942', 23 May 1945, p. 7, OSS History Office, Box 26, File 104, RG 226 National Archives at College Park (henceforth NACP).
26. Sauvage, *Mémoires*, p. 231.
27. *Canberra Times*, 24 March 1941.
28. Baker and Bouillon, *Joséphine*, p. 175.
29. Abtey, *La guerre secrète*, p. 99.
30. Sauvage, *Mémoires*, p. 231.
31. Baker and Bouillon, *Joséphine*, p. 176.
32. Abtey, *La guerre secrète*, p. 99.
33. Kenneth W. Pendar, *Adventure in Diplomacy: Our French Dilemma*, Dodd, Mead & Co., 1945, republished by Simon Publications, 2003, p. 16.
34. Kenneth G. Crawford, *Report on North Africa*, Farrar & Rinehart, 1943, p. 41.
35. Baker and Bouillon, *Joséphine*, p. 176.
36. Abtey, *La guerre secrète*, p. 103.
37. Gavin Maxwell, *Lords of the Atlas, Morocco: The Rise and Fall of the House of Glaoua*, Cassell, 2000, p. 138.
38. Maxwell, *Lords of the Atlas*, p. 137.
39. Maxwell, *Lords of the Atlas*, p. 141.
40. Maxwell, *Lords of the Atlas*, p. 143.
41. Maxwell, *Lords of the Atlas*, p. 154.
42. Maxwell, *Lords of the Atlas*, p. 157.
43. Maxwell, *Lords of the Atlas*, p. 161.
44. Baker and Bouillon, *Joséphine*, p. 176.
45. Abtey, *La guerre secrète*, p. 105; Sauvage, *Mémoires*, p. 234.
46. Sauvage, *Mémoires*, pp. 233–34.
47. Sauvage, *Mémoires*, p. 232.
48. Abtey, *La guerre secrète*, p. 99.
49. Salmsen, 'The one who got away', pp. 34–35, YU.
50. Salmsen, 'The one who got away', p. 35.
51. Bouillon and Baker, *Joséphine*, p. 176.
52. There is no evidence that Paillole or other agents of the Deuxième Bureau were informed about this trip.
53. Abtey, *La guerre secrète*, p. 107.
54. Baker and Bouillon, *Joséphine*, p. 177.
55. 'Teatro de la Zarzuela (Madrid)', *Variety*, 28 May 1941, p. 47.
56. 'Jo Baker goes to Spain sans bananas and patrons ask why', *Chicago Defender*, 14 June 1941, p. 21; also mentioned in 'Josey covers up for Spain', *New York Amsterdam News*, 7 June 1941, p. 20.
57. Sauvage, *Mémoires*, p. 236; she called them secret butterflies.
58. 'Une journée avec Joséphine Baker', *Pour vous*, 28 February 1940, p. 4.
59. Douglas Porch, *The French Secret Services*, Macmillan, 1995, p. 448.
60. Major Bentley, 'Report on Visit to Casablanca, Meknes & Fes July 16–20', 22 July 1941, p. 3, Army Intelligence Project Files, 1941–45, Box 452, French Morocco, File 47, RG 319, NACP.
61. Hal Vaughan, *FDR's 12 Apostles: The Spies Who Paved the Way for the Invasion of North Africa*, The Lyons Press, 2006, p. 54.

62. Pendar, *Adventure in Diplomacy*, p. 3.
63. Pendar, *Adventure in Diplomacy*, p. 11.
64. Reid report, 23 May 1945, NACP.
65. Abtey, *La guerre secrète*, p. 108.
66. Baker and Abtey claim to have worked with the American consuls, but they are not mentioned by name in any of the OSS reports held in the OSS files at NACP.
67. Abtey, *La guerre secrète*, p. 108.
68. Pendar, *Adventure in Diplomacy*, p. 13.
69. 'Joséphine Baker chantait cette semaine au Colisée', *L'Écho d'Alger*, 5 July 1941, p. 3. Baker falls ill in July 1941 (not June, as most commentators say, as she plays the Colisée in Algiers on 1–3 July).
70. Sauvage, *Mémoires*, p. 237.
71. Baker and Bouillon, *Joséphine*, p. 177. It seems likely that she had a history of miscarriages. In late October 1938, several papers reported that Maurice Chevalier had announced publicly that she was pregnant. See 'Joséphine Baker sera bientôt Maman', *Ce soir*, 27 October 1938, and 'Joséphine Baker va être maman Maurice Chevalier l'a annoncé publiquement hier', *Paris-soir*, 27 October 1938. This was denied by Baker the following month, in reports including 'Entre Cour et Jardin: Naissance prochaine', *Excelsior*, 14 November 1938, p. 7 and 'Nègre-blanc', *Marianne*, 16 November 1938, p. 21.
72. Bentley report, 22 July 1941, NACP.
73. Pendar, *Adventure in Diplomacy*, p. 17.
74. Reid report, 23 May 1945, NACP.
75. Pendar, *Adventure in Diplomacy*, p. 32.
76. Pendar, *Adventure in Diplomacy*, pp. 35–37.
77. Pendar, *Adventure in Diplomacy*, p. 21.
78. Reid report, 23 May 1945, pp. 126–127, NACP.
79. Pendar, *Adventure in Diplomacy*, p. 22.
80. Pendar, *Adventure in Diplomacy*, p. 22.
81. Pendar, *Adventure in Diplomacy*, p. 36.
82. Pendar, *Adventure in Diplomacy*, p. 37.
83. Vaughan, *FDR's 12 Apostles*, p. 42.
84. Abtey, *La guerre secrète*, p. 126.
85. Abtey, *La guerre secrète*, p. 128.
86. Abtey, *La guerre secrète*, p. 136.
87. Baker and Bouillon, *Joséphine*, p. 183.
88. Paillole criticised the lack of professionalism of British intelligence. See Kitson, *The Hunt for Nazi Spies*, p. 171.
89. Kitson, *The Hunt for Nazi Spies*, pp. 74–75.
90. Abtey, *La guerre secrète*, p. 126.
91. Gilbert Guillaume, *Mes missions face à l'Abwehr: Contre-Espionnage, 1938–1945*, Plon, 1973, p. 25.
92. He is mentioned by Abtey, *La guerre secrète*, p. 125, and Vice Consul Bartlett wrote a memo about him, referring to him as 'one of my most valuable contacts in French Morocco'. 'French Ex-General Xavier Richert', undated handwritten memo, probably November 1942, COI/OSS Central Files, Sidney Bartlett file, 92A, RG 226, NACP.

93. 'The Pacha of Marrakech is perhaps the only native in the country who is consistently and openly pro-British; to such an extent that he is generally thought to be in their pay.' Political opinions of the natives of French Morocco, 11 June 1942, p. 2, French Morocco file, Box 451, Entry 47, Army Intelligence Project Decimal File 1941–1945, RG 319, NACP.
94. Vaughan, *FDR's 12 Apostles*, p. 67.
95. Vaughan, *FDR's 12 Apostles*, pp. 68–69.
96. Reid report, 23 May 1945, pp. 126–127, NACP.
97. Reid report, 23 May 1945, pp. 126–127, NACP.
98. Pendar, *Adventure in Diplomacy*, p. 78.
99. Murphy never revealed the real reason for his abrupt dismissal, but Bartlett later discovered the truth from a Washington personnel officer. He never made his peace with the notion that his fiancée had been uncovered as a spy and wrote repeatedly to the American authorities requesting to be reinstated or reassigned to North Africa in some capacity. Bartlett's personal file, Memorandum 9 September 1942, Box 11, COI/OSS Central Files, Entry 92A, RG 226, NACP.
100. Abtey claims that Bartlett was recalled in October 1942, when in fact it took place some months before: *La guerre secrète*, p. 145. In 1954, when seeking recognition of his actions, he made a slightly different statement to the military authorities, claiming to have worked regularly with Bartlett until just before the landings: 16 P 2170, SHD.
101. David King, 'Descriptions of individuals and groups in Casablanca', 25 July 1942, p. 6, Box 518, File WN 18767–18775, Entry A1-220, RG 226, NACP.
102. Henry Hyde, 'A brief outline of OSS relationships with Various French Secret Services', 28 December 1943, pp. 4–5, Political opinions of the natives of French Morocco File WN1918 1941–1946, Box 120, RG 226, NACP.
103. Baker and Bouillon, *Joséphine*, p. 181. The outcome was widely reported in the local and African American press: 'Les vedettes devant la cour d'Appel d'Aix', *Le Petit Provençal*, 17 June 1942, and 'Joséphine Baker ... devant la cour d'Appel d'Aix', *Le Petit Marseillais*, 17 June 1942, p. 1. The fine was reported in 'Josephine Baker fined by French', *New York Amsterdam News*, 27 June 1942, p. 1; 'Joe Baker fined for jumping show', *Afro-American*, 27 June 1942, p. 11; 'Josephine Baker runs into non-Aryan trouble abroad', *Pittsburgh Courier*, 8 August 1942, p. 20.
104. These reports appeared between October 1942 and January 1943.
105. Baker and Bouillon, *Joséphine*, pp. 185–186; 'Joséphine Baker est mourante', *L'Ouest-Éclair*, 14 October 1942, p. 3; 'Josephine Baker lies near death in Lisbon hospital', *Chicago Defender*, 17 October 1942, p. 20. Elsewhere, reference is made to Chevalier having seen her some months before 'despondent, feverish, and deserted by all': 'Nous avons de bonnes nouvelles de Joséphine Baker', *L'Effort*, 6 October 1942.
106. 'Josephine Baker dies penniless', *Chicago Defender*, 21 November 1942, p. 1; 'Josephine Baker reported dead in Morocco following long illness', *Afro-American*, 21 November 1942, p. 10.
107. For example, 'Joséphine Baker va mieux', *Aujourd'hui*, 14 October 1942, p. 2; 'Joséphine Baker est en bonne santé', *Le Petit Courrier*, 14 October 1942, p. 1. On 15 November 1942, *Le Réveil du Nord* reassured its readers that a reporter had visited Baker, who had been operated on and was now up and about. She

told the reporter that although she had loved getting to know Morocco, she had decided to 'give up the stage'; once the war was over, she just wanted to do one thing – rest in her superb château in France. Press articles asserting that reports of her death had been in error continued until well after the end of the war.

108. Christopher C. De Santis (ed.), *Langston Hughes and the Chicago Defender: Essays on Race, Politics and Culture, 1942–62*, University of Illinois Press, 1995, p. 195.

109. This was reported in the African American press in 1951, when many of Baker's wartime activities were made known to the American public during Walter Winchell's attack on her wartime record. See, for example, 'Reveals Jo Baker's service to allies', *Cleveland Call and Post*, 10 November 1951, p. 3: 'Josephine Baker was one of the few persons privileged to know the date of the US invasion of North Africa to the exact hour of D-Day.' These events are discussed further in chapter 7.

Chapter 4

1. Baker and Bouillon, *Joséphine*, p. 187.
2. Abtey, *La guerre secrète*, pp. 150–151.
3. Copy of leaflet, OSS History Office, Box 45, File 183, RG 226, NACP.
4. Douglas Porch, *France at War: Defeat and Division, 1939–1942*, Cambridge University Press, 2020, p. 515.
5. Meredith Hindley, *Destination Casablanca, Exiles, Espionage and the Battle for North Africa*, Public Affairs, 2017, p. 245.
6. Abtey, *La guerre secrète*, pp. 153–156; Crawford, *Report on North Africa*, p. 18.
7. A new formation, its mission in combat was 'to protect troops, equipment, and installations from enemy espionage and sabotage'. Operation Torch was its first outing. Counter Intelligence Corps School, *Counter Intelligence Corps History and Mission in World War II*, undated typescript, available at https://irp.fas.org/agency/army/cic.pdf, p. 16.
8. Abtey, *La guerre secrète*, p. 156.
9. Counter Intelligence Corps School, *Counter Intelligence Corps History*, p. 16.
10. 'Ex-US agent says: Jo Baker risked life fighting fascist forces', *Afro-American*, 3 November 1951, p. 7.
11. 'Ex-US agent says: Jo Baker risked life fighting fascist forces', *Afro-American*, 3 November 1951, p. 7.
12. 'Joe Baker helps soldier to win Silver Star', *Arizona Sun*, 2 November 1951, p. 7.
13. Report on ATC Control Marrakech compiled by Major Harry R. Turkel with sections by Lt P.H. Jensen of CIC – considered an A.1 source (i.e. the most reliable). The document refers to a full report by Jensen on Propaganda dated 1 January 1943. Records of the Washington Communications Branch, Box 12, Marrakech File, RG 226, NACP.
14. Counter Intelligence Corps School, *Counter Intelligence Corps History*, p. 18.
15. Counter Intelligence Corps School, *Counter Intelligence Corps History*, p. 18.
16. Baker makes no mention of this event and her part in it in any of the sources.
17. Hindley, *Destination Casablanca*, pp. 322–323.
18. Crawford, *Report on North Africa*, p. 25.

19. Hindley, *Destination Casablanca*, p. 323.
20. C.R. Pennell, *Morocco since 1830: A History*, New York University Press, 2000, p. 260.
21. Abtey, *La guerre secrète*, p. 159.
22. Baker and Bouillon, *Joséphine*, p. 188; Abtey, *La guerre secrète*, p. 161.
23. '"Too busy to die," Jo Baker tells AFRO', *Afro-American*, 23 January 1943, p. 1.
24. Antero Pietila and Stacy Spaulding, *Race Goes to War: Ollie Stewart and the Reporting of Black Correspondents in World War II*, Kindle edition, Now and Then Reader, 2014; Antero Pietila and Stacy Spaulding, 'The Afro-American's World War II correspondents: Feuilletonism as social action', *Literary Journalism Studies*, 5:2 (2013), p. 46.
25. Pietila and Spaulding, 'The Afro-American's World War II correspondents', p. 46.
26. 'Jo Baker wires, I'm alive, thank God', *Philadelphia Tribune*, 9 January 1943, p. 1.
27. Elliott Roosevelt, *As He Saw It*, Duell, Sloan & Pearce, 1946, pp. 109–112.
28. Egya N. Sangmuah, 'Sultan Mohammed ben Youssef's American strategy and the diplomacy of North African liberation, 1943–61', *Journal of Contemporary History*, 27:1 (1992), pp. 129–148; Jamaâ Baida, 'The American landing in November 1942: A turning point in Morocco's contemporary history', *Journal of North African Studies*, 19:4 (2014), pp. 518–523.
29. Carleton Coon, *A North African Story: The Anthropology of an OSS Agent, 1941–1943*, Gambit, 1980, p. 55.
30. Intelligence report, Capitaine du Couedic to the Direction de la Sûreté Militaire, 11 January 1943, GR 28 P 9 390, SHD.
31. Intelligence report probably by agents of the BCRA (therefore Gaullist): Intelligence report, Capitaine du Couedic to the Direction de la Sûreté Militaire, 11 April 1943, GR 28 P 9 390, SHD.
32. Intelligence report, 11 January 1943, SHD.
33. Intelligence report, 11 January 1943, SHD.
34. Undated report in Marrakech dossier, Field Station Files – Casablanca, Box 190, 82–84, RG 226, NACP.
35. Crawford, *Report on North Africa*, p. 41.
36. Crawford, *Report on North Africa*, p. 42.
37. Undated report in Marrakech dossier, Field Station Files – Casablanca, Box 190, 82–84, RG 226, NACP.
38. Undated report in Marrakech dossier, Field Station Files – Casablanca, Box 190, 82–84, RG 226, NACP.
39. Undated report in Marrakech dossier, Field Station Files – Casablanca, Box 190, 82–84, RG 226, NACP.
40. Sangmuah, 'Sultan Mohammed ben Youssef's American strategy', p. 132; Maurice Vaïsse, 'De Gaulle et Mohammed V 18 juin 1940–18 juin 1945', *Guerres mondiales et conflits contemporains*, 241:1 (2011), pp. 97–98.
41. *L'Écho d'Alger*, 20 January 1943.
42. 'Inauguration à Casablanca des clubs de la Croix-Rouge américaine ouverts aux soldats alliés', *Le Petit Marocain*, 21 March 1943, p. 1.
43. 'While officially professing to be racially liberal, the American military authorities in Morocco continue to discriminate against their soldiers on the basis of race', *L'Ouest-Éclair*, 7 April 1943.

44. Abtey, *La guerre secrète*, p. 163. Williams was a pioneer of the civil rights movement and became very active after the war. He was executive director of the Chicago Urban League for eight years. See https://www.chicagotribune.com/news/ct-xpm-1992-03-25-9201270565-story.html

45. *Le Petit Marocain*, 21 March 1943.

46. *Le Petit Marocain*, 21 March 1943.

47. Crawford, *Report on North Africa*, p. 43.

48. 'Josy Baker much alive; entertaining in N. Africa', *Variety*, 21 April 1943, p. 2.

49. Baker and Bouillon, *Joséphine*, p. 190.

50. 'Jo Baker sings "I Want to Make Rhythm" to open Red Cross Club', *Chicago Defender*, 10 April 1943, p. 3; 'Josephine Baker still pitching', *Billboard*, 10 April 1943, p. 6.

51. Crawford, *Report on North Africa*, p. 43; *Chicago Defender*, 10 April 1943.

52. Crawford, *Report on North Africa*, p. 43.

53. Baker and Bouillon, *Joséphine*, p. 190.

54. Baker and Bouillon, *Joséphine*, p. 189; Abtey, *La guerre secrète*, p. 164.

55. Crawford, *Report on North Africa*, p. 46.

56. Abtey, *La guerre secrète*, p. 171; Baker and Bouillon, *Joséphine*, p. 191.

57. Crawford, *Report on North Africa*, p. 42.

58. See Abtey, *La guerre secrète*, pp. 169–172 for a description.

59. He comments on a dinner party which was probably the same dinner, though he dates it as taking place earlier, before the Casablanca conference. Pendar, *Adventure in Diplomacy*, p. 133.

60. Pendar, *Adventure in Diplomacy*, p. 134.

61. Baker and Bouillon, *Joséphine*, p. 192.

62. Fatima Mernissi, *Dreams of Trespass: Tales of a Harem Girlhood*, Perseus Books, 1994, pp. 184–185.

63. Abtey, *La guerre secrète*, p. 170.

64. Baker and Bouillon, *Joséphine*, p. 191.

65. Abtey, *La guerre secrète*, p. 175.

66. Abtey, *La guerre secrète*, p. 166.

67. Baker and Bouillon, *Joséphine*, p. 192.

68. Baker and Bouillon, *Joséphine*, p. 193.

69. Abtey, *La guerre secrète*, p. 181.

70. Abtey, *La guerre secrète*, pp. 183–185.

71. Abtey, *La guerre secrète*, p. 187.

72. 'Jo Baker sings for N. African soldiers', *Afro-American*, 10 July 1943, p. 5.

73. 'Jo Baker loses voice at big Algiers concert: Chicagoan meets Jo Baker in Cairo', *Chicago Defender*, 21 August 1943, pp. 1, 4.

74. 'Josy Baker's tour of No. African bases symbol of a Fighting France', *Variety*, 29 September 1943, p. 26.

75. 'Jo Baker touring camps', *Pittsburgh Courier*, 5 June 1943, p. 20.

76. Abtey, *La guerre secrète*, p. 188.

77. Lieutenant Morton Eustis, 'Double feature in North Africa: Josephine Baker and an air raid', *Theatre Arts*, October 1943, pp. 609–611.

78. Eustis, 'Double feature in North Africa', *Theatre Arts*, October 1943, pp. 609–611.

79. 'She's toast of soldiers now', *Afro-American*, 31 July 1943, p. 8; '"Jo" Baker signs up for the boys', *Omaha Guide*, 17 July 1943, p. 1.

80. 'Says boys overseas want more glamour stars like Josephine Baker', *Pittsburgh Courier*, 3 July 1943, p. 21.

81. 'Quaint Moslem customs bared at elaborate dinner in honor of Josephine Baker', *New Journal and Guide*, 22 May 1943, p. 1.

82. 'Jo Baker sings for N. African soldiers', *Afro-American*, 10 July 1943, p. 5.

83. Hindley, *Destination Casablanca*, p. 327.

84. Brian Edwards, *Morocco Bound: Disorienting America's Maghreb from Casablanca to Marrakech Express*, Duke University Press, 2005, p. 33.

85. Edwards, *Morocco Bound*, p. 37.

86. *Chicago Defender*, 22 May 1943.

87. 'Jo Baker sings "I Want to Make Rhythm" to open Red Cross Club', *Chicago Defender*, 10 April 1943, p. 3; Crawford, *Report on North Africa*, p. 44.

88. Crawford, *Report on North Africa*, p. 44.

89. Pietila and Spaulding, *Race Goes to War*.

90. 'Officers, Moslems meet at party for Jo Baker', *New Journal and Guide*, May 22 1943, p. B1.

91. 'Finds clever star popular with soldiers: Comedienne appears before mixed audiences', *New Journal and Guide*, 22 May 1943, p. B26. At least a dozen French air force officers were also present as well as the Red Cross officials who had organised the event, relatives and friends of the host and the journalist himself.

92. 'Finds clever star popular with soldiers: Comedienne appears before mixed audiences', *New Journal and Guide*, 22 May 1943, p. B26.

93. 'Jo Baker sings for N. African soldiers', *Afro-American*, 10 July 1943, p. 5.

94. 'Jo Baker, proud of colored soldier; sings for them', *Philadelphia Tribune*, 31 July 1943, p. 2; 'Jo Baker sees race making great headway', *Chicago Defender*, 31 July 1943, p. 5; 'Jo Baker, former rage of Paris, new toast of soldiers overseas', *Pittsburgh Courier*, 31 July 1943, p. 21.

95. 'Finds clever star popular with soldiers: Comedienne appears before mixed audiences', *New Journal and Guide*, 22 May 1943, p. B26.

96. Sam Lebovic, '"A breath from home": Soldier entertainment and the nationalist politics of pop culture during World War II', *Journal of Social History*, 47:2 (2013), p. 277.

97. Stephen Papich, *Remembering Josephine*, Bobbs-Merrill, 1976.

98. Papich, *Remembering Josephine*, p. 133.

99. 'Jo Baker, proud of colored soldier; sings for them', *Philadelphia Tribune*, 31 July 1943, p. 2; 'Jo Baker sees race making great headway', *Chicago Defender*, 31 July 1943, p. 5; 'Jo Baker, former rage of Paris, new toast of soldiers overseas', *Pittsburgh Courier*, 31 July 1943, p. 21.

100. 'Joe Baker proud of race soldiers', *Atlanta Daily World*, 25 July 1943, p. 6; 'Jo Baker sees race making great headway', *Chicago Defender*, 31 July 1943, p. 5.

101. 'Songstress warbles lilting tunes for African soldiers', *Algiers Daily Stars and Stripes*, 7 June 1943, p. 2.

102. Baker and Bouillon, *Joséphine*, p. 189.

103. Baker and Bouillon, *Joséphine*, p. 191.

104. Hindley, *Destination Casablanca*, p. 412.

105. Levisse-Touzé, *L'Afrique du Nord*, pp. 314–315.

106. Abtey, *La guerre secrète*, p. 195.

107. 'A l'Opéra, Gala de la Croix-Rouge Française', *L' Écho D'Alger*, 11 and 14 June 1943. Baker performed with a Black American orchestra. She had hoped to see de Gaulle, but it was M. and Mme Giraud who attended the gala in aid of the French Red Cross, with de Gaulle's head of staff, General Billotte, there to represent him. Reviews refer to her performance as offering 'a poignant Parisianism with an exotic touch'.
108. Sébastien Albertelli, *Les services secrets de la France Libre: Le bras armé du général de Gaulle*, Nouveau Monde Editions, 2012, pp. 70–71.
109. Abtey, *La guerre secrète*, pp. 176–177.
110. Intelligence report, Capitaine du Couedic to the Direction de la sûreté militaire, 11 January 1943, GR 28 P 9 390, SHD.
111. Abtey repeatedly complains that he was not listened to and he continued to have problems in gaining recognition for his wartime military record for the rest of his life – see chapter 7. Unsurprisingly, there is no evidence of these 'doubtful morals' in his memoirs.
112. Abtey, *La guerre secrète*, p. 200.

Chapter 5

1. Janes created an archive of his correspondence with Baker and his collection of newspaper cuttings, photos, etc. This was later purchased by Yale University and held in its Beinecke Rare Book and Manuscript Library, Henry Hurford Janes – Josephine Baker Collection (henceforth HHJ-JBC).
2. Merriman, *Greasepaint and Cordite*, p. 165.
3. Merriman, *Greasepaint and Cordite*, p. 165.
4. Merriman, *Greasepaint and Cordite*, p. 165.
5. Merriman, *Greasepaint and Cordite*, p. 179.
6. Merriman, *Greasepaint and Cordite*, p. 180.
7. Merriman, *Greasepaint and Cordite*, p. 164.
8. Merriman, *Greasepaint and Cordite*, p. 176.
9. Handwritten notes by Janes, JWJ MSS 2 Box 4 Folder 151, Series 2. Personal Papers, 1926–86, HHJ-JBC, YU.
10. Abtey, *La guerre secrète*, p. 208.
11. Artemis Cooper, *Cairo in the War: 1939–1945*, Penguin, 1995, p. 250.
12. Photograph of Baker with Dean on the terrace of Shepheard's Hotel in the *Tatler*, 25 August 1943.
13. Noël Coward, *Future Indefinite*, Methuen, 2004, pp. 210–211.
14. 'Jo Baker loses voice at big Algiers concert: Chicagoan meets Jo Baker in Cairo', *Chicago Defender*, 21 August 1943, pp. 1, 4.
15. Abtey, *La guerre secrète*, p. 209.
16. Coward, *Future Indefinite*, p. 217.
17. Merriman, *Greasepaint and Cordite*, p. 186.
18. Noël Coward, *Middle East Diary*, Heinemann, 1944, p. 171.
19. Merriman, *Greasepaint and Cordite*, p. 186.
20. Rémy, J.A.: *Episodes de la vie d'un agent S.R*, pp. 292–293.
21. Typescript by Janes, 'Josephine – and Mr Bull', p. 3, JWJ MSS 2 Box 4, Folder 151, series 2. Personal Papers, 1926–86, HHJ-JBC, YU.
22. 'How ENSA went to war', *United Services Review*, 3 September 1945, pp. 7, 10.
23. Merriman, *Greasepaint and Cordite*, p. 223.

24. '"Thin blue line" to the rescue of Josephine Baker', *Air Force News*, 1:11, 13 July 1943, p. 8.
25. Coward, *Middle East Diary*.
26. Papich, *Remembering Josephine*, p. 133.
27. Janes, 'Josephine – and Mr Bull', p. 3, HHJ-JBC, YU.
28. Handwritten notes by Janes, HHJ-JBC, YU.
29. Baker and Chase, *Josephine*, p. 255.
30. Janes, letters to Baker, 29 June 1945 & 16 July 1943, JWMSS2, Box 1 Correspondence 1938– 1986, HHJ-JBC, YU
31. Abtey, *La guerre secrète*, p. 206. This may be Mena House, which was used for troops during the war.
32. Baker and Bouillon, *Joséphine*, p. 194.
33. Abtey, *La guerre secrète*, p. 208.
34. Abtey, *La guerre secrète*, p. 207; Baker and Bouillon, *Joséphine*, p. 194.
35. 16 July 1943, Janes to Baker, HHJ-JBC, YU.
36. 31 July 1943, Janes to Baker, HHJ-JBC, YU.
37. Handwritten notes by Janes, HHJ-JBC, YU.
38. 1 September 1943, Janes to Baker, HHJ-JBC, YU.
39. Abtey, *La guerre secrète*, p. 206.
40. Abtey, *La guerre secrète*, p. 205.
41. Rémy, *Episodes de la vie d'un agent S.R.*, p. 295; Abtey, *La guerre secrète*, p. 204.
42. Abtey, *La guerre secrète*, p. 207.
43. Albertelli, *Les services secrets de la France Libre*, p. 73.
44. Rémy, *Episodes de la vie d'un agent S.R.*, p. 296.
45. Abtey notes in his memoirs that their mission was not universally supported, and this was almost certainly due to the 'civil war' atmosphere that continued to reign in French intelligence service circles and the uncertainty about whether his loyalties lay with Giraud or de Gaulle.
46. Alla Dumesnil's letter of support for Baker's Légion d'honneur related her *'missions délicates'*, though no detail is provided of what these were: Lettre d'Alla Dumesnil, 3 October 1946, Dossier individuel d'officier, AI 1 P6679 (1), SHD. For speculation on this, see also Létang and Soutet, 'Feux de la rampe', p. 3.
47. Abtey, *La guerre secrète*, p. 212.
48. Abtey, *La guerre secrète*, p. 214.
49. Abtey, *La guerre secrete*, p. 214.
50. Strictly speaking, he was joining the 'Fighting French' at this point, but this is how Abtey refers to it. Abtey, *La guerre secrète*, p. 216.
51. Baker and Bouillon, *Joséphine*, p. 199.
52. Abtey, *La guerre secrète*, p. 216.
53. 'Au cours de son voyage triomphal au Maroc, Casablanca et Meknès ont fait au général de Gaulle un accueil vibrant d'enthousiasme', *L' Écho d'Alger*, 9 August 1943, p. 1.
54. Subtitle: 'Le général de Gaulle prend contact avec l'Islam marocain', *L' Écho d'Alger*, 11 August 1943, p. 2.
55. Intelligence report, 'Trend of Events in Casablanca 1–8 August 1943', 9 August 1943, Field Station Files Casablanca, Marrakech file 83, RG 226, NACP.
56. 'Le général de Gaulle préside le gala des Forces françaises libres', *L' Écho d'Alger*, 14 August 1943, p. 1.

57. 'De Gaulle, parmi ses compagnons', *France-Amérique*, 29 August 1943.
58. Oral interview, Alla Dumesnil, A18Z 232 1, SHD.
59. Abtey, *La guerre secrète*, p. 218.
60. Sauvage, *Mémoires*, p. 334. See chapter 7 for more on this.
61. Baker and Bouillon, *Joséphine*, p. 195.
62. Baker and Bouillon, *Joséphine*, p. 196.
63. 'Jo Baker loses voice at big Algiers concert', *Chicago Defender*, 21 August 1943.
64. Abtey, *La guerre secrète*, p. 221.
65. Baker and Bouillon, *Joséphine*, p. 196.
66. Abtey, *La guerre secrète*, p. 237.
67. Baker and Bouillon, *Joséphine*, p. 196.
68. Abtey, *La guerre secrète*, p. 224.
69. Janes to Captain Harrington, ENSA Entertainment Tripoli & Henry Janes to Captain Jamieson, 2 August 1943, HHJ-JBC, YU.
70. Rose, *Jazz Cleopatra*, p. 200.
71. Baker and Bouillon, *Joséphine*, p. 197.
72. Abtey, *La guerre secrète*, p. 226.
73. Abtey, *La guerre secrète*, p. 227.
74. Abtey, *La guerre secrète*, p. 228; Baker and Bouillon, *Joséphine*, p. 197.
75. See Jonathan Fennell, *Combat and Morale in the North African Campaign*, Cambridge University Press, 2011, pp. 125–150.
76. Coward, *Middle East Diary*, p. 108.
77. Abtey, *La guerre secrète*, p. 232.
78. Abtey, *La guerre secrète*, p. 234.
79. Abtey, *La guerre secrète*, p. 236.
80. Abtey, *La guerre secrète*, p. 236; Baker and Bouillon, *Joséphine*, p. 197.
81. Abtey, *La guerre secrète*, p. 234.
82. Abtey, *La guerre secrète*, pp. 238–239.
83. Abtey, *La guerre secrète*, p. 239; Baker and Bouillon, *Joséphine*, p. 198.
84. Abtey, *La guerre secrète*, p. 241.
85. Baker and Bouillon, *Joséphine*, p. 198.
86. Abtey, *La guerre secrète*, p. 242.
87. Abtey, *La guerre secrète*, p. 245.
88. Abtey, *La guerre secrète*, p. 243.
89. Noël Coward referred to it as a 'glittering new open-air night club': *Middle East Diary*, p. 47.
90. Cooper, *Cairo in the War*, p. 251.
91. Cooper, *Cairo in the War*, p. 252.
92. Abtey, *La guerre secrète*, p. 209.
93. Coward, *Middle East Diary*, 8 September 1943, p. 78.
94. 'Noël Coward reports', *Billboard*, 18 December 1943, p. 4. In *Variety*, 15 December 1943, he commented on the 'wonderful job being done by Baker in entertaining the men of both the British and American armies in the Middle East'.
95. Le Chef d'Escadron Brousset à Monsieur Boniface, Directeur des Affaires Politiques, Résidence Général de France au Maroc, Undated, France Libre de Gaulle, Questions coloniales, 1 Maroc 3AG1/284, AN.
96. Le Chef d'Escadron Brousset à Monsieur le Général Collet, Commandant de la Région de Marrakech, Undated, France Libre de Gaulle, Questions coloniales, 1 Maroc 3AG1/284, AN.

97. Le Chef d'Escadron Brousset à Monsieur Boniface, Directeur des Affaires Politiques, Résidence Générale de France au Maroc, Undated, France Libre de Gaulle, Questions coloniales, 1 Maroc 3AG1/284, AN.

98. James Barr, *A Line in the Sand: Britain, France and the Struggle that Shaped the Middle East*, Simon & Schuster, 2011; Rachel Chin, *War of Words: Britain, France and Discourses of Empire during the Second World War*, Oxford University Press, 2022; Karen Evans, 'The apple of discord: The impact of the Levant on Anglo-French relations during 1943', unpublished PhD thesis, University of Leeds, 1990.

99. Aviel Roshwald, 'The Spears mission in the Levant 1941–1944', *Historical Journal*, 29:4 (1986), pp. 897–919.

100. Abtey, *La guerre secrète*, p. 247.

101. Abtey, *La guerre secrète*, p. 247.

102. 'Déliée par la Victoire du Serment du Silence, L'Espionne Noire Raconte', *Point de vue*, 6 June 1946, p. 8.

103. Abtey, *La guerre secrète*, p. 247: 'France's fate in the Middle East was sealed; the Arab Union had scored its first victory.'

104. Abtey, *La guerre secrète*, p. 263.

105. These photographs were put in a hand-made album and presented to Baker by one of the soldiers. It was one of the very few souvenirs that she kept by her until the end of her life. See Hammond and O'Connor, *Josephine Baker*, pp. 178–179.

106. 'Josy Baker's tour of No. African bases symbol of a Fighting France', *Variety*, 29 September 1943, p. 26.

107. 'Josephine Baker in Jerusalem', *Palestine Post*, 3 October 1943, p. 4.

108. 'Sightseeing with Josephine', *Palestine Post*, 5 October 1943, p. 4.

109. Abtey, *La guerre secrète*, p. 251.

110. Abtey, *La guerre secrète*, p. 253.

111. 'Inauguration de la Saison du Caire: Le Gala de l'Opera', *Images*, 31 October 1943, p. 3.

112. Baker and Bouillon, *Joséphine*, p. 201.

113. Abtey, *La guerre secrète*, p. 253.

114. Abtey, *La guerre secrète*, p. 258.

115. Abtey, *La guerre secrète*, p. 257.

116. Julian Jackson, *A Certain Idea of France: The Life of Charles de Gaulle*, Penguin, 2019, p. 290.

117. Abtey, *La guerre secrète*, p. 270.

118. Baker and Chase, *Josephine*, p. 258.

119. Le Chef d'Escadron Brousset à Monsieur Boniface, Directeur des Affaires Politiques, Résidence Générale de France au Maroc, Undated, France Libre de Gaulle, Questions coloniales, 1 Maroc 3AG1/284, AN.

120. Le Chef d'Escadron Brousset à Monsieur Boniface, France Libre de Gaulle, Questions coloniales, 1 Maroc 3AG1/284, AN.

121. Paul Paillole, *L'Homme des Services Secrets: Entretiens avec Alain-Gilles Minella*, Julliard, 1995, p. 201; Oral Interview, Paillole, SHD.

122. Pierre Péan, *Une jeunesse française: François Mitterrand, 1934-1947*, Fayard, 1994, p. 357.

123. In February 1944, he was assisted by sea to return to France on a Royal Navy boat commanded by Lieutenant Commander David Birkin, father of the

future actress, Jane Birkin. Hammond and O'Connor, *Josephine Baker*, p. 155; Péan, *Une jeunesse française*, pp. 375–376.

124. De Gaulle appears to have acceded to Henri Frenay's wishes in this matter. Curiously, neither Baker nor Abtey makes any mention of this episode in their memoirs.

125. On his *acte d'engagement* for the Corps Franc d'Afrique (Africa Free Corps), signed on 15 December 1942, Lion gives an address in Casablanca. Dossier résistant, GR 16 P 373520, SHD.

126. Sauvage, *Mémoires*, p. 267.

127. Abtey, *La guerre secrète*, p. 278.

128. Rapport no. 1, Capitaine Abtey, France Libre de Gaulle, Questions coloniales, 1 Maroc, 3AG1/284, AN.

129. Abtey, *La guerre secrète*, p. 278.

130. Rapport no. 1, Capitaine Abtey, France Libre de Gaulle, Questions coloniales, 1 Maroc, 3AG1/284, AN.

131. Abitbol, *Histoire du Maroc*, p. 499.

Chapter 6

1. Paillole credits Baker with having had considerable influence on the positions held by the Moroccans, suggesting that her absence in the Middle East contributed to the emergence of a more militant position on the part of the independence movement; Bouillon and Baker, *Joséphine*, pp. 204–205.

2. Vaïsse, 'De Gaulle et Mohammed V', p. 99.

3. Vaïsse, 'De Gaulle et Mohammed V', p. 100.

4. E.G.H. Joffé, 'The Moroccan nationalist movement: Istiqlal, the sultan and the country', *Journal of North African History*, 26:4 (1985), p. 305.

5. Vaïsse, 'De Gaulle et Mohammed V', p. 101.

6. Dumesnil, Légion d'honneur recommendation letter, SHD.

7. Oral interview, Dumesnil, SHD.

8. Baker and Bouillon, *Joséphine*, p. 204.

9. Abtey, *La guerre secrète*, p. 280; Baker and Bouillon, *Joséphine*, p. 280.

10. Baker and Bouillon, *Joséphine*, p. 204.

11. Abtey, *La guerre secrète*, p. 285.

12. Etat Signalétique des Services Dossier de Résistant, GR 16 P 28445, SHD.

13. 'What made the Sammies run: Puritanical Miss Baker eliminates anatomical', *Stars and Stripes* (London edition), 14 May 1945, p. 5.

14. 'Acte d'engagement définitif et déclaration d'abandon de solde', signed by Commandant Dumesnil, 27 May 1944, SHD.

15. 'Autorisation à revêtir la tenue bourgeoise [civilian dress]', signed by Air Force General Bouscat, Chief of Air Staff, Algiers, 31 May 1944, SHD.

16. Some mention is made in Sébastien Albertelli, *Elles ont suivi de Gaulle: Histoire du Corps des Volontaires Françaises*, Perrin, 2020.

17. See Sébastien Albertelli, *Elles ont suivi de Gaulle*, for a detailed history of these formations across all the French forces.

18. Oral interview, Dumesnil, SHD.

19. *France Amerique*, 19 March 1944.

20. 'Historique d'unités (1943–1944) Formations Féminines de l'Air', Undated, 4 D 60, SHD.

21. Text of radio speech by General Martial Valin, 6 March 1943, Z23332, SHD.
22. 'Algiers', *Daily Mail*, 23 December 1943, p. 2.
23. D.B. Wyndham, 'Standing by . . . one thing and another', *Tatler and Bystander*, 12 January 1944, p. 44.
24. 'Déliée par la Victoire du Serment du Silence, L'Espionne Noire Raconte', *Point de vue*, 6 June 1946, p. 9.
25. Oral interview, Dumesnil, SHD.
26. This was one of the first to appear. 'Les Filles de l'Air', *France-Amérique*, 19 March 1944, p. 8. For the original photo, see Images Défense, FFL100722 1944. See also '"Jo" gets commission', *Chicago Defender*, 27 May 1944, p. 1, though the caption is inaccurate about her wartime activities.
27. Propaganda film *Filles de France*, ECPAD Images Défense, Ref. FT7, available on its website.
28. Létang and Soutet, 'Les feux de la rampe', p. 114.
29. Jean-Charles Foucrier and Aurélien Renaudière, 'Les victoires d'une défaite? L'écriture de l'histoire des forces aériennes dans la bataille de France (1940–2020)', *Nacelles*, 10 (2021).
30. See also introduction.
31. Letter from Colonel Gouet to Commandant Colonel of the Air Battalion 117, 10 August 1945, Individual officer's file, AI 1 P 6679 (1), SHD.
32. Projet de décret portant nomination dans la Légion d'honneur (1946) AI 1 P 6679 (1), SHD. See chapter 7 for a full discussion of this.
33. Oral interview, Dumesnil, SHD.
34. 'En mission à Paris Joséphine Baker nous raconte ses "campagnes"', *Ce soir*, 12 October 1944, p. 1.
35. 'What made the Sammies run: Puritanical Miss Baker eliminates anatomical', *Stars and Stripes* (London edition), 14 May 1945, p. 5; 'Josephine Baker may go to Pacific via United States', *Detroit Tribune*, 23 June 1945, p. 13.
36. Text of radio speech by General Martial Valin, 6 March 1943, Z23332, SHD.
37. 'Les Coups d'Ailes', *Les Ailes: journal hebdomadaire de la locomotion aérienne*, 23 December 1944, p. 2.
38. 'Le gala des Ailes; Spectacle brilliant et parfaitement réussi', *L'Écho d'Algers*, 21 May 1944, p. 2.
39. 'Infantry unit in N. Africa awaits Jo Baker's visit', *Afro-American*, 6 May 1944, p. 16; 'Joe gets a kick out of this visit', *Afro-American*, 11 November 1944, photo with caption, p. 6; 'When Jo Baker visited Red Cross Club', *Atlanta Daily World*, 10 November 1944, photo with caption, p. 1.
40. Photos of Baker at Bouscat's residence including AIR 106-1927, 1928 and 1929, held on the website of the ECPAD Images Défense.
41. Abtey, *La guerre secrète*, p. 303.
42. Abtey, *La guerre secrète*, p. 306.
43. Journal de Marche, 6 June 1944, SHD archives; Baker signed the account in 1946. The event is related in Abtey, *La guerre secrète*, pp. 300–308; and Baker and Bouillon, *Joséphine*, p. 205; it was reported in the services press, too: 'Josephine takes a swim', *Daily Newspaper of South East Command*, 26 June 1944.
44. Baker and Bouillon, *Joséphine*, p. 205.
45. Abtey, *La guerre secrète*, p. 309.
46. 'Jo Baker hailed on visit to camps in war zone', *Chicago Defender*, 18 November 1944, p. 9.

47. Sauvage, *Mémoires*, p. 25.
48. According to the *Chicago Defender*, 18 November 1944.
49. Sauvage, *Mémoires*, p. 258.
50. Baker and Bouillon, *Joséphine*, p. 208.
51. Sauvage, *Mémoires*, p. 259.
52. *Hebdomadaire Illustré du M.L.N (Mouvement de Libération Nationale)* V, 21 October 1944, p. 10.
53. ' "Je ne suis qu'un soldat" nous dit Joséphine Baker', *Défense de la France*, 11 October 1944, p. 1.
54. 'Joséphine Baker nous dit', *Regards*, 1 May 1945, p. 3.
55. 'Josephine Baker toasted in Paris', *Chicago Defender*, 28 October 1944, p. 10; 'Josephine Baker a lieutenant', *New York Times*, 11 October 1944, p. 27; 'Jo Baker in Paris; wears air uniform', *New Journal and Guide*, 14 October 1944, p. A10.
56. 'Davis, Jo Baker reach Paris', *Afro-American*, 21 October 1944, p. 1.
57. 'Joséphine en uniforme', *France*, 3 November 1944.
58. Sauvage, *Mémoires*, p. 270.
59. ECPAD Images Défense, Magazine recréatif, 26 April 1945, with sound, MAG200 and ACT333/334 without sound.
60. 'What made the Sammies run: Puritanical Miss Baker eliminates anatomical', *Stars and Stripes* (London edition), 14 May 1945, p. 5.
61. Baker and Bouillon, *Joséphine*, p. 207; Sauvage, *Mémoires*, pp. 267, 270.
62. Sauvage, *Mémoires*, p. 270. She claims she was advised by Yves Bonnat, who was dealing with the purges in music hall but who also seems to have been a journalist who covered her return in several publications. The Bouillon autobiography mentions Bonnat; see Baker and Bouillon, *Joséphine*, p. 208.
63. Sauvage, *Mémoires*, pp. 270–271.
64. Baker and Bouillon, *Joséphine*, p. 208.
65. Sauvage, *Mémoires*, p. 272; Hammond and O'Connor, *Josephine Baker*, p. 156.
66. Baker and Bouillon, *Joséphine*, pp. 208–209.
67. Merriman, *Greasepaint and Cordite*, p. 223.
68. 'Rentrée de Joséphine Baker', *Paris-presse, L'Intransigeant*, 21 November 1944, p. 2.
69. 'Au "Vél'd'Hiv" le 2 décembre Grande Fête', *L'Humanité*, 29 November 1944, p. 2.
70. *France-Amérique*, 24 December 1944, p. 7.
71. Sauvage, *Mémoires*, p. 272.
72. ECPAD Images Défense, 24 January 1945, ACT294.
73. Sauvage, *Mémoires*, p. 273.
74. Sauvage, *Mémoires*, pp. 213–215. The visit is also mentioned in Abtey, *La guerre secrète*, p. 320; Baker and Bouillon, *Joséphine*, p. 209.
75. Baker and Bouillon, *Joséphine*, p. 211.
76. Sauvage, *Mémoires*, p. 276.
77. Janes to Baker, 1 September 1943, HHJ-JBC, YU.
78. Baker to Janes, 5 May 1944, HHJ-JBC, YU.
79. Baker to Janes, 5 May 1944, HHJ-JBC, YU.
80. Letter from Edward Stanley, General Manager, ENSA Entertainments to Basil Dean, Paris, 29 November 1944, HHJ-JBC, YU.
81. Janes to Baker, 17 May 1945, HHJ-JBC, YU.

82. Janes to Dean, 21 April 1945, HHJ-JBC, YU.
83. Report on Baker's factory appearances, 28 May 1945, HHJ-JBC, YU. An article appeared with a photo of Baker in uniform: 'In London', *Daily Mail*, 25 April 1945, p. 1.
84. Reports on Josephine Baker's service and factory visits, HHJ-JBC, YU.
85. Draft typescript, Josephine Baker – Association with 'Harry' Hurford Janes, p. 2, HHJ-JBC, YU.
86. Janes to Baker, 4 May 1945, HHJ-JBC, YU.
87. She also appeared on the BBC on 11 and 12 May 1945: *France*, 11 May 1945.
88. Typescript by 'Harry' Janes, Josephine Baker – Appearances during the war with Noël Coward,12 July 1971, HHJ-JBC, YU.
89. 'Un gala de bienfaisance', *France*, 25 May 1945.
90. 'Josephine Baker gives soldiers a victory song', *Picture Post*, 2 June 1945, pp. 12–13.
91. Press cutting from 'Dusky Flower', *News Review*, 24 May 1945, in HHJ-JBC, YU.
92. 'Jo Baker, former Paris idol, entertains soldiers in England', *Cleveland Call and Post*, 19 May 1945, p. 11A.
93. Pierre-Célestin Delrieu, *Feu du ciel, feu vengeur*, Gerbert, 1984, cited in online article https://yorkshireairmuseum.org/josephine-baker-1945-elvington-york-visit/
94. Typescript entitled 'Josephine Baker', p. 2, HHJ-JBC, YU.
95. Written manuscript, HHJ-JBC, YU.
96. Undated notes, HHJ-JBC, YU.
97. Janes to Baker, 9 October 1944, HHJ-JBC, YU.
98. Janes to Basil Dean, Director of ENSA, 8 May 1945, HHJ-JBC, YU.
99. 'What made the Sammies run: Puritanical Miss Baker eliminates anatomical', *Stars and Stripes* (London edition), 14 May 1945, p. 5.
100. 'Jo Baker to visit troops in Pacific', *Afro-American*, 30 June 1945, p. 1.
101. Janes to Baker, 21 June 1945, HHJ-JBC, YU.
102. Janes to Mrs Newell, 8 June 1945, HHJ-JBC, YU.
103. Mary Newell to Duff Cooper, 15 July 1945, HHJ-JBC, YU.
104. Duff Cooper to Mary Newell, 25 July 1945, HHJ-JBC, YU.
105. John W. Young, 'The Foreign Office, the French and the post-war division of Germany 1945–46', *Review of International Studies*, 12:3 (1986), pp. 223–234.
106. *Les Lettres Françaises*, 11 August 1945, pp. 5–6.
107. Janes to Baker, 29 June 1945, HHJ-JBC, YU.
108. Baker to Janes, Undated, HHJ-JBC, YU.
109. Janes to Mrs Vernon, ENSA Calcutta, 27 July 1945, HHJ-JBC, YU.
110. Janes typescript entitled 'Draft Association with Henry Hurford Janes', p. 2, Box 4, Folder 121, Series 2, Personal Papers 1926–1986, HHJ-JBC, YU.
111. Baker to Janes, 25 June 1945, HHJ-JBC, YU.
112. Vaïsse, 'De Gaulle et Mohammed V', pp. 102–104.
113. 'Le Sultan du Maroc assistera aux fêtes du 18 juin', *Libération*, 9 June 1945; 'Sa Majesté le Sultan va se rendre en France en voyage officiel', *La Vigie Marocaine*, 7 June 1945.
114. 'Few veterans fly home, AFRO reporter discovers', *Afro-American*, 11 August 1945, p. 11.
115. Charles de Gaulle, *Mémoires de Guerre*, Tome 3, *Le Salut 1944–1946*, Plon, 1959, pp. 223–225.

116. Alain-Marie Foy and Jean-Marie Dumont, 'Hommage à Joséphine Baker', *Bulletin Municipal du Vésinet*, no. 31, June 1975, at http://histoire-vesinet.org/ hommage-baker.htm. The event is also described in Baker and Chase, *Josephine*, p. 268.
117. ECPAD Images Défense F 47-82 (Air1).
118. Sauvage, *Mémoires*, p. 327.
119. Vaïsse, 'De Gaulle et Mohammed V', p. 106.
120. Ministre de l'Air to Monsieur le Colonel Commandant le Bataillon Air 119, 10 August 1945, AI 1P 6679 (1), SHD.

Chapter 7

1. Sauvage, *Mémoires*, p. 277.
2. Baker and Bouillon, *Joséphine*, p. 212.
3. Baker and Chase, *Josephine*, p. 269.
4. Baker to Janes, 10 October 1945, HHJ-JBC, YU.
5. Max Roelli in the *Luzerner Tagblatt*, 22 September 1945, translated from text in the Henry Hurford Janes Collection, YU. Her tour is also mentioned in 'Joe Baker dazzles Swiss on opening of world tour', *Afro-American*, 22 December 1945, p. 8.
6. Sauvage, *Mémoires*, p. 274.
7. See programme entitled 'Joséphine Baker, Jo Bouillon et son orchestre', in HHJ-JBC, YU.
8. Baker and Bouillon, *Joséphine*, pp. 216–217.
9. Baker and Bouillon, *Joséphine*, p. 217.
10. Baker and Bouillon, *Joséphine*, p. 207.
11. 'Ils sont rentrés pendant que vous êtes partis', *Claudine*, 28 August 1946, p. 3.
12. Decret portant attribution de la Médaille de la Résistance Française, Paris, 5 October 1946, Josephine Baker Collection, Box 4, JWJ MSS 104, YU.
13. Jacques Soustelle to Baker, Paris, 8 October 1946, Box 4, JWJ MSS 104, JBC, YU.
14. 'Joséphine Baker officier de la Résistance', *France-Illustration*, 19 October 1946, No. 55, p. 1 (photo with caption).
15. 'Décorée parce qu'elle a deux amours: son pays et la France', *France-soir*, 9–10 October 1946.
16. Full text of the letter was reproduced as a preface to Abtey's publication *La guerre secrète*; see later discussion.
17. 'France decorates Josephine Baker', *Afro-American*, 26 October 1946, pp. 1, 15; 'French honor Josephine Baker at nursing home', *Chicago Defender*, 19 October 1946, p. 3.
18. 'Déliée par la Victoire du Serment du Silence, L'Espionne Noire Raconte', *Point de vue*, 6 June 1946, p. 9.
19. *Le Petit Marocain*, 4 July 1946. She also announced she was going to marry Claude Meunier.
20. Charles Onana, *Joséphine Baker contre Hitler*, Editions Duboiris, 2006, p. 100.
21. Projet de décret portant nomination dans la Légion d'honneur, AI 1 P 6679 (1), SHD.
22. Renseignements concernant la candidature à la Croix de la Légion d'honneur de Mme Baker (Joséphine), AI 1 P 6679 (1), SHD.

23. Letter from Alla Dumesnil, 3 October 1946, AI 1 P 6679 (1), SHD.
24. Letter from General Bouscat to Monsieur le Ministre des Armées, 7 October 1946, photocopy held in the Eugene Lerner Josephine Baker archive, SU.
25. Letter from General Pierre Billotte to cabinet militaire du Ministre des Armées, 22 October 1946, AI 1 P 6679 (1), SHD.
26. Decision no. 1347 de la Commission de la Liquidation et Règlement 'Resistance' du Ministère de l'Air, 30 June 1947, AI 1 P 6679 (1), SHD.
27. Fiche à l'attention de Monsieur le Général Plou, AI 1 P 6679 (1), SHD.
28. Létang and Soutet, 'Feux de la rampe', p. 115.
29. 'Miss Baker revealed that she had just recently had a proposal from her former husband ... "I wouldn't remarry the same man," she stressed.' '"My heart belongs to US Doughboys," says Jo Baker', 5 June 1943, *Chicago Defender*, p. 7.
30. Handwritten and other notes, HHJ-JBC, YU.
31. Baker and Bouillon, *Joséphine*, p. 212.
32. Janes written manuscript, HHJ-JBC, YU.
33. Janes to Harold Lars Sorensen, 20 November 1976, HHJ-JBC, YU.
34. Janes notes, HHJ-JBC, YU.
35. Janes to Baker, 13 February 1946, HHJ-JBC, YU.
36. Telegram, Baker to Janes, 19 February 1946, HHJ-JBC, YU.
37. Baker to Janes, 14 April 1946, HHJ-JBC, YU.
38. Janes to Baker, 17 April 1946, HHJ-JBC, YU.
39. 'Je vais être décorée ... et je vais épouser Claude Meunier', *Le Petit Marocain*, 4 July 1946, p. 1.
40. 'Jo Bouillon fiancé à Joséphine Baker', *Combat*, 7 December 1946, p. 4; 'Joséphine Baker va épouser Jo Bouillon', *France-soir*, 7 December 1946.
41. Baker to Janes, March 1947, HHJ-JBC, YU.
42. Janes to Baker, 17 March 1947, HHJ-JBC, YU.
43. Janes notes, HHJ-JBC, YU.
44. Hammond and O'Connor, *Josephine Baker*, p. 158.
45. Sauvage, *Mémoires*, p. 267.
46. Jules-Rosette, *Josephine Baker in Art and Life*, p. 198.
47. Sauvage, *Mémoires*, p. 267.
48. Baker and Bouillon, *Joséphine*, pp. 215, 221.
49. Janes to Baker, 19 February 1946, HHJ-JBC, YU.
50. 'Le mariage de Joséphine et de Jo Bouillon retardé', *France-soir*, 29 April 1947, p. 1.
51. Baker and Chase, *Josephine*, p. 278.
52. 'Je vais être décorée ... et je vais épouser Claude Meunier', *Le Petit Marocain*, 4 July 1946, p. 1.
53. The article offers a rather dubious account of Baker's exploits, including an alleged meeting with Franco; 'Joséphine Baker revient à Paris pour divorcer reprendre ses bijoux chez ma [sic] tante et publier ses aventures de Mata-Hari Noire', *Samedi Soir*, 21 February 1948.
54. *France-soir*, 16 April 1948, p. 2.
55. 'General de Gaulle appreciated her services ... and later on, he prefaced the history of her secret war told by Commander Jacques Abtey with an admiring handwritten letter.' Sauvage, *Mémoires*, p. 27.

56. 'Marcel Sauvage présente . . . Les Mémoires de Joséphine Baker', *Paris-Dakar: hebdomadaire d'informations illustré*, 18 August 1949, p. 3.

57. Rose, *Jazz Cleopatra*, p. 182.

58. Handwritten note from Baker to Janes, wrongly dated by Janes as Easter 1947 (instead of 1948). Here also see an example of the errors Baker would often make in her English grammar. On 20 February 1948, Janes wrote to Baker about the book, as he had read about it in an article in *Samedi Soir* (13 February 1948). He suggested: 'if Captain Abtey is writing your war history, he must not omit what you did for the British'. HHJ-JBC, YU.

59. 'Joséphine Baker est sans rancune mais ne veut pas être "doublée"', *L'Aurore*, 14–15 March 1948, p. 2. Janes also mentions in his papers that Baker wrote to him that Abtey had cheated her. HHJ-JBC, YU.

60. 'Jo Baker's mother will renounce US citizenship', *Afro-American*, 6 November 1948, pp. 1–2; 'Efforts are now under way to have the book translated into English', p. 2.

61. Letter from Janes to Baker, 5 March 1946, HHJ-JBC, YU.

62. Letter from Janes to Baker, 12 March 1946, HHJ-JBC, YU.

63. Janes notes, HHJ-JBC, YU.

64. See discussion of this later in the chapter.

65. Sauvage, *Mémoires*, p. 284.

66. 'Josephine', *Ebony*, Vol. XXIX, No. 2, December 1973, p. 176.

67. Baker and Bouillon, *Joséphine*, p. 211.

68. Pietila and Spaulding, 'The Afro-American's World War II correspondents', p. 48.

69. 'France decorates Josephine Baker', *Afro-American*, 26 October 1946, pp. 1, 15.

70. '3rd mate to be American, actress Jo Baker says', *Afro-American*, 9 November 1946, p. 1.

71. Rose, *Jazz Cleopatra*, p. 208.

72. 'Joséphine Baker déçoit les Américains', *France-soir*, 9 January 1948, p. 2.

73. Sauvage, *Mémoires*, pp. 287–299.

74. 'Josephine Baker's family goes to France to renounce citizenship', *New Journal and Guide*, 6 November 1948, p. 1.

75. Titia Carrizey-Jasick, *Osez Joséphine: La Star, La Femme, Les Milandes*, Evoluprint, Société Editrice HJ Editions, 2019, p. 19.

76. 'Les Milandes, le paradis perdu de Joséphine Baker', *Le Monde*, 23 November 2021.

77. Note from Roger Seydoux, Consul Général de France à New York to Monsieur Henri Bonnet, Ambassadeur de France aux Etats-Unis, 25 May 1951, Questions Politiques et Sociales, Dossier Joséphine Baker 1951–1976, 474PO/3/45, Centre des Archives Diplomatiques de Nantes (henceforth CADN).

78. Note from Roger Seydoux, Consul Général de France à New York to Monsieur Henri Bonnet, Ambassadeur de France aux Etats-Unis, 25 May 1951, CADN.

79. Hammond and O'Connor, *Josephine Baker*, pp. 163–164.

80. Note from Roger Seydoux, Consul Général de France à New York to Monsieur Henri Bonnet, Ambassadeur de France aux Etats-Unis, 25 May 1951, CADN.

81. 'Joséphine Baker chante, danse et combat le racisme', *Femmes Françaises*, 15 September 1951, pp. 12–13.

82. Seydoux telegram, AFP18, CADN.

83. Stephen Papich, *Remembering Josephine*, p. 118.

84. 'Joe Baker helps soldier to win Silver Star', *Arizona Sun*, 2 November 1951, p. 7.
85. 'Ex-US agent says: Jo Baker risked life fighting fascist forces', *Afro-American*, 3 November 1951, p. 7.
86. 'Ex-US agent says: Jo Baker risked life fighting fascist forces', *Afro-American*, 3 November 1951, p. 7.
87. 'Joe Baker helps soldier to win Silver Star', *Arizona Sun*, 2 November 1951, p. 7.
88. These activities have never been mentioned before in any works about Baker.
89. 'Winchell "missed boat" on Jo Baker. Attempted "smear" of her loyalty to allies flops', *Afro-American*, 10 November 1951, p. 7; 'Josephine Baker's services to Allies revealed in report', *Atlanta Daily World*, 4 November 1951, p. 1. Similar reports also appeared in the *Miami Times*, 10 November 1951; *Cleveland Call and Post*, 10 November 1951; and *Jackson Advocate*, 24 November 1951.
90. *Afro-American*, 10 November 1951.
91. See discussion in chapter 3.
92. Seydoux telegram, AFP144, CADN.
93. Baker and Chase, *Josephine*, p. 313.
94. 'Joséphine Baker adopte une famille panachée', *Le Monde*, 10 April 1953, p. 7.
95. Guterl indicates that the story was more complicated, and the boys were not in fact orphans. Guterl, *Josephine Baker and the Rainbow Tribe*, p. 93.
96. Guterl, *Josephine Baker and the Rainbow Tribe*, p. 95.
97. Guterl, *Josephine Baker and the Rainbow Tribe*, p. 118.
98. Conférence de Joséphine Baker sur le racisme, Chalons sur Seine, 4.12.57 13782 F/7/15741, AN.
99. Jules-Rosette, *Josephine Baker in Art and Life*, p. 229.
100. Conférence de Joséphine Baker sur le racisme, Toulouse, 31.1.57, 13782 F/7/15741, AN.
101. Conférence de Joséphine Baker sur le racisme, Reims, 21.1.57, 13782 F/7/15741, AN.
102. Rose, *Jazz Cleopatra*, p. 233.
103. 'Brief account of Major Abtey's Resistance service from June 1940 to July 1943, the date on which he regularised his status with the FFL by signing an enlistment document in Algiers', 16 P 2170, SHD.
104. The committee came to this conclusion as Abtey left mainland France on 24 November 1940, according to his own account; therefore he could not have belonged to a particular FFL unit; 16 P 2170, SHD.
105. Direction du Personnel Militaire de l'Armée de Terre, Section 'Résistance', Summary of his appeal, 20 July 1959, 16 P 2170, SHD.
106. On 10 March 1957, he attended the annual banquet of the 'Amical du Périgord' presided over by Baker and Bouillon. Jean-Claude Bonnal, *Joséphine Baker et le village des enfants du monde en Périgord*, P.L.B. Editeur, 1992, p. 31.
107. Létang and Soutet, 'Feux de la rampe', p. 116.
108. Decree of 9 December 1957, published in the *Journal Officiel*, 14 December 1957, AI 1 P 6679 (1), SHD.
109. Jules-Rosette, *Josephine Baker in Art and Life*, p. 233.
110. Letter from de Gaulle to Baker, 9 January 1958, AG5(1)1114, AN.

111. Baker and Chase, *Josephine*, p. 365.
112. 'Une grande journée pour la châtelaine des Milandes', *Sud Ouest*, 19 August 1961.
113. Baker and Bouillon, *Joséphine*, p. 323.
114. Jules-Rosette, *Josephine Baker in Art and Life*, p. 235.
115. Jules-Rosette, *Josephine Baker in Art and Life*, p. xv.
116. Papich, *Remembering Josephine*, pp. 210–213.
117. Guterl, *Josephine Baker and the Rainbow Tribe*, p. 142.
118. *Le Monde*, 27 August 1963.
119. Hammond and O'Connor, *Josephine Baker*, p. 207.
120. Sauvage, *Mémoires*, p. 334.
121. De Gaulle to Baker, 16 May 1962, AG5(1)1114, AN.
122. Baker to de Gaulle, 2 May 1949, AG5(1)1114, AN.
123. De Gaulle to Baker, 18 May 1949, AG5(1)1114, AN.
124. Official to Baker, 5 June 1964, AG5(1)1114, AN.
125. It seems that de Gaulle did visit the property at one point when he was out of office; see Baker and Chase, *Josephine*, p. 298.
126. Baker to de Gaulle, June 1962, AG5(1)1114, AN.
127. For example, Baker to de Gaulle, 22 June 1963, AG5(1)1114, AN.
128. Baker to de Gaulle, 20 September 1964, AG5(1)1114, AN.
129. Baker to de Gaulle, 17 August 1965, AG5(1)1114, AN.
130. Baker to de Gaulle, 10 December 1963, AG5(1)1114, AN.
131. Baker to Mme de Gaulle, 16 November 1970, AG5(1)1114, AN.
132. Janes to Lars Sorensen, 17 December 1976, HHJ-JBC, YU.
133. Janes to Lars Sorensen, 24 February 1975, HHJ-JBC, YU.
134. *Le Populaire du Centre*, 13 March 1969.
135. Baker and Chase, *Josephine Baker*, p. 486.
136. Hanley, *Naked at the Feast*, p. 325.
137. Hammond and O'Connor, *Josephine*, p. 277.
138. 'Il y a 46 ans, Paris faisait ses adieux à Joséphine Baker', *Le Figaro*, 27 November 2021.
139. Baker and Chase, *Josephine*, p. 487.
140. Baker and Chase, *Josephine*, p. 488.
141. Guterl, *Josephine Baker and the Rainbow Tribe*, p. 191.

Afterword

1. Stovall, *Paris Noir*, p. 120; Charles Glass, *Americans in Paris: Life and Death Under Nazi Occupation*, HarperPress, 2009, p. 55.
2. Stovall, *Paris Noir*, p. 123.
3. P.D. Delano, 'American women in the Vittel internment camp: Religions, morality, and culture', *Historical Reflections/Réflexions Historiques*, 45:3 (2019), pp. 100–123.
4. Ayshka Sené, 'The orphan story of British women in Occupied France: History, memory, legacy', unpublished PhD thesis, Cardiff University, 2018.
5. Glass, *Americans in Paris*, p. 5.
6. Glass, *Americans in Paris*, pp. 5–6.
7. 'Few veterans fly home, AFRO reporter discovers', *Afro-American*, 11 August 1945, p. 11.

8. Jayna Jennifer Brown, 'Babylon girls: African American women performers and the making of the modern', unpublished PhD thesis, Yale University, 2001.
9. 'What made the Sammies run: Puritanical Miss Baker eliminates anatomical', *Stars and Stripes* (London edition), 14 May 1945, p. 5.
10. 'Jo Baker sings "I Want to Make Rhythm" to open Red Cross club', *Chicago Defender*, 10 April 1943, p. 3.
11. 'Josephine Baker & stars for N. Africa', *Billboard*, 24 July 1943, p. 4.
12. 'Josy Baker's tour of No. African bases symbol of a Fighting France', *Variety*, 29 September 1943, p. 26.
13. Baker and Bouillon, *Joséphine*, pp. 185–186. In 'À Joséphine Baker malade Maurice Chevalier apporte Paris dans une chanson', *7 Jours*, 3 May 1942, p. 8, Chevalier relates a supposed visit he made to Baker in Casablanca, where he found her very frail.
14. Baker and Bouillon, *Joséphine*, p. 164.
15. 'Chevalier pro-Nazi, says Josephine Baker', *Los Angeles Times*, 28 May 1943, p. 7. See also 'Inside stuff – Pictures', *Variety*, 2 June 1943, p. 20; 'Jo Baker touring camps', *Pittsburgh Courier*, 5 June 1943, p. 20.
16. Behr describes how badly affected Chevalier was by the accusations that surrounded him, indicating that he never fully recovered and was haunted by it for the rest of his life. Baker's accusations cut deep, and Chevalier retaliated by recalling how he helped make her a star, implying that her venom had been sexually motivated, a clear case of personal revenge because he had once spurned her advances. Edward Behr, *Thank Heaven for Little Girls: The True Story of Maurice Chevalier's Life and Times*, Hutchinson, 1993, pp. 237, 270.
17. Baker to Janes, 18 March 1972, HHJ-JBC, YU.
18. 'Joséphine Baker nous raconte ses "campagnes"', *Ce soir*, 12 October 1944, p. 3.
19. Guillaume Piketty (ed.), *Français en Résistance*, Robert Laffont, 2009, p. 309.
20. Merriman, *Greasepaint and Cordite*, p. 165.
21. Warwick Charlton, 'Alice Delysia', *Brighton Evening Argus*, 9 May 1944, reproduced in Patrick Hamilton, 'An ENSA record Number Two', p. 26, in HHJ-JBC, YU.
22. Coward, *Future Indefinite*, p. 215.
23. 'Barnstorming in the battle zone', *Union Jack*, 12 March 1945, p. 2.
24. Merriman, *Greasepaint and Cordite*, p. 180.
25. 'Gracie in tears as she left' and 'Stars: We want to go to troops', *Daily Mail*, 25 October 1943, p. 3; Merriman, *Greasepaint and Cordite*, p. 180; 'Where were the top-liners?', *Crusader*, 14 June 1943.
26. 'Where were the top-liners?', *Crusader*, 14 June 1943.
27. 'Lift up your voice', *Wings*, 23 May 1944, Vol. 3, No. 4, p. 12.
28. Merriman, *Greasepaint and Cordite*, p. 168.
29. 'Josephine Baker in Beirut', *Palestine Post*, 14 July 1943, p. 3.
30. 'Josy Baker's tour of No. African bases symbol of a Fighting France', *Variety*, 29 September 1943, p. 26.
31. 'Josephine Baker in Beirut', *Palestine Post*, 14 July 1943, p. 3.
32. '"Thin blue line" to the rescue of Josephine Baker', *Air Force News*, 1:11, 13 July 1943, p. 8.

33. 'Girls for Sicily concerts: French would like to entertain', *Eighth Army News*, 23 August 1943, p. 4.
34. '"Thin blue line" to the rescue of Josephine Baker', *Air Force News*, 1:11, 13 July 1943, p. 8.
35. 'Girls for Sicily concerts: French would like to entertain', *Eighth Army News*, 23 August 1943, p. 4.
36. 'From here to yonder', *Afro-American*, 5 August 1944, p. 12.
37. 'From here to yonder', *Afro-American*, 5 August 1944, p. 12.
38. 'Josy Baker's tour of No. African bases symbol of a Fighting France', *Variety*, 29 September 1943, p. 26.
39. 'From here to yonder', *Afro-American*, 5 August 1944, p. 12.
40. Rose, *Jazz Cleopatra*, p. 263.
41. *Journal du Jura*, Bienne, 25 September 1945, in HHJ-JBC, YU.
42. *Journal du Jura*, Bienne, 25 September 1945, in HHJ-JBC, YU.
43. Jeanne Scheper, '"Of la Baker, I am a disciple": The diva politics of reception', *Camera Obscura*, 22:2(65) (2007), p. 85.
44. The Josephine Baker Homecoming Day Speech, 3 February 1952, CADN.
45. Sauvage, *Mémoires*, p. 230.
46. Donald Darling, *Sunday at Large: Assignments of a Secret Agent*, William Kimber & Co. Ltd, 1977, p. 31.
47. Darling, *Sunday at Large*, p. 32.
48. 'Sightseeing with Josephine', *Palestine Post*, 5 October 1943, p. 4.
49. 'Jo Baker, modern Joan of Arc for our boys', *Pittsburgh Courier*, 4 September 1943, p. 21.
50. 'Sightseeing with Josephine', *Palestine Post*, 5 October 1943, p. 4.
51. Sauvage, *Mémoires*, p. 247.
52. 'Josy Baker's tour of No. African bases symbol of a Fighting France', *Variety*, 29 September 1943, p. 26.
53. *Chicago Daily News*, 26 December 1951, quoted in Hanley, *Naked at the Feast*, p. 258.
54. Speech at la Mutualité, Paris, on 28 December 1953, the text of which was published in *Le Droit de Vivre*, January/February/March 1954, and can be found at https://www.licra.org/1-jour-1-texte-numero-53-josephine-baker-discours-a-la-mutualite-paris-28-decembre-1953
55. Gary Younge, 'Giving Josephine Baker a hero's grave won't bury the truth . . . about France's republican racism', *The Nation*, 19 November 2021.
56. Katherina Gerund offers some ways forward for doing this. Katherina Gerund, 'Josephine Baker's routes and roots: Mobility, belonging, and activism in the Atlantic world', in Violet Showers Johnson (ed.), *Deferred Dreams, Defiant Struggles: Critical Perspectives on Blackness, Belonging, and Civil Rights*, Liverpool University Press, 2018, pp. 11–32.
57. Abtey describes her doing this in Corsica in 1944, in *La guerre secrète*, p. 308.
58. Jules-Rosette, *Josephine Baker in Art and Life*, p. 219.
59. 'Joséphine Baker est morte. Une vedette de légende', *Le Monde*, 14 April 1975.
60. There is some exaggeration in the account of her wartime exploits, including gaining promises from Franco and that she sold everything except the Cross of Lorraine given to her by de Gaulle. See 'Quand Joséphine servait la France!', *Ici Paris Hebdo*, 25 April – 1 May 1975, p. 7.
61. Baker and Bouillon, *Joséphine*, p. 13.

62. Rose, *Jazz Cleopatra*, p. 266.
63. Baker and Bouillon, *Joséphine*, p. 13.
64. Bouillon's book was translated into English in 1978: Josephine Baker and Jo Bouillon, *Josephine*, trans. Marion Fitzpatrick, Virgin Books, 1978. It was reprinted in 1988 and revised in 1995. It is currently out of print.
65. Papich, *Remembering Josephine*, p. xv.
66. Papich, *Remembering Josephine*, pp. 120–130.
67. Guterl, *Josephine Baker and the Rainbow Tribe*, p. 195.
68. Margaret Wallace to Janes, 17 October 1976, HHJ-JBC, YU.
69. Guterl, *Josephine Baker and the Rainbow Tribe*, pp. 199–202.
70. Lerner also acquired Rudolph Salmsen's informative account of his wartime experiences, 'The One Who Got Away' (1955), cited here.
71. 'La double vie de Joséphine', Undated, p. 1, Collection Number: M1297 Box 2, Folder 12, File 12, Josephine Baker correspondence: Captain Jacques Abtey Eugene Lerner Josephine Baker Collection, SU.
72. 'La double vie de Joséphine', Undated, p. 1, Collection Number: M1297 Box 2, Folder 12, File 12, Josephine Baker correspondence: Captain Jacques Abtey Eugene Lerner Josephine Baker Collection, SU.
73. Abtey published a book of conversations with his opposite number, Fritz Unterberg-Gibhardt, but neither makes any mention of Baker. *2ème Bureau Contre Abwehr: Commandant Jacques Abtey, Fregattenkapitän Unterberg Gibhardt*, La Table Ronde, 1967.
74. Letter from Lerner to Abtey, 22 January 1976, Eugene Lerner Josephine Baker Collection, SU.
75. On Abtey's engagement, see Baker and Chase, *Josephine*, p. 274. The new print run had a preface by Jacqueline Abtey and was published by Éditions de la Loze, 2002.
76. English: 'A memorial site'.
77. Carrizey-Jasick, *Osez Joséphine*, p. 33.
78. Terri Simone Francis, 'What does Beyoncé see in Josephine Baker?', in Kaiama L. Glover, *Josephine Baker: A Century in the Spotlight*, 6:1–2 (2007/2008), S&F Online.
79. Gerund, 'Josephine Baker's routes and roots'. See also Jules-Rosette, *Josephine Baker in Art and Life*, who offers a lengthy analysis on this aspect.
80. I was widely solicited to talk in France about this aspect of her life at the time.
81. Régis Debray, 'Et si Joséphine Baker entrait au Panthéon?', *Le Monde*, 16 December 2013.
82. 'Emmanuel Macron et l'inflation mémorielle: le chef de l'Etat s'appuie sur l'histoire pour "retrouver du commun"', *Le Monde*, 7 April 2024.
83. 'Petition seeks to honour French Resistance hero Josephine Baker at the Panthéon', France 24, 30 May 2021.
84. 'La leçon de France de Joséphine Baker' (editorial), *Le Monde*, 26 August 2021.
85. Presentation to Journée d'étude Joséphine Baker, Petit Palais, 15 March 2024.
86. Other commentators have been more critical of his account. See Emmanuel de Chambost, 'Guy Penaud sort de Joséphine Baker de la légende pour la remettre dans l'histoire', available at https://hsco-asso.fr/wp-content/uploads/2023/09/HSCO_Guy_Penaud_Josephine_Baker_v2.pdf

87. Presentation to Journée d'étude Joséphine Baker, Petit Palais, 15 March 2024.
88. 'Déliée par la Victoire du Serment du Silence, L'Espionne Noire Raconte', *Point de vue*, 6 June 1946, p. 9.
89. Baker and Bouillon, *Joséphine*, p. 217.
90. 'Déliée par la Victoire du Serment du Silence, L'Espionne Noire Raconte', *Point de vue*, 6 June 1946, p. 9.

BIBLIOGRAPHY

Primary sources: Archives – France

Archives nationales (AN)

France Libre de Gaulle, Questions Colonials, Le Maroc AG3(1)/284
Direction générale de la Police nationale; Direction générale des Renseignements
    généraux, Joséphine Baker F/7/15747
Dossier Joséphine Baker AG/5(1)/540
Correspondence with de Gaulle AG5(1)1114

Service historique de la Défense (SHD)

Joséphine Baker
    GR 16 P 28445
    GR 28 P 9 390
    AI 1 P 6679 (1)
    AI G 8363 (1)
    AI 6 Fi 880
Jacques Abtey
    GR 16 P 2170 390
    GR Z 2000 1618 7959
Jean Lion
    GR 16 P 373520
Alla Dumesnil
    GR 2000 Z 200 13468 RDC
    DE 2013 ZL 144 286
    GR 16 P 199847
    AI Z 39329 (66 Z)
    AI Z 17502/4
    AI Z 39329 (66 Z)X
    Oral interview, A 18 Z 232 1

BIBLIOGRAPHY

Paul Paillole
  Oral interview, GR 3 K 15 1-2
  Historique d'unités (1943–1944) Formations Féminines de l'Air, 4 D 60
  Communiqués du Général Valin pour 1943, Z23332

Centre des Archives diplomatiques de Nantes (CADN)

Questions Politiques et Sociales, Dossier Joséphine Baker 1951–1976
Archives de la direction de l'Intérieur de la résidence générale de France au
  Maroc, sous-série Renseignements et presse 1936–1956
Direction de l'Intérieur – bulletins de renseignements et des dossiers nominatifs
Archives de la direction de l'Intérieur de la résidence générale de France au
  Maroc, sous-série dossiers nominatifs 1912–1961

Archives départementales de la Dordogne (ADD)

Rapports préfectoraux 1 W 1877, 1 W 1812 et 1W 1813-1, 1 W 1813-1 et 2, 1 W 1814 et
  1 W 1815-1, 1 w 1815-2, sous-série 1573 W (papiers du cabinet du préfet)
Dossier Joséphine Baker 1592W art. 43

Primary sources: Archives – United States

National Archives at College Park, MD (NACP)

Records of the Office of Strategic Services, Research Group 226, including:
  OSS Field Station Files, Casablanca
  OSS Field Station Files, Marrakech
  OSS History Office
  Research and Analysis Branch Central Information Division – Morocco, French
  General OSS Personnel Files
  COI/HHJ-JBC YUOSS Central Files
  Sources and Method, Algiers
  OSS Subject Index French Morocco
  Records of the Washington Communications Branch
Military Intelligence Regional Division Regional Files, Research Group 165
  French Morocco, Research Group 162
  French North Africa, Research Group 168
Army Intelligence Project Files 1941–1945
  French Morocco/French North Africa, Research Group 319

Eugene Lerner Josephine Baker Collection, 1926–2001, Stanford University (SU)

Collection number: M1297
Box 2, Folder 12, Sous-Lieutenant Josephine Baker; Lerner and Kaufman
  correspondence with French government and army [1 of 2] 1944–1977 File
  no. 12
Box 2, Folder 13, Sous-Lieutenant Josephine Baker; Lerner and Kaufman
  correspondence with French government and army [2 of 2] 1944–1977 File
  no. 12

Josephine Baker Collections, Beinecke Rare Book and Manuscript Library, Yale University (YU)

Josephine Baker Collection 1940–1960 (JBC) JWJ MSS 108
Henry Hurford Janes–Josephine Baker Collection (HHJ-JBC) JWJ MSS 2
   Series I: Correspondence
   Series II: Personal Papers

Primary sources: Archives – United Kingdom

The National Archives, Kew (TNA)

HS 3/41 French Special Services
HS 3/43 SOE North Africa
HS 7/1236 SOE Personnel files

T161/1163 National Service Entertainments Board

WO 169/21658 Field Entertainment Unit
WO169/ 21659 Entertainment and Propaganda Unit
WO 204/570 Entertainments
WO 204/806 French North Africa: Reports
WO 204/808 & 809. French North Africa: Counter-intelligence
WO 204/815 French North Africa: Counter-intelligence and security
WO 204/12343. French North Africa: Intelligence
WO 220/31 French North Africa: events
WO 252/ 1200 Intelligence notes on French and Spanish Morocco & Tangier

Primary sources: Newspapers and periodicals – French and Francophone

7 Jours
Les Ailes: journal hebdomadaire de la locomotion aérienne
Aujourd'hui
L'Aurore
Ce soir
Claudine
Combat
Défense de la France
Le Droit de Vivre
L'Écho d'Alger
L'Effort
Excelsior
Femmes Françaises
Le Figaro
France
France-Amérique
France-Illustration
France-soir
Hebdomadaire Illustré du M.L.N (Mouvement de Libération Nationale) V

L'Humanité
Ici Paris Hebdo
Images
L'Intransigeant
Le Jour
Le Journal
Les Lettres Françaises
Libération
Marianne
Marie-Claire
Mercure de France
Le Midi socialist
Le Miroir
Le Monde
L'Ouest-Éclair
Paris-Dakar: hebdomadaire d'informations illustré
Paris-presse, L'Intransigeant
Paris-soir
Le Petit Courrier
Le Petit Marocain
Le Petit Marseillais
Le Petit Parisien
Le Petit Provençal
La Petite Gironde
Le Phare de la Loire
Point de vue
Le Populaire du Centre
Pour vous
Le Progrès de la Côte-d'Or
Le Progrès de la Somme
Regards
Le Réveil du Nord
Samedi Soir
Le Sémaphore de Marseille
Sud Ouest
Le Temps
La Vigie Marocaine

Primary sources: Newspapers and periodicals – African American

Afro-American
Arizona Sun
Atlanta Daily World
Chicago Daily News
Chicago Defender
Cleveland Call and Post
Detroit Tribune
Ebony
Jackson Advocate

BIBLIOGRAPHY

Miami Times
Michigan Chronicle
New Journal and Guide
New York Amsterdam News
Omaha Guide
Philadelphia Tribune
Pittsburgh Courier

Primary sources: Newspapers and periodicals – Entertainment

Billboard
Box Office
Motion Picture Herald
Theatre Arts
Variety

Primary sources: Newspapers and periodicals – Forces

Air Force News
Algiers Daily Stars and Stripes
Contact: RAF Weekly News Magazine
Crusader
Daily Newspaper of South East Command
Eighth Army News
Royal Air Force Journal
Stars and Stripes
Union Jack
United Services Review
Wings

Primary sources: Newspapers and periodicals – British, American and overseas

Bystander
Canberra Times
Daily Mail
Guardian
Los Angeles Times
New York Times
News Review
Palestine Post
Picture Post
Tatler and Bystander

Primary sources: Memoirs

Abtey, Jacques, *La guerre secrète de Joséphine Baker*, Editions Sédoney, 1948
— *2ème Bureau Contre Abwehr: Commandant Jacques Abtey, Fregattenkapitän Unterberg Gibhardt*, La Table Ronde, 1967

Baker, Joséphine with Marcel Sauvage, *Mémoires*, Phébus,1949, republished 2022

Baker, Joséphine and Jo Bouillon, *Joséphine*, Robert Laffont-Opera Mundi, 1976

Coon, Carleton, *A North African Story: The Anthropology of an OSS Agent 1941–1943*, Gambit, 1980

Coward, Noël, *Middle East Diary*, Heinemann, 1944

— *Future Indefinite*, Methuen, 2004

Crawford, Kenneth G., *Report on North Africa*, Farrar & Rinehart, 1943

Darling, Donald, *Sunday at Large: Assignments of a Secret Agent*, William Kimber & Co. Ltd, 1977

de Gaulle, Charles, *Mémoires de Guerre*, Tome 3, *Le Salut 1944–1946*, Plon, 1959

Guillaume, Gilbert, *Mes missions face à l'Abwehr: Contre-Espionnage, 1938–1945*, Plon, 1973

Mernissi, Fatima, *Dreams of Trespass: Tales of a Harem Girlhood*, Perseus Books, 1994

Paillole, Paul, *L'Homme des Services Secrets: Entretiens avec Alain-Gilles Minella*, Julliard, 1995

— *Fighting the Nazis: French Intelligence and Counterintelligence, 1935–1945*, Enigma, 2003

Pendar, Kenneth W., *Adventure in Diplomacy: Our French Dilemma*, Dodd, Mead & Co., 1945, republished by Simon Publications, 2003

Roosevelt, Elliott, *As He Saw It*, Duell, Sloan & Pearce, 1946

Werth, Léon, *33 Days: A Memoir*, Melville House Publishing, 2015

Secondary sources

Abitbol, Michel, *Histoire du Maroc*, Perrin, 2009

Albertelli, Sébastien, *Les services secrets du général de Gaulle: Le BCRA 1940–1944*, Perrin, 2009

— *Les services secrets de la France Libre: Le bras armé du général de Gaulle*, Nouveau Monde Editions, 2012

— *Elles ont suivi de Gaulle: Histoire du Corps des Volontaires Françaises*, Perrin, 2020

Andrew, Christopher and Julius Green, *Stars and Spies: Intelligence Operations and the Entertainment Business*, The Bodley Head, 2021

Baida, Jamaâ, 'The American landing in November 1942: A turning point in Morocco's contemporary history', *Journal of North African Studies*, 19:4 (2014), pp. 518–523

Baker, Jean-Claude and Chris Chase, *Josephine: The Hungry Heart*, Random House, 1993, republished by Cooper Square Press, 2001

Barr, James, *A Line in the Sand: Britain, France and the Struggle that Shaped the Middle East*, Simon & Schuster, 2011

Bean, Hamilton, 'Intelligence theory from the margins: Questions ignored and debates not had', *Intelligence and National Security*, 33:4 (2018), pp. 527–540

Behr, Edward, *Thank Heaven for Little Girls: The True Story of Maurice Chevalier's Life and Times*, Hutchinson, 1993

Boittin, Jennifer Anne, *Colonial Metropolis: The Urban Grounds of Anti-Imperialism and Feminism in Interwar Paris*, University of Nebraska Press, 2010

Boittin, Jennifer Anne and Christy Pichichero, '"Ma France, c'est Joséphine": The crucible of race in French and Francophone studies', *Journal of Western Society for French History*, 2 (2022), pp. 1–19

Bonnal, Jean-Claude, *Josephine Baker et le village des enfants du monde en Périgord*, P.L.B. Editeur, 1992

Boyd, Melba Joyce, 'The unconquerable Josephine Baker waging war against Fascism', in Sylvie Eve Blum-Reid (ed.), *Impressions from Paris: Women Creatives in Interwar Years in Paris*, Vernon Press, 2024

Brown, Jayna Jennifer, 'Babylon girls: African American women performers and the making of the modern', unpublished PhD thesis, Yale University, 2001

Capdevila, Luc, François Rouquet, Fabrice Virgili and Danièle Voldman (eds), *Hommes et Femmes dans la France en Guerre (1914–1945)*, Payot, 2003

Carrizey-Jasick, Titia, *Osez Joséphine: La Star, La Femme, Les Milandes*, Evoluprint, Société Editrice HJ Editions, 2019

Chenu, Alain, 'Des sentiers de la gloire aux boulevards de la célébrité', *Revue Française de la Sociologie*, 1 (2008), pp. 3–52

Chin, Rachel, *War of Words: Britain, France and Discourses of Empire during the Second World War*, Oxford University Press, 2022

Cooper, Artemis, *Cairo in the War: 1939–1945*, Penguin, 1995

De Santis, Christopher C. (ed.), *Langston Hughes and the Chicago Defender: Essays on Race, Politics and Culture, 1942–62*, University of Illinois Press, 1995

Delano, P.D., 'American women in the Vittel internment camp: Religions, morality, and culture', *Historical Reflections/Réflexions Historiques*, 45:3 (2019), pp. 100–123

Diamond, Hanna, *Women and the Second World War in France: Choices and Constraints*, Longman, 1999

— *Fleeing Hitler, France 1940*, Oxford University Press, 2007

— 'The starlet-spy', Medium – Truly*Adventurous online, 2021, available at https://medium.com/truly-adventurous/she-was-a-global-superstar-she-was-a-world-class-spy-df5263d51adc

Dyer, Richard, *Stars*, BFI, 1990

Edwards, Brian T., *Morocco Bound: Disorienting America's Maghreb from Casablanca to Marrakech Express*, Duke University Press, 2005

Evans, Karen, 'The apple of discord: The impact of the Levant on Anglo-French relations during 1943', unpublished PhD thesis, University of Leeds, 1990

Ezra, Elizabeth, *The Colonial Unconscious: Race and Culture in Interwar France*, Cornell University Press, 2000

Fennell, Jonathan, *Combat and Morale in the North African Campaign*, Cambridge University Press, 2011

Foucrier, Jean-Charles and Aurélien Renaudière, 'Les victoires d'une défaite? L'écriture de l'histoire des forces aériennes dans la bataille de France (1940–2020)', *Nacelles*, 10 (2021)

Francis, Terri Simone, 'What does Beyoncé see in Josephine Baker?', in Kaiama L. Glover, *Josephine Baker: A Century in the Spotlight*, 6:1–2 (2007/2008), S&F Online

— *Josephine Baker's Cinematic Prism*, Indiana University Press, 2021

Fry, Andy, 'Du jazz hot à "La Créole"': Josephine Baker sings Offenbach', *Cambridge Opera Journal*, 16:1 (2004), pp. 43–75

— *Paris Blues: African American Music and French Popular Culture, 1920–1960*, University of Chicago Press, 2014

Fuligni, Bruno (ed.), *Dans les archives inédites des services secrets: Un siècle d'espionnage français (1870–1989)*, Gallimard, 2014

Germain, F., S. Larcher, and T. Denean Sharpley-Whiting, *Black French Women and the Struggle for Equality, 1848–2016*, University of Nebraska Press, 2018

Gerund, Katherina, 'Josephine Baker's routes and roots: Mobility, belonging, and activism in the Atlantic world', in Violet Showers Johnson (ed.), *Deferred Dreams, Defiant Struggles: Critical Perspectives on Blackness, Belonging, and Civil Rights*, Liverpool University Press, 2018

Gibson, Susan, *A History of Modern Morocco*, Cambridge University Press, 2013

Gillett, Rachel, *At Home in Our Sounds: Music, Race and Cultural Politics in Interwar Paris*, Oxford University Press, 2021

Glass, Charles, *Americans in Paris: Life and Death under Nazi Occupation*, HarperPress, 2009

Gledhill, C. (ed.), *Stardom: Industry of Desire*, Routledge, 1991

Guillemot, Pierre, *Les 12 Vice-Consuls: Afrique du Nord 1942*, Oliver Orban, 1977

Guterl, Matthew Pratt, *Josephine Baker and the Rainbow Tribe*, Harvard University Press, 2014

Hammond, Bryan and Patrick O'Connor, *Josephine Baker*, Jonathan Cape, 1988

Hanley, Lynn, *Naked at the Feast: The Biography of Josephine Baker*, Robson Books, 1981

Higonnet, M.R., J. Jenson, S. Michel and M.C. Weitz (eds), *Behind the Lines: Gender and the Two World Wars*, Yale University Press, 1987

Hindley, Meredith, *Destination Casablanca: Exiles, Espionage and the Battle for North Africa*, Public Affairs, 2017

Jackson, Julian, *France: The Dark Years, 1940–1944*, Oxford University Press, 2001

— *A Certain Idea of France: The Life of Charles de Gaulle*, Penguin, 2019

Jeffrey, Keith, *MI6: The History of the Secret Intelligence Service, 1909–1949*, Bloomsbury, 2010

Joffé, E.G.H., 'The Moroccan nationalist movement: Istiqlal, the sultan, and the country', *Journal of North African History*, 26:4 (1985), pp. 289–307

Jules-Rosette, Bennetta, *Josephine Baker in Art and Life: The Icon and the Image*, University of Illinois Press, 2007

Keaton, T.D., T. Deanean Sharpley-Whiting and T. Stovall (eds), *Black France/France Noire: The History and Politics of Blackness*, Duke University Press, 2012

Kedward, Rod, *The Legacy of the French Resistance*, Bloomsbury, 2022

Kitson, Simon, *The Hunt for Nazi Spies: Fighting Espionage in Vichy France*, University of Chicago Press, 2008

— *Police and Politics in Marseille, 1936–1945*, Brill, 2014

Lacour-Astol, Catherine, *Le genre de la Résistance*, Presses de Sciences-Po, 2015

Lebovic, Sam, ' "A breath from home": Soldier entertainment and the nationalist politics of pop culture during World War II', *Journal of Social History*, 47:2 (2013), pp. 263–296

Létang, Géraud and Natalie Soutet, 'Feux de la rampe et "armée des ombres". A la recherche de l'expérience combattante de Joséphine Baker (1939–1945)', *Revue Historique des Armées*, 304:1 (2022), pp. 107–116

Lévisse-Touzé, Christine, *L'Afrique du Nord dans la guerre, 1939–1945*, Albin Michel, 1998

Lewis, Damien, *The Flame of Resistance: The Untold Story of Josephine Baker's Secret War*, Quercus, 2022

Lochery, Neil, *Lisbon: War in the Shadows of the City of Light, 1939–1945*, Public Affairs, 2011

Lonjon, Bernard, *Maurice Chevalier: le Chéri des Dames*, Editions du Moment, 2012

Lusane, Clarence, *Hitler's Black Victims: The Historical Experiences of Afro-Germans, European Blacks, Africans, and African Americans in the Nazi Era*, Routledge, 2003

Maxwell, Gavin, *Lords of the Atlas, Morocco: The Rise and Fall of the House of Glaoua*, Cassell, 2000

Mencherini, Robert, *Vichy en Provence, Midi Rouge, ombres et lumières 2*, Editions Syllepse, 2009

Merriman, Andy, *Greasepaint and Cordite: How ENSA Entertained the Troops during World War II*, Aurum Press, 2013

Metzger, Chantal, *Le Maghreb dans la guerre, 1939–1945*, Armand Colin, 2018

Mitchell, Robin, *Vénus Noire: Black Women and Colonial Fantasies in Nineteenth Century France*, University of Georgia Press, 2020

Negra, D. and S. Holmes (eds), *In the Limelight and under the Microscope: Forms and Functions of Female Celebrity*, Continuum, 2011

Onana, Charles, *Joséphine Baker contre Hitler*, Editions Duboiris, 2006

Osborne, Deirdre, '"I do not know about politics or governments . . . I am a housewife"': The female secret agent and the male war machine in Occupied France (1942–5)', *Women: A Cultural Review*, 17:1 (2006), pp. 42–64

Pack, Sasha D., *The Deepest Border: The Strait of Gibraltar and the Making of the Modern Hispano-African Borderland*, Stanford University Press, 2018

Papich, Stephen, *Remembering Josephine*, Bobbs-Merrill, 1976

Péan, Pierre, *Une jeunesse française: François Mitterrand, 1934-1947*, Fayard, 1994

Penaud, Guy, *Joséphine Baker: La Résistance en chantant*, Les Livres de l'Ilot, 2023

Pennell, C.R., *Morocco since 1830: A History*, New York University Press, 2000

Perrot, Michelle (ed.), *Une histoire des femmes est-elle possible?* Editions Rivages, 1984

Pietila, Antero and Stacy Spaulding, *Race Goes to War: Ollie Stewart and the Reporting of Black Correspondents in World War II*, Kindle edition, Now and Then Reader, 2014

— 'The Afro-American's World War II correspondents: Feuilletonism as social action', *Literary Journalism Studies*, 5:2 (2013)

Piketty, Guillaume (eds), *Français en Résistance*, Robert Laffont, 2009

Porch, Douglas, *The French Secret Services*, Macmillan, 1995

— *France at War: Defeat and Division, 1939–1942*, Cambridge University Press, 2020

Raphael-Hernandez, Heike (ed.), *Blackening Europe: The Emergence of an African American Europe*, Routledge, 2012

Regester, Charlene, 'The construction of an image and the deconstruction of a star – Josephine Baker racialized, sexualized, and politicized in the African-American press, the mainstream press, and FBI files', *Popular Music & Society*, 24:1 (2000), pp. 31–84

Rémy, J.A.: *Episodes de la vie d'un agent S.R. et du contre-espionnage français*, Editions Gallic, 1961

Roll, David, *The Hopkins Touch*, Oxford University Press, 2013

Rose, Phyllis, *Jazz Cleopatra: Josephine Baker in Her Time*, Vintage, 1990

Roshwald, Aviel, 'The Spears mission in the Levant 1941–1944', *Historical Journal*, 29:4 (1986), pp. 897–919

— *Estranged Bedfellows: Britain and France in the Middle East during the Second World War*, Oxford University Press, 1990

Roslington, James, '"England is fighting us everywhere": Geopolitics and conspiracy thinking in wartime Morocco', *Journal of North African Studies*, 19:4 (2014), pp. 501–517

Sangmuah, Egya N., 'Sultan Mohammed ben Youssef's American strategy and the diplomacy of North African liberation, 1943–61', *Journal of Contemporary History*, 27:1 (1992), pp. 129–148

Scheper, Jeanne, '"Of la Baker, I am a disciple": The diva politics of reception', *Camera Obscura*, 22:2(65) (2007)

Scott, J.W., *Gender and the Politics of History*, Columbia University Press, 1988

Scott, Len and Peter Jackson, 'The study of intelligence in theory and practice', *Intelligence and National Security*, 19:2 (2004), pp. 139–169

Sené, Ayshka, 'The orphan story of British women in Occupied France: History, memory, legacy', unpublished PhD thesis, Cardiff University, 2018

Shahan, Jess, '"Don't keep mum": Critical approaches to the narratives of women intelligence professionals', *Intelligence and National Security*, 36:4 (2021), pp. 569–583.

Sharpley-Whiting, T. Denean, *Bricktop's Paris: African American Women in Paris between the Two World Wars*, State University of New York Press, 2015

Staszak, Jean-François, 'L'écran de l'exotisme. La place de Joséphine Baker dans le cinéma français: Géographie et cinéma', *Annales de Géographie*, 123:695/696 (2014), pp. 646–670

Stenner, David, 'Did *Amrika* promise Morocco's independence? The nationalist movement, the sultan, and the making of the "Roosevelt Myth"', *Journal of African Studies*, 19:4 (2014), pp. 524–539

Stovall, Tyler, *Paris Noir: African Americans in the City of Light*, Houghton Mifflin, 1996

— 'The new woman and the new empire: Josephine Baker and changing views of femininity in interwar France', in Kaiama L. Glover (ed.), *Josephine Baker: A Century in the Spotlight*, 6:1–2 (2007/2008), S&F Online.

Syrett, Nicholas L., *American Child Bride: A History of Minors and Marriage in the United States*, University of North Carolina Press, 2016

Thébaud, Françoise (ed.), *Résistances et Libérations: France 1940–1945*, Presses Universitaires du Mirail, 1995

Toy, R.F. and C. Smith, 'Women in the shadow war: Gender, class and MI5 in the Second World War', *Women's History Review*, 27:5 (2018), pp. 688–705

Vaïsse, Maurice, 'De Gaulle et Mohammed V 18 juin 1940–18 juin 1945', *Guerres mondiales et conflits contemporains*, 241:1 (2011), pp. 91–106

Vaughan, Hal, *FDR's 12 Apostles: The Spies Who Paved the Way for the Invasion of North Africa*, The Lyons Press, 2006

Weber, Ronald, *The Lisbon Route: Entry and Escape in Nazi Europe*, Ivan R. Dee, 2011

Wheelwright, Julie, *The Fatal Lover: Mata Hari and the Myth of Women in Espionage*, Collins and Brown, 1992

Williams, I.C., *Underneath a Harlem Moon: The Harlem to Paris Years of Adelaide Hall*, Continuum, 2002

Williams, Maude and Bernard Wilkin, *French Soldier's Morale in the Phoney War*, Routledge, 2018

Wood, Ean, *The Josephine Baker Story*, Sanctuary Publishing, 2000

Young, John W., 'The Foreign Office, the French and the post-war division of Germany 1945–46', *Review of International Studies*, 12:3 (1986), pp. 223–234

Younge, Gary, 'Giving Josephine Baker a hero's grave won't bury the truth ... about France's republican racism', *The Nation*, 19 November 2021

INDEX

Note: The abbreviation JB refers to Josephine Baker.

Hudson, Carrie (JB's mother) 229
Hughes, Langston 101–2, 242, 256

Ici Paris Hebdo 262
Images (journal) 173
India, thwarted tour 204–8
Infirmières pilotes secouristes de l'air
    (IPSA) 36
intelligence work
  and entertainment 12, 27–8, 48–9,
    115
  female invisibility 8
  in homeless shelters 36–7
  invisible ink 53, 79
  JB's reminder notes 88–9
  microphones 265
  North African travel 78–9
  Spanish transit visa 81
  women's contribution 8
  see also Baker, Josephine,
    INTELLIGENCE WORK; British
    intelligence; French
    intelligence; German
    intelligence; United States
    intelligence
Italy 16–17, 25–6

'J'ai deux amours' 5–6, 29, 117, 122, 143,
    156, 171, 194, 196, 256
Janes, Henry Hurford (Harry)
  on Abtey's memoirs 224–6
  in Algiers 139
  Collection (archives) 10
  ENSA official 137–8, 139
  first meeting with JB 137–8
  friendship with JB 137, 199, 207–8,
    221
  JB biography 264
  JB tours 140, 143, 145–6, 159,
    199–201, 203–4
  on JB's letters 244
  on JB's relationships 221–2
  Menebhi hospitality 148–9
  thwarted tour to India and Burma
    204–8
  on unfortunate incidents in Middle
    East 147–8
Japanese ambassador 27
Jaurès, Jean 271

Jensen, Paul 105–6, 233
Jordan, Jack 241
Jornal Português 81–2

Kaufman, Hank 264–5
Kelly, Grace (Princess Grace) 245, 247,
    270
Kessel, Joseph 253
al-Khoury, Bishara 168, 169
Killearn, Lord 166
King, David 94–5, 99–100
King, Martin Luther, Jr 241
Kupferman, Laurent 268–9

La Créole (operetta) 6–7, 62–4, 65, 73
La Sirène des Tropiques (film) 6, 34–5
Laval, Pierre 65
Le Figaro 35, 246–7
Le Monde 235, 262, 269
Le Petit Marocain 116, 217, 222
Lebanon
  independence ambitions 168–9,
    173–4, 207
  JB's visits 149, 168–70
  political unrest 173–4
Légion d'honneur 217–20, 238–40, 267
Lerner, Eugene 264–5, 266
Levant, Franco-British rivalry 167–72
Liberty Club, Casablanca 116, 128–9,
    131, 134, 193
Ligue internationale contre le racisme
    et l'antisémitisme (LICRA)
    236
Lion, Jean (JB's husband)
  divorce 220–1
  divorce rumours 19–20
  Jewish family vulnerability 42, 51,
    177, 257, 262
  marriage to JB 14, 17–19, 32, 171, 269
  war service 221
Lisbon
  Abtey remains 60
  Abtey/JB joint mission (1940) 48–9,
    52–8
  British-French intelligence link
    64–5
  JB performances 81–2
  JB's first solo mission (1941) 81–2
  wartime conditions 56–7, 81